*RISK MANAGEMENT IN THE BEHAVIORAL
HEALTH PROFESSIONS*

# Risk Management in the Behavioral Health Professions

A PRACTICAL GUIDE TO PREVENTING
MALPRACTICE AND LICENSING-BOARD
COMPLAINTS

*Frederic G. Reamer*

FOREWORD BY

*Robert P. Landau*

COLUMBIA UNIVERSITY PRESS    NEW YORK

COLUMBIA UNIVERSITY PRESS
*Publishers Since 1893*
New York    Chichester, West Sussex
cup.columbia.edu

Library of Congress Cataloging-in-Publication Data
Names: Reamer, Frederic G., 1953– author.
Title: Risk management in the behavioral health professions : a practical guide to preventing
    malpractice and licensing-board complaints / Frederic G. Reamer ; foreword by Robert P. Landau.
Description: 1 Edition. | New York : Columbia University Press, 2023. |
    Includes bibliographical references and index.
Identifiers: LCCN 2022043091 | ISBN 9780231208307 (hardback) |
    ISBN 9780231208314 (trade paperback) | ISBN 9780231557368 (ebook)
Subjects: LCSH: Risk management—United States. | Psychology—United States. |
    COVID 19 (Disease)—Social aspects—United States. | Medical Innovations—United States.
Classification: LCC HD61 .R38 2023 | DDC 362.10973—dc23/eng/20230203
LC record available at https://lccn.loc.gov/2022043091

Cover design: Noah Arlow

FOR DEBORAH, EMMA, AND LEAH

# CONTENTS

▸ ROBERT P. LANDAU

ASSUME YOU HAVE JUST been served with a summons and complaint for a malpractice lawsuit or have just received notice of a licensing-board complaint. I know firsthand how anxiety-provoking these experiences are for practitioners because I have devoted my professional life for more than thirty-nine years to defending health-care providers involved in medical malpractice lawsuits and licensing-board complaints in Rhode Island and Massachusetts. I also provide clients with legal advice about complex risk management issues. Of course, if a lawsuit or board complaint occurs, practitioners need to immediately notify their professional liability insurance carriers and engage competent legal counsel. But what if there were proactive steps you could take to possibly prevent the lawsuit or board complaint from happening in the first place or to maximize your chance of success in case a lawsuit or board complaint does occur? What if you could avoid experiencing that anxiety? What if you could learn essential information about malpractice insurance, how to respond to subpoenas, how to navigate the tension between the duty of confidentiality and the duty to protect, and how to reduce the legal risks associated with providing clinical supervision? What if you could learn how to avoid common documentation errors and how to safely terminate services without abandoning clients? That's where this book comes into play, and that's why I have such a keen interest in the subject of this book.

I have known Dr. Frederic "Rick" Reamer for decades, so long that I do not remember clearly how we first met. We quickly realized that we shared an enthusiasm for risk management—imagine that!—and in 2013 began to co-conduct seminars on ethics and risk management in behavioral health. Gradually, the frequency of these seminars and webinars increased to the point where we have lectured together more than forty-five times to social workers, mental health counselors, psychologists, marriage and family therapists, school counselors, substance use disorder counselors, psychiatric nurses, and psychiatrists who practice throughout the United States. Our audiences have included professionals who work in a variety of clinical, administrative, and educational settings, such as private practices, behavioral health agencies, hospitals, schools, substance use disorder treatment facilities and training programs, recovery houses, military bases, and graduate schools. I am well acquainted with these behavioral health providers, both because of my professional experience representing them as an attorney and because I have been married to a clinical psychologist for forty years.

In addition, I have consulted Rick on numerous occasions over many years regarding licensing-board matters. I rely on his advice, which has played a critical role in obtaining favorable outcomes for my clients. Rick has also served as an expert witness for me and has provided ethics supervision for several of my clients who engaged in boundary violations.

Although my role in our continuing education seminars has been to present the legal issues and explore how they overlap with ethical issues, I realized early on the depth and breadth of Rick's knowledge in this field. Frankly, Rick understands the legal issues better than most attorneys. He explains the issues facing behavioral health providers in an easy-to-understand and compelling manner.

Rick has written many books addressing risk management issues. Some are broad in scope, such as *Social Work Values and Ethics*; *Social Work Malpractice and Liability: Strategies for Prevention*; and *Risk Management in Social Work: Preventing Professional Malpractice, Liability, and Disciplinary Action*. Others tackle specific topics, such as *Boundary Issues and Dual Relationships in the Human Services* and *Ethics and Risk Management in Online and Distance Social Work*.

In this book, Rick provides extensive updated hypotheticals, discussions of cases in which he has served as an expert witness, and formal reports of court decisions. He also explores new issues related to technology and standards and professional literature. This book approaches these topics broadly to appeal to the entire spectrum of behavioral health services and practitioners. I reviewed this text closely and am impressed by Rick's comprehensive and clear coverage of complex legal concepts. He demonstrates an uncanny ability to translate abstract issues into practical real-world situations. His advice, which reflects his extensive experience, serves as an invaluable guide to practitioners. It also encapsulates his empathetic and compassionate understanding of the dilemmas clinicians confront in their practices.

Rick provides practitioners with the risk management tools to help prevent these unpleasant experiences and to enhance the opportunity for successful results. He has immersed himself in this field as a world-renowned expert in behavioral health ethics, having researched, published, and lectured extensively. Rick is the go-to person whom practitioners regularly consult when they find themselves in challenging ethical circumstances. He also provides ethics supervision to behavioral health providers of all backgrounds, helping them to, for example, gain the insight needed to avoid future boundary violations.

But more importantly, Rick's experience serving as an expert witness hundreds of times for plaintiffs, defendants, and licensing boards gives him a unique perspective. This book does not represent the dry views of an ivory-tower academician. Instead, it is packed with substantive information and nuanced, pragmatic advice about how to approach risk management in the behavioral health field. The appendix includes useful templates of forms and agreements that practitioners can readily adapt.

I am confident that you will find this book to be an indispensable resource and will want to keep it in an easily accessible location to consult when you encounter complex ethical dilemmas and decisions. I intend to keep it on my desk.

LET'S START WITH THE GOOD NEWS: relatively few behavioral health practitioners are named as defendants in lawsuits or as respondents in licensing-board complaints. The vast majority of professionals practice ethically and competently, adhering to widely embraced standards of ethics and behavioral health practice designed to protect clients.

And then there's the bad news: some practitioners—a distinct minority, to be sure—practice outside established standards, thus posing significant risk both to clients' well-being and to the practitioners' own careers. These practitioners are much more likely to have lawsuits and licensing-board complaints filed against them. And even the most conscientious, principled, earnest, and ethical practitioners run the risk, however small, that disgruntled clients will file complaints against them, even when no evidence of wrongdoing exists.

That there is a need for this book is unfortunate. After all, what practitioner wants to spend time reading and thinking about being sued or being named in a licensing-board complaint? Sadly, such formal complaints are a fact of modern life, and the costs are significant. I am not referring only to the financial cost, mind you. I am also referring to the emotional cost. Even when a practitioner has done nothing wrong, being named in a lawsuit or licensing-board complaint is psychologically taxing. Moreover, the practitioner will need to consult (and arrange to pay) a lawyer, answer interrogatories, produce documents, attend depositions and hearings, and repair or preserve her reputation. Under the best of circumstances, this arduous process is a miserable experience. Under the worst of circumstances, it can be devastating.

Unfortunately, behavioral health practitioners—including social workers, psychologists, mental health counselors, marriage and family therapists, psychiatrists, substance use disorder treatment counselors, applied
behavior analysts, and psychiatric nurses, among others—get relatively
little training to help them avoid malpractice claims and licensing-board
complaints. Professional education typically includes little on the subject
of what has come to be known in the field as "risk management." Although
more and more behavioral health practitioners are learning about professional ethics, professional and continuing education rarely includes a
systematic introduction to risk management and ways to prevent and
respond to formal complaints. My hope is that this book will help remedy
the situation.

Since the early 1980s, I have had the privilege of speaking about professional ethics to thousands of behavioral health professionals throughout
the United States, Canada, Europe, and Asia. When I started to receive
invitations to deliver lectures and workshops on the topic, my focus was
primarily on ethical issues in the field of behavioral health and the nature of
ethical decision-making when confronted with difficult dilemmas.

Over time, however, I noticed a distinct trend. During conference breaks
and after my presentations, I began to get more and more questions along
the lines of "I was wondering if I can get sued for ____?" or "Can I get in
trouble with my licensing board if I ____?" (Fill in the blanks.) It did not
take me long to figure out that, while I was preoccupied with perplexing
and conceptually complex philosophical issues related to professional ethics, many people in my audiences were understandably consumed by more
pragmatic concerns about the risk of potential lawsuits and other complaints. This should not have been much of a surprise: many ethical issues
that I was presenting raised complicated legal questions as well.

What this meant, of course, was that over time I found myself learning
more and more about the malpractice and licensing-board risks associated
with behavioral health professions. Over the years, I have collected scores
of case examples from conference participants, colleagues, and more than
one hundred court and licensing-board cases in which I have served as an
expert witness and formal consultant.

It is sad, in a way, that the various behavioral health professions have
generated so much concern about risk management. It distracts from their
principal mission, and the level of concern is often out of proportion to

the statistical likelihood of being named in a lawsuit or licensing-board complaint. From my point of view, however, this also represents an important opportunity to educate practitioners about good practice and good ethics, which ultimately prevent lawsuits and licensing-board complaints. My hope is that this book will provide practitioners with an in-depth and practical guide to help them recognize, prevent, and cope with risks they encounter in their work.

It is important to say at the outset that, as important as these risk management issues are, practitioners' first priority—by far—should be protection of the people they serve. Decisions practitioners make in order to prevent lawsuits and licensing-board complaints, while certainly compelling, must be secondary to their efforts to protect clients.

The book is designed to assist behavioral health practitioners involved in direct or clinical practice (especially clinical work with individuals, couples, families, and small groups) and in behavioral health supervision, management, and administration. After I introduce the concepts of negligence, malpractice, liability, and risk management (chapter 1), I turn to a series of discrete topics. These include problems related to privacy and confidentiality (chapter 2); improper treatment and delivery of services (chapter 3); impaired practitioners (chapter 4); supervision (chapter 5); consultation, referral, documentation, and records (chapter 6); deception and fraud (chapter 7); and termination of service (chapter 8). I conclude the book with a series of practical suggestions for practitioners who are named as defendants in lawsuits or as respondents in licensing-board complaints— and some observations about the role of good practice and good ethics in managing and reducing risk (chapter 9).

This book contains considerable case material. I drew the cases from several sources, including legal texts, law reporters (i.e., published summaries of legal cases), court documents, news media accounts, and my own experiences in a wide variety of court and licensing-board cases. Some case material comes from publications that provide periodic updates of litigated cases. I found other case examples in textbooks and original court opinions published in various state, federal, and regional reporters. Most cases that I cite are a matter of public record; in some instances, I could not provide dates for the decisions because I found descriptions of these cases only in secondary sources, and the cases themselves were not published. Legal citations for most of the cases are provided at the end of the book. In several instances, I report case-related details in disguised form to protect the privacy of the parties involved.

Readers should be aware that lower-court decisions I cite do not constitute legal precedents in those jurisdictions. Only appellate cases in the court of last resort are controlling in this way. While I refer to various cases and legal concepts, court decisions vary among the states and therefore a precedent established in a particular case may not apply to your practice. Nevertheless, I have included a number of lower-court and appellate decisions that provide valuable illustrations of concepts addressed throughout the book.

It is important to note that I am not an attorney, and I am not offering legal advice in this book. Although this book includes information and commentary about legal concepts and cases, readers who believe they need or want legal advice should consult an attorney who has expertise in professional malpractice and risk management associated with behavioral health professions and who is familiar with the relevant law in the jurisdiction where the practitioner is licensed. Practitioners should become familiar with the court cases, regulations, and statutes applicable in the state where they work.

Over the years, I have noticed that when I speak to behavioral health practitioners about this subject, their anxiety tends to increase. Contemplating being named in a lawsuit or licensing-board complaint is not exactly fun. What I have found, however, is that whatever anxiety this topic produces can stimulate determined efforts to enhance the quality of behavioral health practice. Perhaps the most effective way for practitioners to protect themselves from formal complaints is to provide competent and ethical service to clients. Sometimes anxiety can serve a useful purpose by inspiring constructive action. As the nineteenth-century Scottish writer Thomas Carlyle said, "Talk that does not end in any kind of action is better suppressed altogether."

# CHAPTER 1

# Professional Risk Management

IMAGINE THAT YOU ARE a counselor employed at a community mental health center. For three months, you have been counseling a twenty-six-year-old man who was referred to you by the staff of a local psychiatric hospital following the young man's inpatient treatment for depression.

Your client has made considerable progress. He is holding down a job for the first time in five years, is living independently in his own apartment, and is romantically involved with a young woman who is also a client at the mental health center; the couple met while participating in group therapy. Your client reports that he is happier than ever.

Your smartphone rings one afternoon, and your client says, in a fearful voice, that he needs to see you as quickly as possible. He explains that he does not want to discuss the matter over the telephone, and you agree to meet him early the next morning.

Your client arrives on time. His affect is flat, and he seems unusually distressed. After you usher him into your office, your client explains that his physician has just informed him that he has tested positive for HIV, the virus that causes AIDS. He explains that he is shocked by the diagnosis and needs help dealing with the news.

Your client is convinced that his lover infected him with HIV. Your client is furious and makes a number of disparaging comments about her. After several minutes of this ranting, your client erupts and says, "She's going to pay for this. She's *really* going to pay for this." Your client then storms out of your office, leaving you to wonder whether he intends to harm his lover imminently.

You pause to collect your thoughts: To what extent do you have an obligation to protect the client's lover, who is also a client at your agency, from harm? Did your client forfeit his right to confidentiality by threatening his lover? Are you permitted to disclose confidential information about the client without his consent to protect the lover, and, if so, how much information can you disclose and to whom should you disclose it? What specific ethical standards and laws govern this disclosure? What steps do you need to take to make a sound decision and minimize risk to everyone involved?

All contemporary behavioral health practitioners need to be acquainted with the nature of risk management, specifically the ways in which their decisions and actions can expose them to lawsuits and licensing-board complaints, in addition to exposing clients and others to harm. What kinds of claims are clients filing against practitioners? With what frequency? What constitutes negligence and malpractice? How can practitioners avoid liability and licensing-board complaints, and what is the most effective way to respond to them, should they be filed? These are the principal questions that will concern us in this chapter.

## PROFESSIONAL MALPRACTICE AND LIABILITY

*Risk management* is a broad term that refers to efforts to protect clients, practitioners, supervisors, and employers.[1] Risk management includes the prevention of lawsuits and licensing-board complaints. Risk management also includes prevention of ethics complaints filed with national professional associations such as the National Association of Social Workers, the American Counseling Association, and the American Association for Marriage and Family Therapy.

Lawsuits allege professional malpractice; licensing-board complaints generally allege violation of standards of practice set forth in licensing laws and regulations. Ethics complaints filed with professional associations allege violation of their respective codes of conduct.

Lawsuits can result in settlements or monetary judgments against practitioners. Licensing-board complaints can result in fines, public notice of findings, revocation or suspension of a professional license, probation, mandated evaluation or supervision (clinical or ethical) and continuing education, reprimand, or censure. Complaints filed against members of professional associations can result in various types of corrective action or sanctions. Corrective action can include training, supervision, consultation censure, restitution, or compensation, among other options. Sanctions can include a reprimand, public notice of findings, membership suspension, membership termination, or notification of licensing boards and malpractice insurers, among other options.

Malpractice payments and health care–related adverse actions are reportable to the federal National Practitioner Data Bank (NPDB), maintained by the U.S. Department of Health and Human Services. The NPDB is a web-based repository of reports containing information on malpractice payments and certain adverse actions related to health-care practitioners, providers, and suppliers. Established by Congress in 1986, the NPDB is a tool that prevents practitioners from moving state to state without disclosure or discovery of previous damaging performance. It can be accessed by authorized users who are responsible for formal peer review, such as hospitals, state licensing boards, and professional societies. Settlements and verdicts are reportable to state licensing boards.

Professional malpractice is generally considered a form of negligence. The concept of malpractice applies to professionals who are required to perform in a manner consistent with the legal standard of care in a given profession, which is generally defined as the way a reasonable and prudent professional should have acted under the same or similar circumstances.[2] Malpractice lawsuits in the behavioral health field are usually the result of a practitioner's active violation of a client's rights (in legal terms, acts of commission, or misfeasance or malfeasance) or a practitioner's failure to perform certain duties (i.e., acts of omission, or nonfeasance).

Some malpractice claims result from genuine mistakes, for example, inadvertent breaches of confidentiality by practitioners (e.g., a clinician sends an email message containing confidential information to the wrong recipient or a clinician neglects to have a client sign a consent-to-treat document specifically designed for distance counseling); other claims arise from a deliberate decision to risk a claim (e.g., a practitioner decides to divulge confidential information about a client without the client's consent in order to protect a third party from harm). A practitioner's unethical behavior or misconduct (such as sexual contact with a client or abandonment of a vulnerable client) can also trigger claims.

In general, malpractice occurs when the following evidence exists:

1. At the time of the alleged malpractice, the practitioner owed a legal duty to the client (as in the example at the start of this chapter concerning the obligation to keep confidential information shared by a client).

2. The practitioner was derelict in that duty, either through omission (the failure to perform a duty) or commission (e.g., divulging confidential information to the client's lover without the client's consent).

3. The client suffered some harm or injury. (The client in the example could allege that he suffered emotional distress and required additional psychiatric care after the unauthorized disclosure, that he lost time and wages at work, and that he was deprived of his lover's affection and companionship.)

4. The professional's dereliction of duty was the direct and proximate cause of the harm or injury (i.e., the client's injuries were the result of the practitioner's unauthorized disclosure of confidential information).

In contrast, in making their decisions, licensing boards need not require evidence that practitioners' actions (commission) or inactions (omission) caused harm. Rather, practitioners can be sanctioned simply on the basis of evidence that their conduct violated standards contained in licensing statutes and regulations, without any evidence of harm. Practitioners also can be disciplined by their licensing boards for conduct unrelated to the care provided to a particular client, such as misrepresentation, fraud, discipline in another jurisdiction, conviction of certain crimes, and impairment. Professional associations that process ethics complaints can sanction members when there is evidence that a member's conduct violated standards in the association's code of conduct or code of ethics.

### KEY CONCEPTS IN RISK MANAGEMENT

Complaints filed against behavioral health practitioners fall into two broad categories. The first includes claims alleging that practitioners carried out their duties improperly or in a fashion inconsistent with the profession's standard of care (so-called acts of commission, or misfeasance or malfeasance). Examples include flawed treatment of a client (incorrect treatment), sexual impropriety or other boundary violation, breach of confidentiality or privacy, improper referral to another service provider, defamation of a client's character (as a result of slander or libel), breach of contract for services, improper civil commitment of a client (false imprisonment/ arrest), improper use of technology to serve clients remotely, wrongful removal of a child from a home (loss of child custody), assault and battery, improper termination of service (abandonment), improper licensing of staff, and improper peer review.

The distinction between misfeasance and malfeasance is an important one. *Misfeasance* is ordinarily defined as the commission of a proper act in a wrongful or injurious manner or the improper performance of an act that might have been performed lawfully. Examples include flawed informed-consent procedures to provide telehealth services to clients or inadvertent disclosure of confidential information. *Malfeasance* is ordinarily defined as the commission of a wrongful or unlawful act. Examples include embezzlement of a client's money, sexual contact with a client, and falsification of client records.

The second broad category includes claims alleging that practitioners failed to carry out a duty that they are ordinarily expected to carry out in accordance with the profession's standard of care (so-called acts of omission, or nonfeasance). Examples include failure to conduct a comprehensive biopsychosocial assessment, failure to prevent a client's suicide, failure to supervise a client properly, failure to protect third parties from harm, failure to treat a client successfully or at all (sometimes known as failure to cure—poor results), failure to properly obtain a client's consent for treatment, failure to refer a client for consultation for specialized treatment, and failure to terminate services properly. In subsequent chapters, I shall explain more fully the specific allegations contained under these broad headings.

Of course, not all claims have merit. Some are frivolous or lack evidence of professional malpractice or misconduct. However, many claims do have merit. In the case of litigation, they may settle out of court or proceed to trial. Some licensing-board complaints settle through consent orders or agreements; others proceed to a full hearing. Some complaints filed with professional associations are settled through mediation, and some proceed to full hearings.

As I noted earlier, malpractice is a form of negligence that occurs when a practitioner acts in a manner inconsistent with the profession's standard of care—the way a reasonable and prudent professional should have acted under the same or similar circumstances. Suits that allege malpractice are civil suits (in contrast to criminal proceedings). Ordinarily, civil suits are based on tort or contract law, and plaintiffs (the individuals bringing the suit) seek some form of redress for injuries that they claim to have incurred. These injuries may be economic (lost wages or the cost involved in seeking psychiatric care), physical (resulting from a suicide attempt or a practitioner's attempt to restrain an impaired client), or emotional (depression or anxiety brought about by the inappropriate disclosure of confidential information). Although this allegation is much less common, a plaintiff may also allege denial of constitutional rights (individuals hospitalized against their wishes may allege abridgement of their rights to liberty and due process).

As in criminal trials, defendants in civil suits are presumed blameless until proved otherwise. In ordinary civil suits, the standard of proof required to find defendants liable for their actions is preponderance of the evidence, meaning that plaintiffs must prove that it is more likely or probable than not that defendants are liable. Think of sufficient evidence as enough to tip the scale. This is in contrast to the stricter standard of beyond a reasonable doubt used in criminal proceedings.

In principle, tort law—which entails rules allowing injured parties to seek compensation through the courts from those allegedly responsible for the harm—performs three important functions in society. First, it deters behavior that causes injuries, in that it exacts a price for injuring another party. Second, tort law provides opportunity for retribution against those responsible for the injury. Finally, tort law provides a mechanism for compensating the injured party.

Most legal actions against behavioral health practitioners involve tort law, or law involving private or civil wrongs or injuries resulting from a breach of a legal duty (as opposed to contract or criminal law). Torts may be unintentional (negligent) or intentional. Unintentional torts, which include the various forms of negligence and malpractice discussed elsewhere in this book, concern allegations that the practitioner's performance fell below the standard of care for the profession. Intentional torts—such as defamation of character or assault and battery—do not require evidence of negligence.

Most tort claims against behavioral health practitioners allege some form of malpractice (unintentional torts). The malpractice suit has its origins in early British common law. In fact, mention of physicians' professional liability dates to the thirteenth century.[3] Since then, a variety of landmark court cases have clarified the nature of malpractice. In a classic eighteenth-century case involving medical malpractice, for instance, the King's Bench stated in *Slater v. Baker and Stapleton* (1767), "He who acts rashly acts ignorantly; and although the defendants in general may be as skillful in their respective professions as any two gentlemen in England, yet the Court cannot help saying that in this particular case they have acted ignorantly and unskillfully, contrary to the known rule and usage of surgeons."[4]

The first malpractice case on record in the United States is *Cross v. Guthry* in 1794. In this case, a physician was found liable for negligence related to surgery performed on a woman who later died.[5]

### THE ELEMENTS OF MALPRACTICE AND LIABILITY

A malpractice claim must meet four conditions to be successful in court. These include evidence that (1) the practitioner owed a duty to the injured party, (2) the practitioner was derelict in that duty, (3) the plaintiff suffered some sort of harm or injury, and (4) the injury was the direct and proximate result of the breach of that duty.

The first element—evidence that the practitioner owed a legal duty to the injured party—is often the easiest to satisfy. In the example I presented at the beginning of this chapter, for instance, the behavioral health practitioner employed at the mental health center unquestionably had a legal duty to the client. The duty was established when the client sought and obtained a service from the formally trained practitioner, who provided that service in the context of a professional agency.

For the second element, determining whether the practitioner was somehow derelict in that duty typically is much more complex. Here questions ordinarily arise that relate to the prevailing standard of care in the profession. While jurisdictions have varying descriptions of the standard of care, the common principle requires the practitioner to do what a "reasonable person of ordinary prudence" would do in the practitioner's place.[6] In the law, standard of care is considered to be an objective, rather than a subjective, standard.

For many years, courts defined standard of care by comparing a practitioner's actions with those of similarly trained professionals in the same community—what is generally known as the locality rule. The assumption here was that levels of expertise and training varied from community to community, as a function of local training programs and access to technology and treatment techniques. One practical consequence of the locality rule was that expert witnesses in a malpractice case usually came from the local community.

Over time, however, many jurisdictions have overturned the locality rule, either by judicial decision or legislation.[7] The rationale has been that changes in modern communication (especially the advent of the Internet), transportation, and education have provided practitioners with much greater access to updated information about developments in their profession. Consequently, courts now typically permit out-of-state expert witnesses to testify in malpractice cases. That is, the standard of care tends to be based on national, rather than local, norms in a profession.

Some departures from the standard of care are relatively easy to show, of course. A behavioral health practitioner who engages in a sexual relationship with a client or discloses confidential information about a client to a client's neighbor, in casual conversation and without the client's permission, has clearly departed from the profession's standard of care. A practitioner in a residential program who neglects to record in case notes a client's obvious suicidal symptoms and ideation has clearly departed from the standard of care. These are the easy cases.

Far more common, however, are those cases in which reasonable people may disagree about the appropriateness of the practitioner's actions; that is, whether they in fact constituted a departure from the standard of care. The practitioner in the opening example, for instance, might argue that disclosing confidential information was essential to protect the client's lover from potential harm. This practitioner might argue that the benefit of the disclosure, to which the client did not consent, outweighed the breach of the client's right to privacy.

Other practitioners might find such an argument unpersuasive. They might argue that the counselor had an obligation to respect the client's right to confidentiality and that, without his explicit consent, disclosure to a third party was unacceptable and constituted a departure from the profession's standard of care.

Further, it is not hard to imagine that expert witnesses drawn from a behavioral health profession might disagree with one another. A jury hearing this case might have to deal with thoughtful, experienced experts who offer diametrically opposite views about the practitioner's actions. One might support the practitioner's claim to a duty to protect a third party from serious harm and say that a breach of confidentiality under such circumstances is justifiable and necessary. Another expert witness might contend that the practitioner's disclosure constituted a clear violation of professional ethics, particularly because the client never uttered an actual threat against his lover.

Unless the negligence is so obvious that a layperson can judge the conduct, courts require expert witnesses to testify as to whether the standard of care has been breached or satisfied. This gives rise to the so-called battle of the experts that typically occurs in a malpractice trial.

The standard of care is not monolithic. Sometimes, more than one approach can satisfy the standard of care. In theory, the issue before the jury is not to determine whether the defendant used the best approach but rather whether the defendant used a reasonable approach that met the standard of care. The standard of care essentially describes a minimally acceptable level of professional competence. In practice, however, the jury will be forced to decide what the standard of care requires and, hence, what conduct or treatment was required. The jury assesses the credibility and experience of the expert witnesses and the parties. This may mean the jury rejects an approach that a respectable minority of a profession endorses.

This is a profoundly important observation, in that it suggests reasonable minds may differ with regard to the most appropriate intervention or course of action. What matters is whether a behavioral health practitioner's conclusion in particular circumstances was a reasonable decision in light of the relevant information available *at that time*, recognizing that some colleagues may have reached a different conclusion.

Note that if practitioners present themselves as specialists within their respective profession—specializing in, for example, treatment of depression, marital conflict, eating disorders, substance use disorders, suicide prevention, or posttraumatic stress disorder—they may be judged by the standard of care applicable to a specialist, even if the practitioner's claim of expertise is a misrepresentation.

Ordinarily, the plaintiff has the burden of producing the evidence in a negligence case. However, in some cases the plaintiff introduces the doctrine of *res ipsa loquitur* ("the thing speaks for itself") to shift the burden of proof to the defendant. Under *res ipsa loquitur*, the plaintiff argues that the negligence is so self-evident that any reasonable person can see it.[8] Imagine, for example, a suit filed on behalf of a child who was injured by an abusive foster parent; the suit proffers evidence that the social service agency placed the child in the foster home without screening the foster parents, who had a known record of abuse.

The 1865 British case of *Scott v. London and St. Katherine Docks Co.* established the doctrine of *res ipsa loquitur*.[9] Several sacks of sugar fell out of a warehouse window and hit a British customs officer on the head. The judges concluded that sacks of sugar do not fall out of second-story windows and hit pedestrians unless negligence is involved.[10]

Courts require that suits based on the doctrine of *res ipsa loquitur* must meet three criteria: the injury sustained does not ordinarily occur in the absence of negligence; elements within the exclusive control of the defendant must have caused the injury; and the injury must not have been the result of any voluntary action or contribution on the plaintiff's part (although states that recognize the concept of comparative negligence, described later, may dispose of the third criterion and apportion liability according to the percentage contributed by the plaintiff and that by the defendant). The procedural effect of successfully invoking the doctrine of *res ipsa loquitur* is to shift the burden of producing the evidence, which normally belongs to the plaintiff, to the defendant, who must then introduce evidence to refute the presumption of negligence.

Demonstrating the third element of malpractice—that the client suffered some harm or injury—can also be difficult in behavioral health. Unlike medicine, for example, where injuries resulting from malpractice are sometimes easy to document (when a fracture is set improperly and evidence of this appears on an X-ray or a physician mistakenly operates on the wrong body part or prescribes a clearly excessive dose of medication), in behavioral health the injuries alleged are often difficult to document empirically. In many instances, plaintiffs claim that they have experienced some form of emotional injury or harm, as opposed to some form of physical injury. In these cases, the plaintiff may have some difficulty substantiating the injury, especially if she or he has a so-called preexisting condition; that is, the plaintiff had been treated for similar symptoms or diagnoses prior to the alleged malpractice. Compelling expert testimony may be required in order to present a strong case that the alleged malpractice caused harm independent of any prior conditions.

This suggests, of course, a plaintiff can find it difficult to satisfy the fourth element of malpractice—that the practitioner's dereliction of duty was the direct and proximate cause of the harm or injury. Some jurisdictions describe the proximate cause requirement by using a so-called but-for analysis; that is, but for the alleged misconduct, the harm would not have occurred. Other jurisdictions may use a "substantial contributing cause" standard for proving proximate cause. Under any approach, however, this element likely will be hotly contested.

Even plaintiffs who can document that they sustained some sort of injury—emotional distress, depression, or physical harm—may have difficulty demonstrating that the practitioner's alleged dereliction of duty was the direct and proximate cause of the injury. For example, strong evidence may exist that a client manifested symptoms of depression after a practitioner inadvertently released confidential information without the client's permission. The practitioner's defense attorney might argue, however, that this client had a long-standing history of depression and that a variety of other stressful events in the client's life at the time of the inadvertent disclosure may account for the depression.

Consider the opening example. Assume for the moment that the client sues you and your agency, alleging that you violated his right to confidentiality. Through his attorney, your client (now presumably your former client) claims that you had a duty to respect his right to privacy and breached this duty by disclosing to his lover details about comments made by the client in a confidential counseling session. In particular, your former client asserts that you violated the standard in your code of ethics concerning your duty to protect clients' confidential information and that your disclosure did not meet threshold criteria that permit disclosure without clients' consent.

In addition, your former client claims that as a result of your disclosure of confidential information about him, he suffered significant harm. Specifically, he alleges that he suffered serious emotional distress and symptoms of depression and anxiety. He spells out how he never intended to harm his lover, you misinterpreted his comments, his lover fled the relationship after your disclosure, and he had to seek psychiatric help at considerable expense as a result. Finally, your former client claims that he lost time at work and wages as a result of this emotional injury.

You can imagine how controversial your former client's claims would be. In his mind, perhaps, is a clear, direct, and unambiguous connection between your alleged violation of his right to privacy and the emotional injury that he claims to have suffered. From your point of view, serious questions can be raised about this connection. In your defense, your attorney may argue that your former client has a history of depression and anxiety symptoms and that he has missed work in the past as a result of his emotional difficulties. Further, at the time of your disclosure to the lover of your former client—which you do not deny—your former client also complained of significant stress in his life because of conflict with his supervisor at work and financial problems. Hence your attorney might argue that your former client cannot demonstrate conclusively that disclosure of the information was the direct cause of his subsequent symptoms of depression and anxiety, missed work, or lost wages. A number of other factors could account for these difficulties.

Your lawyer also might question whether your former client's claims of injury are valid. Although missed days of work and lost wages are easy to document—recognizing that the cause may be debated—claims of emotional injury can be difficult to substantiate, because emotional injuries do not show up on X-rays or laboratory tests. Evidence often takes the form of self-report and evaluations conducted by mental health professionals. As behavioral health practitioners know quite well, even seasoned practitioners may disagree about the validity of evidence presented to substantiate claims of emotional injury.

In many cases involving liability risks, behavioral health practitioners are vulnerable to a lawsuit no matter what course of action they take. In the case example, for instance, the practitioner might be sued for disclosing confidential information without the client's permission. A practitioner also could be sued for *failure* to disclose confidential information without a client's permission (here the distinction between acts of commission and acts of omission is clearly relevant). Imagine that you decide to honor your client's request for privacy. Perhaps you concluded that your client's comments do not pose a serious threat of harm to his lover. Moreover, you do not believe that violating your client's right to privacy without his permission would be ethical.

Shortly thereafter, your client gets involved in a vicious argument with his lover, brings up the HIV infection, accuses his lover of being unfaithful and deceptive, and stabs her. Your client's lover knows that he was in counseling with you and has reason to believe you were aware of his hostile feelings and threatening comments. The lover is so distressed and feels so betrayed that she consults an attorney, who sues you, alleging that you were obligated to take steps to protect your client's lover. Specifically, her attorney argues that you violated widely accepted ethical standards in your behavioral health profession regarding exceptions to clients' confidentiality rights when disclosure is likely to prevent harm. The attorney claims that the risk to her client's safety clearly constituted a compelling professional reason to violate confidentiality and that you were remiss in not taking steps to protect her.

### TWO VIEWS OF THE STANDARD OF CARE: PROCESS AND OUTCOME

Some malpractice cases in behavioral health are relatively clear-cut. A practitioner in a residential setting who simply forgot to enter into the record that a client displayed evidence of suicidal ideation may clearly be liable if staffers on the next shift, unaware of the suicide risk, consequently failed to monitor the resident closely, and the client was injured seriously in an actual suicide attempt. Similarly, a practitioner in private practice who neglects to discuss informed consent with a client, fails to have the client sign a consent form, and then discloses diagnostic information to the client's employer clearly may be liable if the employer then fires the client. In these instances, malpractice and negligence may be relatively easy to establish.

In general, behavioral health practitioners will agree that a practitioner should never strike a client physically (except perhaps in extreme cases requiring self-defense when a client is out of control) and that a practitioner should always obtain informed consent from a client before disclosing confidential information (except in rare cases involving genuine emergencies). The opening case example, however, illustrates a common phenomenon—reasonable behavioral health professionals can disagree about what a practitioner should have done and whether those actions departed from the standard of care in the profession. Some practitioners might argue, for example, that you were ethically obligated to take steps to protect your client's lover from harm and that this might include disclosing confidential information about his threats. They probably would cite relevant ethics standards, statutes, and court decisions, discussed more fully later in this book, to support their argument.

Other practitioners might argue with equal force that you had an obligation to respect your client's right to privacy, that you did not have sufficiently compelling evidence to warrant disclosure of confidential information against his wishes, and that disclosure without the client's consent would not be appropriate. Thoughtful, experienced practitioners have in fact presented such conflicting arguments about this very set of circumstances.[11]

What this suggests is that in many liability cases, a judge or jury can find it quite difficult to determine what, exactly, constitutes the standard of care in the profession with regard to a practitioner's actual decision and actions. The same holds for licensing-board cases, where board members may have difficulty reaching consensus. Attorneys and expert witnesses often present strong arguments in conflicting directions. Attorneys sometimes refer to this as "the battle of the experts."

What can happen, however—and this is a remarkably important point—is that debate about the standard of care may shift away from the practitioner's actual decision and actions related to the substantive issue at hand or the outcome of the decision (in this instance whether the practitioner should have divulged confidential information to the client's lover against the client's wishes) and toward the *process* and *procedures* that the practitioner followed in order to make the decision. That is, the line of questioning may focus instead on the steps that the practitioner took (or should have taken but did not take) to make a sound decision.

In my view, the *procedural* standard of care—the steps a reasonable and prudent practitioner should take in order to make a sound decision in complex circumstances that may lead reasonable practitioners to reach different conclusions—includes eight key elements, which I will explore in detail throughout the book:

1. *Consult colleagues.* Practitioners who face difficult or complicated decisions should consult colleagues who have specialized knowledge or expertise related to the issues at hand, including ethics experts. Practitioners in private or independent practice should participate in peer consultation groups. Practitioners employed in settings that have ethics committees (committees that provide staff with a forum for consultation on difficult cases) should take advantage of this form of consultation when they face complicated ethical issues.[12] Practitioners may be able to

obtain consultation advice from their malpractice insurer or professional association. Moreover, practitioners who are sued or who have licensing-board complaints filed against them can help demonstrate their competent decision-making skills by showing that they sought consultation.

2. *Obtain appropriate supervision.* Behavioral health practitioners who have access to a supervisor should take full advantage of this opportunity. Supervisors may be able to help practitioners navigate complicated circumstances. And practitioners who are sued can help demonstrate their competent decision-making skills by showing that they sought supervision.

3. *Review relevant ethical standards.* It is vitally important that practitioners become familiar with and consult relevant codes of ethics applicable to their respective professions. Contemporary codes provide extensive guidelines concerning ethical issues that often form the basis for malpractice claims and lawsuits; for example, confidentiality, informed consent, conflicts of interest, boundary issues and dual relationships, client records, defamation of character, termination of services, and use of technology to deliver services and communicate with clients.

4. *Review relevant regulations, laws, and policies.* Practitioners who make difficult judgments that have legal implications should always consider relevant federal, state, and local regulations and laws. With respect to the opening case, for example, practitioners should review state laws concerning the disclosure of confidential information by clients during counseling sessions. Many regulations and laws have direct relevance to behavioral health; prominent examples concern the confidentiality of substance use disorder treatment records, the confidentiality of students' educational records (pertaining to school-based counseling), and the confidentiality of health care and mental health treatment records. In addition to state laws, key federal laws and regulations may be relevant to practitioners' ethical decisions (such as the regulation Confidentiality of Substance Use Disorder Patient Records, the Health Insurance Portability and Accountability Act, better known as HIPAA, and the Family Educational Rights and Privacy Act, better known as FERPA). Practitioners employed in military settings must be cognizant of confidentiality provisions in the Military Rules of Evidence and Uniform Code of Military Justice, which include important provisions related to the limits of confidentiality. Practitioners employed by the U.S. Department of Veterans Affairs must be familiar with unique legal regulations pertaining to management of confidential information,

especially pertaining to substance abuse and HIV. In addition, relevant advisories, guidelines, or position papers published by licensing boards should be consulted. Finally, agencies, hospitals, or other employers may have issued relevant policies that should be consulted.

5. *Review relevant practice standards.* National professional associations—such as the American Counseling Association, National Association of Social Workers, American Psychological Association, American Psychiatric Association, American Association for Marriage and Family Therapy, and the National Association of Alcoholism and Drug Abuse Professionals—periodically adopt formal practice standards developed by task forces. Examples include national standards pertaining to the use of technology to serve clients, treatment of adolescent clients, school-based services, military-based services, and supervision, among others. These prominent standards may be introduced as evidence in litigation and licensing-board cases.

6. *Review relevant literature.* Practitioners should always keep current with their professional literature, especially that pertaining to their specialty areas. When faced with challenging decisions, practitioners should make every reasonable effort to consult pertinent literature in an effort to determine what authorities in the field say about the issues and whether they agree or disagree. Such consultation can provide useful guidance and also provides helpful evidence that a practitioner made a conscientious attempt to comply with current standards in the field. That a practitioner took the time to consult pertinent literature—or consult with a colleague who is an expert on this literature—looks good, as a defense lawyer might say. In addition, practitioners can expect that opposing lawyers will conduct their own comprehensive review of relevant literature in an effort to locate authoritative publications that support their clients' claims. Lawyers often submit as evidence copies of publications that, in their opinion, buttress their legal case. Lawyers may use the authors of influential publications as expert witnesses.

7. *Obtain legal consultation when necessary.* Practitioners often make decisions that have legal implications (although many ethical decisions do not require legal consultation; for example, whether to accept a modest gift from a client or accept the client's invitation to attend the client's wedding). This is particularly true with respect to a number of ethical decisions, where statutes, regulations, and court decisions may address, for example, confidentiality, privileged communication, informed consent, conflicts of

interest, remote delivery of services, termination of services, and discussion of abortion. In addition, a practitioner's taking the time to obtain legal consultation provides additional evidence of having made conscientious, diligent efforts to handle the situation professionally. Consultation with skilled lawyers familiar with health-care law and risk management, as opposed to lawyers who are general practitioners or who specialize in other areas of the law, can be extraordinarily helpful.

8. *Document decision-making steps.* Careful and thorough documentation enhances the quality of services provided to clients. Comprehensive records are necessary to assess clients' circumstances; plan and deliver services appropriately; facilitate supervision; provide proper accountability to clients, other service providers, funding agencies, insurers, utilization review staff, and the courts; evaluate services provided; and ensure continuity in the delivery of future services. Thorough documentation also helps to ensure quality care if a client's primary practitioner becomes unavailable because of illness, incapacitation, vacation, employment termination, or death; colleagues who provide coverage will have the benefit of up-to-date information. In addition, thorough documentation can help protect practitioners who are named in ethics complaints and lawsuits (for example, documentation that a practitioner obtained consultation, consulted relevant codes of ethics and ethical standards, referred a high-risk client for specialized services, obtained a client's informed consent for release of confidential information, or competently managed a client's suicide risk can be admitted into evidence).

The extent to which a behavioral health practitioner engaged in these steps when making a decision may become a key issue during a lawsuit. For example, during a deposition (a method of pretrial discovery that consists of a witness's statement and responses to questioning under oath) or actual trial, an opposing attorney in the case might ask which supervisors the practitioner consulted about the decision. Were these supervisors the most appropriate ones to consult, given their areas of expertise? Did the practitioner bring the issue up in peer consultation? Did the practitioner consult a lawyer about the legal implications of the decision? Did the practitioner consult the relevant code of ethics, practice standards, and literature? Did the practitioner document these various steps? Does the case record include evidence that the practitioner actually took these various steps?

What I am suggesting here is that the standard of care in behavioral health can be viewed in two ways. First, the standard of care may focus on a practitioner's specific decisions or actions pertaining to the professional duty, such as the handling of confidential information, entering into friendships with former clients, physical contact with clients, use of technology to provide services remotely, informed consent, and suicide prevention. Second, the standard of care may focus on the process and procedures that the practitioner followed in making the relevant decision or pursuing the controversial course of action (that is, the practitioner's use of supervision, consultation, research, review of code of ethics standards and practice standards).

With regard to the process and procedures, documenting any supervision or consultation that practitioners obtain or research that they conduct is extremely important. Should some question arise about a practitioner's particular decision or actions, being able to demonstrate the kind of prudent supervision or consultation that the practitioner obtained can be quite useful. I have heard many malpractice attorneys say, "If it's not written in the case record, it didn't happen." That may not be literally true, of course, but the absence of detailed, thorough documentation can make it much harder to successfully defend a malpractice claim or licensing-board complaint.

### DAMAGES IN LIABILITY CASES

If the practitioner loses the lawsuit, courts can award two kinds of damages, compensatory and/or punitive. In general, damages include monetary compensation, which the law awards to the party injured by the action of another. Compensatory, or actual, damages include those directly related to the breach of duty and cover losses that can be readily proved to have been sustained and for which the injured party should be compensated as a matter of right, such as past or future earnings lost or the cost of mental health care.

Punitive, or exemplary, damages provide compensation in excess of compensatory or actual damages. They essentially constitute a form of punishment to the wrongdoer and extra compensation to the injured party. They are ordinarily awarded in instances of reckless, malicious, or willful misconduct. Courts award punitive damages much less frequently than compensatory damages.[13]

Courts may adjust monetary awards against behavioral health practitioners on the basis of the concepts of joint liability, comparative negligence, contributory negligence, or assumption of risk. Under the doctrine of joint liability, a court might find that a practitioner and another party are responsible for the injury to the plaintiff. Imagine a practitioner who is sued by a former client who alleges that he was placed in a psychiatric hospital against his wishes, in part because of inaccurate information that the practitioner provided to the committing psychiatrist. If the plaintiff's claim has merit, a finding of joint liability could result—both the committing psychiatrist and the other practitioner who interviewed the client are held responsible.

For example, in an Oregon case, a man whose baby died sued the state and a county mental health agency; he alleged negligent treatment of the infant's mother. The agency had removed the infant from the care of his mother, who struggled with psychiatric challenges, after she inappropriately gave him some of her own medication. After about six weeks, the agency returned the infant to the mother, who several months later shot and killed the baby and then committed suicide. The court awarded the father $150,000, to be paid by the state and the county mental health agencies.[14]

In a Wisconsin case, a woman who had been the victim of sexual abuse was admitted to a hospital psychiatric unit after she learned that a neighbor had sexually abused her son. The patient met a psychiatric nurse at the hospital and later left her husband and two children to live with the nurse. The woman subsequently sued the nurse, claiming the nurse had seduced her into a relationship and that the nurse caused the disruption of the plaintiff's marriage. The jury found the nurse 75 percent negligent and the hospital 25 percent negligent.[15]

This is in contrast to comparative negligence. According to the doctrine of comparative negligence, the court can distribute responsibility for damages between the plaintiff and defendant on the basis of the relative negligence of the two, particularly when there is evidence that the plaintiff's conduct contributed to the injury sustained as a result of the professional's negligence (that is, the client's own actions fell below the standard of self-care that an ordinary and reasonable person would exercise under the same or similar circumstances). As a result, the court may reduce the amount of damages awarded to the plaintiff.

Over the years, the rather strict standard associated with the doctrine of contributory negligence—where a plaintiff who acted negligently may be barred from recovering damages—has given way to the broader doctrine of comparative negligence, where negligent plaintiffs may find their damages reduced by the proportion by which their negligence contributed to their injury.[16] (In some jurisdictions, the court will reduce an award proportionately if a plaintiff was as much as 50 percent at fault, but the plaintiff who is more than 50 percent at fault is awarded nothing.)

Imagine a client who sues a behavioral health practitioner, claiming failure to provide adequate protection in a group home. Another resident assaulted the client, who claims, on the basis of national standards, that the practitioner—the group-home director—should have had at least one other staff person working on that shift to provide the supervision necessary to prevent such an assault. The court could find the practitioner liable in failing to have an adequate staff-to-client ratio but might also find that the plaintiff was negligent because his behavior provoked the assault. Damages may be awarded accordingly, taking into account the comparative negligence of the parties involved.

A number of court cases involving behavioral health professionals have resulted in findings of comparative negligence. For example, in a California case, the surviving son of a man who committed suicide sued his father's therapist. The son claimed that the therapist failed to prevent his father's suicide by not hospitalizing him. The court awarded the son $602,000 but found that the decedent father was 40 percent negligent; the net award was $363,000.[17]

In a Michigan case, a man who had been admitted to a psychiatric hospital sustained serious injuries after he knocked out the window in a seclusion room in which he had been placed, made a rope with sheets, and jumped from the third floor. The man claimed that the hospital staff failed to supervise him properly and placed him in a room that was not escape-proof. The award in the case was $100,000, but it was reduced to $75,000 because of the plaintiff's 25 percent comparative negligence.[18]

Several cases illustrate how awards for damages can address issues of both joint liability and comparative negligence. In a Colorado case, a patient at a psychiatric center became involved sexually with an unlicensed mental health worker on the staff. The patient alleged that the relationship destroyed her marriage. The suit named the mental health worker, the medical director of the center, and the center itself. The award for the plaintiff was $29,145, but the court considered the plaintiff 30 percent negligent (comparative negligence). The court found that the unlicensed worker was 60 percent negligent and the medical director was 10 percent negligent (joint liability).[19]

In a Missouri case, a patient sued a physician for sexual misconduct during therapy. The lawsuit also claimed that the physician was practicing psychotherapy without a license. The gross award in the case was $260,000. The court considered the plaintiff 5 percent negligent (comparative negligence) and split the remaining joint liability between the physician (60 percent) and the physician's employer (35 percent).[20]

The concept of assumption of risk can also influence the outcome of a liability claim. In tort law, defendants can use assumption of risk to claim that plaintiffs were aware that a condition or situation was dangerous to them and yet voluntarily exposed themselves to the hazard or failed to take steps to avoid known danger. Thus contributory negligence arises when a plaintiff fails to exercise due care, while assumption of risk arises regardless of the care used and is based on the concept of consent.[21]

Consider, for example, a client who, while being admitted to an inpatient psychiatric treatment program, voluntarily signs a statement that acknowledges the discussion of personal problems during treatment might trigger emotional distress, depression, and other psychiatric symptoms. If the client subsequently sues the treatment staff and program, alleging that their treatment approach created more psychological symptoms than it alleviated, the defendants might argue that the client assumed the risk.

State legislatures use statutes of limitations to restrict the time period during which someone can file a negligence suit and seek damages. In most cases, the period specified in the statute of limitations begins at the date of the alleged actual injury, while in a small minority of cases it begins at the date that the person reasonably should have learned of the injury. Typically, the statute of limitations applicable to minors begins to run when they reach the age of majority. Minors are not able to sue on their own behalf until they reach the age of majority; until a minor reaches the age of majority, a parent, guardian, or "next friend" of the minor can sue on his or her behalf. Thus adults can sue for injuries sustained during their childhood for a significant number of years after they reach the age of majority.

With some exceptions, the effective statute of limitations, as applied to the treatment of minors, is age of majority plus the relevant state's statute.[22]

Relatively few lawsuits actually reach court. Most malpractice and other professional liability claims (85 to 90 percent) are settled out of court.[23] Some cases are dismissed without payment. Pretrial settlement of a case does not imply that the defendant admitted responsibility or was in any way culpable. Defendants, and more likely their malpractice insurance carriers, may simply decide to cut their losses and settle out of court to avoid further legal and other expenses. For those cases that actually reach court, rulings can be based on statutory law and constitutional law but are often based on common law. Previous court decisions establish common law, which is frequently known as case law. Under the doctrine of *stare decisis* (Latin: "to stand by decided matters"), a judge determines whether a particular case falls within the ruling set forth in the earlier case. A court may also generate a new law, or precedent, on the basis of this particular case.[24]

## MALPRACTICE INSURANCE

Behavioral health practitioners can obtain comprehensive liability insurance that offers legal defense coverage and indemnifies practitioners against liability. Policies are available that cover individual practitioners, behavioral health agencies, corporations, students, and educational programs. These liability policies typically contain options regarding the amount of coverage (for example, the amount of coverage for each wrongful act or series of related wrongful acts and the amount of aggregate coverage during a given policy period, such as a year), coverage during extended reporting periods (that is, coverage for claims filed against a practitioner after the end of the policy period), and coverage of employees (as in a private group practice).

A typical policy is known as a claims-made policy, which means the coverage is limited to liability for only those claims that are first made against the policyholder and reported to the company during the period the policy is in force. Practitioners who also want to be insured for claims made after terminating the policy need to pay an additional premium for extended reporting-period protection; this is known as "tail coverage."

Some insurers also offer what is known as "nose coverage" (also known as prior acts coverage). A basic claims-made policy will only cover claims associated with services that were provided while the policy is in effect.

Nose coverage is a supplement to an expiring claims-made malpractice insurance policy that may be purchased from a new carrier when a practitioner changes carriers and had claims-made coverage with a previous carrier. Nose coverage will provide protection under the new policy if claims are reported in the future for treatment dates going back to the previous policy's inception date.

Behavioral health practitioners also have the option to purchase so-called occurrence coverage. An occurrence policy has lifetime coverage for the incidents that occur during a policy period, regardless of when the claim is reported. A claims-made policy typically is less expensive initially than an occurrence policy; the premium matures over a number of years (for example, five years).

With dramatic increases in behavioral health practitioners' use of digital and other technology to provide services to clients remotely, communicate with clients, and store sensitive information electronically, it is important to have what is known as cyber-liability coverage. This policy provides coverage in the event of a data breach in a practitioner's computer, smartphone, or electronic client records. A data breach or security incident occurs when confidential client data, such as electronic records or personal financial data, are taken, copied, transmitted, viewed, stolen, or used by any individual unauthorized to handle the information. Even if practitioners use a third-party company, such as a warehouse, a mover, or a data storage provider, practitioners can be held responsible for data breaches caused by them. Such a policy may provide coverage for legal expenses, breach notification expenses, and damages and fines in the event of a data breach.

Professional liability policies typically contain certain exclusions. Many policies exclude coverage for any dishonest, criminal, fraudulent, or malicious act or omission; fee disputes; a variety of wrongful acts of a managerial or administrative nature; any claim arising from any business relationship or venture with a former or current client; and a number of other specific activities enumerated in the policy. In addition, most policies contain a special provision regarding coverage for sexual misconduct. Some policies place a ceiling on the amount that the insurance company will pay for damages arising from actual or alleged sexual misconduct. Some policies exclude any coverage for sexual misconduct, and other policies limit coverage to legal defense, up to a specified amount, but do not pay damages for sexual misconduct.

Even behavioral health practitioners employed in settings that provide group liability coverage should seriously consider obtaining their own individual coverage and maximizing the amount of coverage, especially for licensing-board defense. Practitioners may be surprised at the relatively small additional premium charged to increase their licensing-board defense coverage from, say, $10,000 to $100,000. Consider the financial burden of having to pay those legal and expert fees out of pocket instead of having the insurance company pay for these or reimburse you for these. When a liability claim names both the practitioner and the worker's employer, the employer could argue that the practitioner, and not the employing agency, was negligent. This can create a conflict of interest. Individual coverage would thus protect workers who find themselves at odds with their employers in relation to a liability claim, particularly if the employer is not willing to retain separate legal counsel for the practitioner.

Also, individual policies typically include a provision that will cover legal expenses if a practitioner retains an attorney to assist in responding to a complaint filed with a state licensing board. An employer's policy may not provide coverage for this legal representation.

Further, individual coverage protects individual practitioners if claims against their employer's insurance policy exceed that policy's limits (for example, if a case involving client suicide leads to a $5.75 million judgment against an employer's insurance policy that has a $3 million limit). Finally, individual coverage offers protection to practitioners who leave their employment setting before a lawsuit is filed that alleges the practitioner was negligent during the time of employment.

Practitioners also should remember to immediately notify their insurance companies in the event of a potential or actual claim or lawsuit. Failure to do so can void coverage under the policy.

Although liability claims and lawsuits filed against practitioners are relatively rare, professionals must have a keen understanding of legal concepts related to malpractice, negligence, and liability. Statistically, licensing-board complaints filed against practitioners are more common, although most practitioners will complete their careers without being named in one. Fortunately, behavioral health practitioners can take a number of steps to help prevent lawsuits and licensing-board complaints.

# Confidentiality and Privileged Communication

THE CONCEPTS OF PRIVACY and confidentiality are core elements in the field of behavioral health. Practitioners fully appreciate how important privacy and confidentiality are to meaningful therapeutic relationships. Seasoned practitioners also understand that circumstances sometimes arise that require disclosure without clients' consent. Some confidentiality issues emerge during legal proceedings that require application of privileged communication guidelines.

### THE CONCEPT OF PRIVACY

The concept of privacy is central in the behavioral health professions. Practitioners have always had a deep-seated respect for their clients' need for confidentiality. The trust between practitioner and client, so essential to effective help, typically depends on the practitioner's assurance of privacy. The willingness of clients to disclose intimate, deeply personal details about their lives is understandably a function of their belief that their practitioners will not share this information with others.

But privacy is also relevant in other behavioral health domains. Agency administrators need to understand the limits of confidentiality as they pertain to personnel matters or sharing of information with colleagues in other agencies and organizations (e.g., insurance companies, accrediting bodies, utilization review representatives, human services departments, court and law enforcement officials). Protective service workers need to avoid excessive invasion of privacy while investigating reports of abuse and neglect of children and vulnerable adults. Public-sector practitioners in administrative positions need to understand the tension between confidentiality rights and local open-meeting statutes, which may allow the public and media to attend sensitive high-level meetings.

The concept of privacy in professional practice to a great extent is rooted in pronouncements by the Pythagoreans in the fourth century BCE and was later incorporated in the Hippocratic oath: "Whatever I see or hear, in the life of men, which ought not to be spoken of abroad, I will not divulge, as reckoning that all such should be kept secret." The concept of privacy was also an important component of ancient Jewish law, as conveyed in the Talmud. Early English common law also acknowledged the right to privacy associated with the concept of honor among gentlemen.[1]

The new American states legally codified privacy rights in 1791 in the Fourth and Fifth Amendments to the U.S. Constitution. However, medical privacy had no legal basis until 1828, when the state of New York established the physician-patient privilege. In the United States, the first formal statement of the legal concept of privacy appeared in an 1890 essay, "The Right to Privacy," by Samuel Warren and Louis Brandeis. This germinal law-review article ultimately served as the foundation for many court decisions and statutes. Warren and Brandeis defined *privacy* as the right to be left alone or elect not to share information about private matters, habits, and relationships. Since then, the concepts of privacy and confidentiality have assumed a prominent place among clients' most venerable rights.[2]

Clarifying the meaning of, and differences between, *privacy* and *confidentiality* is important. Privacy refers to the right to noninterference in individuals' thoughts, knowledge, acts, associations, and property. Thus behavioral health practitioners' clients have a right to decide whether to share information about their emotional and behavioral challenges, sexual orientation, gender expression, religious beliefs, and political ideology. Confidentiality rights arise when individuals entrust others with private information, usually because of a need to share.

Contemporary behavioral health practitioners recognize that confidentiality cannot be absolute; clients' confidentiality rights have many exceptions. Widely accepted exceptions related to protection of third parties (e.g., mandatory reporting of abuse or neglect of children and vulnerable adults) and clients' threats to harm themselves or others sometimes require disclosure of confidential information. Hence clients have a right to relative (versus absolute) confidentiality.[3]

Many of the earliest legal actions against professionals alleging breach of confidentiality involved physicians. The first recorded appellate decision in the U.S. courts involving a physician's alleged breach of a patient's confidence was decided in 1920 (*Simonsen v. Swenson*). In this case, the Nebraska court ruled that the doctor had a privilege to disclose information required to prevent the spread of a contagious disease.[4]

Over time, most jurisdictions in the United States have recognized legal actions against psychotherapists and other social service professionals in breach-of-confidence cases. Courts have varied, however, with respect to the legal theory on which they have based their rulings. Suits alleging wrongful disclosure of confidential information have been based on theories of (1) invasion of privacy, (2) express or implied statutory violations, (3) breach of implied contract, and (4) tortious violation of the duty to maintain confidentiality.[5] In *Hammonds v. Aetna*—several decades before the Health Insurance Portability and Accountability Act of 1996 (HIPAA) was enacted—a federal district court in Ohio stressed the necessity of privacy in therapeutic relationships when it concluded that "the preservation of the patient's privacy is no mere ethical duty upon the part of the doctor; there is a legal duty as well. The unauthorized revelation of medical secrets or *any* confidential communication given in the course of treatment, is tortious conduct which may be the basis for an action in damages."[6] In *Horne v. Patton*, an Alabama court was even more explicit about invasion of privacy; it concluded that disclosure of confidential information concerning a patient's mental health may constitute "unwarranted publicization of one's private affairs with which the public has no legitimate concern such as to cause outrage, mental suffering, shame or humiliation."[7] The concept of invasion of privacy was also cited in *Doe v. Roe*, in which a New York court found that a therapist violated a patient's privacy rights by publishing a book containing verbatim information that the patient disclosed during therapy sessions.

Some courts have also ruled that wrongful disclosure of confidential information can be based on the theory of express or implied statutory violations, specifically statutes related to licensing, testimonial privilege, and limiting the availability of medical information.[8] In *Berry v. Moench*, a Utah court ruled that patients may sue physicians when they disclose confidential information in violation of a statute that implicitly mandates confidentiality. In *Alberts v. Devine*, the Supreme Judicial Court of Massachusetts ruled that a psychiatrist could be held liable for breach of confidence, based in part on a state statute limiting the availability of hospital records.

Several court decisions have cited the theory of breach of an implied contract.[9] In *Hammonds*, for example, the federal district court ruled that a physician's disclosure of confidential information constituted a breach of an implied contract between physician and patient. The court held that a simple contract is formed whenever a doctor and patient establish a relationship, and one condition of this contract is that information the doctor learns during the course of the relationship will not be disclosed without the patient's permission. The court also said that within the context of such a relationship, patients have the right to rely on the professional's "warranty of silence." Similar references to the theory of implied contract appear in *Horne v. Patton* and in *Doe v. Roe*.

Finally, some courts have cited the theory of breach of fiduciary duty in their opinions in cases involving wrongful disclosure.[10] In *Alexander v. Knight*, *Hague v. Williams*, and *MacDonald v. Clinger*, for example, state appellate courts held that medical professionals have a fiduciary duty to their patients that entails protecting confidential information, and a breach of that duty is actionable as a tort (a wrongful act or an infringement of a right leading to a legal liability). State courts also recognized tort actions in breach of confidentiality in *Vassiliades v. Garfinckel's*, *Alberts v. Devine*, and *Fedell v. Wierzbieniec*.

Liability and malpractice problems related to privacy and confidentiality in behavioral health usually fall into two broad categories. The first includes deliberate disclosure of confidential information, such as sharing with a third party threats that a client made against that person or filing a report of child or vulnerable adult abuse against a client's wishes. The second includes inadvertent, unintentional, or accidental disclosure of confidential information, as in disclosing confidential documents without a client's authorization, posting sensitive information about a client on a social networking site (such as Facebook or Instagram), leaving sensitive information about a client exposed on a table in a semipublic area or on an unsupervised computer screen, or discussing a client's circumstances in the hallway of the agency.

### COMMON CONFIDENTIALITY ISSUES

Behavioral health practitioners encounter many instances when they must make decisions about whether to disclose confidential information to third parties, such as personnel in other social service agencies, clients' family members or employers, law enforcement officials, or managed-care organizations. Key issues include the disclosure of information to protect clients and third parties.

#### Protecting Clients and Third Parties

Judy S. was a mental health counselor at the Ocean State Family Service Agency. Her client, Alan F., had sought treatment three months earlier for symptoms of depression. Alan F. reported that he has had low self-esteem for years, ever since his bitter divorce. He has struggled with alcoholism and has been hospitalized on three occasions following suicide attempts and suicidal ideation.

Alan F. was particularly agitated during one recent session. He told Judy S. that he and his former wife were in the middle of a big dispute about visitation and child custody rights. Alan F. claimed that despite provisions in their divorce settlement, his former wife has been "doing everything she can to keep me from seeing the kids."

During the counseling session, Alan F. went on and on about how his former wife was tormenting him. He was clearly distraught. Toward the end of the session Alan F. said, "I can't begin to tell you how much I hate that woman. She's ruining my life. You have no idea how much I'd like to get rid of her. Maybe I just ought to do it."

Nearly every behavioral health practitioner can identify with the general circumstances presented in this case, a client who may pose a threat to a third party. In some instances the threat is clear and unambiguous, such as when a client explicitly announces an intention to harm a third party. By now there is considerable consensus that behavioral health practitioners need to take steps to protect such third parties; on occasion this may entail disclosure of confidential information against the client's wishes.

In other instances, however, the validity of the threat is less clear. Many clients make vague threats during an intense therapy session. Often, such threats are nothing more than blowing off steam. Yet, as we have learned all too well, such threats sometimes are genuine and purposeful.

By now, most behavioral health practitioners are acquainted with what is widely recognized as the red-letter precedent in so-called duty-to-protect cases: *Tarasoff v. Board of Regents of the University of California*. In 1969, Prosenjit Poddar was a student at the University of California–Berkeley. He became an outpatient counseling client at Cowell Memorial Hospital at the university and informed his psychologist, Dr. Lawrence Moore, that he was planning to kill an unnamed young woman (easily identified as Tatiana Tarasoff) upon her return to the university from her summer vacation. Poddar and Tarasoff had met at a campus dance. Over time, Poddar became disappointed that Tarasoff was not interested in pursuing a relationship with him. After the counseling session in which Poddar announced his plan, the psychologist telephoned the university police and requested that they observe Poddar because he might need hospitalization as an individual who was "dangerous to himself or others." The psychologist followed the telephone call up with a letter requesting the help of the chief of the university police.

The campus police took Poddar into custody temporarily but released him on the basis of evidence that he was rational; the police also warned Poddar to stay away from Tarasoff. At that point, Poddar moved in with Tarasoff's brother in an apartment near where Tatiana Tarasoff lived with her parents. Shortly thereafter, the psychologist's supervisor and the chief of the department of psychiatry, Dr. Harvey Powelson, asked the university police to return the psychologist's letter, ordered that the letter and the psychologist's case notes be destroyed, and directed that no further action be taken to hospitalize Poddar. No one warned Tatiana Tarasoff or her family of Poddar's threat. Poddar never returned to treatment. Two months later he killed Tatiana Tarasoff.

Tarasoff's parents sued the university's board of regents, several employees of the student health service, and the chief of the campus police, along with four of his officers, because their daughter was never notified of the threat. A lower court in California dismissed the suit, saying that sovereign immunity protected the multiple defendants. The court dismissed the civil action against the university, finding that Tarasoff's parents had no basis on which to sue because the university owed no duty of care to Tatiana, as she was not the patient. The California Supreme Court reversed the decision of the lower court and allowed the Tarasoffs to sue the university for failure to warn or protect, returning the case to the lower court for retrial. In its influential 1976 ruling, the California Supreme Court held that a mental health professional who knows that a client plans to harm another individual has a duty to protect the intended victim. In the court's oft-cited words,

> We recognize the public interest in supporting effective treatment of mental illness and in protecting the rights of patients to privacy and the consequent public importance of safeguarding the confidential character of psychotherapeutic communication. Against this interest, however, we must weigh the public interest in safety from violent assault. . . . We conclude that the public policy favoring protection of the confidential character of patient-psychotherapist communications must yield to the extent to which disclosure is essential to avert danger to others. The protective privilege ends where the public peril begins.[11]

This landmark case was ultimately settled out of court for an undisclosed sum. Many practitioners refer to *Tarasoff* as the "duty-to-warn" case. In fact, this phrase is misleading. The court noted practitioners' duty to protect, which is broader than the duty to warn. Warning a potential victim is one way, but not the only way, to protect potential victims. Notifying law enforcement officials of a threat and seeking psychiatric hospitalization of a dangerous client, when warranted, are other ways practitioners can attempt to protect potential victims. (Practitioners should be sensitive to concerns in communities of color about how law enforcement officials might respond.) *Tarasoff* is better described as the "duty-to-protect" case that led to many current confidentiality standards.

Since *Tarasoff*, a number of important duty-to-protect cases in various jurisdictions have clarified the thinking of courts and legislatures about the circumstances under which mental health professionals are obligated to disclose confidential information against clients' wishes. Some cases embrace and reinforce the court's reasoning in *Tarasoff*. Others challenge, extend, or otherwise modify the conclusions contained in the *Tarasoff* opinion.

The discussion below illustrates how states vary widely in the degree to which they follow the *Tarasoff* case. In addition, many states have adopted the guidelines, in the form of statutes and regulations, that were established in *Tarasoff* and other duty-to-protect cases. It is critically important for behavioral health practitioners to understand that some state laws *require* mental health professionals to disclose confidential information to protect a potential victim, while others *permit* disclosure to protect a potential victim. Practitioners should consult their respective state laws for guidance.

For example, in *McIntosh v. Milano*, Lee Morgenstein, a patient of Dr. Michael Milano's, killed Kimberly McIntosh, a young woman with whom Morgenstein once had had a relationship but who no longer wanted to be involved with him. Morgenstein was fifteen when he entered treatment with Milano; a school psychologist had referred Morgenstein's parents to Milano because of their son's drug use.

In treatment, Lee Morgenstein had discussed how overwhelmed he was by his relationship with McIntosh and his intense feelings of jealousy since McIntosh had become involved with another boyfriend. Morgenstein had threatened McIntosh on a number of occasions by firing a gun at her or her boyfriend's car and verbally threatening her and her dates. In addition, Morgenstein had brought a knife into a therapy session and had discussed fantasies of violent retribution against people who frightened him. One day, Morgenstein approached McIntosh, forced her to enter his car, took her to a park, and shot her.

In suing Milano, McIntosh's parents argued that by not warning their daughter, the therapist had departed from the standard of care in the profession. An expert witness, a psychiatrist, supported the parents' position. The defense argued that the *Tarasoff* guidelines should not be applied because the state of New Jersey did not have a duty-to-protect statute. In particular, the defense maintained the following:

> There is no such duty by a therapist to third parties or potential victims, and that *Tarasoff II* should not be applied, and was wrongly decided in that it (a) imposes an "unworkable" duty on therapists to warn another of a third person's dangerousness when that condition cannot be predicted with sufficient reliability; (b) will interfere with effective treatment by eliminating confidentiality; (c) may deter therapists from treating potentially violent patients in light of possible malpractice claims by third persons; and (d) will result in increased commitments of patients to mental or penal institutions.[12]

Consistent with *Tarasoff*, however, the New Jersey Superior Court held that a therapist may have a duty to take whatever steps are reasonably necessary to protect an intended or potential victim of his client when he or she determines, or should determine, in the appropriate factual setting and in accordance with the standards of his profession, that the client is or may present a probability of danger to that person.

In *Davis v. Lhim*, the Michigan courts also reinforced the logic of *Tarasoff*. Ruby Davis, administrator of the estate of Mollie Barnes, sued Dr. Yong-Oh-Lhim, a staff psychiatrist at Northville State Mental Hospital. Barnes, who was shot and killed by her son, John Patterson, had not been warned of a threat against her. Patterson had committed himself to the state hospital voluntarily several times during a three-year period. His problems included depression, insomnia, and schizophrenia. On September 2, 1975, Patterson asked Lhim to release him from the hospital. Lhim complied and released Patterson to the custody of his mother. Patterson initially stayed with his aunt, Ruby Davis, because his mother was visiting her brother, Clinton Bell. As time passed, however, the mother found her son too hard to handle and drove him to Bell's home. Patterson entered the Bell home, found a handgun, and began firing it. Patterson shot and killed his mother when she tried to take the gun from him.

The Wayne County Circuit Court concluded that Mollie Barnes was a foreseeable victim because Lhim knew of a threat that Patterson had made against her. The court found in favor of the plaintiff and ultimately was upheld on appeal.

The *Tarasoff* decision also clearly influenced the outcome of *Chrite v. United States*. In this case, Warner Chrite sued a U.S. Department of Veterans Affairs (VA) hospital in Massachusetts; he alleged that no one had warned his wife, Catherine, about a threat posed by a VA patient, Henry O. Smith, who was her son-in-law. Smith was released from the hospital under a state law that does not permit a patient to remain under supervision, without court permission, for more than sixty days. On the day he was released, Smith wrote a note stating, "Was Henry O. Smith Here Yesterday. He is wanted for murder Mother in Law." Hospital staff recorded the note in Smith's chart but did not warn his mother-in-law, Catherine Chrite. Smith carried out his threat after being released. The federal district court ruled in favor of Warner Chrite, concluding that hospital staff had an obligation to warn Catherine Chrite about the threat. Because of the details in the note, the court ruled, Catherine Chrite should have been considered a foreseeable victim.

*Tarasoff* also had a direct influence in *Jablonski v. United States*. In this case, Meghan Jablonski sued the VA hospital in Loma Linda, California, in the death of her mother, Melinda Kimball. Phillip Jablonski, Kimball's son-in-law, killed her; he was a patient at the hospital at the time of the slaying. Phillip Jablonski had gone to the VA hospital voluntarily for a psychiatric examination, after threatening Isobel Pahls, Kimball's mother, with a knife and attempting to rape her. The police spoke with the head of psychiatric services at the hospital and informed him of Phillip Jablonski's criminal record, including his obscene telephone calls to Pahls, and encouraged the medical staff to place Phillip Jablonski in an inpatient unit. In addition, Kimball informed another physician that Phillip Jablonski had served a prison term for a rape conviction and said that four days earlier Phillip Jablonski had attempted to rape her mother. The federal district court found the government liable, saying that the staff should have concluded, based on the information and previous records available, that Kimball was a foreseeable victim.

In *Mavroudis v. Superior Court*, the California courts further spelled out that the danger of violence to others must be an "imminent threat of serious danger to a readily identifiable victim" in order to justify a duty to warn. In *Thompson v. County of Alameda*, the California courts narrowed the requirement even further by suggesting that a duty to warn exists only when someone has made specific threats against identifiable victims. In this case, a chronic juvenile sex offender, "James," informed authorities that he intended to kill whatever child he next accosted. Nonetheless, a licensed therapist released the youngster, who ultimately carried out his threat. The parents of the slain youth, a five-year-old boy, sued the county authorities, alleging negligence because a dangerous juvenile was released into the community; they further claimed that the county authorities' supervision of James's legal custodian (his mother) was improper and that no one had warned the local police, neighborhood parents, or James's mother about his violent tendencies. The Superior Court of Alameda County ruled that because county officials could not have identified and warned a specific victim, the county had no duty to protect the child who was killed. The court dismissed the case, and the parents appealed. The Supreme Court of California affirmed the lower court's decision.[13]

The federal courts further stressed the importance of foreseeable harm and an identifiable victim in *Leedy v. Hartnett*. Harrison and Gertrude Leedy sued the VA hospital in Lebanon, Pennsylvania, after no one warned them that a patient, John Hartnett, had a tendency to get violent when drinking. Hartnett, a disabled veteran who received treatment at the hospital between 1956 and 1978, had been diagnosed with paranoid schizophrenia and chronic alcoholism. Hospital staffers apparently were familiar with Hartnett's violent tendencies during a period of at least ten years. On September 26, 1977, Hartnett discharged himself from the hospital and told hospital staffers that he would be staying with the Leedys. On March 31, 1978, Hartnett and the Leedys went to a club to celebrate Hartnett's birthday. Hartnett drank twenty-four 12-ounce bottles or cans of beer. Early the next morning at 2:00 A.M., Hartnett assaulted the Leedys at their home.

The Leedys sued the hospital, claiming negligence because no one warned them of Hartnett's violent tendencies. The hospital argued that it could not be held responsible for Hartnett's actions because he never informed the staff of his intent to harm the Leedys. The federal district court ruled in favor of the hospital, concluding that the Leedys were in no greater danger than anyone else who came into contact with Hartnett. The court ruled that Hartnett did not make *specific* threats at the time of discharge and his actions therefore were not foreseeable.

A federal district court in Colorado used similar reasoning when it dismissed *Brady v. Hopper*, in which victims of John Hinckley, Jr.'s, assault on President Ronald Reagan sued, alleging negligence. Hinckley's parents had brought him to Dr. John Hopper after Hinckley attempted to commit suicide. During his treatment with Hopper, Hinckley never specifically mentioned his intention to kill the president. Moreover, the defense argued, Hinckley had no history of violence and no previous hospitalizations because of violence. The court determined that Hinckley's therapist, Hopper, did not have a duty to protect the victims because Hinckley did not make explicit threats against these specific victims.

The absence of specific threats against victims also influenced the decision in *Cairl v. State*. In this case, Steven J. Cairl, who owned a small apartment building, sued Minnesota, the Ramsey County Welfare Department, and Bruce Hedge, the community reentry facilitator at the Minnesota Learning Center, because residents of the building, including Mary Ann Connolly and her two daughters, were not warned of the dangerous tendencies of Connolly's son. Tom Connolly, a resident at the Minnesota Learning Center who had an IQ of 57, was released to his family's home for the Christmas holiday; such home visits were consistent with the center's treatment philosophy. Learning Center staffers knew that Tom Connolly had set fires but concluded that the fires Mr. Connolly had set while at the center were not serious enough to cause concern. Mary Ann Connolly had been informed of the home visit plan, and on December 21, 1977, Hedge drove Tom Connolly to her home. On December 23, 1977, Tom Connolly set fire to the living room couch; one of his sisters was severely burned, another died of her injuries, and Cairl's property was destroyed.

At the initial trial in the District Court of Ramsey County, the court ruled that the hospital staff was not negligent in failing to warn the building's residents because Tom Connolly had not specifically stated that he would injure any of them; further, the court concluded, Mary Ann Connolly was aware of her son's fire-setting history. Cairl appealed the ruling, which was affirmed by the Supreme Court of Minnesota.[14]

The absence of a specific threat also influenced the outcome of *Rogers v. South Carolina*. A woman had been admitted to psychiatric hospitals on nine occasions. She had a substantial record suggesting a long-standing delusion of persecution by her family. After her release from one of her hospitalizations, the woman claimed that her sister was trying to poison her. Two weeks later she shot and killed her sister. The personal representative of the sister's estate filed a wrongful death suit against the patient's psychiatrist, alleging that the doctor had a duty to warn the sister that the patient might harm her. The South Carolina Court of Appeals concluded in part that because there was no evidence that the patient had made specific threats against her sister while being treated by the psychiatrist, the psychiatrist had no duty to warn the sister.[15]

Behavioral health practitioners should be aware, however, that some courts have not insisted on evidence of an identifiable victim to justify disclosure to protect a third party. In *Carr v. Howard, Massachusetts*, for example, a Massachusetts Superior Court judge rejected the traditional *Tarasoff* guidelines that require evidence of "specific threats to specific easily recognizable victims."[16] In this case, a hospital employee was injured by a psychiatric patient who attempted to commit suicide by leaping off the upper level of the hospital's parking garage. According to Lambert:

> The reach of *Tarasoff* has been steadily stretched by other courts to encompass more than "specific threats to specific victims." See, e.g., *Hamman v. County of Maricopa*, 775 P.2d 1122 (Ariz. 1989), 32 ATLA L. Rep. 182–85 (June 1989) (going beyond *Tarasoff*, Arizona rejects specific threat to

specific limit of *Tarasoff* and holds that therapist's or doctor's duty may run to and encompass non-privity third parties who are endangered by a violence-prone patient, here the enraged son's stepfather).[17]

At least one case suggests that therapists may have a duty to hospitalize potentially dangerous clients to protect potential victims. In *Currie v. United States*, a patient at a VA outpatient clinic who was in treatment to address posttraumatic stress disorder threatened to blow up a building owned by IBM, his former employer. The therapist involved in the case believed that the patient posed a threat and contacted IBM, the FBI, local police, and the U.S. attorney's office. The therapist did not, however, believe that the patient met the commitment criteria under North Carolina law. Some time later, the patient took homemade explosives and a gun to an IBM office and killed an employee.

The victim's estate sued the VA, claiming that it had not warned all potential victims and alleging negligence in not seeking the man's commitment. The defense argued that the duty to protect did not pertain because the victim was one of many IBM employees and hence could not have been identified. The defense also argued that the therapist had no duty to commit because the patient did not meet the involuntary commitment criteria. The federal district court held that patients who act out at random or in only broadly predictable ways do in fact create a duty for therapists. The court also ruled that the therapist wrongly interpreted the state's commitment criteria and that the patient was indeed committable.

Similar issues were raised in *Lipari v. Sears, Roebuck*. Ruth Ann Lipari sued Sears, Roebuck because a psychiatric patient, Ulysses L. Cribbs, had bought a gun at a Sears store; also named in the suit was the federal government because Cribbs was a patient at a VA hospital. One night Cribbs entered an Omaha nightclub and fired shots into the room, killing Dennis Lipari and seriously wounding Ruth Ann Lipari. After Lipari filed her suit, Sears, Roebuck and Lipari joined forces in *Sears v. U.S.*, suing the VA hospital because Cribbs had not been detained or committed. Court papers disclosed that Cribbs had been committed to a psychiatric facility and started treatment in a day program at the VA hospital approximately two months before the shooting. The federal district court denied the government's motion for a summary judgment and ultimately agreed with the plaintiffs' argument that the VA was negligent because it had failed to commit Cribbs.

In *Shaw v. Glickman*, a Maryland court did not accept the reasoning of *Tarasoff*. In this case, Leonard Billian, his wife, Mary Ann, and her lover, Dr. Daniel Shaw, were all in treatment with a team led by Dr. Leonard Gallant, who died after the events at issue occurred (Glickman was named as a defendant because he was the personal representative of Gallant's estate). While in treatment, Mary Ann Billian left her husband. One night Leonard Billian entered Shaw's home at 2:00 A.M. and found Shaw and Mary Ann Billian both nude and asleep in the same bed. Leonard Billian shot Shaw five times. Shaw survived and sued Gallant, the team leader, arguing that he was negligent because he had not warned Shaw of Leonard Billian's "unstable and violent condition and the foreseeable and immediate danger that it presented to Dr. Shaw." The Superior Court of Baltimore City ruled in Gallant's favor—concluding that Gallant did not have a duty to warn—and granted him a summary judgment. Shaw appealed. The Maryland appellate court affirmed the lower court decision, concluding that because Leonard Billian never stated his intent to kill or injure Shaw, and Shaw assumed the risk of injury when he went to bed with Mary Ann Billian, Gallant did not have a duty to warn. Moreover, the court argued that it would have been "a violation of the statute for Dr. Gallant or any member of his psychiatric team to disclose to Dr. Shaw any propensity on the part of Billian to invoke the old Solon law and shoot his wife's lover."[18]

A Florida court too apparently challenged the *Tarasoff* doctrine in *Boynton v. Burglass*. In this case, the plaintiff sued a psychiatrist, alleging that the psychiatrist had a duty to warn and did not do so. A patient of the psychiatrist had killed the plaintiff's son. The suit alleged that the psychiatrist had a duty to warn the intended victim, the victim's family, or law enforcement officials of the threat of violence and that the slaying resulted from the breach of that duty. The suit stated that the patient had threatened to kill the plaintiff's son during a therapy session.

The Florida trial court dismissed the suit because it failed to state a claim (i.e., the plaintiff failed to set forth sufficient facts to entitle recovery against the defendant, should the plaintiff win the case); the plaintiff appealed. The appellate court affirmed the trial court's decision, concluding that "it would be fundamentally unfair to impose a duty to warn upon psychotherapists because psychiatry is an inexact science and a patient's dangerousness cannot be predicted with any degree of accuracy."[19] In addition, the appellate court concluded that the psychiatrist would have violated both his duty to his patient and Florida's statutory psychotherapist-patient privilege had he disclosed any threat by the patient to harm the victim. The court opinion also expressed concern about the possibility that patients' trust and confidence would be undermined if a clinician were required to warn potential victims whenever a patient expressed hostile feelings toward a third party.[20]

A widely publicized and controversial Connecticut case, *Almonte v. New York Medical College*, raised several novel duty-to-protect issues. The plaintiff, who was ten years old at the time, was brought to a hospital as a suicide risk. A physician completing his residency in child psychiatry treated the boy. As part of his training, the resident was also in treatment with a psychiatrist, with whom he shared a fantasy about having sex with children—and a trip the resident reported he took to Mexico to find a child. The Connecticut boy alleged that the psychiatry resident fondled and attempted to sodomize him during treatment sessions. The psychiatry resident was found negligent.[21] In addition, the federal district court in Connecticut held that the Manhattan-based doctor who treated the resident had a duty to warn or otherwise prevent the resident from sexually abusing the boy (*Garamella v. New York Medical College*). The court held that "even without breaching the confidentiality of the resident's communications, the instructor was authorized to notify the medical college that . . . the resident had revealed information that made him unsuitable for psychoanalytic training . . . and . . . the college would be advised to review whether the resident should remain in the residency program practicing child psychiatry."[22]

Several courts have been reluctant to extend the *Tarasoff* reasoning to cases involving suicide. In *Bellah v. Greenson*, for instance, a therapist's client committed suicide, and the family members claimed that they should have been warned of this possibility. The California courts held, however, that the clinician had no duty to warn unless there was a risk of violent assault to others. Although the ruling did not conclude that therapists *cannot* provide such warnings, it did assert that therapists are not *required* to violate confidentiality.

Clearly, the *Tarasoff* decision unleashed considerable debate and controversy concerning the limits of clients' right to confidentiality. Proponents argue that it is naive to believe the right to confidentiality is inviolable. Public safety, they assert, sometimes must trump privacy rights, particularly when a third party is at risk of serious or violent harm.

Critics, however, argue that *Tarasoff*-like guidelines are like the camel's nose under the tent. Once the perimeter has been breached, the entire structure is at risk. One commonly cited concern is that mental health practitioners have relatively poor records of predicting clients' violent behavior.[23] Thus it makes little sense to base a practitioner's obligation to disclose confidential information to protect third parties on the assumption that professionals are in fact able to predict future violence accurately. Grossman has been one of the most ardent critics. Referring to the California Supreme Court's ruling in *Tarasoff* soon after it was rendered, Grossman stated,

> The court also keeps using statements such as "to *predict* that Poddar presented a serious danger of violence . . . [and] did in fact *predict* that Poddar *would* kill." It indicates that the *amicus* brief introduced by national professional organizations did bring to their attention from the authoritative source of the treating professions that therapists can *not* predict a violent act. The statistics of studied experiences ran approximately one eventual violent act out of 100 "predictions." None of these studies compared these to the average population incidence of violence. Nor was mention made that therapists can detect thought and emotional processes having a violence theme. At times they may detect a weakening of the ordinary restraints that keep such themes from overt expression, but they certainly cannot predict the future external events that may trigger such an increased weakening of control of the violent emotion or thought that leads to either a verbal or physical assault. They cannot predict whether an act that may take place, should control break, will be verbally or physically assaultive.[24]

In addition, critics question the assumption that providing a warning to a potential victim is likely to, in and of itself, prevent a violent act. According to Grossman, the belief that such warnings are likely to provide real protection is naive:

> Approximately 50 people interested in *Tarasoff* were informally asked, "If you were warned under these circumstances—a psychiatric patient on the loose, who had threatened your life during therapy—how would you protect yourself?" Most first answered, "I'd call the police." When told of the above cases [where warnings seemed not to be effective], they gave one of these replies: "I would hate going into hiding"; "I don't know"; and "I'd kill him if he came near." The warning offers no protection and may well harm the supposed victim.[25]

Over time, the influence of *Tarasoff* as a legal precedent has become more limited because many jurisdictions have adopted specific statutes addressing duty-to-protect issues. Behavioral health practitioners should determine whether their state has such a statute and understand its provisions, which can vary from jurisdiction to jurisdiction.

### Balancing Confidentiality and Protection

The litigation in the various duty-to-protect cases over the years has helped to clarify the precarious trade-offs between practitioners' obligation to respect clients' right to confidentiality and therapists' simultaneous duty to protect third parties from harm. Although some rulings in these cases are inconsistent and contradictory, the general trend suggests that four conditions ordinarily justify disclosure of confidential information to protect a third party from harm. First, the practitioner should have evidence that the client poses a threat of violence to a third party. As the court said in *Tarasoff*, "When a therapist determines, or pursuant to the standards of his profession should determine, that his patient presents a serious danger of violence to another, he incurs an obligation to use reasonable care to protect the intended victim against such danger."[26] Although courts have not provided precise definitions of *violence*, the term ordinarily implies the use of force—by use of a gun, knife, or other deadly weapon—to inflict harm.

Second, the practitioner should have evidence that the violent act is foreseeable. That is, the practitioner should be able to present evidence that suggests significant risk that the violent act will occur. Although courts recognize that practitioners cannot make foolproof predictions, practitioners must be able to demonstrate that they had good reasons for believing that their client was likely to carry out the violent act.

Third, the practitioner should have evidence that the violent act is imminent. That is, the practitioner should be able to present evidence that the act was impending or likely to occur relatively soon. Here too the courts have not provided clear, unambiguous guidelines. *Imminence* may be defined differently by different practitioners, ranging from minutes to hours to weeks from the moment of decision. Ultimately, practitioners need to be able to make a strong case to defend their definition of *imminence*.

Finally, a number of court decisions—although not all—suggest that a practitioner must be able to identify the probable victim. The rationale here is that disclosure of confidential information against a client's wishes should not occur unless the behavioral health practitioner has specific information about the client's apparent intent. This would include knowledge of an actual potential victim. As Lewis observes:

> Though not stated in either opinion, it appeared that both *Tarasoff* and *McIntosh* required that there be a particular or readily identifiable potential victim in order to impose liability for negligent failure to warn. In *Thompson v. County of Alameda*, the California Supreme Court clarified this requirement. The *Thompson* court found no cause of action where the threats uttered by a juvenile offender to county officials did not constitute specific threats against particular individuals, but rather, were directed to an entire class. The court concluded that the county could not be liable for negligent failure to warn or to take other steps to protect an entire class of children to whom the juvenile posed a threat.[27]

Note, however, that when a practitioner can infer the identity of a foreseeable victim from case-related material—even if the client has not specifically named the potential victim—a duty to protect may exist.

Behavioral health practitioners should be aware that court decisions vary considerably concerning whether they must have evidence of an identifiable potential victim in order to incur a duty to protect. This is evident especially in the Washington State Supreme Court decision *Volk v. DeMeerleer*. On July 18, 2010, Jan DeMeerleer entered the home of Rebecca Schiering, his ex-fiancée, and murdered Schiering and one of her sons. Her other son escaped. DeMeerleer then shot and killed himself.

DeMeerleer had been diagnosed with bipolar disorder and had been in psychiatric care on and off with Dr. Howard Ashby of the Spokane Psychiatric Clinic for nine years. Intermittently over the years, DeMeerleer had thoughts of harming himself and others, but he had made no suicide attempts during his nine years of treatment with Dr. Ashby. He had his last appointment with Dr. Ashby approximately three months before the event at issue. At that appointment, DeMeerleer reportedly voiced no thoughts of violence and, specifically, no thoughts of harm directed at Schiering, her children, or anyone else. He denied any intent to harm himself. Subsequently, DeMeerleer's relationship with his fiancée ended.

After the deaths, Schiering's mother and surviving son sued Dr. Ashby and the Spokane Psychiatric Clinic for failure to follow the standard of care, arguing that Dr. Ashby might have prevented the attacks by warning the victims. Citing Washington law, specifically Revised Code of Washington (RCW) 71.05.120 [7], Dr. Ashby asserted that a mental health clinician owes a duty to third parties only when the patient has communicated an actual threat of physical violence against a reasonably identifiable victim or victims, which had not occurred in this case. The trial court agreed and granted summary judgment to Dr. Ashby.

On appeal, the appellate court ruled that the state's statute applied only in the context of involuntary psychiatric treatment and reversed and remanded the trial court's decision. The Washington Supreme Court affirmed the appellate court. According to this court, the outpatient mental health clinician "incurs a duty to take reasonable precautions to protect *anyone* who might foreseeably be endangered by the patient's condition." Once there is a "special relationship" between the patient and clinician, the clinician has a duty because of the patient's dangerous propensities, even if the patient voices no threat of violence and even if no victim is identified (or reasonably identified). Not surprisingly, this court decision sent shock waves throughout the behavioral health community in light of its assertion that there can be a duty to protect even when the practitioner's client has not voiced a threat of violence and has not identified a potential victim.[28]

In another significant case, *Maas v. UPMC Presbyterian Shadyside*, the Pennsylvania Supreme Court ruled that neighbors of a potentially dangerous client are considered readily identifiable third parties, even if the client does not provide the names of the neighbors. Terrance Andrews, a psychiatric client, resided at a supported living facility and received mental health treatment from UPMC Presbyterian Shadyside. Staffers eventually facilitated Andrews's move from the supported living facility to an apartment building and continued to provide supportive services. Andrews then began frequently expressing a desire to kill his neighbors and disclosed a plan to stab a "neighbor" who had knocked on his door in the middle of the night and to "kill the next-door neighbor and everyone." Andrews never identified the potential victims by name.

After expressing homicidal thoughts and receiving outpatient treatment, the patient was sent home by the facility's case manager with medication. Four days later, the patient murdered his neighbor, Lisa Maas, five doors down, with a pair of scissors.

Despite the rulings in *Tarasoff* and subsequent duty-to-protect cases, practitioners and lawyers continue to debate which guidelines should govern practitioners' decisions. By now they generally agree that a practitioner whose client makes a clear threat to violently injure an identifiable victim within the next several hours has a duty to take steps to protect the potential victim. This may include disclosing confidential information against a client's wishes. Other cases, however, are less clear.

Consider, for example, a case in which a behavioral health practitioner's client is HIV positive and seems to pose a threat to his sexual partner, who is not aware of the client's infection. The practitioner does her best to encourage the client to disclose his health status to his sexual partner, but for a variety of complex clinical reasons the client does not share this information with his partner. This set of circumstances is complicated, and there has been considerable disagreement about the relevance of the *Tarasoff* and other duty-to-protect guidelines that have evolved since that decision. When the *Tarasoff* case was decided, no one anticipated its eventual application to AIDS cases. In fact, the final *Tarasoff* decision in 1976 preceded by five years the first AIDS case identified in the United States. Since then, however, the debate about the relevance of *Tarasoff* to AIDS cases has been vigorous.[29] Some argue, for example, that *Tarasoff* is not an adequate precedent because people with AIDS may not specifically and explicitly threaten a third party with an act of violence. People who are HIV positive usually are concerned about their partners and willing to practice safer sex, although they may be unwilling to disclose their HIV-positive status to their partners. In addition, the threat to third parties may not always be imminent, and the victim may not be identifiable.[30] As Francis and Chin argue, "Maintenance of confidentiality is central to and of paramount importance for the control of AIDS. Information regarding infection with a deadly virus, sexual activity, sexual contacts and the illegal use of IV drugs and diagnostic information regarding AIDS-related disease are sensitive issues that, if released by the patient or someone involved in health care, could adversely affect a patient's personal and professional life."[31]

However, some claim that the HIV-positive status of an individual, which merely *poses* a threat to another party, is sufficient to rely on *Tarasoff* and related cases as precedents.[32] As Gray and Harding conclude, "A sexually active, seropositive individual places an uninformed sexual partner (or partners) at peril, and the situation therefore falls under the legal spirit of the *Tarasoff* case and the ethical tenets of 'clear and imminent danger.' "[33] As the president of the American Professional Agency, a major malpractice insurer of behavioral health professionals, said, "We can pay for breach of confidentiality, but we can't bring the dead back to life."[34]

Although precise, unequivocal guidelines governing disclosure of confidential information to protect third parties do not exist, behavioral health practitioners can minimize their liability risks. For example, faced with a client who may pose a threat to a third party, the practitioner should do the following:

- Consult with supervisors and colleagues about the best way to manage the situation, and document the consultation.
- Consult an attorney who is familiar with state law concerning the duty to warn and/or protect third parties (state laws vary considerably on the obligations of health-care professionals with respect to confidentiality and the duty to protect).
- Consider asking the client to warn the victim (unless the practitioner believes this contact would only increase the risk).
- Seek the client's consent for the practitioner to warn the potential victim.
- Disclose only the minimum amount necessary to protect the potential victim and/or the public.
- Encourage the client to agree to a joint session with the potential victim in order to discuss issues surrounding the threat (unless this might increase the risk).
- Encourage the client to surrender any weapons he or she may have.
- Increase the frequency of therapeutic sessions and other forms of monitoring.
- Be available or have a backup available, at least by telephone.
- Refer the client to a psychiatrist if medication might be appropriate and helpful or if a psychiatric evaluation appears to be warranted.
- Consider hospitalization, preferably voluntary, if appropriate.

Throughout this process, practitioners should seek relevant consultation from colleagues who have experience in dealing with dangerous clients and should document this consultation; the nature of their own thinking about the case; their review of relevant literature, ethics standards, and laws; and the rationale for whatever decision the practitioner ultimately makes.

Most important, clients must be informed at the beginning of service that while the practitioner ordinarily respects the right to confidentiality, legal limits do exist. Practitioners should include a brief explanation of confidentiality limits on an information sheet prepared for clients. The form would provide clients with a summary of agency or private practice policy concerning disclosure of confidential information, especially the circumstances under which the practitioner has a duty to warn or protect and behaviors or threats that may require disclosure. Other items on this information sheet might pertain to service hours, fees, payment policies, instructions in case of emergency, and the inability to guarantee success in treatment. Clients might be asked to sign a copy of this document, to be inserted in their file, attesting that they read it, understand its content, and were given an opportunity to ask questions.

When a practitioner concludes that disclosure is necessary, who should be notified or warned is not always clear. Schutz offers sage advice in these circumstances:

> Generally, it is suggested that the authorities and/or the intended victim should be warned. Warning the authorities makes the most sense when the intended victims are the patient's children, since a warning to the victim is ordinarily useless, and the child protective agency often has broader powers than the police—who might say that they cannot detain the patient (particularly after a failed commitment) because he has not done anything yet. If one decides to warn the victim—who is naturally shocked and terrified by the news that someone intends to kill him— and if nothing occurs, one could be liable for infliction of emotional distress by a negligent diagnosis. One way to reduce this risk might be to include as a part of the warning a statement of professional opinion about the nature and likelihood of the threat; to recommend that the victim contact the police, an attorney, and a mental health professional for assistance to detain (or try to commit) the patient; to inform the victim of his legal rights; and to offer assistance with the stress of such a situation.[35]

Many attorneys recommend always notifying law enforcement officials, even when the intended victim is warned. From a legal risk management perspective, notifying law enforcement officials shares the responsibility with other professionals.

Practitioners should be familiar with so-called red-flag laws in their jurisdiction. Red-flag laws, also known as extreme risk protection order laws, aim to prevent individuals who show signs of being a threat to themselves or others from purchasing or possessing firearms. Law enforcement officials, family members, and health-care professionals may be able to petition a court to place the order. The parties permitted to petition the court for an extreme risk protection order and the criteria courts are required to consider vary. Practitioners should review their jurisdiction's provisions.

One potential pitfall is that behavioral health practitioners' concern about liability could lead them to overreact. That is, to avoid risk, practitioners might disclose information too quickly or seek civil commitment of individuals who do not in fact require confinement. Such excessive caution can create its own problems. Unnecessary intrusion and violation of clients' rights can trigger legal claims that allege defamation of character, negligent diagnosis, infliction of emotional distress, false imprisonment, invasion of privacy, and malicious prosecution.

In the end, practitioners must use their judgment about the tension between protecting a client's right to confidentiality and protecting third parties from harm. Explicit, unambiguous guidelines for those decisions do not exist. As M. Lewis notes, "It must . . . be recognized that psychotherapy is an imperfect science. A precise formula for determining when the duty to maintain confidentiality should yield to the duty to warn is, therefore, beyond reach."[36] Although court decisions provide some guidance, behavioral health practitioners ultimately must rely on thoughtful judgment that is based on prudent consultation. After reviewing case law and statutes on the issue, M. Lewis goes on to say:

> The acceptance by many jurisdictions of the duty imposed on psychotherapists to warn or take other reasonable steps for the protection of their patients' potential victims, viewed contemporaneously with an increasing recognition that patients have a right to sue for damages for unauthorized disclosure of confidential information, places mental health professionals in an unenviable predicament. *Tarasoff* and its progeny established that persons harmed by individuals undergoing therapy may sue that patient's psychotherapist for negligent failure to protect them from the patients' dangerous propensities. Case law also makes it clear that mental health professionals have a duty to maintain the confidential nature of their relationships

to those to whom they are rendering treatment. A breach of either duty may result in civil liability. The inquiry that arises out of this conflict is whether therapists can uphold a duty of reasonable care with respect to potential victims while continuing to exercise reasonable care toward their patients.[37]

### Substance Use Disorders Treatment

Behavioral health practitioners also need to be well informed about comprehensive restrictions concerning disclosure of confidential information pertaining to substance use disorder treatment. Strict federal regulations— Confidentiality of Substance Use Disorder Patient Records (42 CFR Part 2)—limit practitioners' disclosure of confidential information. These regulations broadly protect the confidentiality of the records of substance use disorder treatment programs—with respect to the identity, diagnosis, prognosis, or treatment of any client—maintained in connection with any program or activity relating to substance use disorder treatment that is federally assisted. Disclosures are permitted only in a narrow range of circumstances that are set forth in this detailed federal regulation.

### Student Education Records

Behavioral health practitioners employed in school settings should be familiar with the Family Educational Rights and Privacy Act (FERPA) (34 CFR Part 99) as amended and with its attendant federal regulations. This federal law protects the privacy of student education records and applies to all schools that receive money from the U.S. Department of Education. For example, parents or eligible students have the right to inspect and review the student's education records maintained by the school. Generally, schools must have written permission from the parent or eligible student in order to release any information from a student's education record. However, FERPA allows schools to disclose those records, without consent, to certain parties and under specific conditions (e.g., to comply with a court order or lawfully issued subpoena, in cases of health and safety emergencies).

More specifically, FERPA gives parents certain rights with respect to their children's education records. These rights transfer to the student when she reaches the age of eighteen or attends a school beyond the high school

CONFIDENTIALITY AND PRIVILEGED COMMUNICATION

level. Students to whom the rights have transferred are "eligible students." These rights are as follows:

- To inspect and review the student's education records maintained by the school.
- To request that a school correct records that parents or eligible students believe to be inaccurate or misleading. If the school decides not to emend the record, the parent or eligible student then has the right to a formal hearing. After the hearing, if the school still decides not to emend the record, the parent or eligible student has the right to place a statement with the record setting forth his view about the contested information.

Generally, schools must have written permission from the parent or eligible student in order to release any information from a student's education record. However, FERPA allows schools to disclose those records, without consent, to the following parties or under the following conditions:

- School officials with legitimate educational interest
- Other schools to which a student is transferring
- Specified officials for audit or evaluation purposes
- Appropriate parties in connection with financial aid to a student
- Organizations conducting certain studies for or on behalf of the school
- Accrediting organizations
- Compliance with a judicial order or lawfully issued subpoena
- Appropriate officials in cases of health and safety emergencies
- State and local authorities, within a juvenile justice system, pursuant to specific state law

Schools may disclose, without consent, "directory information" such as a student's name, address, telephone number, date and place of birth, honors and awards, and dates of attendance. However, schools must tell parents and eligible students about directory information and allow parents and eligible students a reasonable amount of time to request that the school not disclose directory information about them. Schools must notify parents and eligible students annually of their rights under FERPA. The actual means of notification (special letter, inclusion in a PTA bulletin, student handbook, or newspaper article) is left to the discretion of each school.

School-based behavioral health practitioners should take steps to segregate their clinical notes from students' educational records. School administrators and teachers should not have access to practitioners' counseling notes.

Also, practitioners should be very familiar with the "sole possession records" provision in FERPA. According to this regulatory law, records are exempt from FERPA if they are kept in the sole possession of the maker of the records, are used only as a personal memory aid, and are not accessible or revealed to any other person except a temporary substitute for the maker of the records. Sole possession records may not be reviewed by the student. An example of a sole possession record would be personal notes a school social worker or counselor keeps regarding a student encounter.

### Deceased Clients

Behavioral health practitioners sometimes receive requests for confidential information about former clients who have died. Surviving family members of a client who committed suicide may seek information to help them understand and cope with their loss or practitioners may be subpoenaed in a legal matter involving a dispute among family members concerning the former client's will. A news reporter or law enforcement official may request information about a deceased client who was somehow involved in a serious crime or an Internal Revenue Service official may ask for information about a deceased client's lifestyle.

Clients' confidentiality rights do not end in death; thus practitioners must take careful steps to protect the confidentiality of deceased clients. Practitioners should not disclose confidential information unless they have obtained proper legal authorization to do so (for example, in the form of a court order or permission from the legal representative of the client's estate).

In one case in which I consulted, an experienced clinician made the mistake of granting an interview to a reporter who was investigating the death of one of the practitioner's clients. The clinician specialized in the treatment of sex offenders and inadvertently disclosed confidential information about her deceased client. The state licensing board sanctioned the practitioner.

A widely publicized case involved the nationally known therapist Susan Forward, who had been treating Nicole Brown Simpson, the former wife of

O. J. Simpson. Forward appeared on several national interview programs and was among the first to disclose Nicole Brown Simpson's history of abuse by O. J. Simpson. The regulatory board in California concluded that Forward's disclosure of confidential information about her deceased client violated professional standards and suspended Forward's license to practice for three months. The board also placed Forward on probation.[38]

### Parents and Guardians

Behavioral health practitioners who provide services to children and adolescents sometimes must make difficult decisions about the disclosure of confidential information to third parties. Often, these situations occur when minors are engaging in self-destructive behaviors (e.g., high-risk sexual activity, drug abuse, cutting, suicidal gestures) or threaten to harm others. Also, parents may initiate a request for information about their minor children. This is especially common when parents are involved in a child custody dispute; one parent (or the parent's attorney) may want to inspect the clinical record to assess whether it contains information that can be used in court against the other parent (e.g., when the child shared information during a counseling session about the other parent's allegedly abusive behavior or other misconduct).

State laws and regulations vary with respect to practitioners' obligations in these situations. Practitioners should consult local statutes, regulations, and attorneys to determine the extent to which they are (1) obligated to disclose confidential information to parents and guardians, even without the minor client's consent; (2) permitted—but not obligated—to disclose confidential information to parents or guardians without the minor client's consent; and (3) not permitted to disclose confidential information to parents or guardians without the minor client's consent. In some states, the minor's rights relating to disclosure of confidential information may be determined by the parents' marital status (divorced or separated) or whether the child is deemed a mature minor.

Most states have statutes that explicitly address minors' right to obtain mental health or substance use disorder treatment services without notification of parents or parents' consent. Statutory provisions vary considerably among the states; many states have one law governing minors' right to mental health services and another law regarding substance use disorder treatment services. For example, some state laws permit minors of a certain age (e.g., sixteen) to obtain mental health services without parental notification or consent but permit minors of any age to obtain substance use disorder treatment without parental notification or consent. Some state laws permit behavioral health practitioners to provide services to minors without parental notification or consent if the practitioner believes that notification of the parents without the minor's consent would be harmful to the minor (e.g., if there is evidence that the parents would abuse the child upon learning about the child's substance use). Still other state laws permit practitioners to provide substance use disorder treatment services without parental consent only if two physicians certify that the minor requires addiction services. Given the considerable variation in state laws and that they can change over time, practitioners should be sure to consult their state laws and attorneys as needed.

Various courts have ruled on parents' requests to inspect the clinical records of their minor children. *In the Matter of Kathleen Quigley Berg and Eugene E. Berg*, a New Hampshire case, is illustrative. When Eugene Berg and Kathleen Quigley Berg divorced, Kathleen was awarded primary physical custody of their four children. The parents shared joint legal custody, and Eugene had specific periods of visitation.

After the divorce, Eugene asked the court to find Kathleen in contempt. Eugene alleged that the children were not visiting him as scheduled and that Kathleen had alienated the children from him. Eugene requested records and notes from the children's therapists to determine whether they contained evidence of Kathleen's alleged interference with his relationship with the children. The therapists refused to produce the records on the grounds that disclosure would not serve the children's best interests.

The *guardian ad litem* (GAL) who had been appointed by the court to represent the children's interests asked the court to seal the children's records. Kathleen agreed, but Eugene objected. The marital master denied the request to seal, stating that the legal right of a custodial parent to access his children's medical records overrides the children's privacy rights.

On appeal, the New Hampshire Supreme Court was asked to address three questions:

1. Do children have a right to privacy for their medical records and communications?
2. Does the court have the authority to seal the therapy records of the parties' minor children when one parent demands access to the records for purposes of litigation?
3. Should the court have the authority to seal the therapy records of minor children when the parents are in conflict about the release and access to such records?

The court essentially answered "yes" to all three questions. The court rejected Eugene's argument that a parent's right to raise his or her children overrides the children's privacy interests. The court challenged the assumption that a parent will always act solely with the children's best interests in mind, noting that this assumption may not always be warranted in the context of divorce and child custody proceedings. In fact, in a custody dispute, the interests of the parents may be adverse to the child's interest.

In the end, the New Hampshire Supreme Court stated that the trial court must determine whether waiver or assertion of the privilege is in the child's best interest. The court instructed the trial court to give particular emphasis to preserving the child's ability to engage in treatment in making such a determination. The trial court may exercise its discretion to appoint a GAL to address this issue. It may also grant the GAL the right to inspect the treatment records or it may conduct an *in camera* (private) review.

Out of an abundance of caution, practitioners who counsel minors should clarify whether one or both parents have legal custody. This has implications regarding parental consent to treatment and access to otherwise confidential information about the minor. I recommend that practitioners ask parents for a copy of relevant legal documents, including current and court-approved child custody agreements and divorce decrees.

In an effort to protect the privacy of their minor clients, practitioners should consider asking parents to sign a confidentiality agreement at the outset of counseling. A typical agreement highlights the importance of privacy in counseling and how essential it is for minor clients to trust their clinician. It informs the parents that therapy is most effective when a trusting relationship exists between the therapist and the patient. Privacy is especially important in earning and keeping that trust. As a result, it is important for children to have a "zone of privacy" where children feel free to discuss personal issues without fear that their thoughts and feelings will be immediately communicated to their parents and guardians. Parents and guardians are informed that it is the practitioner's policy for the child's clinician to provide them with general information about the child's treatment, but not to share specific information the child has disclosed to the clinician without the child' consent, including activities and behavior that the parents or guardian would not approve of—or might be upset by—but that, in the practitioner's judgment, do not put the child at risk of serious and immediate harm. The policy states that if the child's risk-taking behavior becomes more serious, the practitioner would need to use his or her professional judgment to decide whether the child is in serious and immediate danger of harm and information needs to be shared with parents or guardians. In turn, minor clients are informed of the practitioner's policy about respecting the minor's privacy and circumstances that may warrant disclosure to parents or guardians.

### Family, Couples, and Group Counseling

Behavioral health practitioners who provide services to families, couples, or groups sometimes encounter difficult ethical dilemmas related to confidentiality. For example, members of a family, couple, or group may not respect other clients' confidentiality or will expect the practitioner to keep secrets from other family, couple, or group members. Many practitioners present clients with forms that explain the importance of confidentiality and request each client's agreement to honor other clients' rights to confidentiality.

Before beginning counseling relationships, practitioners should ensure that their clients fully understand whether and to what extent their therapeutic communications are privileged under the law, and the rights of each party to access and release the practitioner's clinical record. If communications are made in the presence of an unprivileged third party, they may not be privileged, unless the law provides for exemption. Some jurisdictions protect communications made during family or group therapy.

In an effort to prevent this potential conflict of interest, many clinicians who serve couples have the parties sign an agreement including language such as: "All parties acknowledge that the goal of psychotherapy is the amelioration of psychological distress and interpersonal conflict, and that the process of psychotherapy depends on trust and openness during the therapy sessions. Therefore, it is understood by all parties that if they request my services as a psychotherapist, they are expected not to use information given to me during the therapy process for their own legal purposes or against any of the other parties in a court or judicial setting of any kind. If you are involved in a divorce or child custody dispute, I will not provide testimony in court on any subject other than your therapy. You must hire a different mental health professional for any evaluations you require."

Many behavioral health practitioners who provide counseling to couples are not willing to provide individual counseling to one or both members of the couple, because of the possibility of a conflict of interest and challenges managing the parties' confidential disclosures in individuals' counseling sessions. For example, a husband who receives individual counseling from the couple's therapist may disclose sensitive information in an individual counseling session that he does not want the practitioner to share with the husband's spouse (e.g., his involvement in an extramarital affair). This places the practitioner in a difficult and uncomfortable situation. To avoid such predicaments, many practitioners who provide couples counseling insist on referring partners to other clinicians for individual counseling.

### Collateral Agreements

Many behavioral health practitioners arrange to meet with clients' family members and acquaintances during clinical sessions. Meeting with so-called collaterals may be useful to add clinically relevant insights or to arrange support for a client.

It is vitally important for practitioners to explain clearly to collaterals the nature of their rights, especially related to confidentiality. Given that collaterals are not formal clients, they are not entitled to the same confidentiality protections typically afforded clients. This could become an issue if, for example, the practitioner's records are subpoenaed in conjunction with a legal proceeding in which the client is involved (such as a divorce, child custody dispute, or criminal proceeding).

To protect all parties involved in the counseling, it behooves practitioners to develop and share collateral agreements with third parties who are included in counseling sessions. Typically, collateral agreements explain that the collateral is not considered a client, is not the focus of the services, and that the collateral has less privacy protection than the client. Further, practitioners inform the collateral that the practitioner will not maintain a formal record in the collateral's name, and that notes about the collateral may be included in the client's record. The client has a right to access that record; the collateral does not.

### Disclosure to Third Parties

Behavioral health practitioners sometimes receive requests for confidential information from third parties who have some interest in clients' circumstances. Practitioners need to handle these requests carefully, avoiding disclosure without written authorization by the client or other legitimate party (e.g., a court order).

When clients authorize disclosures to reporters (e.g., when a journalist wants to feature a client in a story about how people cope with behavioral health challenges), practitioners should discuss with clients in detail the risks that may be involved in permitting their clinician to talk with a reporter (e.g., the risks associated with publicity) as well as potential benefits. Practitioners should not disclose confidential information to the media without proper authorization. In one case, the court held that a psychiatric nurse's intentional disclosure of confidential treatment records to the media constituted unprofessional conduct.[39]

Practitioners should also be careful when responding to requests for confidential information from law enforcement officials, protective service agencies, and collection agencies. When disclosure is appropriate or required, practitioners should limit the disclosure as much as possible.

There are multiple guidelines pertaining to disclosures to law enforcement officials. These are embedded in various federal laws, state laws, and code of ethics standards. Many practitioners in the United States are governed by disclosure rules contained in HIPAA. According to HIPAA, practitioners may disclose confidential information to law enforcement officials without clients' consent under a number of circumstances:

- To report protected health information (PHI) to a law enforcement official reasonably able to prevent or lessen a serious and imminent threat to the health or safety of an individual or the public.
- To report PHI that the practitioner in good faith believes to be evidence of a crime that occurred on the premises of the entity covered by HIPAA.
- To alert law enforcement to the death of the individual, when there is a suspicion that death resulted from criminal conduct.
- When responding to an off-site medical emergency, as necessary to alert law enforcement to criminal activity.
- To report PHI to law enforcement when required by law to do so (such as reporting gunshots or stab wounds).
- To comply with a court order or court-ordered warrant, a subpoena or summons issued by a judicial officer, or an administrative request from a law enforcement official (the administrative request must include a written statement that the information requested is relevant and material, specific and limited in scope, and de-identified information cannot be used).
- To respond to a request for PHI for purposes of identifying or locating a suspect, fugitive, material witness, or missing person. The information must be limited to basic demographic and health information about the person.
- To respond to a request for PHI about an adult victim of a crime when the victim agrees (or in limited circumstances if the individual is unable to agree). Child abuse or neglect may be reported, without a parent's agreement, to any law enforcement official authorized by law to receive such reports.

In contrast, the strict federal regulation Confidentiality of Substance Use Disorder Patient Records (42 CFR Part 2) prohibits disclosure to law enforcement officials without a court order, and only if the disclosure is necessary to protect against an existing threat to life or of serious bodily injury, including circumstances that constitute suspected child abuse and neglect and verbal threats against third parties; or the disclosure is necessary in connection with investigation or prosecution of an "extremely serious crime," such as one that directly threatens loss of life or serious bodily injury, including homicide, rape, kidnapping, armed robbery, assault with a deadly weapon, or child abuse and neglect.

For school-based counselors, the Family Educational Rights and Privacy Act (FERPA) states that when a significant threat exists—anything from an active shooter to a hazardous weather event to a chemical spill—school officials are permitted to disclose "personally identifiable information" (PII) from education records to appropriate parties, such as law enforcement, to protect the health and safety of students or other individuals. Schools are allowed to share this information only during the period of the emergency, and they must meet certain record-keeping requirements.

Many state laws concerning health-care confidentiality also include language permitting behavioral health professionals to share confidential information with law enforcement officials when there is evidence of serious, imminent, and foreseeable risk. Further, state licensing regulations and codes of ethics governing behavioral health professionals include similar provisions.

### Electronic Records and Communications

A wide range of technological innovations has enabled behavioral health practitioners to transmit confidential information quickly and efficiently, for example, using smartphones, e-mail, and electronic record software. Practitioners should take a variety of steps to protect clients' confidentiality. They should take reasonable steps to ensure that clients' records are stored in a secure electronic location and that clients' records are not available to others who are not authorized to have online access. Practitioners should use applicable safeguards (such as encryption, firewalls, and passwords) when using electronic communications such as e-mail, online posts, online chat sessions, mobile communication, and text messages.

Practitioners who use fax machines should obtain clients' informed consent and inform clients about the potential risks involved (i.e., unauthorized individuals may have access to these unprotected communications). Also, practitioners should notify the intended recipient by telephone that the fax is being sent and obtain the recipient's agreement to immediately retrieve the document from the fax machine. The document's cover sheet should include a statement alerting recipients to the confidential nature of the communication, along with the sender's telephone number.

Further, practitioners should not leave confidential details in voicemail messages intended for their clients if the practitioners are not entirely certain who has access to the messages. As a precaution, practitioners should talk with clients early in their relationship about where and how to leave messages in a way that safeguards the client's privacy and confidentiality. Clients' preferences should be documented in the clinical record to ensure that all staffers who serve the clients honor their wishes.

Internet communications are particularly risky. E-mail messages can be sent to the wrong party and may not be secure. Practitioners should inform clients of their policies related to e-mail. For example, many practitioners have developed what are known as social media policies that inform clients that they are not to use e-mail or social networking sites (such as Facebook) to communicate with practitioners about their clinical concerns. A typical social media policy informs clients that practitioners cannot guarantee a timely response to e-mail or other electronic messages and that these messages may not be secure. Practitioners should discuss their policies with clients at the beginning of their relationship to avoid any misunderstanding.[40]

Practitioners must become intimately familiar with the federal regulations that focus explicitly on electronic communications initiated by health-care providers. HIPAA and its regulations require that personal health information be kept confidential. Failure to comply can result in civil and criminal penalties. Protected health information includes information about a person's health, health care, or payment for health care that identifies a person and is created or received by a covered health-care provider. The term *health* includes behavioral health. Protected health information may not be disclosed by a covered entity without the informed and voluntary written consent or authorization of the client. Disclosure of confidential information must be limited to the minimum amount necessary for the purposes of the disclosure, when providers need access to clients' full records; the exception is the transfer of records for treatment. Clients requesting the information must be given a history of disclosures of their protected health information. To comply with HIPAA regulations, covered health-care providers must designate a privacy official who will develop and implement the privacy policies and procedures of the agency; develop policies and procedures designed to ensure that covered entities are in compliance with the standards and requirements of the regulations; provide privacy training to staff and develop a system of sanctions for employees who violate the agency's policies; meet documentation requirements; and provide written notice of privacy practices in plain English. The notice of privacy practices (templates for which are readily available) must include a description of the client's rights, describe anticipated uses and disclosures of information that may be made without authorization, identify a contact person in the event of a complaint, and inform clients of the right to register a complaint with the secretary of the U.S. Department of Health and Human Services. The agency must post the notice in a visible location, and clients must receive a written copy during their first visit.

Several exceptions under the HIPAA regulations permit disclosure of clients' protected health information without client consent or authorization. Examples include disclosures required by law; disclosures for public health activities (such as reporting diseases, collecting vital statistics); disclosure about victims of abuse, neglect, or domestic violence; disclosures for judicial or administrative proceedings; disclosures for law enforcement purposes (as noted earlier); and disclosures to prevent a serious threat to health or safety.

Practitioners should be aware that under HIPAA regulations, "psychotherapy notes" have special privacy protections. Ordinarily, clients must give written consent before a third party can receive psychotherapy notes. The authorization must be limited to psychotherapy notes and cannot be combined with an authorization for other parts of a clinical record. Clients do not have a right of access to psychotherapy under HIPAA, although the practitioner may decide in her discretion to permit access.

The regulations define *psychotherapy notes* as notes recorded (in any medium) by a health-care provider who is a mental health professional documenting or analyzing the contents of conversation during a private counseling session or a group, joint, or family counseling session and that are separated (physically or electronically) from the rest of the individual's medical record. Excluded from the definition of psychotherapy notes are prescriptions for and monitoring of medication, counseling session start and stop times, modalities and frequencies of treatment furnished, results of clinical tests, and any summary of client diagnosis, functional status, treatment plan, symptoms, prognosis, and progress to date.

The Health Information Technology for Economic and Clinical Health (HITECH) Act, enacted as part of the American Recovery and Reinvestment Act of 2009, was signed into law on February 17, 2009, to promote the adoption and meaningful use of health information technology. Subtitle D of the HITECH Act addresses the privacy and security concerns associated with the electronic transmission of health information, in part through several provisions that strengthen the civil and criminal enforcement of the HIPAA rules. Subtitle D also implements new rules for the disclosure of patient health information if a breach takes place.

Overall, the HITECH Act significantly modifies HIPAA. HITECH expands HIPAA's definition of *business associates* and provides that the HIPAA security standards that apply to health plans and health-care providers will also apply directly to business associates, that is, anyone who must use protected health information, such as billing clerks, as well as the health and mental health professionals with whom practitioners collaborate. The HITECH Act also makes the HIPAA privacy provisions applicable to business associates.

### Integrated Records

One of the most significant developments in the field of behavioral health in recent years is the proliferation of integrated health-care settings. An integrated health-care setting includes deliberate and sustained coordination of care among health-care practitioners (physicians, nurses, nurse practitioners, and physician assistants, among others) and behavioral health professionals (social workers, psychiatrists, psychologists, mental health counselors, and addiction specialists, among others). This important phenomenon reflects professionals' increasingly rich understanding of the complex and essential connections between individuals' physical health and mental health.

Integrating health care and behavioral health services has produced a number of complex ethical and risk management challenges. Administrators in behavioral health organizations may need to segregate some protected health information to comply with relevant laws and limit which employees can access it. For example, an integrated health center may include a specialized program for people who struggle with substance use disorders. If the organization receives any form of federal assistance, clinical records generated by staffers in this program would be governed by 42 CFR Part 2: Confidentiality of Substance Use Disorder Patient Records. Organization staffers who do not work in this program should not be permitted to access these notes, unless the client has authorized the sharing of this information with other organization staffers (e.g., with the client's primary-care physician in this integrated health center). Organizations can protect this sensitive information by creating firewalls in their electronic health records. Many integrated health centers also feature "break-the-glass" protocols in their electronic health records systems, which require staffers to create a digital footprint acknowledging that they have accessed this portion of the client's record and documenting the reasons for accessing the record.[41]

### Privacy Audits

Increasing numbers of behavioral health agencies and practitioners are conducting what are known as privacy audits to ensure compliance with current standards. Many of the current privacy audit standards were developed with two prominent sets of federal standards—HIPAA and the HITECH Act—in mind. Any health-care provider that deals with protected health information (PHI) must ensure that all the required physical and network security measures are in place and followed.

The HITECH Act includes provisions requiring organizations to conduct privacy audits. Subtitle D of the HITECH Act addresses the privacy and security concerns associated with the electronic transmission of health information, in part, through several provisions that strengthen the civil and criminal enforcement of HIPAA rules. Health-care organizations and third-party payers are expected to monitor for breaches of PHI from both internal and external sources.

The U.S. Department of Health and Human Services Office for Civil Rights has established criteria that its auditors use to validate compliance with federal regulations. They provide a useful guide for behavioral health agencies and practitioners. Key audit activities include the following:

- *Determine the activities that will be tracked or audited.* Obtain and review documentation to determine whether audit controls have been implemented over information systems that contain or use PHI.
- *Select the tools that will be deployed for auditing and system activity reviews.* Inquire of management as to whether systems and applications have been evaluated to determine whether upgrades are necessary. Obtain and review documentation of tools or applications that management has identified to capture the appropriate audit information.

- *Develop and deploy the information review/audit policy.* Obtain and review formal or informal policies and procedures and evaluate the content to understand whether a formal audit policy is in place to communicate the details of the entity's audits and reviews to the workforce. Obtain and review an e-mail, or some form of communication, showing that the audit policy is communicated to the workforce.
- *Develop appropriate standard operating procedures.* Obtain and review management's procedures in place to determine the systems and applications to be audited and how they will be audited.

The American Health Information Management Association (AHIMA)—a prominent organization dedicated to improving the management of health-related information—has developed comprehensive protocols for professionals who want to conduct privacy audits.[42] Their guidelines are especially valuable for behavioral health practitioners and agencies. According to AHIMA, privacy audits should produce detailed audit logs that are useful for the following:

- detecting unauthorized access to client information;
- establishing a culture of responsibility and accountability;
- reducing the risk associated with inappropriate access;
- providing forensic evidence during investigations of suspected and known security incidents and breaches to client privacy, especially if sanctions against a workforce member, business associate, or other contracted agent will be applied;
- tracking disclosures of PHI;
- responding to client privacy concerns regarding unauthorized access by family members, friends, or others;
- evaluating the overall effectiveness of the organization's policy and user education regarding appropriate access and use of client information (this includes comparing actual workforce activity to expected activity and discovering where additional training or education may be necessary to reduce errors);
- detecting new threats and intrusion attempts;
- identifying potential problems; and
- addressing compliance with regulatory and accreditation requirements.

A number of behavioral health professionals and their employers have discovered significant security breaches that led to online exposure of clients' sensitive health and behavioral health information. Office for Civil Rights investigations of such breaches can result in significant civil monetary penalties and publicly available disclosure on the agency's website. For example, Sunshine Behavioral Health Group, a network of drug and alcohol addiction treatment facilities in California, Colorado, and Texas, experienced a breach of sensitive patient information because of a misconfigured website. News reports indicate that breached data included billing records that may have contained some combination of full names, birth dates, addresses, telephone numbers, e-mail addresses, credit card numbers, expiration dates, CVV (card verification value) codes, and health insurance information.[43]

In another case, Inmediata Health Group, a provider of clearinghouse services, software, and business processing solutions to health plans, hospitals, and independent practitioners, disclosed a security incident affecting some customer data. The incident was discovered when Inmediata found that a misconfigured webpage was allowing some electronic health information to be viewed publicly. The webpage was allowing search engines to index Inmediata's internal webpages that were used for business operations and not intended for public view. The health information involved in this incident included patients' names, dates of birth, genders, and medical claims information, with some affected individuals potentially having their Social Security numbers exposed.[44]

In addition, personal data of more than 645,000 clients of Oregon's Department of Human Services (DHS) were compromised during a data breach. The breached client information potentially included first and last names, addresses, dates of birth, Social Security numbers, case numbers, personal health information, and other information used in Oregon DHS programs. The data breach occurred as a result of an e-mail phishing attempt when several Oregon DHS employees opened and clicked on a phishing link, thereby giving the sender access to their accounts.[45]

In one widely publicized case, the U.S. Federal Trade Commission (FTC) charged an electronic health records company with deceptive practices that violated patients' privacy and confidentiality.[46] The cloud-based electronic health records company agreed to settle FTC charges that it misled consumers by soliciting reviews for their doctors without disclosing adequately that these reviews would be publicly posted on the Internet, resulting in the public disclosure of patients' sensitive personal and medical information.

According to the FTC complaint, the company made plans to launch a public-facing health-care provider directory. In order to populate the directory with patient reviews, the company began sending e-mail messages to patients of health-care providers utilizing the company's electronic health records service. The e-mails appeared to be sent on behalf of the patients' doctors and asked consumers to rate their provider "[t]o help improve your service in the future."

According to the complaint, consumers who clicked on the five-star rating image in the e-mail were taken to an online survey form with questions about their recent medical visit. The survey included a text box where patients could enter any information they wished within a set character limit. Because patients likely thought the information was only shared with their provider, many of them included in the text box their full name or phone number along with personal health information inquiries. For instance:

- one consumer asked for information on dosing for "my Xanax prescription";
- one consumer included a request for help with a depressed child, writing "I think she is depressed and has stated several times this week that she wishes she was dead";
- and one consumer wrote that "I did a little research and I think I have a yeast infection called candida."

The settlement with the FTC prohibited the company from making deceptive statements about the privacy or confidentiality of the information it collects from consumers. It also required the company, prior to making any consumers' information publicly available, to clearly and conspicuously disclose this fact and obtain consumers' affirmative consent.

### Disclosures for Extreme Risk Protection Orders

Some states have enacted laws that permit professionals governed by HIPAA to disclose protected health information without clients' consent to obtain what is known as an extreme risk protection order (ERPO). Such protection orders may be sought in some states by law enforcement, family members, or others concerned that an individual who is suicidal or otherwise in crisis will use a firearm to seriously injure or kill himself or herself or another person. These laws are sometimes referred to as red-flag laws.

The U.S. Department of Health and Human Services Office for Civil Rights has issued guidance to help clarify how the HIPAA Privacy Rule permits covered health-care providers to disclose protected health information to support applications for extreme risk protection orders that temporarily prevent a person in crisis, who poses a danger to themselves or others, from accessing firearms.[47] This guidance helps implement the U.S. Department of Justice's model extreme risk protection order legislation that provides a framework for states to consider in creating laws allowing law enforcement, concerned family members, or others to seek these orders and to intervene in an effort to save lives. This model legislation provides a framework for states to consider as they determine whether and how to craft laws allowing law enforcement, concerned family members, or others to seek these orders and to intervene to try to prevent a tragedy.

The model legislation includes language that would authorize courts to issue no-firearms orders for dangerous individuals and the concurrent issuance of search warrants to search for and seize their firearms. Further, the model legislation provides that, in qualifying emergency circumstances, the at-risk individual may be served with the order concurrently with or after the search is carried out. The process would be overseen by a court to ensure the protection of the individual's rights.

Under the federal government's guidance, HIPAA permits a covered health-care provider to disclose protected health information (PHI) to support an ERPO application by the provider or another person in certain circumstances, including the following:

- *When the disclosure is required by law.* A covered health-care provider may disclose PHI when the disclosure is required by law (e.g., statute, regulation, court order, subpoena) and the disclosure complies with and is limited to the relevant requirements of such law.
- *When the disclosure is in response to an order of a court or administrative tribunal, subpoena, discovery request, or other lawful process in the course of a judicial or administrative proceeding.* The Privacy Rule places conditions on disclosures for these purposes, including when such disclosures are required by other law. Here are examples:

  **Example 1**: A covered health-care provider receives a court order compelling the provider to produce a client's medical records to the court to support its determination as to whether to issue an ERPO against the provider's client. The Privacy Rule permits the provider to disclose only the PHI that is authorized by the court order.

**Example 2**: A petitioner applies for an ERPO in state court alleging, in an affidavit, that her partner has threatened to shoot her with his firearm and has been receiving care from a behavioral health professional. The state's attorney issues a subpoena compelling the partner's covered behavioral health provider to disclose medical records to determine whether there is a sufficient legal basis to issue the ERPO.

The Privacy Rule permits the behavioral health provider to disclose the minimum necessary PHI to comply with the subpoena that is not accompanied by an order of a court or administrative tribunal if one of the following conditions is met:

- The provider receives satisfactory assurances from the state's attorney that reasonable efforts have been made to ensure that the individual who is the subject of the PHI request has been given notice of the request; or
- The provider receives satisfactory assurances from the state's attorney that reasonable efforts have been made to secure a qualified protective order prohibiting use or disclosure of the PHI for purposes other than the proceeding, and requiring the return to the provider or destruction of the PHI at the end of the proceeding.
- The disclosure is necessary to prevent or lessen a serious and imminent threat to the health or safety of a person or the public. A covered healthcare provider who believes that an individual presents a serious and imminent threat to the health or safety of a person (including the individual) or the public may, consistent with applicable law and standards of ethical conduct, disclose PHI if the provider believes in good faith that the disclosure is necessary to prevent or lessen the threat and the disclosure is made to any person or persons reasonably able to prevent or lessen the threat. The covered health-care provider must make reasonable efforts to limit the PHI disclosed to the minimum necessary to prevent or lessen the threat.

A health-care provider that discloses PHI to prevent or lessen a serious and imminent threat is presumed to have acted in good faith with regard to the belief that the disclosure is necessary to prevent harm if the belief is based on the provider's actual knowledge or in reliance on a credible representation by a person with apparent knowledge or authority. Health-care providers may disclose the necessary PHI, without an individual's authorization, to anyone who is in a position to prevent or lessen the threatened harm. This permission includes the sharing of psychotherapy notes, which otherwise receive special protection under the Privacy Rule.

> **Example 3**: An individual's family member calls the individual's therapist and states that the family is worried because the individual threatened to bring a firearm to the workplace and kill a supervisor. An applicable state law authorizes health-care providers to petition a court for an ERPO to protect the life of a patient or another person. The therapist knows that the individual possesses a firearm and believes the family member's representation is credible. The therapist applies for an ERPO and provides an affidavit that discloses PHI about the individual who poses a threat.

The Privacy Rule permits the therapist to disclose the PHI of the individual to the court in an ERPO application if the therapist believes in good faith that the disclosure is necessary to lessen or prevent the serious and imminent threat to the supervisor. The good faith belief may be based on a credible representation by the individual's family member.

The Privacy Rule also permits the therapist to notify the supervisor that the individual poses a serious and imminent threat if the therapist believes in good faith that the disclosures are necessary to prevent or lessen the threat and the disclosures are to a person or persons reasonably able to prevent or lessen the threat.

### Third-Party Payers

Behavioral health practitioners often receive requests from third-party payers, such as insurance and managed-care companies, for information about clients. This information may concern clients' clinical symptoms and profiles, treatment history, and treatment plan. To comply with prevailing ethics standards and federal regulations under HIPAA, practitioners should obtain clients' consent or authorization before disclosing such confidential information, unless permitted under the law (e.g., for purposes of treatment, payment, and health-care operations). Some practitioners include wording on the informed-consent or release-of-information form for this purpose that acknowledges the client understands that the practitioners cannot be responsible for protecting confidential information once it is shared with the third-party entity and that the client releases the practitioner from any liability connected with a breach of confidentiality by a third-party payer.

### Transfer or Disposal of Clients' Records

Practitioners who transfer a case record or other confidential material to another agency or colleague should take steps to protect the confidentiality of the information. Electronic records containing protected health information should be properly encrypted and protected from unauthorized access. Further, practitioners also should dispose of records (when permitted by relevant regulations, statutes, and standards) in a manner that protects client confidentiality. Confidential paper records should be shredded or otherwise destroyed to prevent access by unauthorized individuals. Electronic records containing protected health information are subject to strict disposal standards under HIPAA.

### Client Confidentiality and the Practitioner's Death, Incapacitation, or Employment Termination

Behavioral health practitioners need to prepare for the possibility that they may not be able to continue working with clients because of disability, illness, employment termination, or death. Practitioners should develop procedures to ensure continuity of service and to protect clients' confidential records. This may include a practitioner arranging for colleagues to assume at least initial responsibility for her cases if the practitioner is unable to continue practicing. Such steps may include oral or written agreements with colleagues or stipulations that appear in a plan that the practitioner develops with the assistance of a lawyer (e.g., designating a personal representative who will manage the practitioner's professional affairs).

Behavioral health practitioners in private or independent practice should prepare a professional will that includes plans for the transfer or disposition of cases if the practitioner dies or becomes incapacitated.[48] The will can provide for an executor or trustee who will maintain records for a certain period of time. Such an arrangement can prevent unauthorized people from gaining access to confidential information.

A professional will enables practitioners to plan for what happens if they die or become incapacitated. It spells out the steps that colleagues or other parties should take to ensure that clients' needs are met in a timely fashion. This guidance can be particularly helpful when death or incapacitation occurs without forewarning. A comprehensive professional will should address several key issues.

*Who will assume responsibility?* Practitioners need to designate an individual or individuals who will take charge in the event of a practitioner's death or incapacitation. This may be a colleague or another trusted party; ideally, this designee is a trained professional who is familiar with ethical standards in the field of behavioral health that pertain to client confidentiality and informed consent. The professional will should include detailed contact information of individuals who may be able to assist in locating/accessing client records; for example, telephone numbers (landline, mobile, fax), office address, e-mail address.

It makes sense to designate one or two backup administrators as well. Practitioners should meet with their designee to ensure that that person fully understands the details of the professional will. Practitioners should provide information about the location of office keys, computer log-in information, and security codes. Administrator-designees should also have information about voicemail access codes in order to review and respond to clients' messages.

*Client records.* Practitioners should inform their designees about the location of clients' physical records and filing cabinet keys. Practitioners who maintain electronic records should ensure that their designees have relevant computer usernames and passwords and information about the names of computer files that hold records. A practitioner's administrator-designee should also know how to access the practitioner's schedules so that clients who have upcoming appointments can be notified. The professional will can state who will store the records until more permanent arrangements can be made.

*Informed consent and client notification.* When practitioners begin working with clients, they should consider obtaining clients' consent to share their contact information and, if necessary, clinical records with the practitioner's designee in the event of an emergency. This can be included in the initial consent to provide services that practitioners have clients sign.

Professional wills may identify specific ways that practitioners' designees can notify clients of the practitioner's incapacitation or death, such as calling each client, placing a notice in the local newspaper, changing the practitioner's outgoing voicemail message to include the announcement, changing the voicemail message to ask clients to call the practitioner's designee for implementing the deceased or incapacitated practitioner's professional will, and sending letters and e-mail messages. Which notification approach is most appropriate depends on the nature of the practitioner's unique practice and clientele.

Ideally, designees who notify clients about the practitioner's death or incapacitation should provide clients with information about steps they can take to arrange other services. This may include the names of other providers and their contact information. Whatever forms of notification are considered, practitioners and their designees should be mindful of clients' right to privacy and confidentiality. Letters, e-mail messages, and telephone or voicemail messages that are not carefully handled can inadvertently disclose to third parties that a person is seeing a clinician. This can be particularly problematic, for example, when the client is a domestic violence victim who sought counseling services without her partner's knowledge; unintentional disclosure to the abusive partner may exacerbate the client's risk.

*Notification of colleagues, insurers, and attorneys.* A professional will should identify members of the practitioner's peer consultation group to notify in the event of the practitioner's death or incapacitation. It should also include information about the practitioner's professional malpractice insurer, policy number, and contact information. Further, a professional will should include the name of, and contact information for, an attorney the practitioner has used for professional consultation.

*Billing information.* The practitioner's designee will need to know where billing records are located, how to access them (whether paper or electronic records), who prepares and processes the bills (e.g., a billing service or office clerical worker), and how pending charges are to be handled.

*Expenses.* Managing a deceased or incapacitated colleague's affairs can be very time consuming. A professional will ought to specify how the practitioner's designee will be compensated. Options include authorizing a customary hourly rate the designee is to be paid, a flat fee, or a token payment. A professional will should include clear instructions about how all expenses are to be paid.

Professional will templates are widely available online and are relatively easy to complete. Some practitioners may wish to have a skilled attorney—particularly one who specializes in health and behavioral health law—help prepare and review a draft of the professional will. Once the professional will has been finalized, the practitioner should give copies to her or his attorney and designee. Practitioners and their attorneys should decide whether to give the designees access to confidential information such as computer usernames and passwords when the professional will is signed or only upon the practitioner's death or incapacitation. Practitioners should review and update their professional wills on a regular basis (e.g., yearly).

### Collection Agencies

It is reasonable for behavioral health practitioners to contact collection agencies when they encounter serious difficulty collecting payment from clients. Before doing so, practitioners should make every effort to provide clients with sufficient notice and reasonable payment plans (some practitioners wisely inform clients at the beginning of service about how they will handle overdue payments).

When practitioners find it necessary to contact collection agencies, they should have strict procedures in place to prevent the inappropriate disclosure of confidential information (e.g., clinical information). Information shared with collection agencies should be limited to the client's name, contact information, and the amount of the debt. Practitioners should confirm that state laws do not prohibit disclosure of information about behavioral health clients to collection agencies.

Practitioners should keep in mind that bill collection efforts sometimes lead to a licensing-board complaint from a disgruntled client alleging incompetent or harmful treatment. If the practitioner sues to collect the debt, he or she should anticipate a counterclaim alleging malpractice. Some practitioners decide to write off uncollected fees to minimize this risk. However, practitioners should not routinely waive co-pays or deductibles because this can violate the federal antikickback statute and subject the practitioner to the risk of being accused of fraud by insurance companies. Attorneys typically advise practitioners to avoid allowing clients to accumulate large bills; when this occurs, practitioners become creditors and run the risk of having a conflict of interest and acting in dual roles. Practitioners should be aware that they can ethically terminate services in the event of nonpayment, although they should not do so if there is evidence at that time that the client poses an imminent danger to self or others.

### Consultants

Practitioners' consultation with colleagues is often reasonable, necessary, and a key risk management step. Practitioners should share with consultants the least amount of information necessary to achieve the purposes of the consultation. Often, it is possible for practitioners to avoid disclosing clients' identifying information.

### Volunteers and Employees

Practitioners who have supervisory responsibilities should take steps to ensure that volunteers and employees have access only to that confidential information necessary in order to carry out their duties (i.e., they should have access to confidential information on a need-to-know basis). Volunteers and employees should be trained to handle confidential information responsibly. For example, volunteers and paid staff should be trained not to disclose the identities of clients and how to avoid inadvertent and unintentional disclosure of confidential information (e.g., responding to a request for confidential information by a police officer or family member, exchanging text and e-mail messages, avoiding hallway conversations about clients or leaving confidential information on a desk or displayed on a computer screen). Many agencies ask volunteers and employees to sign formal confidentiality agreements that spell out their duties and responsibilities.

### Disclosing Information for Teaching or Training Purposes

Behavioral health educators and trainers often present case material for instructional purposes. In such instances, practitioners should not disclose any identifying information without clients' informed consent. Clients' names should not be mentioned, and presenters should disguise or alter case-related details to ensure anonymity. Any written case material should be similarly disguised.

Practitioners who present audio- or video-recorded material should also take careful steps to protect clients. Such material should not be presented unless clients have provided informed consent to the taping itself and to the presentation of the material. With video records, it may be possible to protect client confidentiality by recording clients from an angle that limits their visibility or by blurring their distinguishing characteristics (face and voice, especially).

Practitioners need to assess the ability of clients to make sound judgments about consenting to the disclosure of identifying information or images for teaching or training purposes. Clients who are asked for their consent may feel some pressure, whether intended or not, to accede to their practitioner's request. Practitioners should be careful to avoid any exploitation or the appearance of exploitation.

Classroom and webinar educators should ensure that students understand their obligation to protect client confidentiality when students are asked to include case material in written assignments or presentations. Educators should discuss with students various ways in which they can disguise case material and avoid disclosing identifying information.

### Unauthorized Access

Practitioners employed in agency settings must not access confidential client records without authorization. On occasion, licensing boards have disciplined practitioners when they examined confidential records about people known to them but who were not clients. Practitioners should access confidential records only when they are authorized to do so and on a need-to-know basis.

### THE CONCEPT OF PRIVILEGED COMMUNICATION

The *Tarasoff* case and other duty-to-protect cases litigated since *Tarasoff* raise a variety of complex issues concerning the limits of clients' right to privacy, particularly when third parties appear to be at risk. As I noted earlier, privacy and confidentiality are essential ingredients in therapeutic relationships. Nonetheless, clients' right to privacy and confidentiality have limits. For example, behavioral health practitioners must comply with mandatory reporting laws related to abuse of children and older adults.

To understand the limits of privacy and confidentiality, practitioners must be familiar with the doctrine of privileged communication. The right of privileged communication—which assumes that a professional cannot disclose confidential information without the client's consent—originated in British common law, under which no "gentleman" could be required to testify against another individual in court. Among professionals, the attorney-client relationship was the first to gain the right of privileged communication. Over time, other groups of professionals, such as physicians, psychiatrists, social workers, psychologists, mental health counselors, and clergy, sought legislation to provide them with this right.[49]

Behavioral health practitioners need to understand the distinction between *confidentiality* and *privilege*. *Confidentiality* refers to the professional norm that information shared by or pertaining to clients will not be shared with third parties. *Privilege* refers to the disclosure of confidential information in court or legal proceedings. As Meyer, Landis, and Hays say:

> The terms confidentiality and privilege, though often confused, actually refer to different legal concepts. Confidentiality refers to the broad expectation that what is revealed in a private or "special" relationship based upon trust will not be shared with third parties. Obviously, the kind of information revealed by individuals in therapy fits into this category. Privilege is a narrower concept that concerns the admissibility of information in a court of law, though in practice it really refers to whether courts may legitimately compel revelation of confidential information for the purpose of legal proceedings.[50]

Various groups of professionals have argued that they and their clients or patients need statutory protection from requests to reveal confidential information. Courts commonly accept four conditions, originally proposed by the jurist John Henry Wigmore, as necessary to the consideration of information as privileged:

- The parties involved in the conversation assumed that it was confidential.
- Confidentiality was an important element in this relationship.
- The community recognizes the importance of this relationship.
- The harm caused by disclosure of the confidential information would outweigh the benefits of disclosure during legal proceedings.[51]

Regarding the first condition, behavioral health practitioners can reasonably assume that clients expect the information that they share will be kept confidential. Further, a central tenet of behavioral health practice is that effective assistance depends on clients' willingness to trust practitioners with the most personal details of their lives and that such trust is necessary if this relationship is to be meaningful and productive. In addition, the community at large generally accepts the assumption that relations between clients and practitioners are important and valuable, thus satisfying Wigmore's third condition. The fourth condition, that the injury caused by disclosure of confidential information is greater than the benefit gained from disclosure, is ordinarily the most difficult to satisfy and triggers the greatest debate.

The most significant federal court decision with direct bearing on behavioral health practitioners is the landmark case of *Jaffe v. Redmond*, in which the U.S. Supreme Court ruled that the clients of clinicians have the right to privileged communication in federal courts.[52] In this precedent-setting case, a police officer, Mary Lu Redmond, sought counseling from a clinical social worker after the officer killed Ricky Allen, a man involved in a fight. Redmond had responded to a fight at an apartment complex. She shot Allen believing he was about to stab a man he was chasing. The administrator of Allen's estate filed suit in federal district court alleging that Officer Redmond violated Allen's constitutional rights by using excessive force. During discovery, the plaintiff learned that Redmond participated in many counseling sessions with social worker Karen Beyer. The plaintiff sought access to Beyer's clinical record; Redmond objected arguing that disclosure should be prevented because of a psychotherapist-patient privilege. The district court judge ruled that the Federal Rules of Civil Procedure did not provide for a psychotherapist-client privilege and allowed the discovery of Beyer's clinical record, but neither Beyer nor Redmond complied with the request. The judge advised the jury that the refusal to turn over Beyer's notes could be considered a presumption that the content of the notes would have been unfavorable to the respondent. Ultimately, this case reached the U.S. Supreme Court.

In its decision, the U.S. Supreme Court said that "participants [in therapy] must be able to predict with some degree of certainty whether particular discussions will be protected. An uncertain privilege, or one which purports to be certain but results in widely varying applications by the courts, is little better than no privilege at all."[53] This case is particularly important because it established, for the first time in U.S. legal history, that clinical social worker–client relationships are privileged in federal court proceedings; until the *Jaffe* decision, only some state courts recognized social worker–client privilege.

It is important to note that the *client* holds the privilege, not the behavioral health practitioner; the practitioner has a duty to assert the client's privilege and protect relevant information from disclosure. Over the years, both courts and statutes have identified a number of exceptions to the client's right of privileged communication. A number of these exceptions pertain to judicial proceedings, such as when a client introduces in court information that he has received counseling for emotional problems resulting from an automobile accident that has led to a suit for damages or when a practitioner's testimony about a client is required so the practitioner can defend against a suit filed by the client.

Disclosure of privileged information may also be permissible when a client threatens to commit suicide, shares information in the presence of a third person, is a minor and is the subject of a custody dispute, is involved in criminal activity or has been abused or neglected, is impaired and may pose a threat to the public (an actively alcoholic airline pilot or bus driver), has not paid his or her fees and a collection agency is retained, threatens to injure a third party, or has informed the practitioner about plans to commit a serious crime.[54]

Cases in which clients admit or confess to commission of a crime can be particularly troublesome. On the one hand, practitioners may want to avoid undermining clients' trust by disclosing confidential information. After all, many clients seek counseling for the express purpose of addressing their guilt feelings and sense of remorse about past misdeeds. Practitioners may not want to discourage these constructive efforts. At the same time, however, practitioners can understand the legitimate claim by the public that it has a right and need to know who perpetrated serious crimes, particularly those that have not led to an arrest. According to Madden, however, "the general rule is that mental health workers are not required to report past criminal acts of a client. There is no compelling public policy rationale comparable to the protection of public safety in the duty-to-warn cases."[55] Practitioners must also recognize that codes of ethics in the behavioral health professions prohibit disclosure of confidential information when such disclosure would not prevent serious, imminent, and foreseeable harm in the future (e.g., when a client tells a counselor that she committed a serious crime years earlier and there is no evidence of a contemporaneous threat of harm).

Although statutes are relatively clear that behavioral health practitioners must disclose information shared by clients concerning abuse or neglect of children or older adults, they offer less guidance with respect to other crimes committed by clients. In *Missouri v. Beatty*, a psychiatrist's patient admitted during a therapy session that she had robbed a local service station earlier in the day. The psychiatrist placed an anonymous telephone call to the local Crime Stoppers office and, without identifying his patient, reported that the offender had been employed at the restaurant where his patient worked. The Crime Stoppers staff passed this information on to the police, who eventually arrested the patient.

The patient argued in court that her psychiatrist violated her confidentiality rights and that any related evidence should not be admissible. The Missouri Court of Appeals upheld the patient's conviction, ruling that the psychiatrist had not violated the physician-patient privilege because the law creating that privilege applied only to a psychiatrist's in-court testimony.[56]

In a California case (*California v. Kevin F.*), a resident at a substance use disorder treatment facility confessed to his psychotherapist that six months earlier he had set fire to a friend's home, knowing that people were inside, in an attempt to hide evidence of a theft. A friend of the client's mother and the woman's son were seriously injured. Several months later, the psychotherapist referred to the confession in a report to the client's probation officer. The client was eventually charged with arson and placed in a juvenile correctional facility. He appealed his adjudication, arguing that the psychotherapist's disclosure of the confession violated the state's privileged communication statute. The California Court of Appeal ruled, however, that the confession fell under a statutory exception that permitted disclosure when a psychotherapist had reason to believe an individual posed a danger to himself or others.[57]

In *California v. Cabral*, the California Court of Appeal held that the psychotherapist-patient privilege did not protect a defendant's letter to a therapist in which the patient admitted that he had sexually abused his daughter. The father had written asking to participate in a therapeutic program that the psychologist directed. The psychologist shared the letter with law enforcement officials, and the trial court admitted the letter into evidence. The appeals court held that the letter was not privileged because it did not meet the statutory definition of a confidential communication between "patient and psychotherapist."[58]

Behavioral health practitioners who facilitate group, couples, or family treatment must be especially alert to privileged communication guidelines. Some professionals argue that a client who discloses information to third parties in group, couples, or family treatment forfeits the right to the privilege (because of the client's willingness to share this information with others). Others argue, however, that this sort of disclosure should not invalidate the privilege, and several states have passed laws that protect the privileged content of group and family therapy sessions.[59] In addition, several courts have generally recognized this principle. In *Minnesota v. Andring*, for example, the Minnesota Supreme Court acknowledged that group therapy does involve an expectation of privacy and that the privilege should apply.[60] The court ruled on a defendant's attempt to access the records of group therapy sessions. The court concluded that in a group therapy context, each client is the therapeutic agent of the other, and the presence of third parties is essential to the unique goals of group therapy. Several years later, the California Court of Appeal heard a similar case (*Lovett v. Superior Court*) brought by a father accused of sexually assaulting his teenage daughter. The father wanted to question members of a support group in which the daughter participated to help her cope with her traumatic experiences. The court rejected the father's claim that he should have access to group members' testimony.

Also, in *Hulsey v. Stotts* a federal district court in Oklahoma held that a man who participated in joint counseling with a former girlfriend did not waive the psychotherapist-patient privilege with respect to those sessions. The former girlfriend sought to depose the therapist who conducted the counseling. The court ruled that each member of joint counseling has the right to prevent disclosure by the other: "No division may be made as to where one therapy ends and another's begins."[61]

In a case involving marital therapy (*Cabrera v. Cabrera*), the Connecticut Appellate Court rejected the husband's argument that confidential information shared by the wife with the couple's psychologist was not privileged and should have been disclosed in court. The husband had appealed the outcome of divorce and custody proceedings and wanted to introduce the psychologist's testimony to support his arguments. The husband claimed that the disclosures made by the wife occurred during marital counseling rather than psychological counseling and therefore were not privileged. The appeals court held that the wife's communications were privileged, and, because she had not waived the privilege, the psychologist could not testify about her sessions with the wife or her sessions with the couple. The court concluded that "it would make no sense . . . to divide visits to a psychologist in a case such as this into marital counseling versus psychological counseling and assign privileged status to the latter but not the former."[62]

In contrast, in *Redding v. Virginia Mason Medical Center*, the Washington Court of Appeals held that the therapist-patient privilege did *not* protect statements made by one spouse during joint counseling sessions from being disclosed in a later custody dispute between the couple. The court ruled that the records were not privileged because allegations that the wife had a drinking problem, which were discussed in joint sessions, would be significant to a court deciding the custody dispute.[63]

In several cases, courts have considered allegations that behavioral health professionals disclosed privileged information inappropriately in custody and divorce proceedings. In *Renzi v. Morrison*, the Illinois Appellate Court held that a psychiatrist inappropriately disclosed confidential information about a patient while testifying for the patient's spouse during a child custody hearing. The psychiatrist evaluated the patient and provided her with counseling services. The psychiatrist then testified at the custody hearing and disclosed information about the patient's psychological test results (which the psychiatrist had shared with the husband); the court awarded temporary custody of the child to the husband. The patient won her suit against the psychiatrist on the basis of her claim that the psychiatrist's testimony violated her right to privileged communication.[64] Also, in *Runyon v. Smith*, a New Jersey appeals court ruled that a psychologist breached the client's right to privileged communication by disclosing, without the client's consent, information from a counseling session that led to the client's loss of custody of her children.[65] Such disclosures risk both breach of privilege claims and HIPAA violation claims.

Behavioral health practitioners should also keep in mind the distinction between formal group therapy and self-help groups. A court may recognize therapist-client privilege with respect to group treatment, where the practitioner is functioning in the role of therapist, but not with respect to a self-help group. In a famous New York case, members of an Alcoholics Anonymous (AA) group were subpoenaed to testify in a matter involving a group member accused of brutally murdering two people during an alcohol-induced blackout. The AA group members claimed that they were obligated by the group's rules to avoid disclosure of confidential information shared by group members. The judge in the case rejected the group members' arguments, concluding that a legal privilege did not exist, given that the self-help group was not facilitated by a mental health professional.[66]

A federal district court in Wisconsin held that the psychotherapist-patient privilege did not protect a man's statements to two Alcoholics Anonymous volunteers who advised him to go to a detoxification center. The man claimed that he thought the volunteers were counselors; the volunteers ended up contacting the police and sharing information with them about a gun in the man's possession. The court ruled that the man's disclosure did not fall under the state's law that permits patients to refuse to disclose confidential information shared with licensed clinicians or people believed to be such.[67]

Because statutes vary from state to state and because case law across jurisdictions sometimes is inconsistent, practitioners should consult a lawyer to determine the current status of a particular client's right to privileged communication in their state. Practitioners who serve couples and families should clarify with all parties which individuals are considered clients and the nature of practitioners' professional obligations to the various individuals who are receiving services. Practitioners who anticipate a conflict of interest among these individuals or who anticipate having to perform in potentially conflicting roles (e.g., when a practitioner is asked to testify in a child custody dispute or divorce proceedings involving clients) should clarify their role with the parties involved and take appropriate action to minimize any conflict of interest.

Practitioners should also be careful to seek clients' permission (or, in the case of minors, the permission of a parent or guardian) or a court order before disclosing privileged information. Otherwise, the practitioner might be found liable for violating clients' right to privacy and confidentiality. In *Cutter II v. Brownbridge*, a licensed clinical social worker, Robert Brownbridge, prepared a written document concerning the diagnosis and prognosis of his client, Newell Cutter, in response to a request from Cutter's ex-wife. Brownbridge apparently prepared the document in the absence of a subpoena or other court order. Eventually, the ex-wife's lawyer filed the document as evidence in a dispute between the Cutters concerning visitation rights involving their children. The husband sued Brownbridge, alleging that he had violated his client's constitutional and common law right to privacy, breached an implied covenant of confidentiality, and intentionally inflicted emotional distress. The California Superior Court, which was upheld on appeal, found that the social worker had "violated his client's right to privacy and confidentiality by voluntarily publishing material concerning his client without first resorting to prior judicial determination."[68]

Behavioral health practitioners who supervise unlicensed staff should be clear about the extent to which confidential information shared by clients will be treated as privileged; again, legislation and court opinions vary from state to state. For example, in *Missouri v. Edwards*, the Missouri Court of Appeals held that testimony from an unlicensed counselor, who worked under the supervision of a licensed social worker, about conversations with an alleged sexual abuse victim were not privileged under state law.[69]

Behavioral health practitioners should also pay close attention to the specific contexts in which clients disclose confidential information. The presence of a third party, for example, or a discussion that took place outside a typical counseling session may be significant. For example, the Indiana Court of Appeals held that a defendant's admission to child molestation, made in response to a question by his attorney while sitting in his family therapist's office, was not protected by therapist-client privilege (*Kavanaugh v. Indiana*). The client did not make the comment during a therapy session but rather during a meeting with his attorney, at the therapist's office, to discuss legal issues in the case. Also, the court noted that the defendant made his comment in response to a question from his attorney and that the therapist-client privilege applies only to communications between a therapist and client.[70] Also, a Wisconsin appeals court held that a minor's comments to a psychologist and social worker concerning additional sexual assaults that he had committed were not privileged under state law, because the minor knew that this information could be shared with others outside the treatment setting.[71]

Clearly, behavioral health practitioners often are asked or ordered to disclose confidential information in the context of civil or criminal court proceedings. Prominent examples include practitioners who are subpoenaed to testify in situations such as the following:

- Malpractice cases in which a client has sued another practitioner (e.g., a physician). The defendant's lawyer may subpoena the client's practitioner to gain testimony about the client's mental status or about comments made during counseling sessions. The defense lawyer may attempt to introduce evidence that the client's allegations merely reflect the client's emotional instability, psychiatric illness, vindictiveness, or irrational tendencies. The defense may also try to show that the client had mental health problems that predated the emotional injury that the client claims were caused by the defendant in the case. Defense lawyers may use a similar strategy in other tort or personal injury cases in which a practitioner's client claims to have been injured by the actions of another party (e.g., as a result of an automobile or workplace accident).

- Custody disputes in which one parent subpoenas a practitioner who has worked with one or both parents, believing that the practitioner's testimony will support the parent's claim (e.g., testimony concerning comments made during a counseling session about one parent's allegedly abusive behavior).[72]
- Divorce proceedings in which a practitioner is subpoenaed by one spouse who believes that the practitioner's testimony about confidential conversations will support claims against the other spouse.
- Criminal cases in which a prosecutor or defense attorney subpoenas a practitioner to testify about the defendant's comments during counseling sessions.

### RESPONDING TO SUBPOENAS AND COURT ORDERS

A subpoena is a written document issued by a court clerk or officer of the court (such as an attorney) that commands a person to appear in court at a specific place and time or produce specific documents. While it may appear to be a court order and looks official, it typically is not signed by a judge and is not the same as a court order. Behavioral health practitioners can be subpoenaed in two different ways. A *subpoena ad testificandum*, also known as an ordinary subpoena, literally means "to testify under penalty." It commands a person to appear at a particular location to give testimony. The most common use of a subpoena is to require a witness to attend a deposition or trial.

A *subpoena duces tecum*, also known as a subpoena for production of evidence, literally means "bring with you under penalty." It commands a person to appear at a particular location to bring a specified item, such as a client's clinical record or copies of digital communications, for use or examination in a legal proceeding.

A *subpoena duces tecum* is used most often in civil lawsuits when one party to a lawsuit seeks production of documents from a third party during the discovery process. If a court is convinced that the document request is legitimate, it can order the production and disclosure of documents.

Behavioral health practitioners who are subpoenaed may face a special dilemma concerning the disclosure of privileged information. If the practitioner works in a state that grants the right of privileged communication to behavioral health practitioners' clients, challenging the subpoena may be easier because the legislature has acknowledged the importance of the privilege. Also, contrary to many practitioners' understanding, a legitimate response to a subpoena is to argue that the requested information should not be disclosed or can be obtained from some other source. A subpoena itself does not require a practitioner to disclose information. Instead, a subpoena is essentially a request for information, and it may be without merit. As Grossman has said, "If the recipient knew how easy it was to have a subpoena issued; if he knew how readily the subpoena could demand information when there actually was no legal right to command the disclosure of information; if he knew how often an individual releases information that legally he had no right to release because of intimidation—he would view the threat of the subpoena with less fear and greater skepticism."[73] Further, Grossman says, "In private discussions attorneys admit that the harassing tactic of using these writs is as important in court contests as the legal 'right to the truth.'"[74] Practitioners who are subpoenaed should immediately notify their client and ask the client whether he wants to sign a release-of-information form or contest the subpoena in court.

Challenging a subpoena is appropriate, particularly if practitioners believe that the information is privileged, is not essential to the legal matter, or if they can argue that the information can be obtained from other sources. According to Wilson:

> When data sought by the court can be obtained through some other source, a professional who has been subpoenaed may not have to disclose his confidential data. If the practitioner freely relinquishes his confidential though non-privileged data with little or no objection, the courts may not even check to see if the information can be obtained elsewhere. If the professional

resists disclosure, however, the court may investigate to see if it can get the data from some other source.[75]

Lawyers typically offer several guidelines concerning the proper service of and response to a subpoena:

- Do not release any information unless you are sure you have been authorized in writing to do so.
- Notify your employer (if applicable), so that the employer can notify the malpractice insurer.
- Notify your own malpractice insurer (to determine whether legal representation may be necessary, obtain legal advice about how to respond to the subpoena, and ensure that the insurer is notified in a timely fashion, in accord with policy provisions that require the insured to notify the insurer of a potential claim). The insurance may cover the legal expense of an attorney filing a motion to quash the subpoena or to obtain a protective order.
- Should you employ an assistant or supervise a trainee, it would be wise to claim the privilege to protect confidentiality, even though the court might rule that unlicensed practitioners are not covered by the privilege.
- Determine who served you with the subpoena.
- Determine whether the issuer of the subpoena will pay you a witness fee and cover your travel expenses.
- At a deposition, where there is no judge, you might have your own attorney present or choose to follow the advice and direction of your client's attorney. Your malpractice policy may cover all or a portion of this expense.
- If you feel your information about your client is embarrassing, damaging, or immaterial, you might consider getting written permission to discuss the situation with your client's attorney.
- Unless you are required to produce records only (as with a *subpoena duces tecum*), and are providing all your client records, you must appear at the location stated in the subpoena.[76]

Practitioners can use several strategies to protect clients' confidentiality during legal proceedings.[77] If practitioners believe that a subpoena is inappropriate (e.g., because it requests information that state law considers privileged), they can arrange for a lawyer (perhaps the client's lawyer) to file a motion to quash the subpoena, which is an attempt to have the court rule that the request contained in the subpoena is inappropriate. A judge may issue a protective order explicitly limiting the disclosure of specific privileged information during the discovery phase of the case (discovery is a pretrial procedure by which one party obtains information—facts and documents, for example—about the other). In addition, practitioners, perhaps through a lawyer, may request a review by the judge *in camera* (a review in the judge's chambers) of records or documents that they believe should not be disclosed in open court. The judge can then decide whether the information should be revealed in open court and made a matter of public record.

Despite a local privileged communication statute and a practitioner's attempts to resist a subpoena and disclosure of confidential information, a court could formally order the practitioner to reveal this information. For example, in the New York State case of *Humphrey v. Norden*, a social worker, whose client was presumably protected by the right of privileged communication, was ordered to testify in a paternity case after the court ruled that "disclosure of evidence relevant to a correct determination of paternity was of greater importance than any injury which might inure to [the] relationship between [the] social worker and his clients if such admission was disclosed."[78]

In *Belmont v. California*, a social worker was suspended from her job at the California Department of Social Welfare for willful disobedience of an order to disclose information to the department concerning her clients. The department had requested the information for inclusion in a new computerized database. The social worker, who had provided services to clients who had behavioral health challenges and were receiving public assistance, refused to share the information and was suspended for five days without pay. The California Court of Appeal ruled that social workers employed in this setting do not have a privilege to refuse to disclose confidential information. The court concluded that "the Department's and the legislature's purpose to make 'maximum use of electronic data processing' in the handling and storage of welfare recipient information, under the facts embraced by appellants' offer of proof, flouted neither the 'right of privacy' nor other Fourth Amendment principle."[79]

In the case *In re* Lifschutz, a teacher, Joseph F. Housek, sued John Arabian for damages, alleging that Arabian assaulted him. In a deposition, Housek testified that he received counseling services for approximately six months from a psychotherapist, Joseph Lifschutz. Lifschutz, however, refused to testify in response to a subpoena, even with respect to whether he had treated Housek. Lifschutz claimed that information about any relationship he has with a client is privileged. Both lower and appellate courts held Lifschutz in contempt because the psychotherapist privilege in California does not apply when clients introduce to the court proceedings their emotional or mental condition.[80] Further, the privilege belongs to the client, not the therapist.

The California Supreme Court refused to hear the case, and Lifschutz continued to refuse to testify. Eventually, he was jailed for contempt of court. After a hearing on Lifschutz's challenge of the contempt finding, the California Supreme Court ruled that he was indeed obligated to testify. The court concluded that Lifschutz's client waived the privilege by openly testifying that Lifschutz had treated him. The court also rejected Lifschutz's various arguments concerning, for example, the extent to which his livelihood would be threatened by disclosure of confidential information and the claim that Lifschutz did not receive equal protection under the clergy-penitent-litigant act. This case is particularly important because it recognized that no previous cases had applied the patient-litigant exception to the psychotherapist-client privilege.[81]

A behavioral health clinician was also found in contempt of court for refusing to disclose confidential information in *Caesar v. Mountanos*. Dr. George Caesar, a psychiatrist, was providing treatment to Joan Seebach after injuries she allegedly sustained in an automobile accident. Despite Seebach's willingness to waive in writing the psychotherapist-patient privilege, Caesar refused to answer a number of questions concerning the relationship between Seebach's emotional condition and the accident. Caesar contended that disclosure of this confidential information could be harmful to Seebach. The U.S. Court of Appeals for the Ninth Circuit affirmed the judgment of the federal district court, concluding that there needs to be "a proper balance between the conditional right of privacy encompassing the psychotherapist-patient relationship and [California's] compelling need to ensure the ascertainment of the truth in court proceedings."[82]

Unique issues can emerge when clients share confidential information with student interns. Behavioral health practitioners must determine whether their state's statutes extend the concept of privileged communication to clients seen by student interns. In *California v. Gomez*, a court concluded that privileged communication pertains only to licensed professionals, not to student interns. This case involved information that John

Gomez shared with two student interns about his intention to kill a man with whom his wife had become involved. Gomez argued that the trial court erred by allowing the student interns to testify concerning his comments about wanting to kill his wife's lover. Gomez claimed that the psychotherapist-patient privilege should apply. After the *Gomez* decision, however, the California legislature passed laws that extend the psychotherapist-patient privilege to some registered interns who are completing their practicum requirements.[83]

### UNINTENTIONAL DISCLOSURE OF CONFIDENTIAL INFORMATION

Clearly, in many instances behavioral health practitioners have to make a deliberate decision about whether to disclose confidential information to third parties. Cases involving the duty to protect, suicide, child or elder abuse (or abuse of vulnerable adults), disclosures to law enforcement officials, and fee collection, for instance, sometimes call for difficult judgments about the limits of privacy and the need for others to know details of a client's life.

Far more common, however, are unintentional or inadvertent disclosures of confidential information, with no deliberate intent to breach a client's right to privacy. In these instances, a practitioner typically has simply been absentminded, careless, or sloppy.

Bev E., a mental health counselor at a local family service agency, had an 11:00 A.M. appointment to meet with another counselor, Carl F., at a nearby community mental health center. Bev E. and Carl F. were members of a statewide committee charged with drafting a proposal to fund a collaborative effort between the local police department and behavioral health organizations. Bev E. and Carl F. agreed to meet in Carl F.'s office to map out details related to the draft.

Bev E. arrived at the community mental health center about ten minutes early. She took an elevator to the fourth-floor office, walked into the waiting room, and introduced herself to the receptionist. The receptionist told Bev E. that Carl F. would be with her momentarily, offered her a cup of coffee, and invited her to take a seat. Bev E. sat on a nearby chair and began scrolling through her smartphone. Several minutes later, one of the center's other counselors walked out of her office and through the waiting room, leaving the agency's suite. The receptionist noticed this other worker and said, "Oh, Mary, Sue Smith called a few minutes ago. She said she won't be able to keep her two-thirty appointment. Apparently she has a child-care problem. She said she'd call back to reschedule."

This reminded Bev E. of her own afternoon schedule. She glanced at the schedule on her smartphone and realized she should call a colleague with whom she was planning to meet that afternoon in order to get key details about their meeting. Before calling, Bev E. asked the receptionist whether she could borrow a pen and pad of paper in order to write down the directions. The receptionist said she needed to run down the hall to make a photocopy and invited Bev E. to use the pen and pad on her desk.

Bev E. made her telephone call; as she glanced down at the desk, Bev E. noticed a client's signed consent forms. To avoid staring at the document, Bev E. turned away from the desk, only to find herself staring at a partially typed letter to a client on the receptionist's computer monitor.

At that point, Carl F. walked into the waiting room area to greet Bev E. They met in Carl F.'s office to discuss the grant proposal. After about twenty minutes, Carl F.'s telephone rang. He placed his hand over the mouthpiece and asked Bev E. whether she minded if he took the call. He explained that one of his clients was moving to another state and he was transferring the client to a counselor in that state. Bev E. indicated that he should take the call from the colleague.

Before long, Bev E. heard Carl F. give the caller identifying information about the client's age, family circumstances, treatment history, and presenting problems. During the conversation, Bev E. also gazed around the office and eventually noticed a client's confidential information displayed on the nearby computer screen. As soon as Carl F. hung up the telephone, an exasperated colleague knocked on his door and said he needed to get some advice about the delivery of crisis services to one of the agency's clients, an undocumented immigrant. The visiting colleague mentioned the client's name and circumstances in front of Bev E. Carl F. advised the visiting colleague to fax information about the client's mental health status to the client's attorney. The visiting colleague dialed the wrong fax number, and the confidential material was sent to a local factory, whose fax number was similar to the attorney's, and read by an office worker who recognized the client's unique name.

After the telephone call, Carl F. and Bev E. finished a rough draft of the outline for the proposal. They walked down the hall to make a photocopy. When Carl F. opened the photocopy machine cover, he found part of a case record that a colleague had left in the machine. While Carl F. made a photocopy of the conference schedule, Bev E. glanced down at the waste basket next to the machine. On top of the pile of discarded paper was a slightly crumpled copy of the face sheet of a client's record. Apparently it had been copied on the wrong size paper and thrown out.

At that point, Carl F. asked Bev E. whether she had time for a quick bite to eat at a nearby deli. Bev E. accepted the offer, and the two proceeded to the building's elevator. When they got on the elevator, they were greeted by three other agency workers, who proceeded to animatedly discuss a case in which they were all involved. Bev E. heard one staffer mention the name of a client involved in the case.

Bev E. and Carl F. then walked to the local deli for lunch. They sat at their table and continued to discuss the grant for which they were applying. Before long, however, Bev E. could not help but overhear the three staff members who had been on the elevator continuing their discussion of the case while seated at a nearby booth.

After lunch, Bev E. went on her way, and Carl F. returned to his office. At the end of the day, Carl F. gathered copies of two case records that he wanted to work on at home, tidied up his desk, and went to catch the 5:15 P.M. commuter train. On his way home on the train, Carl F. pulled out a case record. As he reviewed it and made some notes, a passenger seated next to him began reading the exposed material, unbeknownst to Carl F.

Carl F. continued working on the case when he got home. When his wife got home, Carl F. left the record on the kitchen table, and he and his wife went out to a dinner meeting, leaving their children with a babysitter. While Carl F. and his wife were out, the hungry babysitter sat down at the kitchen table to have a snack. She began flipping through the case record.

At about nine o'clock that evening, a custodian entered Carl F.'s office to empty the trash, straighten the furniture, and dust. As the custodian was dusting Carl F.'s desk, he noticed the name on the case record that Carl F. had left on top of the desk. It was the name of the custodian's second cousin, and the custodian sat down and thumbed through the record.

Although this case example is fiction, I have witnessed every component of the vignette. My guess is that many details will be familiar to readers.

Daily pressures in behavioral health settings can exacerbate inadvertent disclosures of confidential information. In these instances, practitioners mean no harm. They do not make deliberate decisions to violate clients' right to privacy. These breaches of confidentiality are mistakes.

Behavioral health practitioners can take a number of steps to prevent these mistakes and the liability risks that they involve. An important step is to provide systematic routine training to all agency staffers. Including professional and nonprofessional staff members (e.g., secretaries, clerks, drivers, cooks for residential programs, and maintenance staff) in a program is especially important because both have access to confidential information. Because of the turnover in behavioral health agencies, the training on confidentiality should be offered periodically. This produces knowledgeable staff and enhances protection of clients' and staff members' rights, and it provides some measure of protection to the agency because it can demonstrate its efforts to ensure that staff members understand how to handle confidential information. The same recommendation pertains to private practitioners, of course.

Training on confidentiality should include two major components: written material (including electronic information) and verbal communication of information related to clients. Written confidential material can take several forms, including such case record items as intake forms, assessment and diagnostic reports, progress notes, billing records, insurance forms, and correspondence. Practitioners need to be acquainted with guidelines concerning access to paper and electronic case records by (1) third parties outside the organization (other service providers, insurance companies), (2) staff within the organization, (3) clients, and (4) clients' families, guardians, executors, and/or significant others. In general, contents of case records should not be released to parties outside the agency without the client's informed consent (see chapter 3 for a discussion of informed-consent procedures). Although some exceptions are permissible (life-threatening emergencies and coordination of care, for example), clients' informed consent ordinarily is essential. Practitioners need to be especially careful when asked for confidential material by close friends of clients or colleagues employed in other agencies who may feel entitled to information because of their unique relationship.

Sharing of information between public agencies can also be a special problem. Staffers at a county or state child welfare department may feel entitled to case record material located in a state child welfare agency when a particular client is involved with both agencies. Unless the agencies have negotiated a clear memorandum of agreement or sharing of information is permitted by law, releasing confidential information without the client's consent is inappropriate.

Agency-based practitioners must also be careful about releasing confidential information to other staff members *within* the organization. Staffers sometimes mistakenly assume that their mere employment in an agency entitles them to information contained in clients' records. Certainly, in many cases various staff members in an agency should have access to the record. In a community mental health center, for example, giving a variety of professionals access to confidential material may be appropriate in order to coordinate services.

In some instances, however, access by staff should be limited; for example, when some agency records are governed by 42 CFR Part 2 and should not be generally available among staffers. On occasion, staff members who are not directly involved in a client's care may be curious about a case, as when an agency is providing services to a celebrity or notorious individual. The governing principle should be that only staff members who are involved in the client's case and have a *need to know* the confidential information should have access in order to carry out their duties. Staffers who cannot satisfy the need-to-know criterion should not have access.

Practitioners also need to be clear about clients' rights to their own records. Professionals' thinking about this has changed dramatically over time. Once, few practitioners believed clients should be able to examine their own records. Behavioral health clinicians typically viewed records as agency property and for staffers' eyes only. However, practitioners have come to appreciate why clients may need or want to see their records and that such disclosure can indeed have therapeutic value if handled properly.

Agencies and private practitioners typically have policies concerning clients' access to records. Clients may be allowed to have photocopied portions of the record, remote access to their electronic record, or may examine the record while in the presence of a staff person. Such policies often spell out the circumstances in which clients may be denied access, such as when the practitioner has reason to believe that the client would be harmed emotionally. In these instances, an alternative is to release the information to the client's legal representative. Of course, practitioners must be careful not to share the contents of a client's case record with family members, significant others, or guardians without proper consent or legal authorization.

Many behavioral health practitioners in the United States are obligated under federal law to provide clients with remote access to the clients' electronic records, free of charge. Under the "open notes" provision in the federal 21st Century Cures Act, which took effect in 2021, various categories of clinical notes created in an electronic health record (EHR) should be made available to clients immediately through a secure online portal. Practitioners and their employers are governed by these requirements if they meet criteria developed by the federal Office of the National Coordinator for Health Information Technology (ONC), which established standards for structured data that EHR programs must meet to become certified. The 21st Century Cures Act does not require practitioners to make their "psychotherapy notes," as defined by HIPAA, available to clients. Thus, practitioners should write every note as if clients will read them or the notes will be disclosed during legal or other proceedings. The law also lists a number of exceptions, including preventing harm and privacy.

Written and electronic information about clients can also be released quite accidentally, as demonstrated by the case example involving Bev. E. Both professional and clerical staff members need to be careful not to leave confidential information on desktops and conference tables to which others may have visual access; not to provide visual access to computer monitors that contain confidential information; or not to leave confidential material in a photocopier. Also, they should not discard hard copies of confidential information in a way that risks exposure (i.e., practitioners should tear up or shred confidential material before disposing of it and ensure proper deletion of electronic records). They need to be sure that passengers on buses, trains, or airplanes cannot read confidential information over the practitioner's shoulder; to take care to not leave confidential information exposed to family members or visitors at home; and to take adequate precautions when disclosing confidential information or when mailing material to a client's home with the practitioner's name and title on the envelope (unless the client says she is not concerned about this form of disclosure). Many practitioners and agencies omit the practitioner's or agency's name from envelopes mailed to a client in order to protect the client's right to privacy. Practitioners should ensure that their electronic devices—laptops, desktop computers, tablets, smartphones, and flash drives—are encrypted and require secure passwords.

Widely available technology, such as fax machines, also poses special problems. Although the practitioner who sends the information may not intend for anyone other than the recipient to read the written communication, fax machines are often located in areas that give others access to the material. Practitioners who fax confidential material should be sure that the recipient is available to retrieve the information immediately and should include a confidentiality notice on the cover sheet. This is one example:

> The documents accompanying this facsimile transmission contain confidential information. The information is intended only for the use of the individual(s) or entity(ies) named above. If you are not the intended recipient, you are advised that any disclosure, copying, distribution, or the taking of any action based on the contents of this information is prohibited. If you have received this facsimile in error, please notify us immediately by telephone at the above number to arrange for return of the original documents.

As the case example also illustrated, inappropriate release of confidential information through verbal communication is a common problem. A great deal of confidential information is divulged inadvertently when third parties seated in waiting rooms hear staff members greet clients by name; hear staffers discuss clients in a hallway, in a waiting room or elevator, at a social gathering, or in a restaurant or other public facility; and overhear practitioners discuss a case on the telephone. Practitioners must also be careful to edit the messages that they leave at a client's workplace and home.

Voicemail can also pose a problem. Although a practitioner may believe that the client or a professional colleague is the only one who will listen to the confidential message, others may have access to the voicemail.

Several other circumstances also warrant special attention to confidentiality. In group or marital therapy and family counseling, practitioners must be careful to respect clients' wishes concerning the disclosure of confidential information. In several cases, a practitioner who has provided both individual and group counseling to the same client has inadvertently (i.e., without the client's consent) divulged confidential information about the client during group counseling.

Marriage or couples counseling can pose other problems as well, particularly when one partner contacts the practitioner and shares confidential information that he does not want disclosed to his partner. Some practitioners permit such confidential disclosures, or secrets, and do their best to respect the confidence. Other practitioners prohibit such secrets, usually for therapeutic reasons. This is a complicated professional debate, one that I cannot settle here. Suffice it to say that practitioners should always be clear ahead of time how they would handle such circumstances, and they should clearly present their policy on this issue to their clients. Those practitioners who permit such secrets ought to share this policy with clients at the beginning of treatment. Clients can then state whether they are comfortable with the arrangement. Practitioners who prohibit secrets should inform clients of this.

Even such clear policies do not prevent problems, however. In one case, a practitioner was providing marriage counseling to a couple. The wife was particularly distressed about the husband's drinking and insisted that he seek treatment. To save the marriage, the husband sought alcohol treatment and talked about his progress in sessions with his wife and the practitioner. Several months after treatment began, the practitioner was attending a professional conference at a local hotel and encountered the husband outside the hotel bar. The husband was clearly inebriated. The husband pleaded with the practitioner not to tell his wife about his drunkenness. The practitioner had to decide whether he had an obligation to share this information with the wife, particularly when the husband refused to do so himself. The practitioner felt uncomfortable participating in therapy sessions in which he knew the husband was actively deceiving his wife. The practitioner also felt he was colluding with the husband and reinforcing the husband's lying and deception. The practitioner resolved the matter by agreeing to work with the husband individually for four weeks to help the husband acknowledge his problem to his wife during subsequent joint counseling sessions.

A final problem has to do with statements about confidentiality that appear on behavioral health organizations' or private practitioners' public-relations materials, such as websites, brochures, pamphlets, and client's rights statements. Many agencies provide information on websites and in brochures that briefly describe agency services, hours, staff, and fees. Often, this information contains statements such as this one, which appears on a mental health agency's website: "All counseling sessions are held in strict confidence." The website does not acknowledge any exceptions. In addition, many agencies and practitioners distribute client's rights statements that spell out confidentiality policy among other policies related to civil rights, grievances, medication, fees, and cancellations. The following is a statement that appears on the client's rights statement prepared by a community mental health center:

> Your privacy is very important to us. No one will be told that you are a client at XYZ Agency without your written permission. Your case record is a confidential document and is protected by federal and state laws. It will be accessible only to clinical staff members responsible for your treatment and support personnel as required during normal business hours. No information about you will be obtained or given out to anyone, including your family or private doctor, without your written authorization.

After reading the statement on the first agency's website and on the second agency's client's rights form, clients might reasonably expect that *everything* they reveal in counseling would be considered confidential. They might be quite surprised to learn of the various exceptions, such as practitioners' need to comply with mandatory reporting laws related to suspected abuse of children and older adults, compliance with court orders, and legal and ethical guidelines in cases in which a client threatens to harm third parties (duty-to-protect guidelines). Therefore, clarifying the legal limits to clients' right to confidentiality is important. Although spelling out these limits in great detail on websites and other broadly worded public-relations documents may not be appropriate, at the very least the statements should state that such limits exist. I advise adding a phrase along the lines of "All information in your record will be considered confidential *to the extent permitted by law.*" At an appropriate time early in the relationship, practitioners should spell out, as gently and diplomatically as possible, the nature of these limits. This discussion should be documented in the client's record.

In sum, formulating comprehensive policies to prevent inappropriate disclosure of confidential information is important. Such policies should address a variety of topics and issues, including the following:

1. Disclosure of information over the telephone, computer (e-mail and attachments), and fax machine
2. Access to agency facilities and clients by outsiders (e.g., to attend meetings or take a tour)

3. Physical safeguarding of paper and electronic records
4. Record retention and destruction
5. Access to client records by staff, clients, significant others, and legal representatives
6. Disclosure of information to outside agencies
7. Audio and video recording of clients
8. Photocopying of confidential information
9. Display of confidential information on computer terminals in public or semipublic areas
10. Discussion of confidential information in waiting rooms, hallways, offices, elevators, and other public and private settings
11. Use of voicemail
12. Statements concerning confidentiality on organization websites, brochures, and other documents
13. Disclosure of confidential information to the news media and law enforcement officials

In formulating confidentiality policies, behavioral health practitioners can find assistance by consulting a variety of documents, including state and federal laws, accreditation standards, union policies, licensing regulations, agency policies, insurance company policies on disclosure, professional literature, and codes of ethics.

Clearly, respect for clients' right to privacy and confidentiality is among the most enduring of professional values in the behavioral health professions. Privacy and confidentiality are essential ingredients in effective practice. Practitioners know, however, that various circumstances may warrant or require disclosure of confidential information. In other instances, practitioners may disclose confidential information unintentionally or inadvertently. Practitioners can avoid liability risks by being aware of the various ways in which confidentiality can be breached appropriately and inappropriately.

CHAPTER | 3

# The Delivery of Services

THE VAST MAJORITY OF BEHAVIORAL health practitioners are competent professionals who provide sound interventions. But on occasion, liability and licensing-board complaints are filed against practitioners alleging that their interventions were somehow flawed. Ordinarily, these claims allege that the practitioner's intervention departed from the standard of care in the profession or violated licensing standards. In a lawsuit, the claimant, usually a client, former client, or family member of a client, sometimes alleges that the practitioner carried out his or her duties in a negligent fashion (acts of misfeasance or malfeasance) and sometimes that the practitioner failed to carry out his or her duties (acts of nonfeasance). In a licensing-board complaint, the complainant alleges that the practitioner violated relevant licensing-board guidelines as reflected in statutes and regulations. Whatever the setting and whatever the practice method, practitioners need to be concerned about the malpractice and liability risks associated with flawed treatment.

Statistically, most malpractice and liability claims and licensing-board complaints alleging improper treatment stem from some sort of clinical practice arising out of work with individuals, families, or treatment groups. Some claims also involve administration, often related to supervision, billing, and personnel matters.

This chapter focuses primarily on risks related to clinical practice. In particular, I discuss risks related to the violation of clients' rights; informed consent; assessment and high-risk intervention; negligent interventions; remote service delivery; boundary issues and dual relationships; undue influence; suicide; commitment proceedings; protective services; defamation of character; technology and remote service delivery.

### CLIENTS' RIGHTS

Especially since the 1960s, state legislatures, the U.S. Congress, and the courts have recognized an increasing number of client rights. Some of these rights have emerged as a result of litigation (e.g., concerning psychiatric patients' right to refuse services), and others are the product of legislative initiatives.

To protect clients' rights and minimize risks, behavioral health practitioners employed in agency settings and independent practice should ensure that they have policies and procedures in place (see the appendix for a sample client rights form):

- Confidentiality and privacy. As I discussed at length in chapter 2, clients have a wide range of confidentiality and privacy rights. Practitioners should have clearly worded confidentiality policies that describe these rights (and exceptions) and procedures to acquaint clients with these rights.

   In addition, practitioners should caution clients about confidentiality risks if clients communicate with practitioners using e-mail, text messaging, or messaging options on social networking sites (such as Facebook and LinkedIn).
- Release of information. Practitioners should have well-established policies and procedures for obtaining a client's (or guardian's) authorization for the release of confidential information.
- Informed consent. As I discuss in detail later in this chapter, practitioners should have sound policies and procedures for obtaining a client's consent to release confidential information, acknowledgment of awareness of treatment options, and permission to conduct activities such as video recording and audio recording or observation by a third party of service provision to the client. Practitioners who provide services to clients remotely should have informed-consent forms and protocols that explicitly address the potential benefits and risks of remote service delivery.
- Access to services. Practitioners should inform clients routinely of their rights to various services offered by their agency. This is particularly important in settings where clients are held or treated involuntarily, such as prisons,

juvenile correctional institutions, psychiatric facilities, and other programs
and supervision to which clients are remanded by a court (e.g., probation).

- Access to records. As I discussed in chapter 2, clients ordinarily have the
  right to inspect their records in-person or remotely. Practitioners who are
  concerned that a client's access to these records could cause serious misunderstanding or harm to the client should provide assistance in interpreting
  the records and consultation with the client regarding the records. Only in
  exceptional circumstances—where the requested information falls under
  HIPAA's psychotherapy notes definition or the evidence is compelling that
  a client's access to these records would cause serious harm to the client—are
  practitioners permitted to limit clients' access to their records (or portions
  of their records). Practitioners' client rights statement should summarize
  the nature of clients' rights to see and obtain copies of information in their
  record. Practitioners who work in settings that are governed by the 21st
  Century Cures Act must ensure that clients have remote access to their
  electronic records.

  Agencies that hire former clients (e.g., addictions programs) should
  ensure that staffers who were once clients do not inappropriately access
  records—their own records or records of other clients they knew during
  their time as clients.

- Service plans. Many practitioners seek to include clients in the development of treatment and service plans as a way to empower clients and engage
  them in the helping process. The client rights statement should explain the
  ways in which clients have an opportunity to participate in the formulation
  of service and treatment plans.

- Options for alternative services and referrals. Clients have the right to
  know whether they can obtain services from other providers. This is consistent with behavioral health practitioners' obligation to respect clients'
  right to self-determination and to give informed consent before services are
  provided to them. The client rights statement should explain to clients the
  options that they have in regard to being referred to, and receiving services
  from, other agencies and providers.

- The right to refuse services. In general, clients have the right to refuse services (recognizing that in some instances clients do not have this right; for
  example, when a court orders a client to receive services). The client rights
  statement should inform clients about the extent of their right to refuse
  available services.

- Termination of services. Practitioners should inform clients about the agency's or practitioner's policies concerning the termination of services; for example, the circumstances under which services may or will be terminated, along with relevant criteria and procedures (see chapter 8 for additional detail).

- Rights to amend records, obtain accounting of disclosures, request restriction of disclosures, request confidential communication, and receive notice of breaches. Under HIPAA, clients have rights to request that protected health information in records be amended, and, if their requests are denied, to respond to rebuttal statements. Clients have the right to request accountings of certain disclosures of protected health information made by practitioners. Clients have the right to request that practitioners restrict or limit use or disclosure of protected health information for treatment, payment, or health-care operations, but practitioners are not required to agree to restrict such disclosure to health plans for purpose of carrying out payment or health-care operations unless they relate to services paid for out-of-pocket. Clients have the right to request that practitioners communicate with them about health matters in a certain way or at a certain location. Clients have the right to be notified about the details of any breach of unsecured protected health information.

- Grievance procedures. In many settings, clients have the right to challenge or appeal decisions with which they disagree and that are related to, for example, accessing records, amending records, treatment plans, benefits, eligibility for services, and termination of services. The client rights statement should explain to clients the extent to which they have the right to appeal adverse decisions and what the relevant grievance procedures are.

- Evaluation and research. Some agencies involve clients in evaluation or research activities (such as clinical research and program evaluations). The client rights statement should inform clients about policies and procedures designed to protect evaluation and research participants (often known as "protection of human subjects" guidelines). These guidelines should be consistent with widely accepted standards related to informing clients about the purpose of the research and evaluation; foreseeable risks, discomforts, or negative consequences; potential benefits to clients and others; alternatives to participation that might benefit the client; confidentiality or anonymity provisions; compensation; provisions for treatment in the event of harm or injury; and contact people available to respond to questions about the research and evaluation.

One practical suggestion is to provide clients with a written summary or "service contract" that summarizes key features of the practitioner's (and agency's) relationship with clients. Typical written agreements summarize the practitioner's areas of expertise; training and education; professional affiliations; privacy, confidentiality, and privileged communication guidelines, as well as clients' rights and responsibilities; boundaries in the practitioner-client relationship; social media policies (policies related to social networking, digital and electronic services, e-mail and other electronic communications, electronic searches, location-based services, consumer review sites); policies related to audio and video recording of clinical sessions; how to handle emergencies; and fee arrangements, billing procedures, and collection methods. The ideal service contract is written in user-friendly, diplomatic language that is not legalistic in tone.

### INFORMED CONSENT

Behavioral health practitioners have always recognized the central importance of a client's consent, whether to services, release of information, medication, or audio/video recording. Because of practitioners' long-standing commitment to the principle of client self-determination, informed consent has been a centerpiece of professional practice.

The historical roots of informed consent trace to Plato, who in *Laws* compares the Greek slave-physician who gives orders "in the brusque fashion of a dictator" with the free physician who "takes the patient and his family into confidence . . . [and] does not give prescriptions until he has won the patient's support."[1] The medieval French surgeon Henri de Mondeville also stressed the importance of obtaining a patient's consent and confidence, although he also urged his colleagues to "compel the obedience of his patients" by selectively slanting information provided to them.[2] Clearly, informed-consent norms have changed since then.

By the late eighteenth century, European and American physicians and scientists had begun to develop a tradition that encouraged professionals to share information and decision-making with their clients. The first major legal ruling in the United States on informed consent came in the landmark 1914 case of *Schloendorff v. Society of New York Hospital*, in which Benjamin Cardozo, then sitting on the New York Court of Appeals (the state's highest court), set forth his oft-cited opinion concerning an individual's right to self-determination: "Every human being of adult years and sound mind has a right to determine what shall be done with his own body."[3] To do otherwise, Cardozo argued, is to commit an assault upon the person.

Current informed-consent legislation and guidelines were devised after revelations of medical experiments performed without consent of the subjects in Germany during World War II and in the United States until 1972. The 1957 case of *Salgo v. Stanford University Board of Trustees* introduced the phrase "informed consent." The plaintiff, who became a paraplegic following a diagnostic procedure for a circulatory disturbance, alleged that his physician did not properly disclose ahead of time pertinent information regarding risks associated with the treatment.

Although the concept of informed consent has its origins in medicine and health care, it has recently been applied legislatively, judicially, and administratively to a wide range of other client groups. Behavioral health practitioners regularly provide services to such client groups as those with psychiatric illness and cognitive impairment, minors, older adults, hospital patients, prisoners, and research participants. In agencies that provide behavioral health services, for example, practitioners must be familiar with consent requirements related to voluntary and involuntary commitment and the rights of institutionalized and outpatient clients regarding the use of psychotropic medication, restraints, aversive treatment measures, isolation, sterilization, and psychosurgery.[4]

Practitioners in agencies that serve children must keep pace with evolving standards regarding consent of minors. State laws vary considerably and are subject to change. Consent issues arise in relation to abortion counseling, contraception, treatment of sexually transmitted diseases, behavioral health services, substance use disorders treatment, and foster care. In *Dymek v. Nyquist*, for example, the custodial parent of a nine-year-old boy was his father. But the boy's mother took him to a psychiatrist, who treated him for one year without the father's knowledge and consent. The suit alleged that the psychiatrist knew that the mother was not the custodial parent and that she had not obtained from the court permission for the psychiatrist to treat the boy. The Illinois court found in the father's favor, ruling that the psychiatrist had no authority to provide psychotherapy to the child.[5]

Traditionally, minors have not been considered capable of giving informed consent or entering into contracts; the consent of parents or someone standing *in loco parentis* has typically been required, unless it is

a genuine emergency.[6] Especially since the 1970s, however, states have recognized the concepts of mature or emancipated minors, which imply that
certain minors are in fact capable of providing their own consent in their
relationships with professionals. Mature minors are those who are "judicially recognized as possessing sufficient understanding and appreciation of
the nature and consequences of treatment despite their chronological age."[7]
Emancipated minors are those who have obtained the legal capacity of an
adult because they are self-supporting, living on their own, married, or in
the armed forces.

States vary considerably in the extent to which they grant minors autonomy and the right to consent. For example, with respect to abortion services, substance use disorders treatment, dispensing of contraceptives, and
treatment of sexually transmitted diseases, some states permit professionals to treat minors without obtaining parental consent; some require that
parents be notified, that their consent be obtained, or both; some require
practitioners to make a "good faith" effort to have the minor notify the parents for purposes of obtaining parental consent; and some merely permit
agency staff members to notify parents, obtain their consent, or both. State
laws also vary in the extent to which parental consent is required to place a
child in an inpatient or outpatient mental health program.

Consent issues related to the care of medical patients have received considerable attention, especially regarding the care of hospital patients and
their right to die, be informed of medical risks, refuse treatment on religious grounds, consent to experimental treatment, participate in research,
and donate organs. Once again, states vary considerably in the amount of
autonomy that they grant patients and the procedures that health-care staff
members are expected to follow when patients request controversial treatment or fail to provide consent. In the famous case of Karen Ann Quinlan
(*In re* Quinlan), the Supreme Court of New Jersey required hospital staff
to consult with a hospital ethics committee, rather than a court of law, concerning the decision to remove extraordinary treatment. This important
court case led to the proliferation of ethics committees in a wide range of
health and mental health settings.[8] However, in *Superintendent of Belchertown v. Saikewicz*, the Massachusetts Supreme Judicial Court rejected
the New Jersey approach, and its reliance on administrative procedures,
in favor of court approval of decisions concerning life-prolonging care of
incompetent patients.

Debate concerning client consent to participate in research has also received much attention. Discussion has been especially vigorous with respect to clients whose competence to consent is considered questionable or who are considered especially vulnerable. Particular attention has been paid to the right of people with mental illness, older adults, minors, and prisoners to consent to participate in research related to drugs, treatment techniques, and program evaluation.[9]

Although states and local jurisdictions have different interpretations and applications of informed-consent standards, what constitutes valid consent by clients depends on prevailing legislation and case law. In general, for consent to be considered valid, six standards must be met: coercion and undue influence must not have played a role in the client's decision; clients must be capable of providing consent; clients must consent to specific procedures or actions; the forms of consent must be valid; clients must have the right to refuse or withdraw consent; and clients' decisions must be based on adequate information.[10]

*Absence of coercion and undue influence.* Behavioral health practitioners frequently maintain some degree of control over the lives of their clients. Access to services, money, time, and attention are but a few of the resources that practitioners control. That practitioners not take advantage of their positions of authority to coerce a client's consent, subtly or otherwise, is especially important. Practitioners who want clients to agree to enter or terminate a program, release information to third parties, participate in a research project, or take medication, for example, need to be aware that clients may be particularly susceptible to influence, which would jeopardize the validity of their consent.

*Reif v. Weinberger* illustrates the inappropriate use of coercion. The evidence showed that a number of clients receiving welfare benefits had been coerced into agreeing to sterilization procedures; they had been told that a portion of their welfare benefits would be withheld unless they agreed to the procedures. A federal district judge in Washington, D.C., issued an order prohibiting the use of tax dollars to pay for some sterilizations because of the use of coercion.

*Capacity to consent.* Although professionals widely agree that only competent clients are capable of giving informed consent, they are in much less agreement about the determination of competence. In its influential 1982 report, *Making Health Care Decisions*, the President's Commission for the

Study of Ethical Problems in Medicine and Biomedical and Behavioral Research considered several different informed-consent standards. These included patients' ability to make choices, comprehend factual issues, manipulate information rationally, appreciate their current circumstances, retain information, and "test reality." After its comprehensive review of various perspectives, the commission decided that competency is determined by the client's recognition of a set of values and goals, ability to communicate and understand information, and ability to reason and deliberate.

Despite the unsettled debate about how to determine competence, practitioners seem to agree that no one should assume that any particular client group, such as children, older adults, or people with mental illness or intellectual disabilities, are incompetent, except for those who are unconscious. Rather, clients in some categories—perhaps children or individuals with severe intellectual disability—should be considered to have a greater *probability* of incapacity. Assessment of a client's capacity should at least consist of such measures as a mental status exam (which accounts for a person's orientation to person, place, time, and situation; mood and affect; content of thought; and perception), as well as determination of the ability to comprehend abstract ideas and make reasoned judgments, of any history of mental illness that might affect current judgment, and of the client's recent and long-term memory. When clients are judged to be incompetent, practitioners should be guided by the principle of substituted, or proxy, judgment, in which a surrogate attempts to replicate the decision that the incapacitated person would make if able to make a choice.[11] An important point for practitioners to consider is that clients whose competence fluctuates may be capable of giving or withdrawing consent during a lucid phase.[12]

*Consent to specific procedures.* Behavioral health agencies often have clients sign general consent forms at a first or second appointment or at the time of admission to a residential program. In a number of precedent-setting cases in the context of medical care, however, clients have challenged such blanket consent forms in court, claiming that they lacked specificity and failed to authorize interventions introduced subsequently. In *Winfrey v. Citizens & Southern National Bank*, a Georgia woman challenged her physician's authority to perform a complete hysterectomy, where the physician performed the hysterectomy on the basis of the patient's consent to an exploratory operation. In *Darrah v. Kite*, the father of a young child challenged a New York neurosurgeon's authority to conduct a ventriculogram on the child when the consent form referred only to "routine brain tests" and a workup. Professionals are thus advised not to assume that general consent forms are valid. Rather, consent forms should include specific details that refer to specific activities or interventions. As Rozovsky has observed, "Reliance on a general consent form may be of questionable merit. Courts have been known to examine the circumstances of a specific case to determine whether the general consent was broad enough to permit the treatment in question."[13]

Practitioners and agency staff should also refrain from having clients sign blank consent forms; this is a practice occasionally used to avoid having to contact clients in person for their signatures at a later date. If challenged in court, these consent forms might not be considered valid, given the absence of information related to treatment or intervention when the client signed the form. Having clients sign blank forms clearly violates the spirit of the concept of informed consent.

In addition, the language and terminology that appear on consent forms must be understandable to clients, and clients should have ample opportunity to ask questions. Practitioners should avoid as much as possible the use of complex and technical jargon. Clients who do not have good command of English need particular care; practitioners should be aware that some clients who are able to speak English reasonably well (expressive language skill) may not be equally capable of understanding the language (receptive language skill). Having access to an interpreter in such instances is important. In addition, practitioners should be certain that clients who have auditory or visual impairments are provided with the assistance they need in order to provide informed consent.

*Valid forms of consent.* Many states authorize several forms of consent. Consent may be written or verbal, although some states require written authorization. In addition, consent may be expressed or implied. Expressed consent entails explicit authorization by a client for a specific intervention or activity such as admission to a residential facility, receipt of remote behavioral health services, or the release of specific information to a third party. Implied consent occurs when consent is inferred from the facts and circumstances surrounding a client's situation. An example is a client who answers questions that are part of an anonymous, mailed, and voluntary client satisfaction survey. A reasonable assumption is that the client has consented to the activity. Another example of implied consent is when a behavioral health agency that serves adolescents informs parents and guardians that agency staffers are administering a client survey and assume that parents and guardians consent to the survey unless they "opt out" or notify the agency that they do not want their child to participate.

*Right to refuse or withdraw consent.* Practitioners should plan for the possibility that clients will refuse or withdraw consent. Of course, clients who do so also should be legally and mentally capable of such a decision, and their decisions need to be informed by details shared by practitioners concerning the risks associated with refusing or withdrawing consent. Taking psychotropic medication or being disabled to some degree by psychiatric illness does not by itself provide ground for being denied the right to refuse or withdraw consent. Rather, practitioners should judge clients' capacity in terms of their ability to think clearly, grasp details relevant to their condition, understand the extent to which their psychiatric history is likely to affect their current judgment, and understand the extent to which they pose a public-health risk. Ordinarily, practitioners serve their own best interests by having their clients sign a release form absolving practitioners or their agencies of responsibility for any adverse consequences stemming from a decision not to give consent. If a client refuses to sign such a form, the client's record should include detailed notes describing the client's decision and the negotiation.

*Adequate information.* Professionals generally agree about the topics that they should cover in discussions with clients before obtaining consent. Commonly cited elements of disclosure include the nature and purpose of the recommended service, treatment, or activity; the advantages and disadvantages of the intervention; substantial, probable, or significant risks to the client, if any; potential effects on the client's family, partner, job, social activities, and other aspects of the client's life; alternatives to the prospective intervention; and anticipated costs to be borne by the client (consistent with the federal No Surprises Act).

This information must be presented to clients in understandable language (taking into consideration clients' learning disabilities, cognitive impairment, literacy, and English comprehension), without coercion or undue influence, and in a manner that encourages clients to ask questions. Consent forms should also be dated and should include an expiration date. Consent forms without an expiration date may be considered invalid if the original signature was obtained long before the form was actually used.

Practitioners must also consider that obtaining informed consent entails more than having clients sign a form. Consent is a process that includes the systematic disclosure of information to a client over time, along with an opportunity for the client to discuss with the practitioner the forthcoming treatment and service. Practitioners should ensure during discussions with their clients that clients understand the risks, benefits, and alternatives to any proposed treatment. As part of this process, practitioners must be especially sensitive to clients' cultural and ethnic differences related to the meaning of such concepts as self-determination, autonomy, and consent.

*Consent for remote delivery of services.* The advent of distance counseling and other remote behavioral health services delivered electronically has enhanced practitioners' ethical duty to ensure that clients fully understand the nature of these services and their potential benefits and risks. Obtaining clients' truly informed consent can be especially difficult when practitioners never meet clients in person. Special challenges arise when minors contact practitioners and request distance or remote services, particularly when practitioners offer services funded by contracts or grants and do not require payment from minor clients' parents or insurance companies; laws around the world vary considerably regarding minors' right to obtain services from behavioral health professionals without parental knowledge or consent.

When behavioral health professionals provide services to clients remotely, the informed-consent form should include statements that address:

- The nature of the services that the practitioner will provide remotely, such as video counseling, text-based counseling, and smartphone applications.
- Possible benefits of remote service delivery. This may include geographical and scheduling convenience.
- Differences between services provided face-to-face and remotely.
- The skills and equipment (such as computer specifications and smartphone applications) the client will need to receive services remotely.
- The importance of privacy for both practitioner and client. Describe steps clients can take to ensure privacy (such as avoiding use of public Wi-Fi during counseling sessions). Describe steps you will take to ensure privacy (e.g., use of encryption, firewalls, and data backup software).
- The possibility of technology failure and transmission interruption, along with instructions in the event these occur (e.g., call-back protocols).

- The possibility that stored data could be accessed by unauthorized people or companies, and the steps you will take to prevent this.
- An emergency response plan to address crises that may arise. Details may include names and telephone numbers of individuals the practitioner can contact, telephone numbers the client can call, and when the client should access care at the client's local hospital emergency department.
- Steps you will take if you believe that the client needs to access face-to-face services because of his or her clinical needs. Include details about referral and termination-of-service protocols.
- Guidelines for clients' use of e-mail and text messaging to communicate with the practitioner (i.e., whether electronic communications should be used only for administrative and scheduling purposes, as opposed to counseling issues).
- Agreement that the client will notify the practitioner of the client's geographical location (to ensure compliance with relevant licensing regulations).
- Agreement that the client will not record any remote counseling sessions or other discussions, unless agreed upon in advance.

*Exceptions to informed consent.* In a variety of circumstances, professionals may not be required to obtain informed consent before intervention.[14] These include instances involving emergencies or a client waiver. In genuine emergencies, for example, professionals may be authorized to act without the client's consent. According to many state statutes and much case law, an emergency entails a client's being incapacitated and unable to exercise the mental ability to make an informed decision. Interference with decision-making ability must be a result of injury or illness, substance use, or any other disability. In addition, a need for immediate treatment to preserve a life or health must exist. As Rozovsky has noted, it is important for practitioners not to assume "that a person who has consumed a moderate amount of alcohol or drugs or who has a history of psychiatric problems is automatically incapable of giving consent: the facts and circumstances of individual cases are essential to such determinations."[15]

As behavioral health practitioners have come to learn, they may be obligated to disclose information to third parties without clients' consent if they have evidence that serious injury to others may otherwise result. As I explained in chapter 2, the *Tarasoff* case and other duty-to-protect cases included circumstances in which a behavioral health professional was expected to disclose confidential information to third parties.

Both statutes and case law have recognized the right of clients to request that they not be informed of the nature of risks associated with impending treatment or services (see, for e.g., *Holt v. Nelson*; *Ferrara v. Galluchio*). In these instances, clients may decide that they are better off not knowing what the services or treatment will entail and thus waive their right to give informed consent. Professionals are generally advised to document such a waiver and to consider having clients sign a waiver form.

*Good faith estimate of costs.* In 2022, the federal No Surprises Act went into effect. This law aims to increase price transparency and reduce the likelihood that clients receive a "surprise" bill by requiring that providers inform clients of an expected charge for a service before the service is provided.

This law requires behavioral health providers to give uninsured and self-pay clients a good faith estimate of costs for services when scheduling care or when the client requests an estimate. Part I of this law protects clients with health plan coverage from surprise bills from out-of-network (OON) providers who provide emergency and nonemergency services at in-network facilities. Part II of this law requires all health-care providers, including behavioral health professionals, and health-care facilities licensed, certified, or approved by the state to provide good faith estimates (GFEs) of expected charges for services offered to uninsured (e.g., not enrolled in any health plan) and self-pay (e.g., not planning to file a claim with their plan) clients.

Any health-care provider or health-care facility subject to state licensure must provide to current and future clients a GFE of expected charges for services and items within specific time frames. These regulations set forth specific requirements for how providers need to inform clients of their right to a good faith estimate, what the estimate must contain, what disclaimers to include, how records are to be maintained, and how to resolve disputes. GFEs do not need to be provided to clients who are enrolled in federal health insurance plans (e.g., Medicare, Medicaid, TRICARE, Indian Health Service, or the Veterans Affairs health system).

Practitioners can meet the notice and consent requirements by providing the patient with written notice and consent seventy-two hours in advance of the client's appointment and a list of in-network providers at the facility and information regarding medical-care management, such as prior authorization. The notice must:

- Alert the client that the provider does not participate in-network.
- Provide an estimate of the OON charges.
- Outline professional service fees.
- Describe a potential range of sessions that may be needed.
- Estimate costs at the end of each range.
- List factors that may influence whether costs ultimately land toward the lower or higher end of the range.
- List in-network providers at the facility.

The good faith estimate can only include recurring services that are expected to be provided within the next twelve months. For additional services beyond twelve months, the practitioner must provide a new good faith estimate and communicate any changes between the initial and the new estimates. Practitioners can update the good faith estimate, and they can cover periods of less than a year. A client's bill will be determined eligible for the client-provider dispute resolution process if the client received a good faith estimate, if the process is initiated within 120 calendar days of the client receiving the bill, and if the bill is substantially in excess of the good faith estimate (e.g., greater than $400). To avoid disputes, practitioners may want to closely monitor charges, compare them with the good faith estimates, and then issue updated good faith estimates as needed.

### CLINICAL ASSESSMENT AND INTERVENTION

Behavioral health practitioners routinely assess clients in an effort to formulate an intervention plan. Particularly in work with individual clients and families, practitioners draw on a wide array of assessment and diagnostic frameworks, reflecting different theoretical orientations. Some practitioners may favor psychodynamically oriented assessments and interventions, while others may favor cognitively or behaviorally oriented assessments and interventions. By now, most practitioners agree that no one theoretical perspective can claim a monopoly. Although practitioners may favor one view or approach over another, many draw on the strengths of various perspectives while keeping in mind their respective limitations and biases.

Whatever the practitioner's ideological or theoretical perspective with respect to assessment and intervention frameworks, every practitioner must be mindful of a range of malpractice and liability risks. As I discussed in chapter 1, claims alleging malpractice or negligence ordinarily argue that the practitioner somehow departed from the standard of care associated with contemporary practice. What matters is whether evidence exists that the practitioner's use and implementation of that approach was somehow flawed or below par (the breach of professional duty) and resulted in injury to the plaintiff (usually the client or the client's legal representative, although the plaintiff may be a third party, such as a client's relative or acquaintance).

Practitioners need to be aware of several potential problems related to assessment and intervention, including failure to diagnose or assess properly and incompetent delivery of service. Well-trained practitioners are expected to have the skill to diagnose (a medical term I prefer to avoid) or assess a variety of client problems. Although not every practitioner may be skilled in all areas of assessment, most practitioners involved in behavioral health are trained to assess common mental health disorders and problems in living.

Problems can arise, however, when practitioners do not conduct thorough assessments consistent with the standard of care in the profession or make erroneous assumptions on the basis of the data available to them. Imagine a client with symptoms of depression who seeks help from a behavioral health practitioner. During the first interview, the client also mentions that she has chronic headaches. The practitioner conducts a cursory assessment and neglects to ask additional questions about the headaches—their intensity, frequency, duration, and so on. As a result, the practitioner does not recommend that the client consult a physician who is trained to assess the organic causes or correlates of headaches. The client turns out to have a brain tumor, and she sues the practitioner, alleging negligence. The client does not expect the practitioner to be able to diagnose a brain tumor, of course. She can claim, however, that the practitioner should ask detailed questions about somatic complaints and, if appropriate, refer her to a physician.

In *Kogensparger v. Athens Mental Health Center*, an Ohio court held a mental health center liable in failing to consider the possibility that organic problems caused a patient's symptoms, which included behavioral disorders and complaints of abnormal discomfort in his head. Staff members maintained that schizophrenia caused the symptoms, which included the patient's consumption of excessive amounts of food and water. The patient, who had been hospitalized for more than three years, suffered a grand mal seizure and died one week later. An autopsy disclosed a brain tumor. Experts agreed that the tumor was slow growing and must have been detectable for several years before the patient died; the court ruled that the center's failure to provide appropriate care was the proximate cause of death.[16]

A number of important legal precedents related to failure to diagnose come from the field of medicine. Most concern problems of misdiagnosis, missed diagnosis (the failure to identify a problem), and improper treatment. Over the years, courts have held physicians liable when they have not used a standard and well-accepted diagnostic test (*Narcarato v. Grob*; *Smith v. Yohe*; *Estate of Davies v. Reese*), interpreted test data incorrectly (*Green v. State*), and have not responded to a patient's adverse reaction to a diagnostic test (*Dill v. Miles*). Doctors have also been held liable for the consequences of inaccurate test results, although they can avoid liability if the misdiagnosis does not affect treatment or if the misdiagnosis is followed by correct treatment.

Other failure-to-diagnose suits have alleged failure to pursue information that seemed relevant and turned out to be essential. In *Merchants National Bank v. United States*, a federal district court in North Dakota found that a psychiatrist was negligent in not pursuing a patient's allegation that her husband had attempted to harm her. Mental health professionals also have been held liable in the failure to forward significant information to another therapist. In *Underwood v. United States*, a U.S. Air Force psychiatrist, who was being transferred off base, did not inform his patient's new psychiatrist of the patient's threats to kill his wife. The new therapist permitted the patient to return to duty and carry a firearm, which he then used to kill his wife. The victim's father won his suit alleging that the psychiatrist's failure to forward the information constituted negligence.[17]

In a Wisconsin case, the plaintiff's mother had dated a man and ended the relationship. Subsequently, the man entered the woman's home by throwing himself through a window; he was armed with a shotgun. The man tortured the woman and then murdered her in the presence of her children. The man then killed himself. During the month before this happened, the man had received clinical services at two counseling centers. The lawsuit alleged that the counselors were negligent in failing to diagnose the man's homicidal intentions and failing to warn the police or the mother. One counseling center settled the case for $400,000 and the second for $600,000.[18]

Not surprisingly, many cases involving failure to diagnose involve allegations that a behavioral health professional did not exercise sound judgment and that as a result the client suffered an injury. In *Chatman v. Millis*, a psychologist was sued by the ex-husband of a woman who sought to terminate his visitation rights with their two-and-a-half-year-old child by alleging that the husband had sexually molested the boy.[19] The psychologist interviewed the mother and son but not the father. As a result of the assessment, the psychologist concluded that the father's visitation rights should be terminated or, at the very least, that his visits with the child should be supervised. Although the Arkansas Supreme Court ruled that the husband could not sue for negligence because he never had a doctor-patient relationship with the psychologist, one justice issued a strong dissenting opinion:

> Defendant was negligent and careless in making such diagnosis by failing to exercise the degree of skill and care, or to possess the degree of knowledge, ordinarily exercised or possessed by other psychological examiners or psychologists engaged in this type of practice ... in that he failed and neglected to ever interview the plaintiff and in fact did not even know him, failed to administer any diagnostic tests ... or to use any of the proper methods that psychologists use in exercising ordinary care to protect others from injury or damage; the defendant acted in a manner willfully and wantonly in disregard to the rights of the plaintiff.[20]

Courts do not expect absolute precision in professionals' assessments. Judges recognize the inexact nature of behavioral health assessment. What they do expect is conformity to the profession's standard of care regarding assessment procedures and criteria. Although the outcome of a case may be tragic and the practitioner's assessment may be inaccurate in some respect, the practitioner may not have been negligent. To be considered negligent, a diagnosis must be wrong (an error in judgment) *and* determined in a negligent fashion. An error in judgment is not by itself negligent.

Many failure-to-diagnose cases involve suicide attempts. Typically, the plaintiff (ordinarily a client who failed in an attempt to commit suicide and was injured in the process or a family member of a client who committed suicide) alleges that the practitioner did not properly diagnose the potential for suicide or manage suicide risk consistent with the standard of care. In a New Hampshire case, the plaintiff was a thirty-one-year-old woman who was admitted to a hospital by two friends who were concerned about her substance use and recent suicide attempt. The suit contended that the hospital staff did not properly assess the woman's suicide risk. During the initial assessment, a hospital staff member noted recent slash marks on the plaintiff's left wrist but accepted her explanation that the cuts were accidental. The staff had not interviewed the plaintiff's friends and therefore did not know of the recent suicide attempt. Shortly after the plaintiff's admission to the hospital, she was found hanging in a bathroom. She suffered permanent anoxic brain damage, although it was unclear whether the damage was entirely the result of the hanging or if she had a preexisting condition that was aggravated by the hanging.[21] The case was settled for $175,000.

In 1991, a federal district court found a VA hospital in Tennessee liable for failure to properly assess the risk of suicide. The plaintiff was a thirty-three-year-old veteran who had been diagnosed with chronic paranoid schizophrenia and whose records showed that he drank as much as a fifth of alcohol per day. The man was taken to the VA hospital by ambulance, and the trip ticket stated that the patient had been seeing demons and intended to kill himself. The VA nurse testified during the trial that she had placed the trip ticket on the chart; however, the resident psychiatrist stated that she did not see the trip ticket when she examined the patient later that afternoon. The resident psychiatrist examined the patient, "who was a little nervous but rational," and the patient was sent home. The next morning, the patient was found dead from a self-inflicted shotgun wound. The court found that the VA hospital had deviated from the standard of care, either by failing to transmit the ambulance trip ticket or by failing to consider its contents, and that the psychiatrist failed to take an adequate history.[22]

*Baker v. United States* demonstrates the difference between an inaccurate judgment and negligence. The suit was filed by the wife of Kenneth Baker. Mrs. Baker was guardian for her husband, a psychiatric patient receiving care at the VA hospital in Iowa City, Iowa. He attempted suicide by leaping into a thirteen-foot-deep window well located on the grounds of the hospital. He was seriously injured, suffering a variety of fractures and complete paralysis of his right side. Mrs. Baker alleged in her suit that the physician who admitted her husband to the hospital failed to properly diagnose his mental illness. According to Mrs. Baker, she had conferred with the acting chief of the neuropsychiatric service at the hospital and had informed him of her husband's suicidal tendencies. She also told the physician that she had found a gun that her husband had hidden several weeks earlier. Mr. Baker was subsequently placed on an open ward; the physician did not think he was a suicide risk.

The federal district court ruled that the admitting physician was not negligent and "exercised the proper standard of care required under the circumstances." In addition, the court concluded, "Diagnosis is not an exact science. Diagnosis with absolute precision and certainty is not possible."[23]

Similar issues related to professional judgment arose in *Boyer v. Tilzer*. The police took a man into custody and transported him to a Missouri state mental health facility where he was involuntarily admitted for a period not to exceed ninety-six hours. An emergency room report described the patient as combative, hyper-religious, and manic. He was apparently hearing voices, seeing demons, and thinking he was God. A psychiatric resident diagnosed the patient as suffering from alcohol abuse and probable PCP (phencyclidine) psychosis and recommended treatment for substance dependency.

The hospital released the patient after three days. One week later, he began having hallucinations and delusions. He stabbed his girlfriend's hand with a knife and fatally stabbed a third party who had come to her assistance. The patient was arrested and diagnosed as having paranoid schizophrenia.

The dead woman's estate sued the psychiatric resident, alleging that the patient had been incorrectly diagnosed and released. The trial court found in favor of the resident, concluding that no proof existed that the resident had acted in bad faith or in a grossly negligent fashion. The estate appealed, and the Missouri appeals court also found no evidence that the psychiatric resident had not performed his duties in good faith and without gross negligence.[24]

In a Virginia case, a twenty-four-year-old mother was admitted to a psychiatric hospital after a suicide attempt involving a gun. About two weeks after the woman's discharge from the hospital, a social worker learned that the gun was back in the woman's house and made a note to "get it out"; however, the record shows that the social worker did not intervene directly. After the woman canceled two consecutive group therapy sessions, the social worker wrote himself a note to "get ahold of Mary right away," but the social worker did not follow through. The woman shot herself in the head as her husband approached the house on the day that he returned from naval duty. The jury awarded the husband and children more than $2 million.[25]

### NEGLIGENT INTERVENTION

Most practitioners provide skilled service to clients that is consistent with prevailing standards in the profession. On occasion, practitioners are negligent. In these instances, their intervention approaches or techniques deviate from the standard of care in the profession. As I noted in chapter 1, many liability judgments against behavioral health practitioners stem from genuine mistakes (e.g., providing remote services across state lines without being properly licensed in the jurisdiction where the client is located) or good intentions (disclosing privileged information without a client's consent in order to protect third parties). Other judgments, however, are triggered by issues related to professional misconduct and impairment, which I address more fully in chapter 4. The emphasis here is on liability risks that pertain to negligent departures from the standard of care.

Practitioners' intervention approaches and techniques can be negligent in many ways. In some instances, practitioners may use techniques for which they have not received proper training, such as biofeedback or hypnosis, or carry them out in some flawed fashion. A practitioner who uses such techniques improperly and whose lack of skill causes injury to a client may be found liable for abuse of the psychotherapeutic process. Using nontraditional approaches can also trigger liability claims and licensing-board complaints. Although practitioners should not feel compelled to limit themselves to commonly used techniques endorsed by the majority of colleagues or to completely avoid experimentation, they should be wary of radical departures from common practices in the profession. For example, in one nationally publicized case, a Colorado social worker was sentenced to sixteen years in prison in the suffocation death of a ten-year-old girl whom she was treating for an attachment disorder. The social worker was convicted of death resulting from reckless child abuse by her use of so-called rebirthing therapy. The therapy included wrapping the child in a flannel blanket, meant to represent the womb; according to the evidence, the child cried when she was not able to breathe and ended up lying in her own vomit and dying of asphyxiation.[26]

In another case, a former client sued a Virginia social worker, who was subsequently disciplined by the state board of social work. According to a published report, the social worker used past-life regression techniques, spiritual guides and masters, and nontherapeutic bodily contact. According to the news story, the social worker also took the client flying in a plane that he had rented and loaned the client money.[27]

In Arizona, a psychologist treated a woman for depression, anxiety, and drug and alcohol abuse. The psychologist allegedly used a variety of unorthodox treatment techniques, including channeling, Holotropic Breathwork, shamanic journeying, spirit depossessions, and soul retrievals. The jury awarded the plaintiff $205,000 in compensatory damages and $120,000 in punitive damages.[28]

A number of malpractice claims filed against behavioral health clinicians claim that they used "recovered memory" techniques and implanted "false memories" of child or sexual abuse. Although some courts have not been willing to admit into evidence testimony about recovered memories because of debate about their validity, others have, recognizing that behavioral health treatment may help clients recall traumatic events. In a prominent California case, a jury awarded damages to a father after finding that a psychiatrist and a social worker had implanted false memories of incest in his daughter's mind while treating her for bulimia. Gary Ramona, a former winery executive, was awarded $500,000.[29]

In a Texas case, parents alleged that their child's psychiatrist negligently produced recovered memories in the child that led him to claim that his father had sexually abused him. The Texas jury awarded the parents $350,000.[30] In another Texas case, a woman alleged that her counselor implanted in her memories of satanic ritual abuse and parental incest and was responsible for her multiple personality disorder and alienation from her family. The jury found the counselor 60 percent negligent and the plaintiff 40 percent negligent.[31]

In *Hammer v. Rosen*, Alice Hammer and her father sued her psychiatrist, Dr. John Rosen. Rosen had treated Alice Hammer, who had been diagnosed with schizophrenia. The plaintiffs claimed that Rosen beat Alice

Hammer during treatment sessions. According to court records, Rosen treated his schizophrenic patients by also acting in a schizophrenic manner at times. Ultimately, the New York Court of Appeals, the state's highest court, reversed the lower court decision and found Rosen liable for improper treatment and malpractice.[32]

A Michigan case raised similar issues. The plaintiff was a legal secretary who went to St. Joseph Hospital with symptoms of panic disorder and agoraphobia. The plaintiff alleged that she was discharged to outpatient treatment without being informed of the diagnosis or given an explanation of her condition. She claimed that attempts to treat her condition were limited to comments about less painful methods of suicide and New Age spiritual guidance. The case was settled for $100,000.[33]

Behavioral health practitioners who use nontraditional or unorthodox intervention approaches must be vigilant in their efforts to adhere to prevailing ethical standards. As Austin, Moline, and Williams urge,

> If you are using techniques that are not commonly practiced, you will need to have a clear rationale that other professionals in your field will accept and support. It is important to consult colleagues when you are using what are considered to be nontraditional approaches to treatment. This is primarily because it is not difficult to prove deviation from average care. Some examples of what may be considered nontraditional therapeutic techniques might include asking clients to undress, striking a client, or giving "far-out" homework assignments.[34]

Another potential source of problems is advice giving. If practitioners give clients advice that departs from the standard of care—such as advising clients about psychotropic medication doses or the therapeutic benefits of herbal remedies for symptoms of clinical depression—they could be held liable (e.g., for practicing medicine without a license). In a Florida case, a clinical social worker was disciplined by the licensing board after evidence was presented that the social worker prescribed the medications Pamelor, Klonopin, and Soma to a client.[35] A Wisconsin practitioner was also accused of prescribing medications to a client and giving the client sample medications. According to the licensing board, "The client has testified that on at least one occasion during the course of Respondent's therapy, Respondent provided the client with a prescription order for medication, which bore the signature of the psychiatrist associated with Respondent in practice. This prescription had been provided to Respondent, pre-signed in blank, and was then filled out by Respondent, on her own authority, and given to the client to fill at a pharmacy."[36]

In a widely publicized case, a New Jersey social worker employed at a mental health clinic told the New Jersey State Board of Medical Examiners that social workers were being allowed to order refills of patients' medication prescriptions because of a shortage of psychiatrists. The social worker said that she and other clinic social workers would order prescriptions by telephone, and staff psychiatrists would later sign the prescription forms. She also alleged that social workers occasionally would change patients' medication—including antipsychotic and antidepressant drugs—and modify dosages without consulting a physician. After she blew the whistle, the social worker said, "I knew that [social workers] prescribing medications was wrong, and I was surprised something like this could be going on, but I was really getting involved in my [psychotherapy] cases and I enjoyed the group I was leading, so I thought I would try to change things from within."[37]

The state board investigated and reprimanded the clinic's consulting psychiatrist, finding that she had inadequately supervised patients who were on prescription drugs. She admitted no wrongdoing but faced $8,000 in penalties. An independent consultant was to monitor the clinic for two years.

In addition, practitioners and the agencies for which they work can be sued for mistreating clients; for example, in the form of verbal or emotional abuse. Consider what happened in a case in Washington, D.C. The plaintiff was a thirty-six-year-old attorney who participated in a five-day program that included lectures, "guided fantasies," and experimental psychological exercises. He experienced psychotic symptoms (hallucinations) during the training, along with hyperactivity and sleep deprivation. He was hospitalized for five days, discharged, and about three months later was readmitted to the hospital, where he was then treated for about three more months. The attorney had no previous history of mental illness. He sued, claiming intentional infliction of emotional distress, negligence, and fraud (in the form of an introductory session that he alleged was misleading). The District of Columbia jury found in favor of the defendant with respect to intentional infliction of emotional distress but found in favor of the plaintiff with regard to the allegations of negligence and fraud. The plaintiff was awarded $297,387.[38]

In another case, the plaintiff sued sponsors of what were known as EST seminars, which were popular in the 1970s and 1980s. These seminars, created by Werner Erhard, were designed for people who sought personal transformation and included controversial treatment techniques. The plaintiff alleged that the treatment caused several psychological problems and a suicide attempt. The plaintiff, who had a history of abuse and psychological difficulties, was recovering from an automobile accident and was depressed because of her injuries. She claimed that during the sessions the trainer and other participants told her that the automobile accident was really her fault and that she chose to be in the accident. The plaintiff claimed that the sponsors should have had a procedure to screen out individuals who were in treatment elsewhere. The Utah case was settled for $50,000.[39]

Of course, many lawsuits alleging negligent intervention are not successful. In *Hess v. Frank*, a New York patient sued his psychiatrist, claiming that the doctor used abusive language and that such language caused anguish and serious injury to the patient. The plaintiff sought $100,000 in damages and $20,000 previously paid to the psychiatrist for treatment but lost the case.[40]

### REMOTE SERVICE DELIVERY

Behavioral health practitioners who provide services remotely must comply with prevailing standards of care to protect clients and themselves. The Coalition for Technology in Behavioral Science (CTiBS) has identified a number of core competencies for behavioral health practitioners who provide behavioral health services remotely.[41] These include the following:

1. Clinical Evaluation and Care: Practitioners must demonstrate how to make evidence-based decisions to protect clients. They must demonstrate working knowledge, skills, and attitudes related to technology-based intake, triage, assessment, diagnosis, and therapeutic services; cultural, linguistic, socioeconomic, and other characteristics related to diversity; and appropriate documentation.

2. Virtual Environment and Telepresence: Practitioners must demonstrate their ability to apply appropriate techniques to maximize therapeutic benefit, including minimizing distraction and interruptions. Practitioners must strive to approximate an in-person relationship and foster spontaneity through remote service delivery.

3. Technology: Practitioners must demonstrate their ability to make informed decisions that reflect understanding their own and their clients' preferences for and experience with use of technology. Practitioners should understand how to responsibly use the technology they choose and demonstrate knowledge of its strengths, applications, and limitations related to privacy, confidentiality, data integrity, and security.

4. Legal and Regulatory Issues: Practitioners must be aware of and demonstrate adherence to relevant federal, state/provincial, and local laws as well as regulations and policies/procedures regarding remote delivery of behavioral health services, including issues such as privacy, confidentiality, data protection/integrity, and security. They must also demonstrate adherence to relevant mandated reporting, informed consent, and documentation requirements. Further, they must demonstrate compliance with legal technology-related mandates, including the appropriate use of business associate agreements.

5. Evidence-Based and Ethical Practice: Practitioners must be aware of and demonstrate adherence to interprofessional and discipline-based professional standards and evidence-based guidelines. Practitioners must also demonstrate adherence to professional boundaries and other best practice guidelines relevant to a virtual setting when engaging in social media and digital information collection sources (such as search engines). Professionals develop written social media and digital information policies and discuss them with clients.

6. Mobile Health Technologies, Including Applications (Apps): Practitioners choosing to work with mobile health technologies, including apps, must be able to demonstrate how these are used in accordance with therapeutic goals; their understanding of potential positive and/or negative effects on the therapeutic relationship; how practitioners adhere to and apply relevant professional standards and state/provincial and/or federal law; how they help clients select options on the basis of evidence; and their understanding of the privacy limitations of mobile technologies utilized/recommended and ways to discuss these with clients.

7. Telepractice Development: Practitioners must demonstrate how to use behavioral health technology and other forms of telecommunication technology to create and maintain one's professional identity and to engage the community at large. Professionals must ensure the accuracy and validity of online and other information disseminated.

The social work profession, in particular, has developed very comprehensive practice standards designed to guide practitioners' use of technology. This is a noteworthy example of how a profession develops standards
of care and may be helpful to other behavioral health practitioners. In
2017, following unprecedented collaboration among key social work organizations in the United States—the National Association of Social Workers (NASW), Council on Social Work Education (CSWE), Association
of Social Work Boards (ASWB), and Clinical Social Work Association
(CSWA)—the profession formally adopted new, comprehensive practice
standards, including extensive ethics guidelines that focused on social
workers' and social work educators' use of technology.[42] Approved by these
respective organizations' boards of directors, these transformational, comprehensive standards address a wide range of compelling ethical issues. In
short, these new standards constitute a sea change in social work practice,
administration, and education.

The standards include four major sections: (1) provision of information to the public; (2) design and delivery of services; (3) gathering,
managing, and storing of information; and (4) social work education
and supervision.

- *Provision of information to the public.* This section summarizes core ethical
  issues involving social workers' use of technology. It also states that social
  workers who use technology to provide information to the public shall take
  reasonable steps to ensure the accuracy and validity of the information they
  disseminate.
- *Design and delivery of services.* This section states that social workers who
  provide electronic social work services shall comply with the laws and
  regulations that govern electronic social work services within both the
  jurisdiction in which the social worker is located and in which the client is located; understand, comply, and stay current with any and all laws
  that govern the provision of social work services and inform clients of the
  social worker's legal obligations, just as they would when providing services in person; inform the client of relevant benefits and risks of services
  provided electronically; obtain and maintain the knowledge and skills
  required to do so in a safe, competent, and ethical manner; establish and
  maintain confidentiality policies and procedures consistent with relevant
  statutes, regulations, rules, and ethical standards; take reasonable steps

to ensure that business associates (e.g., those who process social workers' insurance claims) use proper encryption and have confidentiality policies and procedures consistent with social work standards and relevant laws; maintain clear professional boundaries in their relationships with clients; develop a social media policy that they share with clients; consider the implications of their use of personal mobile phones and other electronic communication devices for work purposes; plan for the possibility that electronic services will be interrupted unexpectedly; be familiar with emergency services in the jurisdiction where the client is located and share this information with clients; refrain from soliciting electronic or online testimonials from clients or former clients who, because of their particular circumstances, are vulnerable to undue influence; and use technology responsibly in conjunction with organizing and advocacy efforts, fundraising, agency administration, supervision, consultation, and program evaluation and research.

• *Gathering, managing, and storing of information.* This section states that social workers who provide electronic social work services shall explain to clients whether and how they intend to use electronic devices or communication technologies to gather, manage, and store client information; ensure clear delineation between personal and professional communications and information when social workers gather, manage, and store client information electronically; take reasonable steps to ensure that confidential information concerning clients or research participants is gathered, managed, and stored in a secure manner and in accordance with relevant federal and state statutes, regulations, and organizational policies; take reasonable steps to develop and implement policies regarding which personnel have access to clients' electronic records, keeping in mind the value of limiting access to those colleagues who truly require it; develop and disclose policies and procedures concerning how they would notify clients of any breach of their confidential records; shall gather information for social work practice or research in a manner that reasonably ensures its reliability and accuracy; take reasonable steps to protect the confidentiality of information that is shared with other parties electronically; ensure that client access to electronic records is provided in a manner that takes client confidentiality, privacy, and the client's best interests into account; not gather information about clients from online sources without the client's consent, except for compelling professional reasons; respect colleagues and verify the accuracy of information before using information gathered online about colleagues; treat colleagues with respect and represent accurately and fairly the qualifications, views, and obligations of colleagues when social workers communicate using electronic tools; be aware of how information that is posted or stored electronically for use by others may be used and interpreted, and take reasonable steps to ensure that the information is accurate, respectful, and complete; develop and follow appropriate policies regarding whether and how they can access electronic client records remotely; and take steps to protect their clients, employer, themselves, and the environment when an electronic device is no longer needed, is phased out, or is outdated.

- *Social work education and supervision.* This section states that social workers who use technology to design and deliver education and training shall develop competence in the ethical use of the technology in a manner appropriate for the particular context; provide information to students and practitioners about the ethical use of technology, including potential benefits and risks; examine and keep current with relevant emerging knowledge related to the use of technology in social work practice; provide students with social media policies to provide them with guidance about ethical considerations; provide clear guidance on professional expectations when evaluating students on their use of technology and how assignments will be graded; provide students with information about how to manage technological problems that may be caused by loss of power, viruses, hardware failures, lost or stolen devices, or other issues that may disrupt the educational process; ensure that practitioners and students have sufficient understanding of the cultural, social, and legal contexts of the other locations where the practitioners or students are located; ensure that students have sufficient access to technological support to assist with technological questions or problems that may arise during the educational process; take appropriate measures to promote academic standards related to honesty, integrity, freedom of expression, and respect for the dignity and worth of all people when using technology for educational purposes; take precautions to ensure maintenance of appropriate educator-student boundaries during electronic interactions; and ensure that supervisors who use technology to provide supervision are able to assess students' and supervisees' learning and professional competence.

## BOUNDARY ISSUES AND DUAL RELATIONSHIPS

Especially since the 1980s, behavioral health practitioners have developed an increasingly mature grasp of a wide range of boundary and dual relationship issues.[43] Boundary issues arise when practitioners encounter actual or potential conflicts between their professional duties and their social, sexual, religious, or business relationships. Some dual relationships are clearly unethical (e.g., engaging in a sexual relationship with one's client or exchanging sexualized text messages with a client); however, other dual relationships may be unavoidable (e.g., when practitioners work and live in small rural communities) and require careful management.

Behavioral health practitioners should be alert to a number of boundary issues that arise in practice and that can be a central issue in malpractice claims and licensing-board complaints[44]:

• Sexual relationships with current and former clients. A significant portion of inappropriate dual relationships entered into by behavioral health practitioners involve sexual contact in some form (although the evidence suggests that only a small percentage of practitioners engage in such conduct). The consensus among practitioners is that sexual relationships with current clients are patently unethical. In general, sexual relationships with former clients also are unethical. Here, however, there are differences in the ethical standards in the various behavioral health professions. Some professions' standards include time frames within which a sexual relationship with a former client is not permitted. For example, the American Psychological Association (APA) Code of Ethics states that psychologists may not engage in sexual intimacies with former clients/patients for at least two years after cessation or termination of therapy. Further, the APA code states that psychologists should not engage in sexual intimacies with former clients/patients even after a two-year interval except in the most unusual circumstances.[45]

The American Counseling Association's ethics code extends this time period to five years.[46] In contrast, the NASW Code of Ethics does not permit such relationships, regardless of the amount of time that has passed since termination of the practitioner-client relationship. According to the NASW Code of Ethics, "If social workers engage in conduct contrary to this prohibition or claim that an exception to this prohibition is warranted because of extraordinary circumstances, it is social workers—not their clients—who assume the full burden of demonstrating that the former client has not been exploited, coerced, or manipulated, intentionally or unintentionally."[47]

• Counseling of former sexual partners. Moving from an intimate sexual relationship to a practitioner-client relationship (e.g., when a practitioner's former lover seeks the practitioner's professional advice or services) can be detrimental to the client. Former lovers who become clients are likely to find it difficult to shift from the role of an egalitarian partner in an intimate relationship to a party who, to some degree, is in a dependent or subordinate position.

• Sexual relationships with clients' relatives or acquaintances. Widely accepted ethical standards also prohibit sexual activities or sexual contact with clients' relatives or other individuals with whom a client maintains a close personal relationship, particularly when risk of exploitation or potential harm to the client exists.

• Sexual relationships with supervisees, trainees, students, and colleagues. Practitioners must also avoid sexual relationships with staff members whom they supervise and other individuals (such as trainees and students) over whom they exercise some form of authority. The power differential in these relationships exposes supervisees, trainees, and students to potential exploitation and harm.

• Physical contact with clients. Practitioners must be careful to distinguish between appropriate and inappropriate physical contact. Briefly holding the hand of a distressed client or a brief good-bye hug at the end of a long-term clinical relationship may be appropriate in some circumstances and contexts. Sustained physical contact is not appropriate. Practitioners should be mindful of clients' religious, cultural, and ethnicity norms pertaining to physical contact. For example, some religions and cultures prohibit physical contact—including handshakes—between unmarried individuals of another sex.

• Friendships with current and former clients. Friendships that develop between practitioners and their clients sometimes arise out of genuine affection; in some instances, however, friendships reflect practitioners' own emotional needs and personal crises. Practitioners must be alert to the ways in which friendships with current clients are unethical and the ways in which friendships with former clients may constitute inappropriate dual relationships. As with sexual relationships, friendships with clients have the potential to harm clients and interfere with their ability to benefit from behavioral health services.

• Encounters with clients in public settings. Practitioners sometimes encounter clients in public settings, such as stores, festivals, or receptions at social events. This is especially likely in rural and other small communities such as military bases. Practitioners should discuss this possibility with clients in advance, focusing on constructive, ethical ways of handling these encounters. Such proactive measures can help clients and practitioners avoid awkwardness and misunderstanding about the nature of their relationship.

• Attendance at clients' social, religious, or life-cycle events. Practitioners hold many and varied opinions concerning their attendance at these events (such as weddings, graduations, baby-naming events, and funerals). Some practitioners believe that such attendance can be therapeutically beneficial and supportive; they argue that refusal to attend may damage the clinical relationship and lead to clients feeling betrayed. Practitioners' understanding of clients' religious and cultural norms around attendance at such events may influence their judgment. In contrast, many practitioners worry about the potential for blurred boundaries when practitioners attend social, religious, or life-cycle events. Practitioners should address the issue explicitly and establish clear guidelines, taking into consideration current ethical standards concerning dual relationships and the potential for ethics complaints and litigation. Practitioners who face such decisions would be wise to seek and document consultation, thereby demonstrating their good faith effort to manage the boundaries responsibly.

• Gifts from clients. Challenging boundary issues sometimes emerge when clients offer gifts or special favors to practitioners. Some gifts (such as a plate of homemade cookies at holiday time) may be completely innocent and harmless; others may be loaded with clinical meaning and may be a precursor to an inappropriate dual relationship (e.g., an expensive piece of jewelry or item of intimate clothing). Practitioners should develop guidelines to distinguish between circumstances in which they may accept modest, token gifts from clients and circumstances in which accepting gifts is inappropriate. It is also helpful to develop procedures to help practitioners respond skillfully and sensitively to clients who offer gifts.

• Gifts to clients. In most instances, it is unethical for practitioners to give clients gifts because of the implication of an inappropriate dual relationship.

Some practitioners and agencies have acknowledged unique exceptions; for example, when clients in an independent living program for youth aging out of foster care invite agency staffers to see their new apartment. In these instances, practitioners should develop clear guidelines to minimize harm (e.g., ensuring that the client understands that the modest gift is from the agency rather than an individual staff member as an acknowledgment of this milestone event and the client's emerging independence). In an Ohio case, the state licensing board disciplined a social worker for giving a client two significant sums of money.[48]

• Favors for clients. A variety of circumstances may tempt practitioners, for altruistic reasons, to offer clients favors (e.g., giving a stranded client a ride, lending money to a destitute client, giving a vulnerable client one's personal mobile telephone number). Although such gestures may be completely innocent and relatively innocuous, practitioners should be aware of the ways in which their altruistic instincts may generate boundary issues. In some instances, clients may interpret such gestures as an indication of the practitioner's interest in a nonprofessional relationship.

• The delivery of services in a client's home. Practitioners who provide services in clients' homes (e.g., in home-based family intervention programs or home-based crisis intervention programs) must be particularly alert to potentially problematic boundary issues. Providing services in such nonoffice, informal, and relatively intimate settings may confuse clients and practitioners about the nature of the practitioner-client relationship. One can imagine a practitioner visiting a chaotic, noise-filled home to meet with a client during a crisis and the only private space available is in a bedroom. Practitioners must be prepared to respond appropriately in these unique circumstances and, also, to manage family members' invitations to join them for meals, family outings, and other social events.

• Financial conflicts of interest. Introducing financial transactions into the practitioner-client relationship (e.g., when practitioners invest in a client's new business venture or borrow money from an affluent client) is likely to distract both practitioners and clients from the clinical or other agenda with which they began their work, compromise clients' interests, and introduce conflicts of interest (where the practitioner's judgment and behavior are affected by the financial considerations). Entering into a business relationship with a client is clearly unethical. In addition, practitioners should not take advantage of their relationships with clients to advance their own financial interests. In one case in which I consulted, a social worker provided clinical services to terminally ill clients with AIDS. On the weekends, the practitioner moonlighted as an antiques dealer. Through her work with terminally ill clients, the social worker learned of antiques that would become available at estate sales after the clients' deaths. The social worker understood that she had to be very disciplined about not taking advantage of this information.)

Also, staff, administrators, and board members should not enter into financial relationships with their agencies or other organizations in a manner that would constitute a conflict of interest (e.g., having a personal financial stake in the organization's business transactions). Agencies should have clear policies about staff members' employment in other settings (e.g., whether clinical staff members at a community mental health center can establish their own part-time private practice) and delivery of services to former clients when staff members terminate their employment (e.g., when clients choose to transfer their care to their practitioners' new employment setting).

• Delivery of services to two or more people who have a relationship with each other (such as couples or family members). As I discussed briefly in chapter 2 with respect to confidentiality issues, practitioners sometimes provide services to two or more people who have a relationship with each other, typically in the context of family, marital, or couples counseling. In these situations, a practitioner should clarify with all the parties involved which individuals will be considered clients and the nature of the practitioner's professional obligations to the various individuals who are receiving services. Practitioners who anticipate a conflict of interest among the individuals receiving services or who anticipate having to perform in potentially conflicting roles (e.g., when a practitioner is asked to testify in a child custody dispute or divorce proceedings involving clients) should clarify their role with the parties involved and take appropriate action to minimize any conflict of interest.

• Barter with clients for goods and services. Practitioners hold many opinions about the use of barter. Many believe that barter is appropriate in limited circumstances when they can demonstrate that such arrangements are an accepted practice among professionals in the local community, considered essential for the provision of services, negotiated without coercion, and entered into at the client's initiative and with the client's informed consent. Others argue that barter is fraught with risk, particularly when defects in the bartered goods or services lead to conflict in, and consequently undermine, the practitioner-client relationship. Practitioners who consider barter arrangements should do so cautiously, mindful of potential boundary complications, review relevant ethical standards, and seek and document consultation.

• Management of relationships with clients in rural or small (e.g., remote military bases where practitioners live and work) communities. As I noted earlier, the likelihood of unanticipated boundary issues and dual relationships increases in geographically small communities, especially in rural areas. Practitioners in these communities often report how challenging it is to separate their professional and personal lives. Clients may be the proprietors of local businesses that practitioners must patronize or may end up being practitioners' service providers in other contexts (e.g., when a client is the only fourth-grade teacher in town and the practitioner's child is enrolled in that class). Practitioners in these circumstances must be vigilant in their efforts to protect clients, by taking into consideration such factors as the practitioners' own comfort level and confidence in their ability to manage the overlapping relationships; clients' opinions about and perceptions of the boundary issues and their ability to handle them; and the type and severity of the clients' presenting problems. Similar issues can arise in small cultural, ethnic, and religious communities; for example, when a religiously observant practitioner employed by a mental health center is actively involved in her religious community and provides services to some members of that community or a lesbian clinician is actively involved in her local lesbian community and receives requests for services from members of that community.

• Self-disclosure to clients. Practitioners' self-disclosure to clients is a complex topic. Practitioners generally agree that relatively limited and superficial self-disclosure, handled judiciously, may be appropriate and therapeutically helpful. Practitioners also recognize that self-disclosure can harm clients, particularly when the self-disclosure occurs primarily to meet a practitioner's emotional needs. For example, practitioners in recovery from substance abuse face unique challenges when they encounter clients at recovery meetings (such as Alcoholics Anonymous or Narcotics Anonymous) or share details about their recovery with clients who struggle with substances.

• Collegial relationships with a former client. On occasion, practitioners may encounter former clients who have become professional colleagues (e.g., former clients who decide to enter the behavioral health field as a result of their personal experiences). In these situations, practitioners should discuss with their former clients any problematic boundary issues and ways of dealing with them. In some instances, professional relationships with a former client may not be harmful or risky and may require no special accommodations; in other instances, however, the intensity and complexity of the former practitioner-client relationship may make a collegial relationship difficult and challenging. In these situations, practitioners may need to make special arrangements (such as resign from a professional task force on which both parties serve).

• Hiring former clients. Some behavioral health programs, such as community mental health centers and substance use disorder treatment programs, consider hiring former clients or consumers. This practice usually stems from professionals' belief that, because of their personal experiences, former clients may provide unique and valuable empathy and services to current clients. Many also view hiring former clients as a way to empower these individuals, promote client growth, and provide current clients with valuable role models.

Practitioners need to carefully consider the ethical and clinical implications of this practice. In addition to a range of potential benefits, hiring former clients poses several risks. Hiring former clients may complicate relationships between practitioners and the former clients who are now agency employees and who must relate to their former service providers as colleagues or employment supervisors. Unique challenges may arise if a former client who is now a staff member needs to reenter treatment and become a client again. Also, former clients who were not hired may feel resentful and hurt. Further, hiring former clients may introduce complex issues related to former clients' access to confidential agency records.

• Interacting with clients online and remotely. Practitioners' use of digital technology has introduced new and complicated boundary issues. Many practitioners receive requests from current and former clients asking to be online social networking "friends" or contacts. Electronic contact with clients and former clients on social networking sites can lead to boundary confusion. Electronic message exchanges between practitioners and clients that occur outside of normal business hours, especially if the practitioner uses a personal social networking site or e-mail address, may confuse practitioner-client boundaries. Practitioners who choose not to accept a client's "friend" request on an online social networking site to maintain clear boundaries may inadvertently cause the client to feel a deep sense of rejection. Practitioners should anticipate this possibility and explain to clients how they handle clients' online "friend" requests.

Also, clients who search online for information about their service provider or who are able to access a practitioner's publicly available social networking sites may learn a great deal of personal information about their practitioner (such as information about the practitioner's personal and family relationships, social and religious activities, and political views); this may introduce complex boundary challenges in the practitioner-client relationship. Some practitioners have managed this risk by creating two distinct Facebook sites; for example, one for professional use and one for personal use. Behavioral health professionals who do not maintain strict privacy settings on their online social networking sites expose themselves to considerable risk. Also, clients' postings on their own social networking sites may also lead to inadvertent or harmful disclosure of private and confidential details; for example, sensitive information shared by others in group therapy sessions.

Further, some forms of distance counseling may introduce conflicts of interest that were previously unknown in the field of behavioral health. For example, some video counseling websites are offered free to practitioners; the sponsors of these websites pay for the development and maintenance of the sites. In return, sponsors post electronic links on a practitioner's counseling screen that take users to sponsor websites providing information about the products and services offered by sponsors. Clients may believe that their practitioners endorse these products and services or benefit from sales.

Novel boundary and dual relationship challenges in the digital age that can expose behavioral health practitioners to risk are appearing in three forms: ethical judgments, ethical mistakes, and ethical misconduct.

*Ethical judgments.* In some instances, competent, principled, and well-meaning practitioners find themselves faced with ethical decisions about whether and how to use technology in their relationships with clients, in light of potential boundary challenges. In these scenarios, clinicians recognize that technology has the potential to enhance their delivery of services to clients—especially among those clients who have crises, live in remote geographical areas, or struggle with severe disabilities that limit their ability to travel—and that their use of technology may introduce complex boundary issues. These clinicians must make deliberate ethical decisions about how to use technology in ways that maintain clear, ethical practitioner-client boundaries. Following are several examples:

- A counselor provided services to a couple that was experiencing marital tension. One of the clinical issues the couple identified was their chronic distress about their lack of sexual intimacy. The counselor, who specialized in sex therapy, considered sending the couple an e-mail message containing links to a number of websites that offer advice on ways to enhance sexual intimacy. The clinician was unsure about whether it was appropriate for her to send clients an online message containing sexually explicit material. The clinician realized that the clients would be able to forward the counselor's message to others electronically, and that other recipients might misunderstand the nature of the relationship and the purpose of the message.

- A clinical psychologist counseled a sixteen-year-old teen who was struggling with depression and sexual orientation issues. During one session, the teen talked with deep emotion about the intense distress in her life. Later than night, around 10:30 P.M., the psychologist decided to search the client's Facebook site to see whether there was any evidence of suicidal ideation in the teen's online postings. The psychologist was concerned about several postings and sent the client private Facebook messages inquiring about the client's emotional state. The psychologist and client engaged in a lengthy online exchange late at night.

- A marriage and family therapist and his wife wrote sexually explicit novels that are available online (e-books). The therapist uses a pseudonym for these publications in an effort to separate his professional and personal lives. Nonetheless, the therapist is aware that clients may learn of the link and that this could introduce untoward boundary issues in his clinical relationships.

*Ethical mistakes.* In contrast, some competent, principled, and well-meaning practitioners have found themselves in ethics hot water because of technology-related errors that created boundary problems in their relationships with clients where there was a sexual component. Some of these errors have led to licensing-board complaints and lawsuits filed by disgruntled clients or third parties. Here are several actual examples:

- A clinical psychologist received an unsolicited Facebook request from a client who had sought treatment for her anxiety symptoms. The client had searched for the psychologist's Facebook site and discovered several of the psychologist's postings about his recent divorce. The psychologist thought he understood how to use Facebook's privacy settings to limit access to such postings to his closest friends. However, the client was able to access many of the psychologist's postings about his personal relationships. Before the psychologist blocked the client's access to his Facebook site, the client had sent the clinician a series of flirtatious, intrusive, and intimate Facebook messages about the psychologist's personal life. Because of these boundary complications, the psychologist decided to terminate the clinical relationship, against the client's wishes, and refer the client. The client became enraged and filed a licensing-board complaint alleging that the psychologist had abandoned her. The licensing board reprimanded the psychologist for failing to maintain proper boundaries online and failing to obtain proper consultation with colleagues. The board required the psychologist to enroll in supplemental continuing education courses on boundary issues and use of technology. The board also required the clinician to consult with a local ethics expert regarding his management of this case, focusing especially on how the psychologist might have processed these boundary issues with his client in order to avoid termination of services.

- In his private life, a mental health counselor was a member of an online creative writing group that included erotica. Group members posted drafts of their work in their Google Docs accounts so that they could be accessed by other group members. Inadvertently, the counselor did not limit access to his Google Docs postings. His client, who sought counseling to help her cope with the breakup of a long-term relationship, searched Google for information about the counselor and was able to open several of the counselor's erotic writings. The client, who had been harboring sexual fantasies about the counselor, told the counselor about how much she enjoyed reading about his sexual fantasies. The counselor was stunned by this boundary crossing and unsure about whether he could continue to work with the client. The counselor sought ethics consultation from his national professional association's ethics office and a local professor who specializes in professional ethics.

*Ethical misconduct.* As in all professions, some behavioral health practitioners—a distinct minority—engage in ethical misconduct. Practitioners' use of technology has expanded the ways in which unscrupulous counselors can engage in sexualized relationships with clients. In some instances, the unethical conduct is limited to online communications. In others, electronic communications are a prelude to a sexual relationship. In some cases, evidence suggests that electronic communications were part of a deliberate, calculated effort by clinicians to groom clients for an eventual sexual relationship. Here are examples:

- A psychologist at a prominent outpatient mental health clinic provided counseling services to clients with co-occurring symptoms (substance use and mood disorders). Most of his clients had trauma histories that contributed to their challenges. Over time, the psychologist engaged in sexual relationships with two of his clients. One of the clients disclosed the relationship to the police after the psychologist suddenly ended their intimate relationship. The clinician's arrest was publicized in the local media, after which the second client disclosed her sexual relationship with him. The psychologist was charged in criminal court and sued by the two clients. During the criminal and civil trials, the prosecutor and the plaintiffs' attorneys introduced a collection of "electronically stored information" (ESI), including text messages and e-mail messages between the clinician and his clients that included sexualized content, which provided compelling evidence of the psychologist's unethical conduct. The clinician—who was not aware that his electronic communications left a digital footprint—was convicted, sentenced to prison, lost his professional license, and was found liable for professional negligence.
- A psychiatrist provided medication prescriptions and brief counseling to a woman who struggled with symptoms of depression and anxiety. During the course of the counseling the patient's husband died, which exacerbated her symptoms. The patient often talked about her intense loneliness. The psychiatrist told the patient that he could help fill the emotional void in the patient's life. The psychiatrist began sending text messages to the patient, allegedly to check on her well-being. Over time, the text message exchanges between the pair became increasingly informal. On several occasions, the

pair met for coffee. Eventually, they began a sexual relationship. During this period of time, the psychiatrist continued to prescribe psychotropic medication to the patient. The intimate relationship ruptured and the patient filed a licensing-board complaint. The board suspended the psychiatrist's license.

- A counselor worked at a school sponsored by a mental health center. The school served adolescents who had difficulty functioning in traditional high school settings; all of the students struggled with behavioral health issues. The counselor spent most of an academic year counseling a seventeen-year-old student who became clinically depressed following the sudden death of his father in an automobile accident. Over time, the counselor and student developed an intense emotional connection; at times the counselor shared with the student details about her marriage and children. The counselor encouraged the teen to text her for support when he was feeling despair. One day, the teen sent the counselor a text message in which he shared his "loving" feelings toward her. The counselor responded with her own text message that told the teen how much she cared about him and how special he is. Gradually, the counselor and teen spent time together away from the school and, eventually, engaged in sex. The teen's mother disclosed the relationship to the school's director after discovering inappropriate text messages on her son's phone, including several graphic, explicit photos that the two had exchanged ("sexting"). The principal fired the counselor and notified her licensing board. The licensing board revoked the counselor's license.

To practice ethically and minimize risk, practitioners who use digital and other technology to provide distance services should develop protocols concerning boundaries, dual relationships, and conflicts of interest that include several key elements. Practitioners must develop sound guidelines governing their contact with current and former clients on social networking sites (e.g., Facebook, LinkedIn, Twitter, Instagram) and their willingness to provide services to people they first met socially on online social networking sites. Practitioners must be careful to avoid inappropriate disclosure of personal information in digital communications (e.g., e-mail messages, text messages, and social network postings) and should establish clear guidelines concerning interactions with clients online and via other digital and electronic means at various times of day and night, weekends, and holidays. Developing a comprehensive social media policy and sharing it with clients can help reduce risk.

### Managing Boundary Risks

Effective risk management concerning dual relationships and boundary issues should provide both conceptual guidance and practical steps that enhance protections of all parties involved. The following is a decision-making model that is based on several available frameworks and which practitioners can use when they encounter potential or actual dual relationships and boundary issues:[49]

1.  Attempt to set unambiguous boundaries at the beginning of all professional relationships.
2.  Evaluate potential dual relationships and boundary issues by considering (a) the amount of power the practitioner holds over the client, (b) the duration of the relationship, (c) the clarity of conditions surrounding planned or actual termination, (d) the client's clinical profile, and (e) prevailing ethical standards. How much power does the practitioner have over the client? How likely is it that the client will return for additional services? In clinical relationships, to what extent do the client's clinical needs, issues, vulnerabilities, and symptoms increase the risk that the client will be harmed? To what extent does the dual relationship breach prevailing ethical standards? Especially risky are relationships that entail considerable practitioner power (such as a parole officer or a practitioner who provides court-ordered services), are long lasting, do not involve clear-cut termination, involve clinical issues that render clients vulnerable, and are not consistent with relevant ethical standards.
3.  On the basis of these criteria, consider whether a dual relationship in any form, including digital and online contact, is warranted or justifiable. Recognize that gradations exist between the extreme options of a full-fledged dual relationship and no dual relationship. For example, a practitioner may decide that attending a client's graduation ceremony at a substance use disorder treatment program is permissible and important therapeutically but that attending the post-ceremony party at the client's home is not. A practitioner may decide to disclose to a particular client that he is a new parent without disclosing intimate details concerning his struggle with infertility. A practitioner may accept e-mail messages from clients to reschedule appointments but not engage in online conversations that include clinical or personal content. A grant administrator may collaborate on a joint project with a

private agency in which her husband is employed but recuse herself from all decisions at her agency concerning funding of her husband's program.

4. Pay special attention to potentially conflicting roles in the relationship, or role incompatibility. For instance, a practitioner should not agree to counsel her secretary or have a Facebook relationship with a former client. An administrator should not supervise her spouse. Of course, sometimes practitioners do not agree about the extent of role incompatibility, which entails divergent expectations and power differentials; among the best examples is the debate among practitioners about whether practitioners in recovery should attend twelve-step meetings, such as those sponsored by Alcoholics Anonymous or Narcotics Anonymous, at which a client is present, and whether community-based mental health programs should hire former clients as staff members.

5. Whenever there is any degree of doubt about dual relationships or boundary issues, consult thoughtful, principled, and trusted colleagues. It is important to consult with colleagues who understand one's work, particularly in relation to services provided, clientele served, and relevant ethical standards.

6. Discuss the relevant issues with all the parties involved, especially clients. Clients should be actively and deliberately involved in these decisions, in part as a sign of respect and in part to promote informed consent. Fully inform clients of any potential risks.

7. Work under supervision whenever boundary issues are complex and the related risk is high.

8. If necessary and feasible, refer the client to another professional in order to minimize risk and prevent harm.

9. Document key aspects of the decision-making process; for example, colleagues consulted, documents reviewed (codes of ethics, agency policies, statutes, regulations, relevant literature), and discussions with clients.

### UNDUE INFLUENCE

On occasion, liability problems arise in the delivery of behavioral health services because of the phenomenon of undue influence. Undue influence occurs when practitioners use their authority improperly to pressure, persuade, or sway a client to engage in an activity that may not be in the client's best interest or that may pose a conflict of interest. Undue influence may take several forms. Examples include persuading a client in a hospice program to include the practitioner in his will after the two have developed a close relationship, pressuring a vulnerable individual to contract for unnecessary services, and convincing a client to include the practitioner, during treatment, in a lucrative investment or business partnership. Gifis offers the legal definition of undue influence:

> It is established by excessive importunity, superiority of will or mind, the relationship of the parties (e.g., priest and penitent or caretaker and senior citizen) or by any other means constraining the donor or testator [one who makes and executes a testament or will] to do what he is unable to refuse. . . . The elements of undue influence are susceptibility of testator/ donor to such influence, the exertion of improper influence, and submission to the domination of the influencing party.[50]

This issue arose in an Alabama case in which the licensing board revoked the license of a public-health social worker who was found guilty of soliciting significant funds from a client as payment for not reporting information to Medicaid that would cause the client to lose his coverage.[51]

A lower court case from New York, *Geis v. Landau*, illustrates how subtle issues involving undue influence can be. Dr. Jon Geis, a clinical psychologist, had provided counseling services to Betsy Landau for approximately eight years. During this period, Landau was going through a divorce and explained to Geis that she was having difficulty paying his fees. When the therapy terminated, Landau had an outstanding bill of $8,000. Geis sued Landau for the unpaid fees. In her defense, Landau contended that Geis, who allowed her fees to build up unpaid, failed to discuss with her the problem that she was "getting in over her head." At one point, Geis wrote Landau a note stating "not to worry about the bill"; according to testimony, Geis had confidence that Landau would eventually pay the bill. According to court records, Geis also stated that he had decided that referring Landau to a low-cost mental health clinic would be unwise. According to the court, Geis "made a unilateral decision that only he could help the defendant." The judge ruled that Geis had exercised excessive power over his client, who was dependent upon him for resolution to her problems. The judge stated that he had doubts that no other alternative (low-cost clinic) was available to Landau to assist her with further treatment. The judge stated that his decision to grant judgment to the defendant (Landau) did not mean that a therapist can never "extend credit to a patient," but, when a therapist knows that the client has no means by which to pay the account, such credit is not considered fair.[52]

In 1979, the *New York Times* reported a highly unusual case involving a social worker who exerted undue influence. A social worker in New York City was convicted of killing his sixty-eight-year-old client after stealing a substantial sum of money from her by persuading the woman to withdraw more than $13,000 from a bank and then throwing the woman's weighted body into the East River. He was sentenced to a minimum of twenty-five years in prison.[53]

Undue influence can be difficult to prove, as illustrated by the classic case of *Patterson v. Jensen*. Although this Wisconsin case involves a physician rather than a behavioral health practitioner, it contains many issues broached in undue influence cases. Mary Faulks named her personal physician, a Dr. Patterson, as the primary beneficiary in her will. In addition to serving as her physician, Patterson had borrowed money from Faulks to buy a house. Faulks had also given Patterson money for an airplane hangar, partial payment on an airplane, and a family vacation. In response to one gift, Patterson promised Faulks that he would attend to her medical needs for the rest of her life. The man whom Faulks and her husband had raised as a young boy, Will Jensen, objected to the relationship between his guardian and Patterson. He argued that it was not in her best interest and that she was "susceptible to undue influence." The court ruled that Faulks was not impaired when she had her last will drafted and that it had no clear evidence that Patterson influenced the contents of the will or became the primary beneficiary as a result of undue influence. The court concluded that influence that resulted from kindness and affection was not undue "if no imposition or fraud be practiced, even though it induced the testator (Mrs. Faulks) to make an unequal and unjust disposition."[54]

Lawsuits against behavioral health professionals alleging undue influence are rare. Nonetheless practitioner-client relationships certainly pose the potential for the exercise of undue influence.

### SUICIDE

Many cases alleging improper assessment and intervention involve suicide.[55] As I discussed earlier, a distressingly large number of liability cases allege that a behavioral health professional did not adequately assess for suicide risk and therefore did not take proper precautions to prevent a suicide. In a federal court case, the plaintiff's husband was admitted to a hospital after showing signs of depression and slitting his wrists. The man was released about two-and-a-half weeks later after receiving medication and psychotherapy. Several months later, the man was admitted to a VA hospital after buying a shotgun with the intention of killing himself. The hospital staff made no attempt to obtain the patient's earlier records or contact the physicians who had treated him. In addition, staff members did not take a complete history at the time of admission and did not conduct a thorough interview with the patient's family about his history. The patient then attempted suicide for the third time, unsuccessfully, by jumping in front of a truck while out of the hospital on a weekend pass. Two months after his admission to the VA hospital, the patient walked out of the facility and committed suicide by throwing himself under the wheels of a bus directly in front of the hospital and on the hospital grounds. The VA hospital was found liable, and the plaintiff was awarded $570,841.[56]

In another case raising similar issues, a patient sued a psychiatric facility, two psychiatrists, two psychiatric nurses, and a psychiatric social worker in Massachusetts. The plaintiff, a nineteen-year-old patient who jumped from the sixth floor of a psychiatric facility, alleged that the defendants did not properly diagnose his suicidal ideation and did not take precautions to prevent a suicide attempt. Before his suicide attempt, he had a one-year history of psychiatric illness and previous psychiatric hospitalization. He had hallucinations, delusions, and symptoms of depression. A note by a nurse reported that the patient had said that he had given his body to Satan. Three days after his admission, the patient was released on a pass to attend a psychiatric group therapy session on the sixth floor of the building. After the therapy session, the patient was left momentarily unattended. He walked to an open atrium foyer and jumped. He suffered severe injuries, including hip and leg fractures, brain damage, and loss of an eye, a kidney, and his spleen. The jury found the defendants 85 percent negligent and the plaintiff 15 percent contributively negligent; the plaintiff ultimately settled for $3 million during the damages phase of the trial.[57]

As I discuss more thoroughly in chapter 5, in still other cases plaintiffs allege that practitioners did not provide adequate supervision of a suicidal client. As Meyer, Landis, and Hays conclude,

While the law generally does not hold anyone responsible for the acts of another, there are exceptions. One of these is the responsibility of therapists to prevent suicide and other self-destructive behavior by their clients. The duty of therapists to exercise adequate care and skill in diagnosing suicidality is well-established (see *Meier v. Ross General Hospital*, 1968). When the risk of self-injurious behavior is identified an additional duty to take adequate precautions arises (*Abille v. United States*, 1980; *Pisel v. Stamford Hospital*, 1980). When psychotherapists fail to meet these responsibilities, they may be held liable for injuries that result.

Not every completed suicide or gesture is cause for liability—only those which could reasonably have been prevented. Demonstrating negligence requires proof that the patient should have been identified as suicidal based on widely recognized criteria used by most other therapists of the same training.[58]

As Meyer, Landis, and Hays suggest, *Meier v. Ross General Hospital* sets an important precedent in litigation involving suicide.[59] The widow and children of the patient, Kurt Meier, brought a wrongful death suit against the California hospital and Dr. James Stubblebine, director of the psychiatric unit, after Meier committed suicide while a patient in the hospital. The family had brought Meier to the hospital after he had attempted suicide by cutting his wrists. The hospital had what it described as an "open-door" policy for its psychiatric patients in order to provide a homelike atmosphere. The patients were free to move about the hospital and even to leave if they so wished. Staff members recognized that this open-door policy lessened security and exposed potentially suicidal patients to greater risk, but they believed that ultimately the enhanced freedom of movement improved the prospects for rehabilitation.

Approximately one week after Meier slashed his wrists, he committed suicide by jumping head first from an open window in his second-floor room. The trial court found in favor of the hospital and psychiatrist. On appeal to the California Supreme Court, however, the decision was reversed, and the court ordered a new trial. The California Supreme Court opinion contains important language concerning professionals' responsibility when they perceive a risk of suicide:

> If those charged with the care and treatment of a mentally disturbed patient know of facts from which they could reasonably conclude that the patient

would be likely to harm himself in the absence of preclusive measures, then they must use reasonable care under the circumstances to prevent such harm [*Wood v. Samaritan Institution* (1945)]. Given this duty and the fact that defendants placed decedent, following an attempted suicide, in a second floor room with a fully openable window, the jury could find from the fact of decedent's plunge through this window that defendants more probably than not breached the duty of care owed to decedent. Even in the absence of expert testimony which describes the probability that the death or injury resulted from negligence, the jury may competently decide that defendant more probably than not breached his duty of care when the evidence supports a conclusion that the cause of the accident (here, the openable window) was not inextricably connected with the course of treatment involving the exercise of medical judgment beyond the common knowledge of laymen.[60]

Similar reasoning appears in *Sayes v. Pilgrim Manor Nursing Home*. This case involved a police officer who was injured when he dove into the water in an effort to rescue a nursing-home patient who was attempting suicide by wading toward deep water. In his suit against the nursing home, the police officer alleged that his injury was caused by its negligent care of the woman. The Louisiana Court of Appeal ultimately held that the nursing home was negligent in allowing the woman to leave the facility unattended. In its ruling, the appellate court made three main points:

First, the nursing home's voluntary acceptance of the resident, after her release from a state mental hospital, with full knowledge of her mental and physical disorders, obligated it to take extra care and precautionary measures to assure that she would not injure herself or others.

Second, the nursing home had allowed the resident complete freedom to leave the home's premises, despite the fact that she had been rehospitalized on four occasions due to her violent and/or destructive outbursts.

Third, immediately preceding the suicide attempt, the resident had exhibited behavior that should have placed the nursing home on notice that she was likely to engage in violent, combative and destructive behavior. These warning signs were ignored.[61]

As is often the case, courts do not expect behavioral health professionals to have the ability to always predict accurately whether a client is likely to commit suicide. Rather, what is required is competent assessment, consistent with the standard of care in the profession and a good faith effort to protect the client from harm.

*Porter v. Maunnangi* illustrates this reasoning concerning good faith effort. The mother of a former state hospital patient filed a wrongful death suit alleging that psychiatrists at the hospital to which her son had been involuntarily committed did not diagnose his suicidal condition and did not provide adequate psychiatric treatment for him. The hospital won the suit because Missouri law provided that licensed physicians cannot be civilly liable so long as their decisions are made "in good faith and without gross negligence."[62] The plaintiffs had not alleged that the psychiatrists had acted in bad faith or were grossly negligent.

A number of suicide cases allege that staffers in a psychiatric facility did not remove from a client's possession or supplied patients with dangerous objects—particularly those that could facilitate suicide. A Minnesota case is prototypical. A forty-two-year-old man appeared at a hospital emergency room and reported that he was fantasizing about killing his parents, his family, and himself. He had been depressed because his employer had transferred him to another city. He agreed to be admitted to the locked psychiatric unit of the hospital, where his room was checked every thirty minutes. The nurse who interviewed him shortly after admission removed his safety razor, nail clippers, and cologne bottle. She did not, however, take away a thirty-inch leather shoulder strap that could be detached from his personal luggage. At that point, the nurse decided the man should be placed on suicide precautions with fifteen-minute room checks. During the evening after he was admitted, staff members noted that the patient was pacing the room, wringing his hands, clenching his fists, holding his head, and sighing. A nurse also observed the man hunched over and rigid. Staff members administered Haldol and left the man alone. Ten minutes later, staff members found the patient hanging by his luggage strap.

A wrongful death suit alleged that hospital staff did not take reasonable precautions to prevent suicide. The man's family argued that the staff should have removed the luggage strap, and the patient should have been placed on constant observation or in a room where self-destructive behavior would be minimized or eliminated. The hospital argued that belts and straps are less lethal than sharp objects and to take the former away might antagonize patients and interfere with the patient-staff relationship. The jury awarded $940,000 to the plaintiffs.[63]

A Georgia case raises similar issues. A forty-nine-year-old nurse with a history of severe psychiatric problems, for which she had been hospitalized several times, had been admitted to a substance use disorder treatment facility. For several weeks before her admission, the patient had experienced hallucinations and had attempted suicide. She also stopped taking the medication that had been prescribed for her. Her family took her to the substance use disorder treatment facility, where she was placed in a single room. According to testimony, the patient was not treated for depression, despite signs of depression. About one week after she was admitted, the hospital staff provided the patient with a hair dryer, which had a long extension cord that the patient used to commit suicide. The family sued the hospital, claiming that the staff did not properly diagnose and monitor the patient and that staffers had provided the extension cord. The jury awarded the plaintiff $750,000.[64]

A lawsuit filed against a psychiatric hospital also involved allegations that the hospital should not have permitted a suicidal patient access to a dangerous object, but the defense was rather novel. The plaintiff's twenty-seven-year-old son, who had a history of schizophrenia, was admitted to the hospital for psychiatric treatment for suicidal ideations. About six months after admission, the patient committed suicide by hanging himself with fishing line that his treating psychiatrist had permitted him to keep in his room. The hospital denied any negligence, claiming that because the patient was an outdoorsman, the fishing line was therapeutic. The Texas case was settled for $320,000.[65]

Madden summarizes current thinking about liability risks associated with suicide:

> There is no general duty to protect a client from self-harm. In fact, some mental health professionals have argued for a right of individuals to commit suicide (Knuth 1979). Even for those who take the self-determination position, the legal analysis rests on whether the reasonable actions of the professional could have prevented the harm.
>
> When a client is evaluated as needing protection due to age or mental disability, the duty to intervene so as to prevent the harm is implicated most strongly. The legal issues that therapists face are related to the quality and

thoroughness of the evaluation as well as the degree of control the worker maintained over the client. Just as in duty-to-protect cases, the therapist duty is greater when the client is in a controlled, residential, or institutional setting than when he or she is in an outpatient clinic.[66]

To prevent malpractice and liability claims related to suicide, behavioral health practitioners should take a number of precautions and preventative steps:[67]

- Practitioners should be familiar with their agency's manual containing policies and guidelines for dealing with suicidal clients. Agencies that do not have a manual containing such policies and guidelines should develop one.
- Practitioners in private practice should obtain regular peer consultation that reviews guidelines and policies for dealing with suicidal clients.
- Early in the therapeutic relationship, practitioners should obtain information from clients about significant others who should be contacted in case of emergency. Clients should also be asked to sign a written consent form, giving their practitioner permission to contact these individuals, should the practitioner determine that the client is or may be suicidal. In general, clients should be informed when the practitioner contacts significant others about the client's risk of suicide.
- Practitioners should use a formal assessment form to assess the likelihood or probability of suicide. The assessment should obtain information related to the client's treatment history and history of suicidal thoughts and/or attempts. The practitioner can explain that completion of the intake form is standard procedure for every new client. This may help to avoid situations in which clients conclude that the practitioner is worried that the client is suicidal.[68]
- Practitioners should document in writing in the case record all their observations, impressions, and courses of action related to suicide risk.
- Practitioners dealing with minors should consider having each minor and parent or guardian sign a written contract specifying the procedures to be followed if the practitioner believes the client is suicidal.
- Practitioners should obtain proper consultation when faced with a client who is or may be suicidal. Documenting the consultation sought and received is important.
- Practitioners must be careful to ensure that suicidal clients with whom they have terminated treatment have access to competent care (see the discussion of abandonment in chapter 8).

- When the risk of suicide is high, practitioners are obligated to take proper steps to control the client, as in seeking emergency treatment or hospitalization. The practitioner should thoroughly document these efforts.
- Practitioners should be familiar with local statutes concerning their duty to protect and duty to warn when a client is or may be suicidal.
- Practitioners should explain and clarify their availability to clients and how to handle emergencies and absences during the practitioner's vacations or illness. This includes sharing the practitioner's social media policy with clients so they are clear about how to contact the practitioner in the event of a crisis (e.g., instructing clients not to notify the practitioner of a crisis via text message or e-mail).

Behavioral health practitioners should follow widely accepted guidelines for managing a suicidal client:[69]

1. Elicit from the client, if possible and credible, a promise that he will control his impulses or will call the therapist or a local emergency number (many practitioners draw up a "suicide contract" with suicidal clients).
2. Ask the client whether he possesses any weapons and make sure that any weapons in the client's possession are placed in the hands of a third party.
3. Increase the frequency of treatment sessions.
4. Contact significant others in the client's social network (with consent, if possible) and ask them to assist in supporting the client between sessions or in joint sessions.
5. Use a call-in system between sessions to monitor the client's stability.
6. Obtain psychiatric consultation in regard to the possibility of using medication as an adjunct to treatment. Bear in mind, however, that antidepressants may initially increase the risk because the seriously depressed client may become sufficiently energized to make an attempt. Also, a client may hoard the medication to collect a lethal dose.
7. Consider taking steps to have the client hospitalized, preferably voluntarily but, if necessary, involuntarily.

### INVOLUNTARY CIVIL COMMITMENT

Behavioral health practitioners are sometimes involved in civil commitment decisions. Practitioners are often consulted by psychiatrists and relied on for information related to commitment proceedings. Cases involving potential suicide often lead in this direction.

The stakes in these cases are high. Hospitalization, whether voluntary or involuntary, can be traumatic. It restricts the clients' freedom, and they may experience significant emotional distress. Clients also could be abused in the process.[70]

A substantial number of lawsuits in the behavioral health field are responses to attempts to commit clients to psychiatric facilities. Some suits allege that a behavioral health professional failed to conduct a proper, thorough assessment and that the commitment therefore was inappropriate. This may constitute false imprisonment, which arises from the "nonconsensual, improper, or unlawful restraint or confinement of one person by another for any period of time."[71]

Other cases allege that a behavioral health professional made an error in judgment about the client's mental health and vulnerability or relied on hearsay evidence. In *Kleber v. Stevens*, the plaintiff claimed that a psychiatrist's commitment papers were improper because they were based on hearsay. The New York trial court awarded the plaintiff $20,000 in damages.

Some suits allege that behavioral health professionals did not confine a client in the least restrictive alternative. In the classic case of *Lake v. Cameron*, Catherine Lake challenged her confinement at St. Elizabeths Hospital in Washington, D.C. A police officer had found her wandering the streets and took her to Washington General Hospital. Twelve days later, Lake filed a writ of verbal habeas corpus in federal district court; a judge concluded that she was "of unsound mind" and authorized her transfer to St. Elizabeths Hospital. Staff concluded that Lake was a danger to herself and in need of care and supervision that her family was not able to provide.

At the district court commitment hearing and the habeas corpus hearing, Lake testified that she was competent to be free. At the federal court of appeals hearing, Lake also stated that, consistent with the newly enacted District of Columbia Hospitalization of the Mentally Ill Act, she would be willing to consider a less restrictive alternative to the psychiatric institution. The court ultimately concluded that "the government, while seeking to provide some sort of custodial care, could not compel Mrs. Lake to accept its help at the price of her freedom. She had a right to be treated with the least restrictive alternative."[72]

Several important cases also demonstrate that hospitalized clients are entitled to treatment while detained. In *O'Connor v. Donaldson*, the plaintiff, Kenneth Donaldson, then forty-nine, was civilly committed to the Florida State Hospital in Chattahoochee with a diagnosis of paranoid schizophrenia. He was confined to the hospital against his will for fifteen years. On several occasions during his hospitalization, Donaldson unsuccessfully petitioned state and federal courts for his release, claiming that he did not pose a threat of danger, was not mentally ill, and that the hospital was not providing him with treatment.

When he was sixty-four, Donaldson filed suit again in federal district court, alleging that the hospital's superintendent and staff had deprived him of his constitutional right to liberty. Evidence presented during the trial demonstrated that Donaldson received primarily custodial care rather than treatment. The jury found in favor of Donaldson. The U.S. Supreme Court stated that "regardless of the grounds for involuntary civil commitment, a person confined against his will at a state mental institution has 'a constitutional right to receive such individual treatment as will give him a reasonable opportunity to be cured or to improve his mental condition.'"[73]

Psychiatric patients also have a right to *refuse* treatment in some circumstances, particularly when coerced treatment violates their Eighth Amendment rights to protection from cruel and unusual punishment. *Rennie v. Klein* addressed the right to refuse treatment. Rennie, who had been hospitalized on twelve previous occasions, had refused to take medication ordered by his psychiatrist. A federal district court in New Jersey ruled that involuntary psychiatric patients *may* have the right to refuse medication or other forms of treatment in the absence of an emergency, consistent with the constitutional right to privacy. In addition, the court ruled, due process must be followed in order to coerce medication. To overrule the patient's refusal, an objective independent party should consider four factors: the patient's capacity to decide on his particular treatment; the patient's physical threat to other patients and staff; whether any less restrictive treatment exists; and the risk of permanent side-effects from the proposed treatment. On the basis of these four criteria, the court ultimately overruled Rennie's refusal. Nonetheless, this decision has been influential in right-to-refuse-treatment cases.[74]

Finally, some lawsuits contend that behavioral health staff members did not adequately monitor a client's progress and condition. In *Whitree v.*

*State*, a patient who had been hospitalized in a state institution for fourteen years alleged that he had been falsely imprisoned. A lower court in New York found in his favor, noting in particular the infrequent examinations of the patient and the lack of depth of the examinations that were conducted. The court also concluded that "the lack of psychiatric care was the primary reason for the inordinate length of this incarceration, with the concomitant side effects of physical injury, moral degradation, and mental anguish."[75] The plaintiff was awarded $300,000 in damages.

As Austin, Moline, and Williams[76] suggest regarding best practices:

- Before seeking involuntary commitment, practitioners should inform clients of their rights regarding detainment.
- Practitioners should develop a good working relationship with a psychiatrist whom they can consult when necessary.
- Treatment plans should respect clients' right to be treated with the least restrictive alternative. Practitioners should be familiar with available resources, both institutional and noninstitutional, the restrictions that they impose, and their therapeutic value.
- Practitioners should ensure that hospitalized clients are receiving proper treatment in addition to appropriate custodial care. They should also be familiar with clients' right to refuse treatment.
- Practitioners should monitor the care that clients are receiving in residential settings to which they have been admitted.
- Practitioners should ensure that clients' progress is reviewed and updated regularly.
- Practitioners should be familiar with local statutes concerning criteria for commitment and commitment procedures. Practitioners should be particularly familiar with the role that they are permitted to assume in commitment proceedings.

As Meyer, Landis, and Hays state with respect to practitioners' involvement in commitment proceedings:

Psychotherapists can serve as petitioners; in fact, in many states they may bypass some of the paperwork involved and arrange for the person to be taken to the hospital simply by calling the authorities. For example, if a client disclosed an intent to commit suicide, a licensed therapist can generally ask the police to take him or her to an inpatient facility immediately, leaving the paperwork for later. Practicing therapists should acquaint themselves with the pragmatics of commitment procedures in their communities *before* a crisis arises. Magistrates and clerks of court are usually very cooperative in explaining the relevant laws and procedures and may "walk through" a petition to illustrate the entire process. Therapists should understand whom to call to arrange a mental health warrant, the criteria that apply in their jurisdiction, how and where to complete the necessary paperwork, and the location of the community evaluation center. Further, they should be able to explain all of the above to members of the community.[77]

### PROTECTIVE SERVICES

During their careers, many behavioral health practitioners face protective service issues involving vulnerable children, older adults, and people with disabilities. Every state has a statute obligating mandated reporters to notify local protective service officials when they suspect abuse or neglect of a child, and most have comparable statutes pertaining to suspected abuse or neglect of older adults and people with disabilities or other vulnerabilities. States typically mandate reporting of suspected physical abuse, physical neglect, sexual abuse, emotional maltreatment, and institutional maltreatment. The terms used in states' statutes vary but usually include language such as physical battering, physical endangerment, physical neglect, medical neglect, sexual abuse, sexual exploitation, emotional abuse, developmental neglect, emotional neglect, improper supervision, educational neglect, abandonment, and institutional maltreatment. Some states have mandatory reporting statutes that pertain to employees in specific settings (e.g., schools).

Not surprisingly, cases involving mandatory reporting and protective services are highly charged. Allegations of the strongest and most provocative kind are often leveled by and against clients' family members, partners, and close acquaintances. Otherwise-trusted professionals are obligated to report suspected abuse or neglect against a client's wishes. Reports of abuse and neglect may also be used as a weapon in child custody disputes.

One understandable consequence of false allegations, harassment, and so on is that the accused will hire a lawyer and sue mandated reporters and protective service workers. As a result, behavioral health practitioners need to be particularly knowledgeable about and sensitive to related liability and malpractice risks. These include four broad areas of risk: reporting of abuse and/or neglect, inadequately protecting a child or other vulnerable person, violating parental and caregiver rights, and inadequate foster care services.

### Reporting of Abuse and/or Neglect

With respect to reporting of abuse and/or neglect, a common claim is failure to report. Since 1964, all states have passed laws that require the reporting of suspected child abuse and neglect. The list of mandated reporters varies from state to state (as do definitions of what constitutes reportable abuse and neglect); however, behavioral health practitioners are mandated reporters in all states. Despite this clear mandate, the evidence suggests that practitioners sometimes fail to notify authorities of abused and neglected individuals whom they encounter.[78]

In some instances, practitioners who fail to report suspected abuse can be charged criminally. In addition to criminal penalties that may be imposed for failing to report suspected abuse or neglect, practitioners risk civil penalties and lawsuits. A suit brought in Arizona accused a social worker of failing to report, even though she had urged the mother of the child to report to the police an allegation involving molestation. The social worker believed that she had complied with state law by urging the mother to report what happened and that reporting it against the client's wishes might harm the client and jeopardize the therapeutic relationship. Although the charges were eventually dropped because the state's haphazard record-keeping system could not be relied on to prove that a report was not made immediately, the case makes clear the real possibility of criminal liability if a mandated reporter fails to make a report.[79]

A number of important civil suits allege negligence, stemming from failure to report, on the part of mandated reporters. Thirty-nine adolescent boys who were residents in a group home in the state of Washington sued independent therapists who were retained to provide mental health counseling. The plaintiffs claimed that the therapists failed to report sexual and physical abuse occurring in the group home. The case was settled for $8 million.[80]

In a California case, a father sued the police, two hospitals, and individual doctors, claiming that no one notified child protective services about a child with severe injuries consistent with abuse. The five-month-old had been taken to the hospital on several occasions with such injuries as a fractured skull, contusions, blood blisters on his penis, marked swelling and discoloration of the left arm and fingertips, burned fingers, puncture wounds and strangulation marks, and welts. The infant's father, who was separated from the mother, sued the defendants, claiming that the hospital did not report and that the lack of report was the cause of the infant's permanent brain damage. The California case was settled out of court for $600,000.[81]

Wrongful reporting can also expose practitioners to liability risks. All states grant immunity from civil and criminal liability to people who report. Almost all states require that professionals report suspected abuse and neglect *in good faith* if they are to be granted immunity from liability. Hence "bad faith" reporting may expose practitioners to liability. In a California case, for example, a father and daughter sued a psychologist who, the plaintiffs alleged, reported to authorities in bad faith that the father had molested the daughter. As a result of the reports, the father was unable to see his daughter for more than eighteen months. The jury awarded the plaintiffs $1.9 million.[82]

A suit against a Virginia physician accused the doctor of maliciously reporting a child who had various bruises on his body. The doctor allegedly berated the parents on two occasions for their treatment of the child and made "unnecessarily irresponsible and defamatory" remarks toward the parents. It was eventually demonstrated, however, that the bruising was the result of the child's hemophilia.[83]

In contrast, the mental health counselor sued in *Lux v. Hansen* for filing a report of child abuse was not found liable, even though her conclusion that the child had been sexually abused by her father was erroneous. The U.S. Court of Appeals for the Eighth Circuit concluded that the counselor had reason to suspect child abuse, in light of comments made by the child, and that under the qualified immunity doctrine, "liability may be found only if a defendant's conduct reflects bad faith or violates clearly established statutory or constitutional rights."[84]

Similar issues emerged in *Vineyard v. Craft*, in which a Texas appellate court held that a father could not sue a psychotherapist for harm to the family relationship after the therapist erroneously concluded that the father had sexually abused the child and reported the suspicion to the child protection agency.[85] The court held that the risk of harm to the family's interests that may result from an erroneous child abuse report was outweighed by the public's interest in protecting children by obtaining professionals' opinions when sexual abuse is suspected.

Controversy surrounding reports of abuse and neglect can sometimes trigger what are known as adverse employment action lawsuits. An example would be a suit filed by a worker in a residential program who claims that actions she took to report institutional abuse resulted in some form of disciplinary action against her by agency administrators. Besharov presents a compelling case summary of this phenomenon:

> I was fired from my position as the only social worker at [a center for the treatment of cerebral palsy] because I was advocating for a child who attended the center. The child, an eleven year old who was fully ambulatory, was tied into a wheelchair from 9 to 3 each day for the past three years in order to prevent his acting out [with] self abusive behavior. A helmet was placed on his head and tied to the back of the wheelchair and his upper arms were tied behind him. No motion was possible. In addition, he was heavily sedated. On the basis of my previous, extensive work with handicapped children, examination of the reports in the child's file and discussions with my colleagues at the agency, I believed that the child had, in addition, been misdiagnosed as severely retarded and was in the wrong program at the Center. After trying, without success, for four months to convince the Center administration, the psychologist and the doctors to untie the boy, to reevaluate him and to plan a proper educational program for him, I contacted the Chairman of the Board of Trustees of our agency and asked him to intervene. Three weeks after contacting him, the child's situation was unchanged and I then notified [the state agency that had placed the child and the state agency responsible for investigating reports of child abuse].
>
> I did not seek support from the child's parents because staff members had reported that the child was tied and kept in a closet at home. I had met the mother and believed that she could not, at that time, be helpful to the child.
>
> I then gave information to the [state agency] and was immediately suspended from my job. I received my salary for 55 days and was then fired, with a dismissal letter containing false statements that will totally damage my professional reputation as a social worker. I asked for an evaluation of my work at the agency the day I was fired and was refused. I also utilized all of

the grievance procedures that were available to me according to the agency's written Personnel Policies, but my efforts were ignored.[86]

The social worker accepted a settlement after realizing that she might end up paying her lawyer far more than any additional payment she might receive.

### Inadequately Protecting a Child

Behavioral health practitioners are frequently in a position to investigate reports of abuse and neglect and then arrange, provide, or monitor substitute care for children who have been abused or neglected. Such care may be provided in foster care, group homes, or other residential settings. This daunting task overwhelms many public and private child welfare agencies. In many programs, budgets and resources cannot keep pace with ever-growing caseloads.[87]

One unfortunate correlate of strained programs and practitioners is litigation related to protective service professionals' failure to accept a report for investigation. *Mammo v. Arizona* is a classic example. In this case, the father of an infant filed a wrongful death suit against the Arizona Department of Economic Security; he alleged that the department had failed to carry out its duty to accept and investigate reports. The infant died as a result of an apparent homicide. Both the police and the father—the noncustodial parent—had contact with the department, conveying their concern about the possibility of child abuse. During two weekends, the father had observed bruises on the bodies of the infant's two older siblings. After the father spoke with an intake unit supervisor in the department's child protective services division, the department took no action except to recommend that the father retain an attorney to contest the mother's custody of the children. The jury awarded the father $1 million in damages, although the trial judge reduced the award to $300,000 (the judge believed the award was excessive).[88]

Issues related to allegations of inadequate protection of a child were central to the landmark case of *DeShaney v. Winnebago County Department of Social Services*. In this case, the U.S. Supreme Court ruled that the Winnebago County [Wisconsin] Department of Social Services and several of its staffers could not be held liable for damages in not protecting a child who had been severely abused by his father. *DeShaney* raised a number of important constitutional issues, primarily related to the Fourteenth Amendment, which forbids the state or its agents from depriving individuals of their right to life, liberty, or property without due process of law. In this case, the U.S. Court of Appeals for the Seventh Circuit held that "the state's failure to protect people from private violence, or other mishaps not attributable to the conduct of its employees, is not a deprivation of constitutionally protected property or liberty."[89] That is, a state's failure to protect an individual against a private act of violence does not constitute a violation of the due process clause.

Behavioral health practitioners can also incur liability risks in returning at-risk children to dangerous foster parents and in providing inadequate case monitoring. Practitioners must be careful to ensure that children are returned home only when the evidence is substantial that the parents no longer pose a danger. Practitioners must also be sure to monitor children's progress carefully. In an Iowa case, for example, the noncustodial father claimed that the state Department of Social Services was negligent in the monitoring of his thirty-four-month-old daughter's safety after he reported his suspicion of abuse. Although the staff had decided to leave the child in the home and provide supportive services, no follow-up visit to the family was made. The mother's lover later killed the child. The case was settled for $82,500.[90]

### Violating Parental Rights

Child protective service workers must be careful not to violate parents' rights during investigations and must be sure to provide social services after reports of abuse or neglect. Because of the volatility of family emotions surrounding allegations of abuse and neglect, practitioners must be particularly alert to any violations of parents' rights.

An investigation can be unnecessarily intrusive if the practitioner's investigative methods are excessive, harassing, or constitute an unreasonable invasion of privacy. In a Virginia Beach case, for example, a father who was investigated sued two workers and the agency, alleging that the workers harassed him, threatened him with prosecution, and publicized false remarks about him to third parties. The case was settled.[91]

Of course, investigations of abuse and neglect sometimes result in the removal of children from the home. Often, these placements are in the children's best interest, and the parents do not contest the decision. On other occasions, however, parents vehemently object to the children's removal. In some cases parents sue, alleging wrongful removal. Besharov cites a Minnesota case that illustrates this phenomenon. Parents sued Hennepin County, alleging that the child protection agency unjustly removed their child from the home. The court found that the parents had made a "sufficient showing that fact questions exist concerning whether defendants' actions were reasonable and in good faith."[92]

### Inadequate Foster Care Services

Once children are placed in foster care, practitioners have a responsibility to ensure the safety and overall quality of this substitute care. Sometimes children are placed with abusive foster parents.[93] A number of court cases document this tragic phenomenon.[94]

Of course, foster children can also pose a risk to foster parents. Lawsuits against practitioners and child welfare agencies have alleged that foster children have killed a foster parent (*Snyder v. Mouser*), damaged or destroyed property (*Seavy v. State*), and infected a foster parent with a serious virus (*Vaughn v. North Carolina Department of Human Resources*). Clearly, practitioners must do their best to identify risks that foster children may pose and either inform potential foster parents of the risk or seek alternative placements.

Once children are placed in foster care, practitioners may be held accountable if they do not provide proper treatment services to the children and in some cases their parents. Although relatively few lawsuits make these allegations, some do. In *Little v. Utah State Division of Family Services*, for example, the state agency was found liable after a child with autism died; the court found that the agency had failed to adequately train the girl's foster parents and other substitute caretakers, make timely evaluations of her condition, provide appropriate safety equipment (such as headgear), and arrange for proper supervision. In *Cameron v. Montgomery County Welfare Services*, one claim of the plaintiff, a foster child, was that the child welfare agency had prevented parental supervision and failed to provide services to the mother that might have helped the child return home. The federal district court case was settled.[95]

## DEFAMATION OF CHARACTER

Behavioral health practitioners have to be particularly careful to avoid defamation of character. Practitioners must avoid unwarranted characterizations of clients and other parties—whether oral or written—that might be considered defamatory.

Defamation occurs as a result of "the publication of anything injurious to the good name or reputation of another, or which tends to bring him into disrepute."[96] Defamation can take two forms: libel and slander.[97] Libel occurs when a statement is in written form. Slander occurs when a statement occurs in oral form. Practitioners can be liable for defamation if three conditions are met: (1) they say or write something that is untrue, (2) they knew or should have known that what they said or wrote was untrue, and (3) the statement caused some injury to the plaintiff. The practitioner's defense against an allegation of defamation may be that the statement was true, the client signed a valid consent form authorizing the release of information, or the practitioner had a legal responsibility to disclose the information, for example, to comply with a mandatory reporting law.[98]

In the well-known Utah case of *Berry v. Moench*, Berry sued Dr. Moench, a psychiatrist, because the psychiatrist wrote a letter that Berry alleged included false and derogatory information about him. Berry had been Moench's patient seven years before. Moench had written a letter to a Dr. Hellewell concerning Berry's emotional stability and background. Berry was engaged to the daughter of former patients of Hellewell, who had requested the letter from Moench. In his letter to Hellewell, Moench made the following comments about Berry:

> He was treated here in 1949 as an emergency. Our diagnosis was Manic [*sic*] depressive depression in a psychopathic personality. . . . The patient was attempting to go through school on the G.I. bill. . . . Instead of attending class he would spend most of the days and nights playing cards for money. . . . During his care here, he purchased a brand new Packard, without even money to buy gasoline. . . . He was in constant trouble with the authorities during the war. . . . He did not do well in school and never did really support his wife and children. . . . My suggestion to the infatuated girl would be to run as fast and as far as she possibly could in any direction away from him.[99]

Moench acknowledged that much of the information contained in the letter was based on information obtained from Berry's ex-wife, his referring doctor, and Berry's former sister-in-law. The court ruled that Moench had committed libel.

Practitioners involved in protective services must be especially aware of defamation issues. In the Virginia case involving the child with hemophilia, for example, the physician accused of wrongful reporting of child abuse also was accused of making "unnecessarily irresponsible and defamatory" remarks toward the parents.[100] Similar allegations were made in the Virginia Beach case, discussed earlier in relation to unnecessarily intrusive investigations. In this case, the plaintiff alleged that the workers "maliciously and falsely addressed remarks to third persons, the substance of which were [sic] that the plaintiff was an alcoholic; that the plaintiff was mentally unstable and was a 'very sick man'; that he was guilty of child molestation; that they were going to take his child or children away from him; and that he would be prosecuted criminally."[101]

## TECHNOLOGY AND REMOTE SERVICE DELIVERY

Widespread use of digital technology—including practitioners' and clients' use of online and remote counseling, social networking sites, text and instant messaging, and e-mail—has created unprecedented risk management challenges, particularly with respect to self-disclosure, privacy, confidentiality, and practitioner availability.[102] As Zur notes:

> The technological explosion toward the end of the 20th century, with its widespread use of cell phones, e-mails, and more recently, Instant Messaging (IM), chat rooms, video teleconferencing (VTC), text messaging, blogging, and photo-cell technology, has changed the way that billions of people communicate, make purchases, gather information, learn, meet, socialize, date, and form and sustain intimate relationships. Like global, national, and cultural boundaries, therapeutic boundaries are rapidly changing as a result. . . . Telehealth and online therapy practices challenge boundaries both around and within the therapeutic relationship. Telehealth or online therapy transcends the physical boundaries of the office as phone or Internet-based therapies take place in the elusive setting we often refer to as cyberspace. Nevertheless, telehealth is subject to exactly the same federal and state

regulations, codes of ethics, and professional guidelines that define the fidu-ciary relationship in face-to-face and office-based therapy.[103]

Some practitioners are enthusiastic supporters of these technologies as therapeutic tools. Others are critics or skeptics, arguing that heavy reliance on online interventions and social media compromises the quality of behav-ioral health services and could endanger clients who are clinically vulner-able and who would be better served by in-person care. Practitioners who consider engaging with clients remotely and electronically would do well to develop comprehensive policies and guidelines that address relevant risks.

### Social Media Policies

Behavioral health practitioners are well advised to carefully construct a social media policy that they share with their clients. Ideally, a comprehen-sive social media ethics policy should address the most common forms of electronic communication used by clients and practitioners: online social networking sites, search engines, e-mail and text messages, location-based services, and consumer review sites.[104]

*Social networking sites.* Practitioners sometimes receive electronic requests from clients who want to be "friends" or contacts on social network-ing sites such as Facebook and LinkedIn. Although some practitioners—a distinct minority, it appears—seem comfortable with these electronic rela-tionships with clients, most agree that a social media policy should inform clients that their practitioner does not interact with clients as electronic friends or contacts on social networking sites. Clients should understand the difference between a Facebook page that a clinical group practice might maintain to provide information to the public and clients and a Facebook profile, which is for personal purposes.

*Search engines.* Practitioners must decide whether it is ethical to conduct electronic searches for information about their clients. To respect clients' privacy, an ethics-based social media policy should explain to clients that their practitioner will not conduct electronic searches about them unless there is, for example, a genuine emergency where information obtained electronically might protect the client from harm. Practitioners who con-duct online searches without their clients' consent should document the rationale for the search.

*E-mail and text messaging.* Practitioners who correspond with clients via e-mail or text messages about sensitive, clinically relevant information may expose a client to confidentiality and privacy breaches. E-mail correspondence and text messages are not 100 percent secure. Further, informal e-mail and text message exchanges, especially during what are customarily nonworking hours, may confuse clients about the boundaries in their relationships with practitioners. A social media policy should explain to clients that practitioners limit such electronic messages to appointment scheduling and other routine correspondence. Clients should understand that e-mail and text message communications may not be secure and that any electronic messages may become part of the clinical record.

*Location-based services.* Many clients use location-based services to enable friends and acquaintances to follow their itinerary via their mobile telephones. A social media policy should inform clients that their use of location-based services, especially if their mobile telephones are GPS enabled, may inform friends and acquaintances that they are visiting a therapist, thus jeopardizing their privacy.

*Consumer review sites.* Some clients choose to post publicly available comments on Internet-based business review sites such as Healthgrades and Yelp about the practitioners from whom they receive services. A social media policy should alert clients that posting comments on these websites with identifying information would compromise their privacy and confidentiality. Practitioners should avoid responding to clients' online reviews, whether they are negative or positive, since any response may disclose that there was a clinical relationship.

### Online Counseling

*Chat counseling.* The Internet now features hundreds of online counseling services. People who struggle with depression, substance use, marital and relationship conflict, anxiety, eating disorders, grief, and other behavioral health challenges can use electronic search engines to locate practitioners who offer counseling services through live online chat, video counseling, and other remote services.

Live online chat is an example of what computer experts call *synchronous* communication, meaning it occurs simultaneously in real time. This contrasts with *asynchronous* communication, where communication is not synchronized or occurring simultaneously (e.g., when a client sends a practitioner an e-mail message regarding a clinical issue and waits for a response).

*Telephone counseling.* Some practitioners provide local and long-distance counseling services that cross state lines entirely by telephone to clients they never meet in person. After providing a counselor with a username and credit card information, clients receive telephone counseling. These may be regularly scheduled or crisis calls.

*Video counseling.* Many practitioners offer clients live distance-counseling using webcams, pan-tilt zoom cameras, monitors, and such services as Skype, Zoom, or encrypted videoconferencing services. Some clinicians offer video counseling services to clients they never meet in person. Other clinicians may supplement their face-to-face counseling with video counseling; for example, when a client who is ordinarily seen face to face is going to be out of town for an extended period and feels the need for clinical sessions.

*Cybertherapy.* Some clinicians offer individual and group counseling services to clients by using a three-dimensional (3-D) virtual world in which clients and practitioners interact with each other visually through avatars rather than real-life photos or live images. An avatar is a digitally generated graphic image, or caricature, that clients and practitioners use to represent themselves in a virtual world that appears on their computer screens. Clients and practitioners join an online therapy community, create their avatars, and electronically enter a virtual therapy room for individual or group counseling.

*Self-guided Web-based interventions.* Practitioners now have access to a wide variety of online and remote interventions designed to help people who struggle with diverse behavioral health issues, such as alcoholism. For example, users complete online questionnaires concerning their drinking use, patterns, and habits and then receive electronic feedback and resources that can help them decide whether to change their alcohol use.

Some websites are designed for behavioral health professionals who provide services to adolescents. Recognizing that, given their preoccupation with digital technology, many adolescents find online services more appealing than in-office services, some practitioners use well-known therapeutic principles, such as solution-focused therapy, to help adolescents address challenges in their lives, sometimes in the form of online therapeutic games.

*Online social networks.* Social networking sites, such as Facebook and LinkedIn, are now pervasive in both clients' and practitioners' lives. Some clinicians believe that maintaining online relationships with clients on social networking sites can be a therapeutic tool; they claim that informal contact with clients on social networking sites humanizes the relationship and makes practitioners more accessible.[105]

The National Suicide Prevention Lifeline has worked with social media platforms and digital communities to establish recommended best practices in suicide prevention for social and digital media. Many social media outlets, including Facebook, Twitter, YouTube, Tumblr, and Google+, have ways to report suicidal content and get help for the content creator.

*E-mail.* Multiple websites offer people the opportunity to receive behavioral health services by exchanging e-mail messages with clinical practitioners. Typically, these practitioners invite users to e-mail a therapy-related question for a flat fee and guarantee a response within twenty-four to forty-eight hours. Some practitioners offer clients monthly e-mail packages that include a set number of e-mail exchanges (e.g., six to eight). Other practitioners choose to exchange occasional, clinically relevant e-mails with clients as an extension of their office-based services.

*Text messages.* Some practitioners have chosen to exchange text messages with clients informally; for example, when clients wish to cancel or reschedule an appointment or provide the practitioner with a brief update during a crisis. Other practitioners and some behavioral health programs have incorporated text messaging as a formal component of their intervention model. For example, staffers in some programs that serve adolescent clients have concluded that they should follow the long-standing behavioral health axiom "start where the client is" and engage adolescents by using text messaging because that is many adolescents' communication medium of choice.

### Risk Management Challenges

A number of compelling risks are emerging as practitioners make increasing use of a wide range of digital and other electronic technology. Key issues include practitioner competence, client privacy and confidentiality, informed consent, conflicts of interest, boundaries and dual relationships, consultation and client referral, termination and interruption of services, and documentation.

*Practitioner competence.* Practitioners have a duty to meet minimum standards of competence when providing services to clients, particularly when clinicians use novel and emerging intervention protocols. Thus, practitioners who choose to use digital and other electronic forms of technology to serve clients should review pertinent research and practice literature and become familiar with rapidly emerging ethical standards.

Comprehensive practice standards were developed jointly by the National Association of Social Workers (NASW), Association of Social Work Boards (ASWB), Council on Social Work Education (CSWE), and Clinical Social Work Association (CSWA).[106] These standards include the following:

- Encourage social workers to discuss with clients policies concerning use of technology in the provision of professional services. Clients should have a clear understanding of the ways in which social workers use technology to deliver services, communicate with clients, search for information about clients online, and store sensitive information about clients.

- Encourage social workers who plan to use technology in the provision of services to obtain client consent to the use of technology at the beginning of the practitioner-client relationship.

- Advise social workers who use technology to communicate with clients to assess each client's capacity to provide informed consent.

- Advise social workers to verify the identity and location of clients they serve remotely (especially in case there is an emergency and to enable social workers to comply with laws in the client's jurisdiction).

- Alert social workers to the need to assess clients' ability to access and use technology, particularly for online and remote services. Encourage social workers to help clients identify alternate methods of service delivery if the use of technology to deliver services is not appropriate.

- Advise social workers to obtain client consent before conducting an online search for information about clients, as a way to respect clients' privacy (unless there are emergency circumstances).

- Highlight the need for social workers to understand the special communication challenges associated with electronic and remote service delivery and how to address these challenges.

- Advise social workers who use technology to comply with the laws of both the jurisdiction where the social worker is regulated and located and where the client is located (given that social workers and clients might be in different states or countries).

- Advise social workers to be aware of, assess, and respond to cultural, environmental, economic, disability, linguistic, and other social diversity issues that may affect delivery or use of services.
- Discourage social workers from communicating with clients by use of technology for personal or nonwork-related purposes, in order to maintain appropriate boundaries.
- Advise social workers to take reasonable steps to prevent client access to social workers' personal social networking sites and personal technology, again to avoid boundary confusion and inappropriate dual relationships.
- Suggest that social workers should be aware that posting personal information on professional websites or other media could cause boundary confusion, inappropriate dual relationships, or harm to clients.
- Remind social workers to be aware that clients may discover personal information about them through their personal affiliations and use of social media.
- Suggest that social workers should avoid accepting requests from or engaging in personal relationships with clients on online social networks or other electronic media.
- Advise social workers to take reasonable steps (such as use of encryption, firewalls, and secure passwords) to protect the confidentiality of electronic communications, including information provided to clients or third parties.
- Advise social workers to develop and disclose policies and procedures for notifying clients of any breach of confidential information in a timely manner.
- Advise social workers to inform clients of unauthorized access to the social worker's electronic communication or storage systems (e.g., cloud storage).
- Advise social workers to develop and inform clients about their policies on the use of electronic technology to gather information about clients.
- Advise social workers to avoid posting any identifying or confidential information about clients on professional websites or other forms of social media.
- Advise social workers using technology to facilitate evaluation or research to obtain clients' informed consent for the use of such technology. Encourage social workers to assess clients' ability to use the technology and, when appropriate, offer reasonable alternatives.

*Client privacy and confidentiality.* For decades, behavioral health practitioners have understood their obligation to protect client privacy and confidentiality and to be familiar with exceptions (e.g., when mandatory reporting laws concerning abuse and neglect require disclosure of information without client consent or when laws or court orders require disclosure without client consent to protect a third party from harm). However, the pervasiveness of digital technology and other electronic media to deliver services has added a new layer of challenging privacy and confidentiality issues. For example, practitioners who deliver services using e-mail, avatars, live chat, and video counseling must be sure to use sophisticated encryption technology to prevent confidentiality breaches (hacking) by unauthorized parties and comply with the strict guidelines of the Health Insurance Portability and Accountability Act (HIPAA). In fact, such encryption can provide significantly more protection than do traditional paper records. Practitioners are wise not to assume that all Internet sites and electronic tools they use are necessarily encrypted; the ethical burden is on the practitioner to ensure trustworthy encryption.

*Informed consent.* The advent of distance-counseling and other social services delivered electronically has enhanced practitioners' ethical duty to ensure that clients fully understand the nature of these services and their potential benefits and risks. As noted earlier, this can be difficult when practitioners never meet their clients in person. Special challenges arise when minors contact practitioners and request distance or remote services, particularly when practitioners offer free services and do not require credit card or parents' insurance information; state laws vary considerably regarding minors' right to obtain mental health services without parental consent.

Although state and federal laws and regulations vary in their interpretations and applications of informed-consent standards, in general professionals agree that the following standards must be met for consent to be considered valid when providing distance or remote services:

1. *Coercion and undue influence must not have played a role in the client's decision.* Practitioners often maintain some degree of control over clients' lives (e.g., by approving benefits, admission into programs, and the termination of services). Practitioners must ensure that clients do not feel pressured to grant consent to services provided remotely.
2. *A client must be mentally capable of providing consent.* Clearly, some clients (e.g., young children and individuals who suffer from serious mental illness

or dementia) are unable to comprehend the remote consent procedure. Other clients, however, may be only temporarily unable to consent, such as individuals who are under the influence of alcohol or other drugs at the time consent is sought or who experience transient psychotic symptoms. In general, practitioners should assess clients' ability to reason and make informed choices, comprehend relevant facts and retain this information, appreciate current circumstances, and communicate wishes. Clients who are unable to consent to online and distance services at a given moment may be able to consent in the future if the incapacity is temporary.

3. *Consent forms and procedures must be valid.* Practitioners sometimes present clients with general, broadly worded consent forms that may violate clients' right to be informed and may be considered invalid if challenged in a court of law. Practitioners should include details that refer to specific activities, information to be released, or interventions. Typical elements include details of the nature and purpose of a service or disclosure of information; advantages and disadvantages of an intervention; substantial or possible risks to clients, if any (including risks uniquely associated with online and remote behavioral health services); potential effects on clients' families, jobs, social activities, and other important aspects of their lives; alternatives to the proposed intervention or disclosure; and anticipated costs for clients. All this information should be presented to clients in clear, understandable language and in a manner that encourages clients to ask questions for clarification. Consent forms should be dated and include a reasonable expiration date.

4. *A client must have the right to refuse or withdraw consent.* Practitioners should be prepared for the possibility that clients will exercise these rights, particularly with respect to the delivery of online and distance behavioral health services. Practitioners should inform clients of their rights and help clients make thoughtful and informed decisions that are based on all available facts and information about potential benefits and risks.

More specifically, when behavioral health professionals provide services to clients remotely, the informed consent form should include statements that address the following:

- The nature of the services that the practitioner will provide remotely, such as video counseling, text-based counseling, and smartphone applications.
- Possible benefits of remote service delivery. This may include geographical and scheduling convenience.

- Differences between services provided face to face and remotely.
- The skills and equipment (such as computer specifications and smartphone applications) the client will need to receive services remotely.
- The importance of privacy for both practitioner and client. Describe steps clients can take to ensure privacy. Describe steps you will take to ensure privacy (e.g., use of encryption, firewalls, and data backup software).
- The possibility of technology failure and transmission interruption, along with instructions in the event these occur (e.g., call-back protocols).
- The possibility that stored data could be accessed by unauthorized people or companies, and the steps you will take to prevent this.
- An emergency response plan to address crises that may arise. Details may include names and telephone numbers of individuals the practitioner can contact, telephone numbers the client can call, and when the client should access care at the client's local hospital emergency department.
- Steps you will take if you believe that the client needs to access face-to-face services because of his or her clinical needs. Include details about referral and termination-of-service protocols.
- Guidelines for clients' use of e-mail and text messaging to communicate with the practitioner (i.e., whether electronic communications should be used only for administrative and scheduling purposes, as opposed to counseling issues).
- Agreement that the client will not record any remote counseling sessions or other discussions, unless agreed upon in advance.

*Boundaries and dual relationships.* Throughout the history of the behavioral health professions, practitioners have understood their duty to avoid conflicts of interest that may harm clients. Practitioners' use of digital technology has introduced new and complicated boundary issues. Many practitioners receive requests from current and former clients asking to be social networking "friends" or contacts. Electronic contact with clients and former clients on social networking sites can lead to boundary confusion. Electronic message exchanges between practitioners and clients that occur outside of normal business hours, especially if the practitioner uses a personal social networking site or e-mail address, may confuse practitioner-client boundaries. Practitioners who choose not to accept a client's "friend" request on an online social networking site to maintain clear boundaries may inadvertently cause the client to feel a deep sense of rejection.

Practitioners should anticipate this possibility and explain to clients how they handle clients' Facebook requests.

Also, clients who are able to access practitioners' publicly available social networking sites may learn a great deal of personal information about their practitioners (such as information about a practitioner's personal and family relationships, social and religious activities, and political views); this may introduce complex boundary challenges in the practitioner-client relationship.

Clients' postings on their own social networking sites may also lead to inadvertent or harmful disclosure of private and confidential details; for example, sensitive information shared by others in group therapy sessions. Behavioral health professionals who do not maintain strict privacy settings on their online social networking sites expose themselves to considerable risk. In one highly publicized case, a social worker was disciplined by her regulatory board in response to a complaint filed by a client who discovered that the social worker posted publicly available comments about the client on the social worker's personal Facebook site. At the time, the client had a child protective services case pending in court. The social worker posted on Facebook: "I'm in court tomorrow for a case where there is a high level of domestic violence amongst many things . . ." and after the trial concluded posted: "It's powerful to know that . . . children's lives have just massively changed for the better and now they are safe and protected from harm and have every hope for the future . . ." One of the social worker's online posts was accompanied by a small map, pinpointing the location of the court.

The social worker's defense during the board hearing was that "she had believed that her Facebook page was accessible only to her 'friends,' not the wider public as a result of her privacy settings." However, the post was publicly available and was found by her manager through a Google search of her name.[107]

To practice ethically, practitioners who use digital and other technology to provide distance services must develop protocols concerning boundaries, dual relationships, and conflicts of interest that include several key elements. Practitioners must develop sound guidelines governing their contact with current and former clients on social networking sites (for e.g., Facebook, LinkedIn) and their willingness to provide services to people they first met socially on social networking sites. Practitioners must be careful to avoid inappropriate disclosure of personal information in digital communications (e.g., e-mail messages, text messages, and social network postings) and should establish clear guidelines concerning interactions with clients online and via other digital and electronic means at various times of day and night, weekends, and holidays.

The 24/7/365 access that digital communications make possible creates elastic boundaries that are newer to behavioral health professionals who otherwise have been able to maintain clear boundaries when services are provided in person during traditional working hours. Practitioners must also think carefully about maintaining digital and electronic relationships with former clients; easy access via electronic means can introduce ethical and clinical challenges related to boundaries and dependency.

*Consultation and client referral.* Practitioners who provide online and electronic services to clients they never meet in person must take assertive steps to ensure that clients are familiar with the information they would need to locate and access emergency, counseling, case management, and other supportive services. In addition, ethically competent practitioners are assertive about collaborating with clients' other service providers and facilitating ancillary services when needed. This may be difficult or impossible to do when practitioners never meet their clients in person, do not live in the same community, and do not have professional relationships with clients' other service providers. The result may be inadequate coordination of services and incomplete or inaccurate clinical assessments, particularly when clients are at risk of harming themselves or others.

*Termination or interruption of services.* Practitioners who provide online and electronic services also face unique risks related to what lawyers refer to as abandonment. Abandonment occurs when a practitioner-client relationship is terminated or interrupted and the practitioner fails to make reasonable arrangements for the continuation of services, when needed.

Online and electronic services could be terminated for a variety of reasons. Clients may terminate services abruptly, disappear, or otherwise fail to respond to a practitioner's e-mail, text messages, or telephone messages. Practitioners may terminate or interrupt services, perhaps inadvertently, because of computer or other electronic equipment failure or because a practitioner fails to respond to a client's e-mail, text, or telephone message in a timely fashion.

*Documentation.* There are compelling reasons for practitioners to document clinically relevant information electronically; this is convenient, and, in principle, properly encrypted electronic records are more secure than traditional paper records. Yet practitioners' use of online and other electronic services has posed unprecedented documentation challenges. Practitioners must develop strict protocols to ensure that clinically relevant e-mail, text, social networking (e.g., Facebook), and telephone exchanges are documented properly in case records.

Practitioners who use digital and other technology to provide distance services must develop records and documentation protocols that include several key elements. Practitioners must develop guidelines that ensure proper encryption; reasonable and appropriate access by clients and colleagues to electronic records and documents (e.g., when a practitioner is incapacitated and a colleague provides coverage); documentation of video counseling sessions, e-mail, text messages, and cybertherapy communications; compliance with laws, regulations, and agency policies concerning record and document retention and access (e.g., the requirements under the 21st Century Cures Act that obligates practitioners to provide clients with access to their records); and proper disposal and destruction of documents and records.

Many insurance companies cover remote counseling and require practitioners to comply with strict documentation guidelines to protect client privacy and confidentiality. Many behavioral health professionals subscribe to HIPAA-compliant online software packages to ensure proper protection.

Practitioners who maintain electronic records should be familiar with HIPAA's specific protection of what this law (45 CFR 164.501) refers to as "psychotherapy notes." As I discussed earlier, HIPAA defines psychotherapy notes as notes recorded by a health-care provider who is a mental health professional documenting or analyzing the contents of a conversation during a private, group, joint, or family counseling session and that are separate from the rest of the client's health record (e.g., a separate tab in the electronic record labeled "psychotherapy notes"). Psychotherapy notes, also called process or private notes, are notes taken by a mental health professional during a session with a client. Psychotherapy notes usually include the practitioner's impressions regarding diagnosis, observations, and any thoughts or feelings the practitioner has about a client's unique situation. After clinical encounters, practitioners can refer to their notes when determining an effective treatment plan.

To be considered "psychotherapy notes" under the law, these notes must be kept separate from clients' general records and billing information, and practitioners are not permitted to share psychotherapy notes with third parties without a client's authorization—even if the client does not have the right to access these notes. In general, psychotherapy notes might include clinical observations, hypotheses, questions to ask supervisors, and any thoughts or feelings relating to the counseling session. Unlike traditional progress notes, psychotherapy notes are private and do not include medication details or records, test results, summaries of diagnosis or treatment plans, summaries of symptoms and prognosis, and summaries of client progress.

It is not surprising that practitioners' use of online and other electronic tools to provide services includes potential benefits and risks. Clients who struggle with anxiety or extreme shyness, for example, may prefer to engage with a practitioner remotely, at least initially. Also, clients who are severely disabled physically or who live great distances from practitioners' offices may benefit from receiving services electronically that they would otherwise have great difficulty accessing. In addition, people who feel the need for help during nonworking hours or whose work schedules do not align conveniently with practitioners' office hours can access services remotely any hour of the day or night. And people who are in crisis typically can access assistance by telephone or Internet almost immediately, often at a cost that is lower than fees for in-person services. Denying services to people in need simply because practitioners are not comfortable with reputable digital and electronic technology is not consistent with behavioral health practitioners' ethical obligation to meet the needs of vulnerable people.

However, online and other distance services also come with considerable risks. Practitioners fully understand how important visual and nonverbal cues are when providing clinical services; it is easy to miss these cues entirely when services are provided only online and by telephone. The risk of misunderstandings may increase when practitioners and clients are not together in person. Also, some clients, such as those who struggle with severe and persistent mental illness, may not be well served by clinical services delivered by practitioners they never meet in person. Further, there is always the possibility, although perhaps not the probability, of technology failure and confidentiality breaches that could harm clients.

In addition, clients who e-mail or text practitioners may not have realistic expectations of a reasonable turnaround time for responses, and this may lead to misunderstandings and conflict in the practitioner-client relationship. Practitioners who provide digital and telephone counseling services across state lines run the risk of violating licensing laws that require practitioners to be licensed in the state in which the client resides. Finally, practitioners who provide services using digital and other electronic technology run the risk of encountering identity fraud perpetrated by clients they never meet in person.

Zur encourages practitioners to make the following disclosure to clients regarding the use of digital and other technology to serve and communicate with clients:

> It is very important to be aware that computers, e-mail, and cell phone communication can be relatively easily accessed by unauthorized people and hence can compromise the privacy and confidentiality of such communication. E-mails, in particular, are vulnerable to such unauthorized access because servers have unlimited and direct access to all e-mails that go through them. Additionally, Dr. XX's e-mails are not encrypted. Dr. XX's computers are equipped and regularly updated with a firewall, virus protection, and a password. He also backs up all confidential information from his computers on CDs on a regular basis. The CDs are stored securely offsite. Please notify Dr. XX if you decide to avoid or limit in any way the use of any or all communication devices such as e-mail, cell phone, or faxes. Unless Dr. XX hears from you otherwise, he will continue to communicate with you via e-mail when necessary or appropriate. Please do not use e-mail or faxes for emergencies. Although Dr. XX checks phone messages frequently during the day when he is in town, he does not always check his e-mails daily.[108]

Zur also offers a series of practical guidelines to prevent problems when using technology to provide clinical services:

1. Identify the client and obtain basic information such as full name, address, age, gender, phone, fax, emergency contacts, and so on.
2. Provide clients with a clear informed-consent form detailing the limitations of telehealth [the delivery of health-related services using telecommunication technology, such as e-mail, social media, videoconferencing, telephone], in general, and confidentiality and privacy, in particular.

3. Inform the clients of potential limitations of telehealth when it comes to crisis intervention and dealing with dangerous situations.
4. Practice within your limits of clinical and technological competence.
5. Have a crisis intervention plan in place, including ways to reach local emergency services, and make referrals to local psychotherapists, psychiatrists, and psychiatric hospitals in the client's vicinity.
6. Provide thorough screening when considering which clients may not be suited to this kind of medium.
7. Have a clear agreement with regard to what is being charged, how it is being charged, and the rates and method of payment.
8. Do not render medical or psychiatric advice by giving a diagnosis or proposing a course of treatment except to those with whom you have established professional psychotherapeutic relationships.
9. Follow your state laws, your licensing-board rules, and your state and national professional association guidelines, and practice within the standard of care.
10. Screen clients for technical and clinical suitability for telehealth.
11. Telehealth is one of the fastest growing fields in medicine. Update yourself on the latest research on telehealth.[109]

### Electronically Stored Information

Behavioral health practitioners should be aware that all online and other electronic communications, including social networking posts, may be subpoenaed during legal proceedings. So-called electronically stored information (ESI) is now a routine component of what lawyers refer to as the discovery phase of a case. Lawyers use the pretrial discovery process to gather information in preparation for trial. In the context of litigation, ESI is any document or information stored in an electronic form, common examples of which include the following:

- Word-processing documents
- Spreadsheets
- Digital photographs
- Videos
- E-mails and their attachments
- Text and instant messages

- Messaging incorporated into workplace collaboration tools
- Call logs
- Voicemails
- Information stored in databases
- Electronic records of online activity, such as social media postings and other activity
- Data generated by connections between sensors, software, and other technologies for the purpose of connecting and exchanging data with other devices and systems over the Internet

Information may be electronically stored on and retrieved from many sources, including:

- Computer hard drives
- Agency or organization network servers
- Thumb (USB) drives
- Databases
- The cloud (servers that are accessed over the Internet, and the software and databases that run on those servers)
- Mobile devices, such as mobile phones and tablet computers
- Social media websites, such as Facebook, Twitter, and LinkedIn

# CHAPTER 4

# Impaired Practitioners

Some liability claims and licensing-board complaints against behavioral health practitioners are the result of honest mistakes. Careless oversight, such as forgetting to get a client to complete a consent form before releasing confidential information to another agency or failing to protect an electronic record, can lead to a lawsuit or licensing-board complaint. Other complaints may result from well-intentioned, deliberate decisions, as when a practitioner decides to breach a client's privacy in order to protect a third party from harm or attempts to manage complex boundary issues when living and working in a small community. However, many complaints result from incompetent practice by a relatively small percentage of practitioners who are impaired.

> George M. was the director of clinical services at Family Services Associates, Inc., a local mental health agency. He had been clinical director for six years, after serving as a family counselor at the agency for five years. George M. had also worked for three years as a mental health coordinator at a local community mental health center. George M. was in the process of divorcing his wife, which caused him a great deal of stress and seriously impaired his judgment.
>
> In addition to supervising clinical staff, George M. usually carried three or four cases of his own. One involved a twenty-six-year-old woman who sought counseling for anxiety symptoms and problems with self-esteem. George M. conducted the initial intake interview and decided to handle the case himself. He and his client spent several weeks fruitfully exploring a number of family-of-origin issues that concerned the client.

During the eighth week of treatment, the client mentioned that she wanted to talk about an event that occurred when she was seventeen, when her older brother sexually molested her. In her judgment, a considerable portion of her present-day anxiety could be traced to that event and subsequent sexual contact with her brother. George M. and his client spent several weeks exploring these issues.

At the end of the twelfth session, the client began crying, following some discussion about the sexual assault. George M. got up from his chair and embraced the client, as he had during several other therapy sessions when the client was distraught. He also began to kiss her. The client did not resist George M.'s caresses and kisses. George M. then said that he thought he could be helpful to his client by showing her what unconditional, sincere lovemaking was like. He dimmed the lights in his office and made love to his client.

George M. and his client continued to have sexual contact for about two months, at which point the relationship became strained. About two months later, the client began treatment with a new therapist in a different agency. The client disclosed to the new therapist that she and George M. had been sexually involved during their professional relationship. The client brought this up during a discussion of the times in her life when men took advantage of her.

After considerable discussion with her client, the therapist encouraged her to think about filing an ethics complaint against George M. with his state licensing board and to consult an attorney about suing him. After giving it some thought, the client filed a lawsuit and licensing-board complaint against George M. The licensing board conducted a formal investigation and concluded that George M. was too impaired to practice. The board revoked his license. The lawsuit was settled.

### THE NATURE OF IMPAIRMENT

In the 1970s and 1980s, various professions began to pay increased attention to the problem of impaired practitioners.[1] In 1972, for example, the Council on Mental Health of the American Medical Association released a statement that said physicians have an ethical responsibility to recognize and report impairment among colleagues. In 1976, a group of attorneys recovering from alcoholism started Lawyers Concerned for Lawyers to address chemical dependence in the profession, and in 1980 a group of recovering psychologists inaugurated a similar group, Psychologists Helping Psychologists.[2] In 1981, the American Psychological Association held its first open forum on impairment at its annual meeting.[3]

Social work's first national acknowledgment of the problem of impaired practitioners came in 1979, when the National Association of Social Workers (NASW) released a public-policy statement on alcoholism and alcohol-related problems.[4] By 1980, a small nationwide support group for chemically dependent practitioners, Social Workers Helping Social Workers, had formed following a gathering of fifty recovering social workers (by 1987, however, it had only sixty-five members). In 1982, NASW established the Occupational Social Work Task Force and charged it with developing a "consistent professional approach for distressed NASW members."[5] In 1984, the NASW Delegate Assembly issued a resolution on impairment, and in 1987, NASW published the *Impaired Social Worker Program Resource Book*, prepared by the NASW Commission on Employment and Economic Support, to help practitioners design programs for impaired social workers. The introduction to the resource book states:

> Social workers, like other professionals, have within their ranks those who, because of substance abuse, chemical dependency, mental illness or stress, are unable to function effectively in their jobs. These are the impaired social workers.... The problem of impairment is compounded by the fact that the professionals who suffer from the effect of mental illness, stress or substance abuse are like anyone else; they are often the worst judges of their behavior, the last to recognize their problems and the least motivated to seek help. Not only are they able to hide or avoid confronting their behavior, they are often abetted by colleagues who find it difficult to accept that a professional could let his or her problem get out of hand.[6]

Organized efforts to address impaired workers began in the late 1930s and early 1940s after Alcoholics Anonymous was formed and because of the need to retain a sound workforce during World War II. These early occupational alcoholism programs eventually led, in the early 1970s, to the emergence of employee assistance programs (EAPs), which are designed to address a broad range of problems experienced by workers. More recently, strategies for dealing with professionals whose work is affected by problems such as substance abuse, mental illness, and emotional stress have become more prevalent and visible.

### EXTENT OF IMPAIRMENT

Both the seriousness of impairment among behavioral health practitioners and the forms it takes vary. Impairment may involve failure to provide competent care or violation of the ethical standards of the profession. It may also take such forms as providing flawed or inferior psychotherapy to a client, sexual involvement with a client, or failure to carry out professional duties as a result of substance abuse or mental illness. Lamb and colleagues provide a comprehensive definition of impairment among professionals:

> Interference in professional functioning that is reflected in one or more of the following ways: (a) an inability and/or unwillingness to acquire and integrate professional standards into one's repertoire of professional behavior; (b) an inability to acquire professional skills in order to reach an acceptable level of competency; and (c) an inability to control personal stress, psychological dysfunction, and/or excessive emotional reactions that interfere with professional functioning.[7]

No precise estimates of the extent of impairment among behavioral health practitioners are available. No one has conducted comprehensive surveys. Only rough estimates (at best) of the extent of the problem have been made, and there are sparse recent data. For example, in the foreword to the *Impaired Social Worker Program Resource Book*, published by the NASW Commission on Employment and Economic Support, Ruth Antoniades, who chaired the commission, states, "Social workers have the same problems as most working groups. Up to 5 to 7 percent of our membership may have a problem with substance abuse. Another 10 to 15 percent may be going through personal transitions in their relationships, marriage, family, or their work life."[8] The report goes on to conclude, however, that "there is little reliable information on the extent of impairment among social workers."[9] A survey sponsored by the NASW Indiana Chapter found that of impairments reported among social workers, 26 percent were alcohol or drug related. Results of a survey of NASW members in New York City found that 43 percent of respondents reported knowing a colleague with a drinking or drug abuse problem.[10]

Prevalence studies conducted among psychologists, for example, suggest a significant degree of distress within that profession. In a study of 749 psychologists, Guy, Poelstra, and Stark found that 74.3 percent reported "personal distress" during the previous three years, and 36.7 percent of this group believed that their distress decreased the quality of care that they provided to clients.[11] Pope, Tabachnick, and Keith-Spiegel reported that 62.2 percent of the members of Division 29 (Psychotherapy) of the American Psychological Association admitted to "working when too distressed to be effective."[12] In their survey of 167 licensed psychologists, Wood and colleagues found that nearly one-third (32.3 percent) reported experiencing depression or burnout to an extent that interfered with their work.[13] Wood and colleagues also found that a significant portion of their sample reported being aware of colleagues whose work was seriously affected by drug or alcohol use, sexual overtures toward clients, or depression and burnout. In addition, evidence exists that psychologists and psychiatrists commit suicide at a rate five to six times higher than that for the general population.[14] Deutsch found that more than half of her sample of social workers, psychologists, and master's-level counselors reported significant problems with depression. Nearly four-fifths (82 percent) reported problems with relationships, approximately one-tenth (11 percent) reported substance abuse problems, and 2 percent reported suicide attempts.[15] Bissell and Haberman report that 24 percent of a sample of fifty alcoholic social workers whom they surveyed reported overt suicide attempts, a rate higher than that reported by dentists, attorneys, and physicians in the Bissell and Haberman sample of alcoholics.[16]

In a comprehensive review of a series of empirical studies focused specifically on sexual contact between therapists and clients, Pope concluded that the aggregate average of reported sexual contact is 8.3 percent by male therapists and 1.7 percent by female therapists.[17]

Not all sexual abuse engaged in by behavioral health practitioners involves clients. A compelling example of this appeared in Rhode Island's *Providence Journal-Bulletin:*

A social worker who at one time counseled abused children was sentenced yesterday to serve 20 years in prison for sexually assaulting two minors.

Lawrence F. Coleman, 41, of 1540 Douglas Ave., North Providence was sentenced by Judge John F. Sheehan. The judge imposed a 30-year sentence but suspended 10 years.

The victims, who are now adults, were not in any counseling program with Coleman.

One of the victims addressed the court before sentencing. Her voice choked with emotion, she said that the sexual assaults had devastated her and given her low self-esteem. . . .

In January Coleman was arraigned on 10 counts of first degree sexual assault before Superior Court Judge John P. Bourcier. He was freed on $100,000 surety bail. In March he pleaded guilty before Judge Sheehan, who kept bail at the same amount. . . . He worked as a counselor at a health center in Greenville, counseling children who were victims of physical and sexual abuse.[18]

### CAUSES OF IMPAIRMENT

Several studies report a variety of forms and sources of impairment among mental health professionals. Guy, Poelstra, and Stark[19] and Thoreson, Miller, and Krauskopf[20] found clinicians reported diverse sources of stress in their lives, including their jobs, the illness or death of family members, marital or relationship problems, financial problems, midlife crises, personal physical or mental illness, legal problems, and substance abuse.

Lamb and colleagues argue that professional education itself can produce unique forms of stress and impairment, primarily as a result of the close clinical supervision to which students are typically subjected, the disruption in their personal lives that is often caused by the demands of schoolwork and internships, and the pressures of their academic programs.[21] These authors found that the most common sources of impairment are personality disorders, depression and other emotional problems, marital problems, and physical illness. It is interesting that those surveyed rarely cited academic problems and alcohol or drug abuse as sources of impairment.

This review of research suggests that distress among clinicians generally falls into two categories: environmental stress, which is a function of employment conditions (actual working conditions and the broader culture's lack of support for the human services mission), or professional training and personal stress, caused by problems with marriage, relationships, emotional and physical health, and finances. Of course, these two types of stress are often interrelated.

With respect to psychotherapists in particular, Wood and colleagues note that professionals encounter special problems from the extension of their therapeutic role into the nonwork aspects of their lives (such as relationships with friends and family members), the absence of reciprocity in relationships with clients (therapists are "always giving"), the frequently slow and erratic nature of the therapeutic process, and personal issues that are raised as a result of their work with clients.[22] As Kilburg, Kaslow, and VandenBos conclude:

> [The] stresses of daily life—family responsibilities, death of family members and friends, other severe losses, illnesses, financial difficulties, crises of all kinds—quite naturally place mental health professionals, like other people, under pressure. However, by virtue of their training and place in society, such professionals face unique stresses. And although they have been trained extensively in how to deal with the emotional and behavioral crises of others, few are trained in how to deal with the stresses they themselves will face. . . . Mental health professionals are expected by everyone, including themselves, to be paragons. The fact that they may be unable to fill that role makes them a prime target for disillusionment, distress, and burnout. When this reaction occurs, the individual's ability to function as a professional may become impaired.[23]

A recurring theme in cases involving practitioner impairment is the problem of professional boundaries.[24] Particularly in cases involving sexual involvement with clients, practitioners typically display confusion about what constitutes appropriate boundaries between themselves and their clients and about the need to clearly delineate the practitioner's and client's involvement in each other's lives. The combination of a needy practitioner and needy client can be disastrous. In these instances, both parties are more likely to be confused about, or will simply ignore warning signs and risks related to, inappropriate involvement that may take the form of sexual contact, socializing, or business involvement unrelated to treatment. These dual relationships have generated a wide range of ethical problems and liability risks. As A. Brodsky notes:

> A sexual intimacy between patient and therapist is one example of a dual relationship. Dual relationships involve more than one purpose of relating. A therapy relationship is meant to be exclusive and unidimensional. The therapist is the expert, the patient the consumer of that expertise. Once a patient accepts an individual as a therapist, that individual cannot, without undue

influence, relate to that patient in any other role. Relating to the patient as an employer, business partner, lover, spouse, relative, professor, or student would contaminate the therapeutic goal. The contamination is much more intense in a psychotherapy relationship than it would be in the relationship between a client and a professional in any other field—for example, between a client and an internist, a dentist, a lawyer, or an accountant.[25]

The problems of confused boundaries and dual relationships were readily apparent in a case on which I consulted. In this case, a thirty-seven-year-old woman with a history of childhood sexual abuse sought counseling from a clinician. They worked together for a number of months. Over time, however, the clinician and the client began spending time together outside counseling sessions. Ultimately, the client sued the clinician, alleging that the clinician's improper maintenance of boundaries was injurious. In addition, the state attorney general's office filed an action in administrative court seeking to revoke the clinician's license. Evidence presented in the suit and in depositions filed in the case suggested that the clinician and client shared a motel room while the clinician attended a professional conference, the clinician provided the client with a number of gifts and wrote affectionate and intimate notes to the client, they dined together in the clinician's home, they had inappropriate physical contact, the clinician disclosed personal details of her own life to the client, and together they viewed a videotape while both were on the clinician's bed in the clinician's home. In her defense, the practitioner argued that all the actions that she took in the case were for "therapeutic purposes."

Practitioners who violate sexual boundaries sometimes target particularly vulnerable clients. In a Michigan case, a clinical social worker who provided services to individuals with serious brain injuries became sexually involved with multiple clients. These severely compromised clients testified that the social worker, who was sentenced to prison following his conviction in criminal court, groomed them over time in his effort to develop sexual relationships with them.[26]

In recent years, the two problems of sexual contact between behavioral health practitioners and clients and of substance abuse among practitioners have begun to receive particular attention. These two phenomena have figured prominently in a significant number of malpractice claims and licensing-board complaints against practitioners.

### SEXUAL ABUSE OF CLIENTS

A significant percentage of liability claims and licensing-board complaints against behavioral health practitioners involve allegations of sexual contact between practitioner and client. Clearly, this is a serious problem, although evidence suggests a relatively small percentage of practitioners engage in such misconduct. Here are several prominent examples:

- After pleading guilty, Utah social worker Donavan Faucette was sentenced to serve five years to life in prison for having sex with a sixteen-year-old client. Faucette was a clinical social worker who had worked at a community mental health center.[27]
- An Arkansas prison psychologist was sentenced to prison for three years following her conviction on charges of having sex with an inmate who was under her care. Prison officials said they had hired Anna Clark despite knowing of at least one previous allegation that she had had sex with a client.[28]
- A former social worker with the Mississippi Department of Child Protection Services was sentenced to eight years in prison for sex crimes involving two teenage boys under her care. According to evidence presented in court, Lauren Cavness had sex with two sixteen-year-old boys. Investigators found a photograph of one boy's genitals on her phone, leading to the second charge. Her phone also had texts with adult friends in which she admitted the relationships.[29]
- Georgia child psychologist Kenneth McPherson was sentenced to five years in prison following a child molestation conviction involving a client. McPherson was initially named in two indictments accusing him of committing acts of child molestation in 2005, 2008, 2010, and 2011. He was arrested in March 2011 and charged with five counts of child molestation and one count of sexual exploitation of a minor in one indictment and two counts of child molestation in the second indictment.[30]
- An Illinois social worker was sentenced to jail for engaging in sex with a client. Christy Lenhardt was employed at a mental health center. She pleaded guilty to sexual misconduct with a person with disabilities.[31]
- California marriage and family therapist Edgar Villamarin was sentenced to four years in prison for sexually abusing seven of his clients. Villamarin was first arrested after a woman reported she was sexually assaulted during

an appointment. A second victim later reported a similar incident during a visit to his office.[32]

- Wyoming psychologist Joshua Popkin admitted to sexually assaulting clients and was sentenced to two consecutive three-to-five-year prison terms. At his sentencing, Popkin stated, "During my brief time as a therapist, I did more harm than good and acted in ways that will reverberate in these women's lives for years to come."[33]
- Michigan social worker Thomas Higgins, who worked in a university-based traumatic brain injury program, was sentenced to serve two to ten years in prison after pleading guilty to charges that he had sexual relationships with three clients. Records showed that the incidents occurred in his office, in the patient's homes, and, in some cases, in a university van he secretly used to run errands around Ann Arbor beginning in the summer of 2006.[34]
- Lamarr Edgerson, a New Mexico therapist, was sentenced to serve twelve years in prison for raping multiple clients. Edgerson pleaded guilty to sexually assaulting clients who were under hypnosis.[35]
- William Dale Robinson, a Wyoming counselor, was sentenced to prison after pleading guilty to having sex with a client during a regularly scheduled counseling session. Robinson was also convicted of fraud; he billed the state Medicaid program for the counseling session during which he had sexual contact with the victim.[36]

All the available data suggest that the vast majority of cases involving sexual contact between professionals and clients involve a male practitioner and female client.[37] Gartrell and colleagues report in their nationwide survey of psychiatrists that 6.4 percent of respondents acknowledged sexual contact with their own patients; 90 percent of the offenders were male.[38]

A relatively small number of cases involve sexual contact between a female practitioner and male client and between a practitioner and client of the same gender. A. Brodsky suggests in her discussion of offending psychologists that there is a prototypical perpetrator profile:

> The following characteristics constitute a prototype of the therapist being sued: The therapist is male, middle aged, involved in unsatisfactory relationships in his own life, perhaps in the process of going through a divorce. His patient caseload is primarily female. He becomes involved with more than one patient sexually, those selected being on the average 16 years younger than he is. He confides his personal life to the patient, implying

to her that he needs her, and he spends therapy sessions soliciting her help
with his personal problems. The therapist is a lonely man, and even if he
works in a group practice, he is somewhat isolated professionally, not sharing in close consultation with his peers. He may have a good reputation
in the psychological or psychiatric community, having been in practice for
many years. He tends to take cases through referral only. He is not necessarily physically attractive, but there is an aura of power or charisma about
him. His lovemaking often leaves much to be desired, but he is quite convincing to the patient that it is he above all others with whom she needs to
be making love.[39]

Brodsky also describes other sexually abusive therapists, including those
who tend to be inexperienced and in love with one particular client, and
therapists with a personality disorder (typically antisocial personality disorder) who manipulate clients into believing that they—the therapists—
should be trusted and that they have the clients' best interest at heart.

The case of *Walker v. Parzen* typifies the sexual abuse of a client by a
therapist. According to court records, Dr. Parzen, a psychiatrist, had sex
with Walker during a two-and-a-half-year period, all the while charging her
an hourly rate per session. The plaintiff eventually divorced her husband,
lost her rights under California community property law, and lost custody
of her two children. Parzen had also prescribed excessive medication for
Walker, who claimed that she had tried to commit suicide more than a
dozen times by using pills obtained from Parzen or his office, according
to court records. Parzen ultimately referred Walker to another physician,
referring to her as a "borderline psychotic." The jury awarded the client
$4.63 million in damages.[40]

Another representative case involved a social worker who developed a
sexual relationship with a woman he had seen in both individual and group
therapy. The social worker was treating the client for bipolar disorder and
substance abuse. The client eventually attempted suicide and claimed that
the clinic that employed the social worker was negligent in hiring, training,
and supervising the social worker.[41]

Many licensing-board cases involve allegations of sexual misconduct
with current clients. For example, in a Wisconsin licensing-board case, a
social worker's recorded telephone conversations documented a sexual relationship with a client who visited the social worker's home.[42] The Alabama

licensing board revoked the license of a social worker who became involved sexually with a client.[43] In a New Jersey case, the licensing board disciplined a social worker who was convicted of having sexual contact with a "mentally disabled" client.[44]

A number of licensing-board cases involve allegations that behavioral health practitioners entered into sexual relationships with former clients. For example, in a Louisiana case, a counselor who provided substance abuse counseling services became sexually involved with a former client.[45] In a Maryland case, the licensing board disciplined a clinician who admitted having a sexual relationship with a former client who was being treated for posttraumatic stress disorder and adjustment disorder. The record indicates that the practitioner invited the client and members of the client's family to the practitioner's home and that the practitioner had visited the client at the client's workplace.[46]

A handful of therapists who have been sued have tried to defend their sexual contact with clients by offering two arguments that strain credibility.[47] The first is that the sexual contact was an essential and legitimate component of therapy. The therapist typically claims that he was merely trying to be helpful to the client. The defense offered by a Dr. Cooper in a California case is illustrative:

> Dr. Cooper is a firm believer in the fact that the body has a tremendous significance and influence on our actions; and the awareness of one's body is one of the keys to personal health; mental health; and his techniques may be considered new, revolutionary, and even bizarre perhaps to some people. But none of us knows the potential of the human body in relation to the human mind, and to explore that and make a person whole is Dr. Cooper's dedicated professional goal.[48]

A second defense is that the sexual relationship was conducted independently of the therapeutic relationship. In these instances, the defendant-therapist usually argues that he and the client were able to separate their sexual involvement from their professional relationship. As Schutz suggests, however, this argument "has not been a very successful defense, since courts are reluctant to accept such a compartmentalized view of human relationships. A therapist attempting to prove the legitimacy of sexual relations between himself and a patient by establishing that two coterminous-in-time but utterly parallel relations existed has a difficult task."[49]

Listed here is a mere sample and diverse cross section of other court cases and disciplinary hearings involving allegations of sexual misconduct:

- A psychiatrist hospitalized a thirty-year-old housewife and had sexual contact with her in the hospital and subsequently during office visits. A psychologist involved in the case was accused of encouraging the woman to have sexual relations with the psychiatrist. The psychiatrist did not deny the sexual contact but claimed that he was in love with the plaintiff. The psychologist argued that she did not encourage their relationship. This Pennsylvania case was settled.[50]

- The patient of a Colorado psychiatrist claimed that she had sexual relations in the psychiatrist's office. The plaintiff alleged that the psychiatrist told her that they could not have a sexual relationship if she was his patient and that the psychiatrist orchestrated a phony termination process. Under the doctrine of comparative negligence, the jury found the defendant 82 percent liable and the plaintiff 18 percent liable.[51]

- A fifty-five-year-old housewife claimed that she and her psychiatrist had a sexual relationship for thirteen years during office visits. The psychiatrist admitted the sexual relations but claimed that the relationship had been consensual. The plaintiff was awarded $3 million in this Oregon case.[52]

- A woman sought counseling from a marriage therapist. Her husband also attended three sessions. When the husband mentioned suicide during one session, the therapist suggested that he should go ahead and kill himself, the suit claimed. Ten months after the wife moved from the area, the therapist contacted her and convinced her to meet with him again, according to the suit. They began to have sexual relations. Both the wife and husband sued, the latter claiming loss of consortium, professional malpractice, outrageous conduct, and reckless infliction of emotional distress. The wife settled for $375,000 during trial. The California jury awarded the husband $1.85 million in compensatory damages and $1.53 million in punitive damages. After the verdict, the parties settled for $850,000.[53]

- A woman sought counseling from a psychologist regarding the effects of childhood sexual abuse by her father. The woman sued the psychologist, alleging that within weeks after treatment began, the psychologist had her sitting near his feet, then on his lap, and then began stroking her hair and back. According to the suit, shortly thereafter the two were involved in sexual relations. The suit claimed that as a result the woman would not be able to hold a meaningful job, was unable to maintain a normal relationship with men, attempted to commit suicide, and would require treatment for the rest of her life. The New York case was settled for $2.6 million.[54]

- A woman sought counseling from a counselor, a lesbian, to address issues related to a sexual problem that she was having with her female roommate and occasional lover. The client believed that the counselor's own sexual orientation would help her deal with the issues. During the course of treatment, the client invited the counselor to have dinner with her and three other women. The counselor and client became sexually involved while the counselor was still providing the woman with counseling services. The California Board of Behavioral Science Examiners found that the counselor was grossly negligent and revoked her license.[55]

- A fifteen-year-old was admitted to a residential treatment center for substance abuse counseling. One month before the youngster's discharge, he and his father learned that the boy's counselor was having an affair with the boy's mother. The Texas jury awarded $3.34 million, including $3 million in punitive damages.[56]

A number of lawsuits and licensing-board complaints involve clients' claims that they were harmed by sexual relationships that began *after* the termination of the practitioner-client relationship. In *Heinmiller v. Department of Health*, the Washington Supreme Court affirmed sanctions against a social worker who engaged in a sexual relationship with a client the day after the formal practitioner-client relationship had ended. In a California case, a therapist acknowledged a sexual relationship with her client but argued that it occurred after termination of the practitioner-client relationship. The case was settled for $220,000.[57] In an Illinois case, a psychiatrist claimed that he ended the patient's therapy, with her full agreement, and did not begin his sexual relationship with her until the following year. The Illinois Appellate Court affirmed a six-month license suspension.[58] In another licensing-board case, *Elliott v. North Carolina Psychology Board*, the North Carolina Court of Appeals affirmed the suspension of a psychologist's license because he had a sexual relationship with two former clients shortly after terminating the practitioner-client relationship and because he had dated two other former clients.[59]

Several authors believe that clinicians who engage in sexual misconduct can be categorized conceptually. Twemlow and Gabbard characterize therapists who fall in love with clients—a particular subgroup of clinicians who become sexually involved with clients—as lovesick therapists.[60] Lovesickness includes several key elements: emotional dependence; intrusive thinking—the therapist thinks about the client almost constantly; physical sensations like buoyancy or pounding pulse; a sense of incompleteness, of feeling less than whole when away from the client; an awareness of the social proscription of such love, which seems to intensify the couple's longing for each other; and an altered state of consciousness that fosters impaired judgment on the part of the therapist when in the presence of the loved one.

According to Schoener, he and his colleagues base their widely cited classification scheme—which includes a broader range of offending therapists—on empirical evidence gathered from psychological and psychiatric examinations of sexually exploitative therapists.[61] These clinical clusters (the italicized terminology is Schoener's) include the following:

1. *Psychotic and severe borderline disorders.* While few in number, these practitioners have difficulties with boundaries because of problems with both impulse control and thinking. They are often aware of current ethical standards but have difficulty adhering to them because of their poor reality testing and judgment.

2. *Manic disorders.* Most typically this applies to practitioners diagnosed with mania who go off medication and become quite impulsive.

3. *Sociopaths and severe narcissistic personality disorders.* These are self-centered exploiters who cross various boundaries when it suits them. They tend to be calculating and deliberate in their abuse of their clients. They often manipulate the treatment by "blurring the professional boundaries with inappropriate personal disclosure that enhances and idealizes transference, and by manipulating the length or the time of the sessions to facilitate the development of a sexual relationship with the client. . . . If caught, they might express remorse and agree to rehabilitation to protect themselves or their professional standing, but they will show minimal or no character change through treatment.[62]

4. *Impulse control disorders.* This includes practitioners with a wide range of paraphilias (sexual disorders in which unusual fantasies or bizarre acts are necessary for sexual arousal) and other impulse control disorders. These professionals often have other impulse control problems in other areas of their lives. They are typically aware of current ethical standards, but these

do not serve as a deterrent. These practitioners often fail to acknowledge the harm that their behavior does to their victims and show little remorse.

5. *Chronic neurotic and isolated.* These practitioners are emotionally needy on a chronic basis and meet many needs through their relationships with clients. They may suffer from long-standing problems with depression, low self-esteem, social isolation, and lack of confidence. At times, these practitioners disclose personal information to clients inappropriately. Typically they deny engaging in misconduct or justify the unethical behavior as their therapeutic technique designed to enhance their suffering client's self-esteem. They may also blame the client's claims on the client's pathology. Such practitioners are often repeat offenders.

6. *Situational offenders.* These therapists are generally healthy with a good practice history and free of boundary violations, but a situational break-down in judgment or control has occurred in response to some life crisis or loss. These practitioners are generally aware of current ethical standards. According to Olarte, "Their sexual contact with a client is usually an isolated or limited incident. Frequently at the time of the boundary violation, these therapists are suffering from personal or situational stresses that foster a slow erosion of their professional boundaries. They most often show remorse for their unethical behavior, frequently stop such violations on their own, or seek consultation with peers."[63]

7. *Naive.* These therapists are not pathological but have difficulty understanding, and operating within, professional boundaries because they suffer from deficits in social judgment. Their difficulties stem in part from their lack of knowledge of current ethical standards and their confusion about the need to separate personal and professional relationships.

In contrast to this framework, Simon offers a typology that includes somewhat different clinical dimensions.[64] Simon places vulnerable therapists in five categories:

- *Character disordered.* Therapists diagnosed with symptoms of borderline, narcissistic, or antisocial personality disorder.
- *Sexually disordered.* Therapists diagnosed with frotteurism (recurrent intense sexual urges and sexually arousing fantasies in regard to a nonconsenting person), pedophilia, or sexual sadism.
- *Incompetent.* Therapists who are poorly trained or have persistent boundary blind spots.

- *Impaired.* Therapists who have serious problems with alcohol, drugs, or mental illness.
- *Situational reactors.* Therapists who are experiencing marital discord, loss of important relationships, or a professional crisis.

On the basis of his extensive experience with vulnerable and offending therapists, Simon argues that boundary violations are often progressive and follow a sequence, or "natural history," that leads ultimately to a therapist-client sexual relationship.[65] Although the sequence is not always this linear, the general pattern is common. The sequence unfolds as follows:

- The therapist's neutrality gradually erodes. The therapist begins to take special interest in the client's issues and life circumstances.
- Boundary violations begin between the chair and the door. As the client is leaving the office, and both client and therapist are standing, the therapist and client may discuss personal issues that are not part of the more formal therapeutic conversation.
- Therapy becomes socialized. More time is spent discussing nontherapy issues.
- The therapist discloses confidential information about other clients. The therapist begins to confide in the client, communicating to the client that she is special.
- Therapist self-disclosure begins. The therapist shares information about his own life, perhaps concerning marital or relationship problems.
- Physical contact begins (e.g., touching, hugs, kisses). Casual physical gestures convey to the client that the therapist has warm and affectionate feelings toward her.
- The therapist gains control over the client. The client begins to feel more and more dependent on the therapist, and the therapist exerts more and more influence in the client's life.
- Extratherapeutic contacts occur. The therapist and client may meet for lunch or for a drink.
- Therapy sessions are longer. The therapist extends the customary fifty-minute session because of the special relationship.
- Therapy sessions are rescheduled for the end of the day. To avoid conflict with other clients' appointments, the therapist arranges to see the client as the day's final appointment.
- The therapist stops billing the client. The emerging intimacy makes it difficult for the therapist to charge the client for the time they spend together.

- Dating begins. The therapist and client begin to schedule times when they can be together socially.
- Therapist-client sex occurs.

Celenza studied a sample of therapists who engaged in sexual misconduct and found a number of common precursors related primarily to the therapist's personality, life circumstances, past history, and the transference-countertransference dynamics of this particular therapist-client pair.[66] More specifically, Celenza found that clinicians who manifest the following traits are more likely to engage in sexual misconduct:

- Long-standing narcissistic vulnerability. Therapists reported a lifelong struggle with a sense of unworthiness, inadequacy, or outright feelings of failure.
- Grandiose (covert) rescue fantasies. Therapists presented a mild-mannered, self-effacing, and humble exterior that hid underlying (and unchallenged) beliefs in powers of rescue and omnipotence.
- Intolerance of negative transference. Often as a result of fragile self-esteem, some therapists have difficulty tolerating and exploring disappointments, frustrations, and criticisms that the client may have about the services she or he is receiving.
- Childhood history of emotional deprivation and sexualized overstimulation. Some therapists reported sexualization of their relationship with a primary caregiver (usually the mother), often in the form of overstimulation of the child in a sexualized manner rather than outright sexual abuse.
- Family history of covert and sanctioned boundary transgressions. Some therapists' families showed evidence of high moralism accompanied by hypocrisy; for example, in the form of marital infidelity or fraudulent financial activity.
- Unresolved anger toward authority figures. Some therapists appeared to engage in sexual misconduct as a way to rebel against the authority of their profession and as a result of an underlying desire to break the rules, perhaps because of anger toward an authoritarian parent.
- Restricted awareness of fantasy (especially hostile/aggressive). Many therapists, especially those who felt intense guilt and remorse, were unable to admit to or access hateful or desirous wishes except in conventional or muted ways. These therapists had difficulty perceiving aggression in themselves or others.

- Transformation of countertransference hate to countertransference love. Some therapists had difficulty tolerating their own aggression and perceiving themselves as depriving clients or not nurturing them. These therapists harbored the unrealistic belief that they should love and help every client.

### PRACTITIONER SUBSTANCE ABUSE

Most studies related to substance abuse among behavioral health professionals focus on alcohol. Relatively little research has been conducted on other drug use among practitioners. Here is an illustrative case example:

Miss Jones was the clinical supervisor for an off-site social work follow-up counseling service of a large public hospital. She was 61 years old, and she had recurring mild back pain resulting from a herniated disk, a problem that could be managed without surgery through diet control, exercise, and correct posture. She had worked for the agency for approximately 8 years, serving for the last 2 as supervisor of the off-site outpatient counseling and guidance service. She supervised a clinical staff of four social workers, one psychologist, and three counselors, all of whom were between 25 and 45 years old. Miss Jones had gradually become the agency's resident "alcohol expert" because she had been sent to a number of seminars and workshops on alcohol-related problems during the last 5 years.

Some months after Miss Jones had transferred to the off-site office, individual staff members began to note an apparent deterioration in her work performance. She became less available for supervision of and consultation with staff members, less systematic in the review of cases, and erratic in keeping supervision appointments, and she began to end supervision sessions abruptly after only 10 to 15 minutes. Moreover, clinical staff also was beginning to hear complaints from clients who had direct clinical contact with Miss Jones. Furthermore, Miss Jones's administrative functioning seemed to be deteriorating; she seemed unable to produce needed administrative reports, was erratic and inconsistent in administrative decision making, and was unable to systematically follow through on administrative details.

Concurrently, her co-workers noted an apparent change in personality and behavior. She seemed to have withdrawn and become aloof. She spent less time informally chatting with staff, and she stopped sharing lunch hours with her co-workers. Her absences from work increased, and it became more and more frequent that she would arrive at work late or leave work early because of "not feeling up to par." Clinical and clerical staff began to note a pattern of Miss Jones's having alcohol on her breath during the afternoon and to appear more frequently to be behaviorally "under the influence of alcohol."

Initially individual staff members commented in private to Miss Jones about one or another concern about her behavior. Her response to such comments or expressions of concern was defensive. She attributed all of her present difficulty to her "back problems," subtly suggested a lack of empathy on the part of the given staff member, and intimated that the staff member's "concern" was placing more pressure on her. . . .

After administrative staff found liquor bottles in her desk and filing cabinets, the program director placed Miss Jones on indefinite administrative leave with the option that if she sought "appropriate help" (still undefined) and adequately demonstrated a return to "normal functioning," she could return to her previous position. Miss Jones decided to seek voluntary hospitalization in a facility specializing in the treatment of stress disorders. While in the facility, she ultimately decided to seek early retirement for "health reasons."[67]

Estimates of the prevalence of alcoholism among professionals vary. Many are based on data from treatment groups or impressions from practitioners' clinical experience. A precise way to measure the incidence of substance abuse among professionals does not exist. The more thorough, detailed estimates suggest that roughly 5 to 6 percent of professionals are alcoholic, with a somewhat higher incidence among men.[68]

Professionals, like the general public, manifest various signs of impairment because of alcohol use. Freudenberger claims to have found a recognizable pattern among many alcoholic professionals:[69]

I have worked with at least 60 impaired professionals, psychologists, social workers, dentists, physicians, and attorneys during the past ten years and have found certain personality characteristics to be common. For the most part, impaired professionals are between 30 and 55 years of age. This is in essential agreement with Farber and Heifetz (1981) who suggested that "suicides of physicians, when they happen, are most likely to occur in the 35–54 age group" (p. 296). Early childhood impoverishment is another common characteristic. This is in agreement with Vaillant, Brighton, and McArthur (1970), who pointed to the "lack of consistent support and concern from their parents" in his study of drug-using physicians.

Most, if not all, of the patients I worked with led consistently unhealthy lifestyles. They tended to be masochistic, to have low self-images, and to be self-destructive in their personal and professional lives. Eighteen of the 60 had been married more than one time, 10 were bachelors, and the remainder were separated or divorced. Those who were married had frequent extra-marital affairs. They all worked excessively long hours and, as Pearson and Strecker (1960) suggested, "had poor organizational habits . . . seldom took vacations, lunch hours and had few outside interests" (p. 916).

Their masochism made them prone to their patients [sic] beyond their own personal limits. All tended to be perfectionists and were usually never pleased with their work. "I know I can be better, I'm not good enough, I could have done more" are frequently heard refrains. They tended to con-duct their lives, both at home and in the office, in such a way that they found little, if any, relief from their chores. They had a desperate need to be needed and rationalized taking drugs as doing something for themselves. . . . They rationalized, denied, and overcompensated to an excessive degree.

While expressing a sense of dedication and commitment, they denied that abusing drugs or alcohol or sexually abusing clients might eventually lead to their destruction. As a group they were risk takers with their own as well as their patients' lives.

As with other forms of impairment, relatively little is known about the prevalence of alcoholism among behavioral health practitioners. Although various estimates have been made of the incidence of substance abuse among practitioners—generally about 5 to 15 percent—no one really knows how widespread the problem is.

A number of licensing boards have disciplined practitioners who abused substances. For example, the Iowa licensing board suspended the license of a clinician on the basis of evidence of significant substance abuse–related impairment.[70] A Texas practitioner was disciplined by the licensing board on the basis of evidence that she used substances at work.[71] The Arkansas licensing board disciplined a social worker on the basis of evidence that she provided "social work services while under the influence of alcohol, other mind-altering or mood-altering drugs."[72] In an Alabama case, the licens-ing board disciplined a practitioner who admitted to "habituation to drugs or to habit forming drugs that impair the ability to perform social work duties."[73]

### RESPONSE TO IMPAIRMENT

To minimize liability and disciplinary risks, behavioral health practitioners must devise ways to prevent impairment and respond to impaired colleagues. Little is known about the extent to which impaired practitioners and other professionals voluntarily seek help for their problems. A comprehensive search of the literature produced few empirical studies of impaired practitioners' efforts to seek help. Guy, Poelstra, and Stark found that 70 percent of the distressed clinical psychologists whom they surveyed sought some form of therapeutic assistance.[74] One-fourth (26.6 percent) entered individual psychotherapy, and 10.7 percent entered family therapy. A small portion of this group participated in self-help groups (3.4 percent) or was hospitalized (2.2 percent). Some were placed on medication (4.1 percent). Exactly 10 percent of this group temporarily terminated their professional practice.

These findings contrast with those of Wood and colleagues, who found that only 55.2 percent of clinicians who reported problems that interfered with their work (substance abuse, sexual overtures toward clients, depression, and burnout) sought help.[75] Two-fifths (42 percent) of all those surveyed, including impaired and unimpaired professionals, reported having offered help to impaired colleagues at some time or having referred them to therapists. Only 7.9 percent of the sample said they had reported an impaired colleague to a local regulatory body. Approximately two-fifths (40.2 percent) were aware of instances in which they believed no action was taken to help an impaired colleague.

We can draw several hypotheses concerning impaired behavioral health professionals' reluctance to seek help and the reluctance of their colleagues to confront them about their problems. Some professionals are hesitant to acknowledge impairment within their ranks because they fear how practitioners will react to confrontation and how such confrontation might affect the future relationships of colleagues who must work. VandenBos and Duthie present the problem succinctly:

> The fact that more than half of us have not confronted distressed colleagues even when we have recognized and acknowledged (at least to ourselves) the existence of their problems is, in part, a reflection of the difficulty in achieving a balance between concerned intervention and intrusiveness.

As professionals, we value our own right to practice without interference, as long as we function within the boundaries of our professional expertise, meet professional standards for the provision of services, and behave in an ethical manner. We generally consider such expectations when we consider approaching a distressed colleague. Deciding when and how our concern about the well-being of a colleague (and our ethical obligation) supersedes his or her right to personal privacy and professional autonomy is a ticklish matter.[76]

Thoreson and colleagues also argue that impaired professionals sometimes find it difficult to seek help because of their mythical belief in their infinite power and invulnerability.[77] Because many psychotherapists are in private practice, the reduced opportunity for colleagues to observe their unethical or inept practice exacerbates the problem.

In a valuable study by Deutsch, a diverse group of therapists who admitted to personal problems gave a variety of reasons for not seeking professional help, including believing that an acceptable therapist was not available, seeking help from family members or friends, fearing exposure and the disclosure of confidential information, concern about the amount of effort required and about the cost, having a spouse who was unwilling to participate in treatment, failing to admit the seriousness of the problem, believing they should be able to work their problems out themselves, and believing that therapy would not help.[78]

Rehabilitation of behavioral health professionals who have been sexually involved with clients is particularly daunting. One-time offenders who made an isolated mistake with an individual client can often be helped through therapy and education. However, the rehabilitative prospects for chronic offenders and professionals with personality disorders, such as antisocial personality disorder, are often grim. As A. Brodsky concludes, "The therapist whose motives were less than honorable, who had intimacies with several patients, and who, in the case of men, is chronically problematic in relationships with women outside of therapy is probably not easily rehabilitated. In some cases of personality disorder, it is questionable whether or not retraining of the therapist is possible."[79]

As I mentioned earlier, in recent years several organized efforts have been made to identify and address the problems of impaired professionals. The consensus is growing that a model strategy for addressing impairment among professionals should include several components.[80] First, behavioral health practitioners need adequate means to identify impaired practitioners. Professionals must be willing to assume some responsibility for acknowledging impairment among colleagues. And, as Lamb and colleagues note, it certainly would help to develop reasonably objective measures of what constitutes incompetent skills, impaired professional functioning, and failure to live up to professional standards.[81]

Second, a practitioner's initial identification and documentation of a colleague's impairment should be followed by exploration of the causes and by what Sonnenstuhl describes as "constructive confrontation."[82] Third, once a practitioner decides to confront the impaired colleague, the practitioner must decide whether to help the impaired colleague identify ways to seek help voluntarily or to refer the colleague to a supervisor or local regulatory body (such as a licensing board).

Assuming the data are sufficient to support a rehabilitation plan, the impaired practitioner's colleague, supervisor, or local regulatory body should make specific recommendations. The possibilities include close supervision, personal psychotherapy, and treatment for any form of impairment, such as addiction. In some cases, a licensing board may need to impose some type of sanction such as censure, probation, limitations on the professional's practice (e.g., concerning clientele that can be served and required supervision), or loss of license. Whatever action is taken should be monitored and evaluated. Here is an illustration of effective intervention with an impaired professional:

> Mr. Brown was the director of a community-based county work release/ rehabilitation program in a medium-sized town. He was 34 years old. Mr. Brown was noted for his friendliness, his openness with colleagues and community leaders, his dedication to making the program work for the community and those enrolled, and his well-balanced approach in solving problems and in instructing others about how best to approach the participants in the program. Due to a cut in state funding to be made available to the county, the county board of administration found it necessary to reallocate funds for the next year's budget in such a way that several programs, including the program directed by Mr. Brown, would have to be redefined or possibly even eliminated. Mr. Brown prepared extensive documentation on the success of his program and presented it to the board, making an impassioned plea for its continuation. The board began its deliberations.

Although not directly involved in the decision-making process, Mr. Brown was well known to many of the board members and, as the board's deliberations progressed, some board members formed factions representing a range of opinions about what should happen to the program and shared information on the board's day-to-day deliberations, which were marked by continual changes in opinions, with Mr. Brown. As a result, over a period of six months, Mr. Brown became progressively more frustrated, uncertain, and stressed about the eventual outcome.

Mr. Brown's co-workers began to notice him gradually withdrawing from those around him. Rather than having his lunch in the cafeteria with his colleagues, he began to eat alone in his office, declaring that he was too busy to do otherwise, and he participated less and less in the ordinary social activity of the staff. He also began to limit "business" contact with his colleagues and members of the community to meetings that were as brief as possible. Several of his co-workers as individuals expressed concern about these changes to him. Mr. Brown's explanation was that the uncertainty about the outcome of the board's deliberations was creating a great deal of pressure on him and, as a result, it was difficult for him to concentrate, and he had to focus more intensely on getting his work done.

Others also noted the changes in Mr. Brown. In particular, these changes were noted by an industrial/organizational psychologist working for a large company, which had participated in the work release program for many years, and who considered Mr. Brown to be both a colleague and a friend. His colleague asked Mr. Brown to conduct a training session for several new employees on the staff on how to work effectively with participants in the work release program. On the day following the session, she called Mr. Brown and asked to meet with him in order to share feedback on the session, and they set a meeting time. During the meeting, she expressed concern about the changes she had noted in Mr. Brown's behavior both personally and professionally and her feeling that those changes seemed to represent a pattern of behavior indicating depression. She went on to say that it was apparent that the depression was not being attended to by Mr. Brown.

As an example of what had caused her to be concerned, she pointed out that during the training session Mr. Brown, who was ordinarily a patient, flexible individual, had responded to members of the group with anger and hostility when they challenged or even questioned elements of his presentation and when they expressed disagreement with his interpretations of material. She noted that this was very inconsistent with his usual behavior. At the same time, she mentioned in passing that she had overheard comments by others—including co-workers and community members—regarding his apparent inaccessibility, both professionally and emotionally. She suggested that Mr. Brown's attempts to control and cope with his distress were not being fully effective and that she and his co-workers wanted to offer whatever support they could. At the same time, she suggested that Mr. Brown might consider entering therapy. Initially, Mr. Brown reacted defensively and angrily. He expressed his feeling that his colleague was intruding. However, after continued discussion, it became apparent to him that her concern was genuine and that she expressed the shared caring and frustration of herself, his co-workers, and others. The effect of her simultaneously confrontational and supporting approach was to break through Mr. Brown's defensiveness and denial. He began to identify and acknowledge other indications of depressive symptomatology. He also mentioned that his rumination about possible "political outcomes" and his withdrawal from others was further complicating the situation for him. Following this confrontation, he went into short-term therapy and his depression was quickly resolved—Mr. Brown again became his friendly, open, effective self.[83]

Relatively little research has focused on the effectiveness of efforts to rehabilitate impaired professionals. Moreover, the few published empirical evaluations—which report mixed results for various treatment programs—focus primarily on impaired physicians.[84] Studies typically report only whether the practitioner is still alive, still licensed, or in practice. Many investigations have serious methodological flaws or limitations. Few studies compare the outcome of efforts to treat impaired professionals with control groups or even other patient groups, and follow-up periods tend to be relatively short. The results of the handful of outcome studies on the treatment of impaired professionals are as follows:

- Goby, Bradley, and Bespalec report on their follow-up survey of forty-three alcoholic physician-patients treated over a ten-year period at Lutheran General Hospital in Illinois.[85] One was in prison, and seven had died (one committed suicide, one died of lung cancer, three died drinking excessively, and two died from unknown causes). Nineteen of the forty-three (44 percent) had been abstinent since discharge from the program; nine reported some drinking but were abstinent for a full year or more at the time of the survey. Only eight did not report a significant decrease in alcohol consumption. Most of the physicians reported good physical and emotional health and were working.

- Kliner, Spicer, and Barnett reported on results of a mail survey of fifty-seven alcoholic physicians treated at the Hazelden Foundation in Minnesota one year after discharge.[86] Fifty-one of the fifty-seven reported abstinence since discharge, five reported serious difficulty with continued drinking, and one reported continued drinking but no related problems. The respondents also reported improvements in self-image, health, professional performance, and personal adjustment.

- Morse and colleagues reported on outcomes for fifty-three alcoholic physicians who had been treated for at least two weeks at the Mayo Clinic.[87] One to five years after discharge, 83 percent of the physicians reported complete abstinence or having been in relapse for no more than one week—and as abstinent when surveyed—compared to 62 percent of a nonphysician "general group" of patients. Eighty-nine percent of the physicians resumed their practice.

- Herrington and colleagues reported on a study of forty alcoholic physicians and dentists treated in an impaired-physician program in Milwaukee, Wisconsin.[88] The treatment included a thirty-day inpatient program, Alcoholics Anonymous and/or Narcotics Anonymous, and follow-up. Seven physicians dropped out of treatment early. Of the thirty physicians and three dentists who remained in treatment, twenty-two reported abstinence since discharge and six reported only a single relapse. The majority continued to practice.

- Pearson reported on the treatment of 250 physicians over a thirty-six-year period.[89] Slightly more than one-third (36 percent) had a history of substance abuse, about one-fifth (18 percent) were diagnosed with psychotic symptoms or affective disorders, and slightly more than one-fourth (28 percent) manifested neurotic or situational problems. Of the 160 who received actual treatment, 42 percent were classified as recovered or much improved, 22 percent as slightly improved, and 36 percent as worse or unimproved.

- Shore reported on a study of twenty-seven alcoholic or drug-addicted physicians treated in Oregon under state-board supervision.[90] The Oregon Board of Medical Examiners had placed all on professional probation. Data suggested that twenty-two of the twenty-seven improved, with fourteen reporting no relapse. Seventy-nine percent returned to practice, but during an average 3.6 years on probation, 53 percent had relapses.

## RISK MANAGEMENT STRATEGY

Behavioral health practitioners can take various steps to protect clients and to minimize the likelihood of lawsuits and ethics complaints associated with boundary problems and impairment. With specific respect to sexual misconduct, Simon highlights five basic principles underlying constructive boundary guidelines:[91]

1. Rule of abstinence. Practitioners should strive, above all else, to avoid sexual involvement with clients and to resist acting on sexual attraction toward clients.
2. Duty of neutrality. Practitioners should seek to relate to clients as neutrally as possible. Neutrality entails the absence of favoritism, preferential consideration, and special treatment.
3. Client autonomy and self-determination. Practitioners should respect clients' right to self-determination, which means avoiding any manipulative behaviors or behaviors that might promote clients' dependence or constitute "undue influence."
4. Fiduciary relationship. Fiduciary relationships are based on trust. Clients must be able to trust their therapists and to assume that their therapists would not engage in manipulative, exploitative, or seductive behaviors for self-interested purposes.
5. Respect for human dignity. Practitioners must maintain deep-seated respect for their clients, act only in a caring and compassionate manner, and avoid engaging in destructive behaviors.

More concretely, practitioners should adhere to a number of guidelines to protect clients and minimize risks associated with sexual attraction:[92]

- Maintain relative therapist neutrality (the absence of favoritism). Foster psychological separateness of the client.
- Protect client confidentiality.
- Obtain informed consent for treatments and procedures. Interact with clients verbally.
- Ensure no previous, current, or future personal relationship with the client. Minimize physical contact.
- Preserve relative anonymity of the therapist. Establish a stable fee policy.
- Provide a consistent, private, and professional setting for treatment. Define the time and length of the treatment session.

Beyond these broad guidelines, practitioners should pay special attention to clients' unique clinical issues that may complicate boundary phenomena. For example, if a therapist senses that a client is feeling attracted to him, the therapist might avoid scheduling the client at times when no one else is in the office suite. As Gutheil and Gabbard observe, "From a risk-management standpoint, a patient in the midst of an intense erotic transference to the therapist might best be seen, when possible, during high-traffic times when other people (e.g., secretaries, receptionists, and even other patients) are around."[93] Therapists in solo private practice must be especially careful because of professional isolation and the absence of institutional or collegial oversight and restraints.[94]

Further, behavioral health practitioners who sense potential boundary issues involving sexual attraction should avoid out-of-the-office contact with clients. A common example includes counseling sessions conducted during lunch in a restaurant:

> This event appears to be a common way station along the path of increasing boundary crossings culminating in sexual misconduct. Although clinicians often advance the claim that therapy is going on, so, inevitably, is much purely social behavior; it does not *look* like therapy, at least to a jury. Lunch sessions are not uncommonly followed by sessions during dinner, then just dinners, then other dating behavior, eventually including intercourse.[95]

Boundary violations can also arise from seemingly innocent gestures, such as offering a stranded client a ride home after a counseling session. Clinically relevant discussion may continue during the ride and while the therapist and client are parked in front of the client's home. Conducting sensitive discussion in the context of the therapist's personal space can lead to boundary ambiguity, confusion, and, ultimately, violation: "From a fact finder's viewpoint, many exciting things happen in cars, but therapy is usually not one of them."[96]

One must consider these guidelines in relation to different treatment approaches and ideologies. Some treatment techniques assume that therapists will spend time with clients outside the office. As Gutheil and Gabbard note:

> It would not be a boundary violation for a behaviorist, under certain circumstances, to accompany a patient in a car, to an elevator, to an airplane, or

even to a public restroom (in the treatment of paruresis, the fear of urinating in a public restroom) as part of the treatment plan for a particular phobia. The existence of a body of professional literature, a clinical rationale, and risk-benefit documentation will be useful in protecting the clinician in such a situation from misconstruction of the therapeutic efforts.[97]

Simon urges practitioners to conduct an "instant spot check" to identify whether the therapist has committed or is at risk of committing a boundary violation.[98] Using this approach, the first question to ask is whether the treatment is for the benefit of the therapist or for the sake of the client's therapy. Second, is the treatment part of a series of progressive steps in the direction of boundary violations (e.g., inviting the client to have lunch after a counseling session in order to continue discussion of compelling clinical issues)? Simon argues that an affirmative answer to either question should put the therapist on notice to desist immediately and take corrective action.

Practitioners who are at risk of impairment should be particularly mindful of self-care options as a preventative. Self-care includes various elements: physical well-being, psychological well-being, spiritual well-being, support, and workplace changes. Ideally, practitioners who find themselves struggling will take assertive steps to enhance their personal well-being.

# CHAPTER 5

# Supervision

*CLIENTS AND STAFF*

The concepts and practice of supervision have always been central in behavioral health. Practitioners' training typically includes considerable attention to theory and skills related to supervision.[1] Over the years, the behavioral health literature has addressed a variety of issues related to supervision, including the administrative and clinical responsibilities of the supervisor, the challenge in moving from practitioner to supervisor, and the importance of leadership qualities in supervision.

Not surprisingly lawsuits and licensing-board complaints sometimes name practitioners who have supervisory responsibilities. Although supervisors may not have been directly involved in the event or circumstances immediately surrounding the case, they may be found responsible, at least in part.

Liability claims and licensing-board complaints related to supervision tend to be of two types. The first includes cases involving client supervision; that is, instances in which practitioners are alleged to have failed in their duty to properly supervise clients. The second includes cases involving staff supervision. These cases usually allege that a practitioner failed to properly supervise a staff member who was negligent or who committed some act of misfeasance, malfeasance, or nonfeasance. In addition to an agency being held liable for failure to supervise, other potential related forms of direct liability include failure to hire, train, and retain competent employees.

### CLIENT SUPERVISION

Howard C. was a counselor in a residential facility for adolescents with behavioral challenges. He had worked at the facility for three years; during that time he had worked as a child-care worker and, most recently, a unit supervisor. In his position as unit supervisor, Howard C. supervised three child-care workers on his shift and also had responsibility for helping to supervise the youngsters on the unit. Most youths on the unit had been admitted with such symptoms as severe depression, violent behavior, self-mutilation, hallucinations and delusions, and attempted suicide.

On one particular Thursday morning, only two child-care workers and Howard C. were on the unit. The third child-care worker had called in sick. As a result, Howard C. was expected to put his administrative duties aside and assume the responsibilities of the third child-care worker. That is, Howard C. was to be physically present on the unit instead of spending much of his time in the corner office where the unit supervisors shared a desk.

Howard C. began the shift on the unit. The residents were engaged in various activities. Several were involved in counseling sessions, some were being tutored on their schoolwork, and others were working on their journal entries. The youths for whom Howard C. was primarily responsible were relaxing, watching television.

Howard C. decided to use this time to finish up some paperwork that each unit supervisor was expected to complete (incident reports). He told the youths for whom he was responsible that he would be in his office. After about twenty minutes, two youths began to argue about the television station that they were watching. They could not agree on what show to watch and began screaming at each other. One youth picked up a chair and hit the other over the head with it. The youth who was assaulted fell to the floor unconscious. He was rushed to the hospital with a serious brain injury.

The youth suffered permanent brain damage. His parents sued Howard C. and the program, alleging that supervision of residents was inadequate and that Howard C. in particular failed to carry out his supervisory responsibilities as called for by the program's policies.

The behavioral health field is filled with cases in which individual practitioners and their agencies have been sued because of alleged failure to supervise clients adequately. Ordinarily, the plaintiff alleges that staff did not monitor clients' activities closely enough or that, according to national standards, the staff-client ratio was inadequate for proper supervision. As cases cited in this chapter will show, these lawsuits often describe instances in which clients attempted suicide, assaulted one another or staff, or were injured when restrained by staff, actions that plaintiffs allege proper supervision could have prevented (chapter 3 also addresses issues related to supervision of suicidal clients).

In Iowa, the parents of a resident of a hospital for people with intellectual disabilities filed suit alleging that staff members should be held responsible for injuries to their son during an assault at the hospital. The man was bitten by his roommate at least fourteen times and suffered a broken jaw, broken foot, and various cuts and bruises. Some inflictions of injuries were not witnessed by staff or occurred under circumstances in which staff members could not protect the injured resident. The judge found that the staff should have separated the roommates four months earlier. A court awarded the plaintiffs $146,000.[2]

After a patient raped a fourteen-year-old girl, a suit brought on her behalf claimed that the Colorado hospital and a doctor failed to supervise the patient who attacked her. The fourteen-year-old girl had been admitted to a psychiatric facility after attempting suicide. The suit claimed that the girl was not adequately protected while at the facility, and that a sixteen-year-old male patient sneaked into her room and assaulted her. Upon her admission, the staff had been concerned that she might attempt suicide and placed her on a fifteen-minute watch schedule. On the night of the assault, however, staff members were not watching the girl because, the staff claimed, her condition had improved. Her attorney contended that she was in a facility in which she was supposed to feel safe and that she would never feel safe again. A jury awarded her damages.[3]

A case against a Florida hospital raised similar issues: the plaintiff, a psychiatric patient, alleged that another patient raped her and that the hospital was negligent when that patient gained access to her room. The court awarded the plaintiff damages.[4]

In contrast, in the case of *Hothem v. Fallsview Psychiatric Hospital*, the Ohio courts did not find the hospital negligent in an assault on one patient by another. One patient was admitted to the hospital for treatment of organic delusional syndrome. The second patient was admitted several days later with a diagnosis of paranoid schizophrenia. The second patient accused the first patient of communicating with the devil, threatened to kill her, and then assaulted her. The courts found, however, that the hospital did not have reason to anticipate the second patient's actions and was not negligent in its supervision of him.[5] Similarly, a Texas appeals court affirmed that a state school and its staff were not liable for injuries that a resident with intellectual disabilities incurred when attacked by another school resident. The appeals court found sufficient evidence to support the jury's conclusion that the staff had followed the violent resident's treatment plan and that staff followed proper procedure when the violent resident's behavior was out of control.[6]

Many cases involve allegations that staff members failed to properly supervise clients in residential facilities who attempted suicide. A state of Washington case against a physician and a hospital involved a forty-year-old woman who was admitted to the hospital for psychiatric treatment and who was allowed to make telephone calls in an interview room with an unscreened window. This occurred one day after admission. The patient claimed that she had a panic reaction and attempted to escape from the hospital through the window. She suffered fractured vertebrae, neurogenic bowel and bladder dysfunction, and head and foot injuries. The patient claimed that being left alone in a room with an unscreened window constituted negligence on the part of the staff. The defendants argued that the woman showed no suicidal ideation and that the family had failed to provide a complete psychiatric history. The case was settled.[7]

The circumstances in another case against a hospital are also commonplace. In this Texas case, parents took their daughter to the hospital after she told them that she was going to commit suicide. The parents told hospital staff that their daughter had tried to commit suicide previously by hanging herself while a patient at another hospital. Shortly after her parents left, the daughter walked out of her room, left the building, climbed to the top of a nearby parking garage, and jumped to her death. The plaintiffs argued that hospital staff members should be adjudged negligent in failing to supervise or control a patient whom the staff had been told was suicidal. The case was settled.[8] Other cases that present similar allegations of improper supervision and suicides committed by hospitalized patients include *McNamara v. Honeyman* and *Bramlette v. Charter-Medical-Columbia*.

Some cases also involve allegations that staff at a secure residential setting did not properly supervise clients who as a result escaped and then attempted suicide. In a case brought against the Commonwealth of Virginia and its mental health agency, the plaintiff, a woman diagnosed with schizophrenia, claimed that she was not supervised adequately after she was committed involuntarily to an inpatient mental health facility. The woman attempted to escape four times during the last three days of her two-week hospitalization. On the fourth attempt, she walked onto a busy highway and into the path of an oncoming car. The plaintiff suffered compound fractures of both legs and permanent nerve injury. A jury awarded her damages.[9]

In some instances, courts may find behavioral health staffers and agencies liable when clients injure themselves accidentally. A woman's family sued the hospital after the thirty-nine-year-old homemaker and mother died; the Minnesota suit claimed that she was not adequately supervised and monitored. The woman had been admitted to a locked psychiatric ward with a diagnosis of schizoaffective disorder. During lunch, a nurse and an orderly supervised the woman and nine other patients. The woman stuffed large amounts of food in her mouth; the nurse offered to cut the woman's food, but the woman refused. The woman ate all the food on her plate. She subsequently choked on her food and died shortly thereafter. The jury awarded damages to the woman's family.[10]

### STAFF SUPERVISION

Sue S., a mental health counselor, was the clinical director at North County Mental Health Services, a local community mental health center. Sue S. was responsible for supervising five clinical staffers at the center. One of her supervisees was Scott M.

Scott M.'s caseload was diverse, including people recently discharged from a nearby state psychiatric hospital and clients referred by the local school district. Scott M. was working with a ten-year-old boy who had been referred by the local grade school. The boy had been having a number of problems in school, including several instances of fire setting and self-mutilation. Scott M. had been working with the boy for about three months. Scott M. also had extensive contact with the boy's family. Scott M. and Sue S. spent considerable time during supervision discussing this clinically complex case.

One afternoon, the principal of the boy's school, who had initially referred the case to the mental health center, called Scott M. and asked him how the boy and his family were doing. The principal asked whether Scott M. could summarize the boy's progress and forward it to her. The next week, Scott M. prepared a case summary, which included details of the boy's allegation that his father had sexually abused him.

During a subsequent conversation with the school principal, the father learned that Scott M. had disclosed this information to the school without his consent. The father sued Scott M. and his supervisor, Sue S., alleging that they had breached his right to privacy with respect to sharing the information with the school. The father specifically alleged that Sue S. had failed to properly perform her supervisory duties in that she did not ensure that his consent had been obtained before disseminating Scott M.'s report to the school principal. The father also filed a licensing-board complaint against Scott M.

Large numbers of behavioral health practitioners supervise staff. A clinical director in a family service agency may supervise caseworkers and counselors. A unit supervisor in a residential treatment facility may supervise mental health or child-care workers. An assistant director of a substance use disorders treatment program may supervise administrative staff. In each setting, supervisors must carry out a variety of tasks, which may include monitoring workers' activities, providing feedback about workers' performance, conducting personnel evaluations, and teaching.

Supervision in the field of behavioral health has historical roots in the nineteenth-century Charity Organization Society, when a master exercised control over the tasks and activities of an apprentice. The staffs of the Charity Organization Society's agencies provided what was essentially oversight for the large numbers of people (then called visitors) who aided people in need.[11] Over time a variety of norms, related primarily to the content and implementation of supervision, have emerged, especially related to the goals, functions, tasks, and styles of supervision.[12]

Although literature on supervision has matured considerably over the years, relatively little addresses malpractice and liability risks. Many supervisors, I have found, do not fully understand the ways in which they may be held responsible for the actions or inactions of the staff that they supervise.

Although many malpractice claims allege mistreatment of a client by a practitioner, a number of claims also implicate the practitioner's supervisor. Such claims typically cite the legal doctrine of *respondeat superior*, which means "let the master respond." According to *respondeat superior*, supervisors are responsible for the actions or inactions of their supervisees that occur during the course of employment and over which the supervisor has some measure of control. As Gifis notes:

> This doctrine is invoked when there is a master-servant relationship between two parties. The "respondeat superior" doctrine stands for the proposition that when an employer, dubbed "master," is acting through the facility of an employee or agent, dubbed "servant," and tort liability is incurred during the course of this agency due to some fault of the agent, then the employer or master must accept the responsibility. Implicit in this is the common law notion that a duty rests upon every person to conduct his or her affairs so as not to injure another, whether or not in managing the affairs he or she employs agents or servants.[13]

Although the doctrine of *respondeat superior* may lead to liability on the part of the supervisor for the actions or inactions of supervisees, the supervisee also may be held liable. Thus, *respondeat superior* simply provides a client-plaintiff with an additional party to sue. If both supervisor and supervisee are negligent or responsible for the plaintiff's injuries, the finding may be one of joint liability. In these instances, the court may divide responsibility for damages between the parties on a percentage basis. For example, if client sued a counselor and clinical supervisor because the counselor allegedly released confidential information to a third party without the client's consent, and evidence shows that the supervisor had not addressed the issue of consent properly in supervision, the finding could be of joint liability with, say, the supervisor held 35 percent responsible and the counselor 65 percent responsible. If the court awarded the plaintiff $240,000 in damages, the supervisor would be responsible for $84,000 and the caseworker for $156,000.

Of course, the agency's insurance company might cover both sets of damages and related legal expenses, although this is not always the case. In some instances, the agency's insurer may want to distance itself from both the supervisor and the supervisee or the insurer may want to defend only the supervisor by arguing that the supervisee was grossly negligent (having acted outside the scope of her employment duties) and therefore may argue that the supervisor is not responsible for the supervisee's actions. Given that supervisor and supervisee can become adversaries in such proceedings, *all* employees should carry their own individual malpractice and liability coverage. As I noted in chapter 1, relying only on an agency's group policy can be risky.

In principle, supervisors can be found liable under the theory of vicarious liability, even if the supervisor adequately fulfilled his supervisory duties. Failing to provide proper supervision (e.g., by not meeting with a supervisee regularly, addressing relevant issues, or delegating supervision to another party) may be a separate cause of legal action.

Areas of potential liability for behavioral health supervisors are numerous, including failure to provide information necessary for supervisees to obtain clients' consent; to catch supervisees' errors in all phases of client contact, such as an inappropriate disclosure of confidential information; to protect third parties; to prevent defamation of character; to provide remote services properly; to detect or stop a negligent treatment plan or treatment carried beyond its effectiveness; to determine that a specialist is needed for treatment of a particular client; to meet regularly with the supervisee; to review and approve the supervisee's decisions; and to provide adequate coverage in the supervisee's absence. In addition, supervisors can be held liable if a supervisee is involved sexually with a client or exerts undue influence on the client or if the client's record is inadequate and the supervisor does not seek to improve it.

Behavioral health supervisors must also avoid inappropriate dual relationships with supervisees. In one case on which I consulted, a residential treatment program was sued by a former client who claimed she was mistreated by agency staffers. The client also filed licensing-board complaints against senior staffers. The complaints alleged that the program staffers disciplined the former client and terminated services unethically. During my consultation, I discovered that the agency director and clinical director had developed an intimate relationship. The former client alleged that this dual relationship, which the client learned about from an acquaintance who worked at the program, compromised the quality of the agency director's supervision of the clinical director. The dual relationship significantly weakened the defense attorney's ability to defend the case. In another case, the Louisiana licensing board disciplined a social work supervisor who engaged in physical and sexual contact with a supervisee.[14]

### SUPERVISION CASE LAW

One particularly complex liability lawsuit on which I consulted raises various issues about a behavioral health practitioner's responsibility—and liability—in the actions of a counselor she had hired to work in her group private practice. Some years earlier, the practitioner and her colleague had started a private practice. A number of their cases involved children with eating disorders. The partners decided to hire a former nurse to provide assessments and evaluations of children. The woman was also enrolled in a master's-level degree program in counseling at a local state university.

The group practice became involved in a case in which one member of the practice saw the child and the former nurse saw the mother. In time, the former nurse began providing counseling services to the mother, although this was before the former nurse had received her counseling degree and before she was licensed as a counselor. In her deposition, the former nurse acknowledged that at this time, she had a "therapist-patient" relationship with the mother.

The mother and her husband sued, alleging that the former nurse was negligent in that she failed to properly handle boundaries between herself and the mother and that the mother was seriously injured as a result. The suit alleged, for example, that the former nurse employed the mother in the former nurse's side business, which was completely unrelated to counseling. In addition, the suit claimed that the former nurse and the client-mother had taken care of each other's children during their professional relationship and on one occasion had traveled out of state together.

The mother claimed in her lawsuit that the former nurse had mishandled the relationship between professional and client and that this caused her great psychological damage, resulting in her hospitalization and lengthy psychiatric treatment. The husband claimed that his relationship with his wife was severely damaged as a result of the former nurse's actions.

Also named in the lawsuit were the practitioner who had started the practice and had hired the former nurse and the practitioner's business partner. The claim alleged that the practitioner was liable in several respects. First, the plaintiffs claimed that the practitioner knew or should have known that the former nurse was providing counseling services without the requisite formal training or credentials, in the form of a graduate degree and license. Second, the plaintiffs alleged that under the doctrine of *respondeat superior*, or vicarious liability, the practitioner's supervision of the case was not adequate. The plaintiffs argued that the practitioner was aware that the client-mother was suicidal and in need of competent skilled care by a trained professional and that the practitioner should have arranged for someone with considerably more expertise than the former nurse to care for the mother-client. A claim filed against the practitioner's partner made similar allegations. According to the lawsuit:

Defendant breached applicable psychological and counseling principles in the following nonexclusive particulars:

(A) Violating boundary standards between therapist and patient;

(B) Failing to utilize appropriate therapeutic and counseling skills;

(C) Failing to properly diagnose and treat plaintiff;

(D) Engaging in unethical duality violations;

(E) Interfering with plaintiff's relationship with her husband, children and other friends;

(F) Inducing, causing or allowing plaintiff to become exceedingly reliant and dependent upon defendant;

(G) Encouraging, soliciting and inducing plaintiff to participate in defendant's independent . . . business while defendant was plaintiff's therapist;

(H) Borrowing money from plaintiff to operate defendant's independent . . . business;

(I) Causing, inducing and allowing an excessively social and personal relationship to develop and continue while still serving as plaintiff's therapist;

(J) Otherwise breaching ethical and professional standards of conduct with regard to her relationship with plaintiff.

As a result of the aforestated medical negligence of defendant, plaintiff has suffered severe psychiatric disorders including severe depression, panic, mental anguish, inconvenience, humiliation, disruption of marital relationship, suicidal tendencies, rage, helplessness and a severe deterioration of her mental and emotional well being. . . .

Upon information and belief, plaintiff shows that [the practitioner and her partner] were defendant's direct supervisors charged with responsibility for supervising, directing and overseeing the quality of counseling provided by defendant to plaintiff.

Upon information and belief, plaintiff shows that [the practitioner and her partner] either knew or should have known of the aforestated medical negligence, conflict of interest and ethical breaches by defendant.

Plaintiffs further show that [the practitioner and her partner] breached their independent duty to plaintiffs by failing to properly supervise, guide, direct and oversee the counseling and therapy provided by defendant to plaintiff and further in failing to respond appropriately to the multiple acts of medical negligence on the part of defendant set forth hereinabove.

Plaintiffs further show that [the group private practice, as a corporate entity], as the employer of defendant, is directly responsible to plaintiffs for all damages resulting from the aforestated medical negligence of defendant under the doctrine of *respondeat superior* or, alternatively, under the doctrine of actual or apparent authority.

The practitioner's partner and the practitioner settled the case out of court. The practitioner was vulnerable because she knew that the former nurse had not completed her training to be a counselor and was not licensed. Moreover, the suit alleged that although the practitioner knew of the client's severe symptoms, including suicidal ideation, she did not become more closely involved in the client's treatment and made no referral.

Other cases also raise a variety of important issues related to supervisor liability. In some instances, clients have sued the practitioner, the supervisor, and the employing agency. In some of these cases, the court found only one defendant liable, although a judge or jury commonly establishes joint liability.

The court cases that I have described thus far have addressed three sets of circumstances. Their outcomes suggest that behavioral health supervisors may be legally responsible for actions of supervisees who ordinarily are directly under their supervision, actions of supervisees who ordinarily are not under the practitioner's direct supervision, and the delegation of responsibility by the behavioral health practitioner to a paraprofessional or unlicensed assistant.

For example, in the classic case *Rule v. Chessman*, a surgeon who taught medical residents at a hospital was sued when a resident he had supervised and advised during surgery left a sponge in a patient's abdomen. The Kansas Supreme Court found the supervisor and supervisee jointly liable in the errors of the supervisee, who was under the direct supervision of the surgeon.

In *Cohen v. State*, a widow sued after her husband committed suicide the same day that he was released from a voluntary inpatient stay in the psychiatric department of Downstate Medical Center in New York. Alan Cohen had been diagnosed as having paranoid schizophrenia and had been hospitalized for four months. The suit alleged that his medical care, particularly that related to the decision to release Cohen, was not properly supervised, despite the involvement of several physicians. At issue was "whether or not a qualified psychiatrist was actively supervising the care of the decedent."[15]

In some instances, the agency itself may be found vicariously liable. In a Michigan case, for example, a social worker entered into a sexual relationship with a client who was being treated for bipolar disorder and alcoholism. A court awarded damages against the social worker and the agency; the finding against the agency was based on the concept of *respondeat superior*.[16] In *Samuels v. Southern Baptist Hospital*, a Louisiana court found that a hospital was liable after a nursing assistant sexually assaulted a sixteen-year-old psychiatric patient.[17]

In Colorado, a court found that a drug and alcohol rehabilitation center was partially liable after a female client became involved in a sexual relationship with the center's assistant director within a month after the client left the program. The woman sued, alleging that the center and its executive director were aware that the assistant director had been involved in another similar relationship but did not reprimand him or take steps to prevent a recurrence. The award to the plaintiff included funds from the center and its executive director on the negligent supervision claim.[18]

An Alaska court made a similar finding in *Doe v. Samaritan Counseling Center*. According to the plaintiff, a pastoral counselor at a counseling center made sexual advances toward her during two counseling sessions and had sexual contact with her after treatment ended. The Alaska Supreme Court ruled that under the doctrine of *respondeat superior*, the agency may be held liable for the therapist's sexual contact with the client.[19]

An important issue in many of these cases is whether the practitioners' actions fall within the scope of their employment. If they do, the employer and/or supervisor may be found liable. In *Birkner v. Salt Lake County*, for example, the Utah Supreme Court ruled that a mental health facility could *not* be held liable in an employee's sexual misconduct with a client. The plaintiff claimed that a social worker had a sexual relationship with her during treatment. The trial court found that the social worker was negligent. However, the Utah Supreme Court reversed the trial court's ruling on the issue of *respondeat superior* and vicarious liability, concluding that the social worker's actions did not fall within the scope of his employment. The Utah Supreme Court noted that neither the plaintiff nor the social worker viewed their sexual contact as part of the therapeutic relationship, that these actions are not the type of activities that a therapist is hired to perform, and that the actions did not further the employer's interests.[20]

A practitioner who temporarily depends to some extent on assistance by another agency employee or colleague can also incur liability, even if the assistant is not ordinarily under the direct supervision of the practitioner. In *Minogue v. Rutland Hospital*, a nurse who was assisting an obstetrician was considered a "borrowed servant" of the obstetrician. The Vermont obstetrician was found liable after the nurse pressed on the rib of a woman during childbirth, thereby causing a fracture. Courts made similar determinations in *Yorsten v. Pennell* and *Norton v. Argonaut Insurance Co.* In *Yorsten*, a patient claimed a resident supervised by the surgeon had made an error. The resident had removed a nail from a worker's leg and prescribed penicillin. Earlier, however, a fourth-year medical student had taken the patient's history and noted that the patient was allergic to penicillin. The patient had a severe allergic reaction to the penicillin. A Pennsylvania court found that the surgeon was liable for damages.

In *Norton*, a nurse injected in a patient a medication that the physician had intended to be administered orally. The physician, however, did not note in the patient's chart that the medication was to be administered orally. As a result, the patient received about five times the intended dosage and died. A Louisiana court found the physician liable in the nurse's actions. These rulings have implications for behavioral health practitioners who provide services in an agency as outside consultants and who occasionally might rely on the assistance of an agency employee not ordinarily under their direct supervision.

However, in *Marvulli v. Elshire*, a California court found that the supervisor, a physician, was not liable in the actions of an assistant, an anesthesiologist. The court reasoned that because the anesthesiologist had been selected in the normal course of events from among available, qualified, reputable, and competent anesthesiologists, the surgeon had no control over his performance. (The case against the anesthesiologist was settled out of court.) The ruling in *Marvulli* suggests that careful and diligent screening of assistants by behavioral health practitioners may prevent findings of liability. If a practitioner takes on an assistant or supervisee without adequately checking that person's training, license status, and references, and the supervisee is incompetent, the supervisor may be liable under what is known as the tort of negligent entrustment.[21]

A number of cases involving supervisory liability concern the delegation of responsibility or specific duties to paraprofessionals and unlicensed supervisees. A number of popular behavioral health interventions—for example, biofeedback, group treatment, and peer support—may involve the use of unlicensed assistants. As a psychiatrist commented after he had been involved in four malpractice suits alleging negligence on the part of supervisees:

> I never saw three of these plaintiffs, nor did I talk to the families. In the other case I saw the plaintiff patient only for ½ hour. My associates and partners were not negligent in these cases, but the plaintiff thought so.
>
> The point is that as a senior partner I was considered responsible for the actions of my associates, even though I had never seen the patients. This is an important point to be remembered by every senior physician.
>
> The senior officer in every organization is legally responsible for every act of his juniors, both omission and commission.[22]

Laws are vague about how much responsibility professionals can legally delegate to unlicensed assistants. Clearly, however, these laws do not permit behavioral health professionals to delegate all their responsibilities to an unlicensed person. In addition, the assistant or supervisee must be competent to perform the delegated duties.[23]

Particular problems can arise when an unlicensed employee of a professional is functioning in a way that leads reasonable people to mistake the employee for a licensed professional. This practice is referred to as "lending out a license," and the professional may be held liable and subject to disciplinary action. Many states consider an assistant to a licensed professional to be legally an extension of the professional.[24]

Another major source of risk involves situations in which psychiatrists sign a form attesting to the supervision of a behavioral health professional, when such supervision never occurred; for example, in order to qualify for reimbursement from an insurance company. In a New Jersey case, a psychiatrist signed a social worker's written statement that a client was not dangerous, although the psychiatrist had never interviewed the client. The client subsequently killed his wife and children.[25] Of course, a supervisee could simply fail to share with the supervisor all the case-related details required for competent supervision. In principle, however, the supervisor may be at risk.

## SUPERVISION OF VOLUNTEERS

Behavioral health practitioners in agencies that serve people who are in crisis, experiencing homelessness, disabled, victims of domestic violence, or vulnerable in other ways often recruit, train, and supervise volunteers. Volunteers may provide emergency assistance, crisis intervention services, home-based care, and various other supportive services.

Practitioners who supervise volunteers face two kinds of risks. First, volunteers may be injured on the job and sue their supervisor and other agency administrators. This could occur, for example, if a volunteer is attacked by an unstable client. Second, agency clients may allege that they were harmed by volunteers; clients who claim they were harmed by volunteers may allege that volunteers' supervisors failed to provide proper training and supervision.

Volunteers are vitally important to the mission of many human service agencies. However, many volunteers, while well meaning, have not received formal education or training related to behavioral health and relevant ethical standards. Unlike formally educated behavioral health practitioners, a typical volunteer has not spent years studying standards and related nuances concerning the complexities of, for instance, client confidentiality and its exceptions, minor clients' right to privacy and to receive services without parental notification or consent, boundaries and dual relationships, conflicts of interest, and proper use of social media. In principle, volunteers may expose the agency to risk if they breach confidential information without proper authorization (perhaps to a police detective who appears at the agency and asks the volunteer whether a particular suspect has been there recently or to the volunteer's family members who happen to know a particular client), befriend a client inappropriately (in person or online), or accept gifts or social invitations from clients in a way that constitutes a boundary violation.

Volunteers enjoy individual protection under the federal Volunteer Protection Act of 1997 (42 USC §14503). Generally speaking, this act provides immunity from tort claims that might be filed against the volunteers of nonprofit organizations and governmental entities, where the claim alleges that the volunteer carelessly injured another party in the course of helping the agency. (A tort is a wrongful act or an infringement of a right, other than under contract, leading to legal liability.) It is important to emphasize that the Volunteer Protection Act does not provide immunity to the nonprofit agency itself; agency supervisors and administrators can be sued under the doctrine of *respondeat superior*.

Before federal legislation was passed, under the law of most states a volunteer who negligently hurt someone would be personally liable. Now the Volunteer Protection Act preempts all such laws, and the volunteer is immune from suit, which may increase the likelihood that people will offer to volunteer for nonprofit agencies. The law applies only to uncompensated volunteers who help nonprofits and governmental entities.

The act provides qualified immunity and protects the volunteer only against claims of negligence and not against claims of gross negligence, willful or criminal misconduct, reckless misconduct, or conscious and flagrant indifference to the rights or safety of the individual harmed by the volunteer. Nonprofit agencies can purchase insurance to protect themselves in the event of a lawsuit alleging that a volunteer was negligent and to compensate parties harmed by volunteers. More specifically, the act states the following:

> No volunteer of a nonprofit organization or governmental entity shall be liable for harm caused by an act or omission of the volunteer on behalf of the organization or entity if—

1) the volunteer was acting within the scope of the volunteer's responsibilities in the nonprofit organization or governmental entity at the time of the act or omission;

2) if appropriate or required, the volunteer was properly licensed, certified, or authorized by the appropriate authorities for the activities or practice in the State in which the harm occurred, where the activities were or practice was undertaken within the scope of the volunteer's responsibilities in the nonprofit organization or governmental entity;

3) the harm was not caused by willful or criminal misconduct, gross negligence, reckless misconduct, or a conscious, flagrant indifference to the rights or safety of the individual harmed by the volunteer; and

4) the harm was not caused by the volunteer operating a motor vehicle, vessel, aircraft, or other vehicle.

To protect clients and reduce risk, behavioral health practitioners and agency administrators should design and offer comprehensive training to volunteers regarding relevant standards of care and ethical guidelines pertaining specifically to the nonprofit agency's mission, clientele, and services. The training curriculum should ensure that volunteers have the knowledge and skills to carry out their duties and have mastered relevant ethics guidelines, especially related to client privacy and confidentiality, informed consent, boundaries and dual relationships, conflicts of interest, and use of social media and other technology. Practitioners and agency administrators should mandate and document volunteers' attendance.

## LIABILITY AND PROFESSIONAL EDUCATION

Special liability concerns arise with respect to internship supervision of students enrolled in behavioral health education programs. Traditionally, behavioral health faculty based at colleges and universities and the staffs of agencies in which students carry out their internships share some responsibility for student supervision. However, little consensus exists about which parties have primary liability if a student causes some form of harm during the internship. Although the doctrine of *respondeat superior* probably would apply in liability cases involving students, the extent to which the internship supervisor and the college or university would be regarded as supervisors is not always clear.

In a Pennsylvania case, surviving relatives of a man who committed suicide sued a mental health center. The client had admitted himself voluntarily to a psychiatric unit after he swallowed a large number of drugs from the family's medicine cabinet. The client was discharged to an outpatient clinic and was treated by a social work student who allegedly did not review the client's psychiatric history or arrange for any treatment by a psychiatrist. The client killed himself in his own home. The lawsuit alleged that a psychiatrist rather than a relatively untrained social work student should have treated the client. A jury awarded the family $317,500.[26]

Behavioral health educators and internship supervisors in education programs should be familiar with ethics standards that pertain to internship supervisors' relationships with students. First, supervisors should be careful not to supervise outside their area of expertise and should provide instruction and supervision on the basis of the most current information and knowledge available in their profession. Second, internship supervisors should evaluate students' performance in a manner that is fair and respectful, avoiding capricious grades, and should take reasonable steps to ensure that clients are routinely informed when services are being provided by students. Finally, practitioners who function as internship supervisors for students should not engage in any dual or multiple relationships with students in which there is a risk of exploitation or potential harm to the student. Internship supervisors are responsible for setting clear, appropriate, and culturally sensitive boundaries.

### PREVENTING SUPERVISORY LIABILITY

Case law on supervisory liability suggests that behavioral health practitioners can take various preventative measures. In particular, a good working relationship between the supervisor and supervisee is essential. If they collaborate closely and constructively, they can avoid many problems. As Cohen and DeBetz observe:

> Under ordinary circumstances, supervisory success stands or falls on the quality of the relationship between the participants. The most carefully prepared didactic presentation of material will fall on deaf ears if the learner is alienated from the teacher. Conversely, the least hint of theory or casual reference to the literature may suffice to motivate the inspired trainee to independently research and creatively expand on his teacher's ideas. Therefore the *responsive mutuality*, the sensitivity and respect shared by the supervisor and the supervised, is perhaps the most potent tool in the supervisory repertoire.[27]

Supervisors must give special attention to the frequency and scheduling of supervision. Setting up a pro forma supervision session once a week or once a month, without sufficient structure or rigor, risks legal liability.

Supervisors should not assume that such routinely scheduled sessions comprise adequate supervision in all cases, although such supervision may suffice for nearly all supervisees. Rather, supervisors must anticipate the possibility of cases with extenuating circumstances that may require more frequent and lengthier supervision than is customary. Further, some supervisees may need more supervision time and closer monitoring according to their experience and skill level. In short, provisions need to be made for extraordinary supervision.

Special mention should be made of behavioral health practitioners in solo private practice because they face a special challenge with respect to supervision. Solo private practitioners do not always have easy access to regular, sustained supervision. Some solo private practitioners contract for supervision with a respected colleague or mentor and/or participate in peer supervision or peer consultation groups. Once again, although neither case law nor statute spells out the standard of care with regard to these forms of supervision and consultation, established norms demand some form of supervision or consultation, whether it is peer or otherwise, for solo practitioners. A private practitioner who is sued for negligence and found to be completely without any form of supervision or consultation may be vulnerable. The form of supervision also is important. If a supervisor relies only on brief cursory conversations with a supervisee, the supervisor may be at risk in failing to obtain detailed information from a supervisee. Relying on sparse case summaries or case record material, for example, may not be sufficient, even if this is supplemented by a brief verbal report.

One function of supervision is to provide the supervisor with information on which to base personnel or performance evaluations. The process of personnel or performance evaluation also raises several risk management and liability issues. Staff members who receive negative evaluations— and who are disciplined, demoted, released, or simply not promoted as a result—may sue the supervisor and agency, challenging the employment action, alleging discrimination, defamation of character, and so on. This is another reason for the supervisor to carefully document the nature of all supervision provided and the information upon which the supervisor based the personnel evaluation.

In addition, supervisors must understand the extent of supervisees' right of access to their personnel records. Most behavioral health settings now recognize staff members' right to review the contents of their personnel files. What this means is supervisors should be careful about the content, wording, and language used in performance evaluations (indeed, supervisors should be careful even if for some reason staff members do *not* have access to their evaluations). Presumably, all employees are concerned about how their work is evaluated, and they often view performance evaluations with hypersensitivity. Supervisors must be careful to avoid language and terminology that are defamatory, derisive, or otherwise inappropriate.

Although exhortations about preventative measures related to supervision of staff are appropriate, given the possibility of liability suits against behavioral health supervisors, it is important to recognize that many practitioners already are so overwhelmed with responsibility that adding the additional burden of closer and more frequent supervision may be difficult. This goes for the supervisor as well as the supervisee. Therefore, agency administrators must acknowledge the importance of enhanced supervision and provide the necessary resources and staff assistance to make it feasible.

Behavioral health agencies and staffers with supervisory responsibility should also conduct training sessions with line staff. These sessions should include a discussion and review of issues related to professional ethics and liability, along with a review of relevant federal, state, and local statutes and regulations. In particular, training should cover the concepts of professional liability and malpractice, licensing-board standards, clients' right to confidentiality and the prevention of inappropriate disclosure, the limits of clients' right to confidentiality, the concept of privileged communication, improper treatment, high-risk interventions, the impaired practitioner, defamation of character, consultation with and referral to specialists, documentation, and fraud and deception. Training also should cover such topics as emergency assistance and suicide prevention, proper supervision of clients in residential and nonresidential settings, informed-consent procedures, guidelines for terminating intervention, boundaries and dual relationships, interaction with clients who are acting out, and practitioners' use of digital and online technology. Agency administrators and supervisors need to be able to document that they provided staff with this training if someone files suit alleging negligence on the part of the agency as a result of the actions of a staff member.

Supervisors should consider developing a written understanding that clarifies the nature of supervision and the relationship between the supervisor and supervisee, possibly in the form of a supervision agreement.[28] Key elements include the following:

- Supervisory context: where supervision will be conducted, by whom, with what frequency, using what methods, for what duration
- Which clinical cases will be reviewed (whether all cases or a sample)
- Learning plan: goals and objectives of supervision
- Format and schedule: type of supervision (e.g., face-to-face supervision, telephone or remote supervision; video recording, audio recording, or

written records; individual or group supervision) and length, frequency, and duration of supervision

- Accountability: requirements related to the use of supervision for personnel evaluation, licensure, third-party payment
- Issues and questions that supervisees should raise during supervision, especially related to high-risk circumstances and ethical challenges
- Documentation and recording: format for documentation by the supervisor (e.g., date of contact, progress toward learning goals, specific recommendations) and supervisee (e.g., date of contact, questions and issues brought to the supervisor's attention, the supervisor's recommendations, follow-up plans); clarification of details to be documented in clients' record (e.g., the client's knowledge that supervision is taking place, the nature of information shared with the supervisor, verification that the client has the name, address, and contact information of the supervisor or other responsible contact person)
- Conflict resolution: procedures for resolving disagreements about issues addressed in supervision
- Compensation: details concerning the ways in which the supervisor will be compensated for her services, if warranted
- Client notification: plans for notifying clients about the nature and purposes of supervision obtained by the clients' clinician
- Duration and termination: details concerning the time frame for the supervision agreement and the process for termination of supervision

In summary, behavioral health practitioners should be aware of a number of specific liability and licensing-board risks related to supervision:

- Failure to provide information necessary for the supervisees to obtain an informed consent or to provide an adequate disclosure to a client
- Failure to catch an error
- Negligent or incorrect misdiagnosis that a client poses a danger to others or himself or has a serious mental illness
- A treatment plan that is negligent or treatment carried out beyond its effectiveness, and the supervisor is responsible for the error or does not detect it
- Failure to determine that a new worker needs to be assigned, treatment terminated, or specialists consulted
- Workers who are involved socially or sexually with clients or exert undue influence on the client

- A client's record that does not contain adequate information about the care that the client has received, and the supervisor does not review the record and require its improvement
- Supervision that is negligent because the supervisor does not meet regularly with the supervisee, review the presented material, or elicit the information necessary to adequately supervise the case
- Workers who are negligent in caring for clients—for example, who did not adequately supervise a suicidal client, who released a dangerous client prematurely, or who failed to provide coverage when unavailable—and supervisors who failed to review and approve these decisions
- Failure to assess the competence of supervisees as to what clienteles and types of cases they can handle
- Supervision of so many supervisees that competent supervision is impossible
- Failure to summarize, record, or otherwise document what occurs in supervision
- Involvement in a dual relationship with a supervisee
- Failure to give detailed written and verbal evaluations to supervisees
- Failure to review supervisees' records for accuracy and completeness
- Signing of insurance or other forms for cases that supervisors have not supervised or otherwise documenting supervision that did not occur
- Failure to provide consistent, regularly scheduled supervision to supervisees
- Use of defamatory or otherwise inappropriate language in performance evaluations of supervisees
- Failure to maintain comprehensive malpractice coverage associated with one's supervisory role

Clearly, supervision is essential to effective behavioral health services. Since the earliest days of the field of behavioral health, professionals have recognized that competent supervision is necessary in order to transmit the values and methods of the behavioral health professions and to monitor the performance of supervisees. No competent professional questions the appropriateness of at least some form of supervision.

Risks related to behavioral health supervision continue to emerge. Behavioral health practitioners must enhance their understanding of liability issues and seek clarification of ambiguous circumstances that arise in supervision. In the end, the best interests of clients depend on the success of these efforts.

# CHAPTER 6

# Consultation, Referral, Documentation, and Records

Behavioral health practitioners often consult with colleagues about their work with clients. Colleagues can provide valuable insights and suggestions, especially with respect to complex and challenging clinical and ethical circumstances.

Practitioners should understand the differences between supervision and consultation. Supervision typically entails a chain of command, such that the supervisor has some responsibility over the supervisee and the supervisee is accountable to the supervisor. Supervisees are often expected to accept a supervisor's advice, although consultees are not necessarily expected to accept a consultant's advice. Consultation is often much more collegial in nature.

Consultation and supervision are differentiated in four ways:

- Consultation involves a relationship voluntarily entered into by both parties wherein the consultant offers her best advice, which the consultee can either accept or reject.
- Although adherence to ethical standards characterizes the consultation relationship, no legal statutes regulate the relationship.
- The authority of the consultant is her expertise; legal responsibility for the clinical (or other) service remains with the consultee.
- Because of the limitations in authority and the voluntary nature of the consultation relationship, consultation does not meet the requirements of many credentialing bodies or insurance companies.[1]

Clearly, behavioral health practitioners are wrong to attempt to provide forms of treatment and intervention outside their range of skill. Although practitioners typically receive broad-based education and are rather versatile, for a practitioner to claim specialized skill in an area for which she has little knowledge and training would be unethical. If a client presents a particular problem that is beyond the practitioner's skill range, she should seek consultation or make a referral. Failure to do so risks liability. In some instances, it is appropriate for the practitioner to continue working with the client, with consultation necessary for only some specific aspect of the case. In other instances, however, it may not be appropriate for the practitioner to continue handling the case at all; instead, the practitioner should refer the client to a colleague who has the specialized education and knowledge required for competent intervention.

### CONSULTATION IN THE FIELD OF BEHAVIORAL HEALTH

The nature of consultation in the field of behavioral health has changed over time.[2] Consultation was not formally recognized as an important component in behavioral health professions until after World War II. Not until recent years, however, have the professions had substantial literature on consultation.

Kadushin provides a classic definition of *consultation*:

Consultation is regarded as an interactional helping process—a series of sequential steps taken to achieve some objective through an interpersonal relationship. One participant in the transaction has greater expertise, greater knowledge, greater skill in the performance of some particular specialized function, and this person is designated *consultant*. The *consultee*, generally a professional, has encountered a problem in relation to his job which requires the knowledge, skill, and expertise of the consultant for its solution or amelioration. Consultation is thus distinguished from other interpersonal interactional processes involving the giving and taking of help, such as casework, counseling, psychotherapy, by virtue of the fact that its problem-solving focus is related to some difficulties encountered in performing job-related functions and by virtue of the fact that the identity of the consultee is generally restricted to someone engaged in implementing professional roles.[3]

Consultation in the field of behavioral health can produce two major liability risks. The first involves situations in which a practitioner should seek consultation but fails to and a client is harmed as a result. The argument in such cases is that the practitioner breached the standard of care by failing to seek appropriate consultation, an act of omission or nonfeasance.

> Maryann B. was a counselor at the Woodholme Family Service Agency. She specialized in couples and marriage counseling. Maryann B. began working with a young married couple who were having some difficulty managing the behavior of their four-year-old son. Maryann B. spent considerable time helping the couple to use simple behavioral techniques, such as positive reinforcement and extinction, to manage their son's behavior. In addition, Maryann B. helped the couple explore several sources of tension and conflict in their marriage.
>
> After several months in treatment, the husband in the couple disclosed that about eight years earlier he had been diagnosed as having schizophrenia, including symptoms of paranoia. He told Maryann B. that he feared that some of his symptoms were reappearing. Maryann B. had neither experience with nor training for treatment of schizophrenia.
>
> Maryann B. continued working with the couple, although she did not seek consultation related to management of schizophrenia. She believed that she had sufficient knowledge and skill to be able to work with her client, although he began complaining more and more about what he believed to be symptoms of the disorder.
>
> About ten weeks after his first complaints about the psychotic symptoms, the husband stabbed his wife. The couple had gotten into a heated argument about disciplining their son. According to the wife, during the stabbing the husband spoke about how government agents were going to kidnap the family.
>
> The wife sued the counselor, claiming that she failed to seek appropriate consultation related to the treatment of schizophrenia. The lawsuit claimed that had the counselor sought proper consultation, the husband would not have assaulted his wife.

Case law highlights the liability risks when a professional does not refer a client to a specialist for consultation. A Texas man claimed that his wife's death was the result of a lack of referral for consultation. The twenty-four-year-old woman's regular physician was treating her for depression. The physician prescribed medication for several months without referring her to a psychiatrist or psychologist for consultation and the possibility of treatment.

After the depressive symptoms worsened, the physician referred the woman to a psychiatrist and psychologist in the same clinic. The woman committed suicide after two visits to the clinic psychiatrist. The woman's husband alleged that the physician who did not refer his wife to a psychiatrist for timely consultation was negligent. The court awarded the woman's family $460,000.[4]

Behavioral health practitioners can also incur liability risks when they fail to consult an organization for advice. This may occur when, for instance, a practitioner does not consult with or report to the local public child protection agency in a case in which abuse or neglect is suspected. As I noted in chapter 3, practitioners and other mandated reporters do not report suspected abuse and neglect in a distressingly large percentage of cases. Often, the mandated reporters are confident that they can handle the situation without the public agency's involvement, do not have confidence in the protection agency staff, and/or do not want to jeopardize their therapeutic relationship with their clients. The legal risk, however, is that the mandated reporter could be held liable in failing to consult with a specialist—the protection agency (in addition to being subjected to whatever statutory criminal or civil penalties may exist)—along with otherwise failing to adhere to standards of care regarding mandated reporting. In one prominent case, a Connecticut psychologist was arrested on a charge of failing to disclose information about alleged abuse or neglect to state authorities as required by law.[5]

Behavioral health practitioners should select their consultants carefully to ensure that the experts have the requisite education, training, license, knowledge, and expertise to be truly helpful. This is a form of due diligence. Practitioners should not rely on consultants who do not have the credentials and demonstrated expertise pertaining to the issue at hand. Practitioners should especially seek consultation when their work with a particular client seems to be stalled or going nowhere. Clients who are frustrated with the progress, or lack of progress, that they are making in treatment may be particularly prone to sue. As Schutz notes:

> When therapy reaches a prolonged impasse, the therapist ought to consider consulting another therapist and possibly transferring the patient. Apart

from the clinical and ethical considerations, his failure to seek another opinion might have legal ramifications in the establishment of proximate cause in the event of a suit. While therapists are not guarantors of cure or improvement, extensive treatment without results could legally be considered to have injured the patient; in specific, the injury would be the loss of money and time, and the preclusion of other treatments that might have been more successful. To justify a prolonged holding action at a plateau, the therapist would have to show that this was maintaining a condition against a significant and likely deterioration. Consultation at this point would establish the reasonableness of one's approach and help establish criteria for when to terminate one's efforts to treat a patient.[6]

Behavioral health practitioners need to be particularly alert to the need for medical consultation, when appropriate. Consider the case of a counselor who was working with a client who claimed to have chronic low self-esteem. For months, the counselor and client focused on family-of-origin issues and issues related to the client's intimate relationships as an adult. On occasion, the client would also complain that she was having a hard time remembering things, such as friends' and colleagues' names, appointments she had made, and so on. Periodically, the client would complain of incapacitating headaches.

Several months after the client began complaining of headaches, she blacked out while shopping at a local mall. The client was rushed to the hospital, where she was diagnosed with a brain tumor. Surgery removed the tumor, but the client suffered some moderate brain damage.

Shortly after surgery, one of the client's doctors told her that had she been seen by a physician one or two months earlier, there was a good chance they could have treated the tumor without surgery. Once the client completely recovered from her surgery, she was angry that the counselor had not referred her to a physician for a medical exam. The client shared her frustration with her sister, who suggested the client talk to an attorney about a negligence suit.

Behavioral health practitioners cannot be expected to be knowledgeable about organic and other medical problems that clients may have. They are, however, obligated to be alert to the need for medical consultation. As Meyer, Landis, and Hays observe in their discussion of liability risks faced by psychologists, "The standard has generally been that others in the same discipline would seek the help of a specialist in the same circumstances."[7] In addition, these authors state:

> Failure to refer is a type of negligence if it leads to some injury to the client. For example, a client consulting a psychologist who describes a recent blow to the head followed by recurrent headaches, personality changes, and difficulty with memory and concentration, may have sustained a neurologic injury. Alternatively he may be displaying a conversion syndrome. The psychologist would be expected to ascertain whether a neurologist or other physician was involved in the case, and either consult with that person or make an appropriate referral to help in the diagnostic process. If the psychologist proceeded on the assumption that no organic damage was present, he could be held liable for negligently failing to refer the patient to a practitioner capable of treating his problem.[8]

The second liability risk related to consultation has to do with the consultation itself. In these cases, typically the claim is that the consultation that a behavioral health practitioner provided was somehow flawed or negligent and that the consultation or advice stemming from it caused some injury. This may occur, for example, if consultants provide training, advice, or guidance on a topic outside their area of expertise.

> Barbara C. was a psychotherapist in private practice. Her practice was devoted primarily to the treatment of eating disorders.
>
> One afternoon, Barbara C. received a telephone call from a social worker employed at a small local private school. Occasionally, the school relied on Barbara C.'s advice concerning management of students' complex behavioral health challenges. The social worker told Barbara C. that a student, a fourteen-year-old girl, manifested symptoms of an eating disorder. The student had been losing weight, not eating at lunchtime, exercising excessively, and had been found in the lavatory inducing her own vomiting. The school social worker, who did not have much experience treating eating disorders, asked Barbara C. to consult on the case. Barbara C. agreed and met with the social worker and two of the student's teachers. For the next two months, the school social worker and Barbara C. met weekly to discuss the case and to review the school social worker's intervention.
>
> Over time, it became clear that the student was also cutting her arms, albeit superficially, it appeared. Barbara C., in her role as clinical consultant,

advised the school social worker to ignore the cutting so as not to reinforce it. The cutting, however, got worse and worse. About three weeks after the cutting became more serious, the student slashed her wrists in an apparent suicide attempt.

The student's parents sued the school, the school's social worker, and the clinical consultant, claiming that they failed to provide proper treatment to their daughter. In particular, the plaintiffs argued that the consultant provided advice outside her area of expertise. Although the plaintiffs acknowledged that the consultant had considerable expertise related to eating disorders, an area in which the consultant had received extensive training, they challenged her ability to give advice related to self-mutilation, an area in which the consultant had received no formal training.

When behavioral health practitioners seek consultation, they should be sure to protect clients' confidential information. Practitioners should not assume that consultants should have access to client-related confidential information. Ideally, practitioners should obtain clients' informed consent before disclosing confidential information to consultants. In addition, practitioners should limit their disclosure of confidential information as much as possible, disclosing the least amount of information necessary to achieve the purposes of the consultation.

Not all liability risks related to consultation involve clinical or case consultation. Practitioners can also encounter problems when they provide consultation to agencies and programs. For example, behavioral health practitioners who have little skill related to program evaluations should not present themselves as experts. A program that relies on the practitioner's claim of skill in this area may be injured if the practitioner conducts a poorly designed study or evaluation, which may ultimately hurt the program's chances for funding. Clearly, practitioners should provide consultation only with respect to those subjects and skill areas for which they can demonstrate competence and expertise.

### REFERRAL IN THE FIELD OF BEHAVIORAL HEALTH

In some cases, behavioral health practitioners find that they do not have sufficient expertise to continue working with a particular client. While it makes sense in some instances for a practitioner to continue working with a client while seeking consultation on a particular aspect of the client's treatment (e.g., a counselor who is trained to intervene in a client's depression but needs consultation regarding the client's eating disorder), in other instances practitioners may need to consider referring the entire case to a professional colleague. Practitioners should refer clients to other professionals when the other professionals' specialized knowledge or expertise is needed to serve clients fully or when practitioners believe that they are not being effective or making reasonable progress with clients and that additional service is required.

In such cases, behavioral health practitioners have an obligation to exercise due care in the process that they use to refer clients to colleagues. Practitioners should not make referrals to others indiscriminately or where there is a conflict of interest (e.g., when practitioners refer clients to close friends or relatives for reasons other than the friends' or relatives' expertise, such as to help the friends or relatives build a private practice). Instead, practitioners should be diligent in their efforts to refer clients to colleagues with solid reputations, who have proper credentials, and in whom they have confidence. Otherwise, a practitioner may risk a claim of negligent referral; that is, a referral that was not made using standard procedures. A news article about a mental health professional in Providence, Rhode Island, illustrates this risk:

> A Providence psychiatrist has been disciplined for referring a patient to an unqualified counselor.
>
> The state Board of Medical Licensure and Discipline last month imposed, but stayed, a three-month suspension on Dr. Lee H. Goldstein, an osteopathic physician [and psychiatrist] at 15 Benefit St. The board also fined him $1,500.
>
> Dr. Milton W. Hamolsky, the board's administrator, said that a stayed suspension is like probation. The board, he said, believed that Goldstein's infraction was not serious enough to prohibit him from practicing, but it did warrant a more rigorous penalty than a reprimand.
>
> According to the disciplinary board, a patient saw Goldstein for weekly psychotherapy sessions for 15 months but terminated therapy and complained to the board when Goldstein referred her to an unlicensed counselor. The board considers it unprofessional conduct for a psychiatrist to refer a patient to someone who is not licensed or certified to provide mental health care.

Hamolsky said there was no evidence that Goldstein had a pattern of making inappropriate referrals.[9]

A Utah case dealt with similar issues related to referral to an unqualified service provider. The defendant was a counselor who had worked with a woman and her sons (the plaintiffs). During the counseling, the defendant referred the plaintiffs to a colleague for additional counseling. The colleague was described as the defendant's associate. The associate, however, did not have specialized training that would qualify him as a counselor. The plaintiffs claimed that the associate's counseling was incompetent, that it caused confusion, bewilderment, anger, and frustration, and that his services were worthless and counterproductive. The defendant settled the suit for an undisclosed sum.[10]

In an Arizona case, a husband and wife claimed that a psychologist was negligent in referring them to a master's-level therapist. The therapist began by seeing the couple together and then provided clinical services to them individually. The therapist eventually entered into a personal relationship with the wife. The couple sued, claiming that when the wife sought to end her relationship with the therapist, the therapist entered her home without permission while the husband was away and verbally assaulted her while she was in the shower. Although the referring psychologist denied liability, a confidential settlement was reached.[11]

R. Cohen also comments on the legal ramifications that can arise from a negligent referral: "If a referral is indicated, the professional has a duty to select an appropriate professional or institution for the patient. Barring any extraordinary circumstances, the professional making the referral will not incur any liability for the acts of the person or institution that he refers the patient to, provided that the person or institution is duly licensed and equipped to meet the patient's needs."[12]

Behavioral health practitioners who refer clients to another professional should not expect to be compensated merely for the referral. This would constitute a conflict of interest.

Practitioners can also be found liable for *failing* to refer clients to specialists when needed (an example of an act of omission, or nonfeasance). In a Florida case, the plaintiffs alleged that a man's health-care provider was negligent in failing to refer him to a psychiatrist and recommend hospitalization—the man committed suicide.[13]

## DOCUMENTATION AND RECORDS

Behavioral health practitioners who consult with other professionals about a client or refer a client to another professional must provide careful documentation of the consultation/referral in the case record. I have been involved in a number of cases over the years in which practitioners were conscientious about obtaining consultation and making referrals. Some practitioners have encountered problems, however, because they failed to document the consultation and referrals in the client's or in an administrative record. When clients alleged that these practitioners neglected to obtain proper consultation or make an appropriate referral, the practitioners were unable to produce evidence or sufficient documentation. Lawyers sometimes offer the axioms, "If it isn't recorded, it didn't happen," and "Work not written is work not done." This is not true literally, of course, but practitioners who do not document carefully can face an uphill climb when defending against allegations.

In fact in one case (*Whitree v. State*), a court determined that an inadequate record was negligent in itself because such a record does not provide guidance for adequate care in the absence of the professional and contributes nothing useful to the client's treatment history, which could affect a client's subsequent care. Victor Whitree, forty-six, was arrested in New York City on a charge of stabbing another man. Whitree was placed on probation and subsequently ordered to Bellevue Hospital for a psychiatric examination. He was then placed in maximum-security confinement for more than four years and kept in a locked cell except for exercise and visits to the bathroom. Whitree eventually sued the state for wrongful confinement and for injuries he sustained as a result of his hospitalization and as a result of various attacks and beatings by patients and guards.

In addition to commenting on the negligence that it determined was involved in Whitree's care, the court found that "the hospital record . . . maintained by the State for claimant was about as inadequate a record as [the judge had] ever examined" and that the "record did not conform to the standards in the community . . . the inadequacies in this record militated against proper and competent psychiatric and ordinary medical care." Further, the lower court concluded, "To the extent that a hospital record develops information for subsequent treatment, it contributed to the inadequate treatment this claimant received." Whitree was awarded $300,000 in damages for the negligence and false imprisonment.[14]

Behavioral health practitioners who fail to document properly expose themselves to considerable risk. For example, a Texas licensing board disciplined several social workers for "failure to keep accurate records."[15] An Arkansas board disciplined a practitioner for "failing to keep proper records and documentation of services."[16] A Louisiana licensing board disciplined a hospice social worker who documented services to clients that she never provided.[17]

Documentation is one of those skills that behavioral health practitioners should learn early in their careers. Proficient documentation enhances the quality of services provided to clients. Records identify, describe, and assess clients' situations; define the purpose of service; document service goals, plans, activities, and progress; and evaluate the effect of service.[18] Recording also demonstrates the practitioner's thoughtful attention to detail. While proofreading documents may seem mundane, failure to do so can have devastating consequences. For example, in a case where I served as an expert witness, a practitioner conducted an initial assessment of a mother who lost custody of her child because of the mother's mental health and substance use challenges and wrote in the record, "Based on this assessment, it is highly unlikely that this mother will be able to parent this child." I address later in the chapter whether this was a prudent statement, but my point here is that this statement was auto-populated into every subsequent entry in the voluminous chart. Months later, when the provider subsequently concluded that the mother should regain custody, the record still contained the quoted language. The failure to accurately edit the chart led to a verdict of $45 million.

In addition, recording enhances continuity of care. Carefully written notes help practitioners recall relevant detail during service delivery and can facilitate coordination of services and supervision among staff members within an agency. Recording also helps to ensure quality care if a client's primary worker becomes unavailable because of sickness, vacation, departure from the agency, or death.

Of course, competent recording is not only good practice. Recording also provides some measure of protection against negligence claims and licensing-board complaints. As Kagle states with specific regard to social workers, "By keeping accurate, relevant, and timely records, social workers do more than just describe, explain, and support the services they provide. They also discharge their ethical and legal responsibility to be accountable.

This accountability extends beyond the individual agency (and the organizations that fund and accredit it) to the profession as a whole, the community, and, ultimately, the client."[19]

Discussions of documentation in the field of behavioral health are no longer limited to clinicians who need to record their interactions with clients to facilitate the delivery of services. Practitioners have come to recognize the usefulness of documentation for risk management purposes in supervision, management, and administration. Documentation in behavioral health—whether it concerns clinical, supervisory, management, or administrative duties—now serves several primary functions: (1) assessment and planning; (2) service delivery; (3) continuity and coordination of services; (4) supervision; (5) service evaluation; and (6) accountability to clients, insurers, agencies, other providers, courts, and utilization review bodies.

### Assessment and Planning

In clinical contexts, clear and comprehensive documentation of all case-related facts and circumstances is essential. Careful and thoughtful information collection ensures that practitioners have an adequate foundation for their clinical reasoning and intervention plans. In addition, the data provide a reliable source of measuring performance and outcomes. Incomplete records may lead to inadequate planning and intervention, critical judgment errors, and poor outcomes for clients.

### Service Delivery

Comprehensive records are necessary for competent delivery of behavioral health services. Thorough documentation provides a solid foundation for practitioners' efforts to design and deliver high-quality services, whether they involve clinical intervention, supervision, or agency administrators' management and evaluation of personnel and programs.

### Continuity and Coordination of Services

Similarly, documentation facilitates professional and interdisciplinary collaboration and coordination of services. For example, practitioners employed in health care, school, and correctional settings often need to share their observations and coordinate services with professionals in other disciplines, such as doctors, nurses, counselors, teachers, and administrators. In clinical settings, documentation ensures that staff members have up-to-date information about clients' needs. Administrative records facilitate coordination among supervisors, managers, and administrators in programs and agencies.

### Supervision

As discussed in chapter 5, under the legal doctrines of vicarious liability and *respondeat superior* ("let the master respond"), supervisors, as well as administrators and agencies, can be held liable for the errors and omissions of their staff if there is evidence of flawed supervision. Thus, it behooves behavioral health supervisors to carefully document the supervision they provide. Further, supervisees should be certain to document supervision they have received.

### Service Evaluation

In addition to facilitating clinical evaluation in individual cases (so-called single-case or $N = 1$ designs), records also provide essential data for broader program evaluations. Measured outcomes and program effectiveness are central to high-quality behavioral health services. At their core lie data and information recorded throughout the case management process. Practitioners must strive to continually strengthen their documentation and record-keeping practices to maintain the integrity of their programs. Program evaluation data can be helpful in the event a behavioral health agency is sued for allegedly failing to provide quality care.

### Accountability

Client requests, insurance contracts, interagency collaboration, litigation, licensing board and ethics committee oversight, and utilization review bodies periodically require practitioners to include fine-grained details about the services they provide, the meetings they attend, the supervision they offer, and the consultation they obtain. These new demands clearly illustrate the importance of documentation for accountability purposes.

## RISK MANAGEMENT STANDARDS AND GUIDELINES

Over time, behavioral health practitioners have developed elaborate risk management standards related to documentation designed to enhance the delivery of services to clients and protect practitioners in case they have to defend themselves against ethics complaints or lawsuits that allege professional negligence. This section provides a summary of these guidelines on the basis of extant literature, prominent court decisions, and my experience as an expert witness in many licensing-board cases and court cases throughout the United States.

Risk management guidelines related to documentation and case recording can be placed into conceptually distinct categories: (1) the content of documentation, (2) language and terminology, (3) credibility, and (4) access to records and documents.

### Content of Documentation

Too much content, too little content, or the wrong content can harm clients and expose behavioral health practitioners to considerable risk of liability. The days when practitioners could proclaim "I was taught not to keep detailed notes to avoid a problematic paper trail" are long gone. As Berner, a lawyer and social worker, observes with respect to documentation in clinical settings:

> Because the practice of clinical record-keeping is of such long standing, and because courts in particular understand that the reason for clinical documentation is, in fact, not for the convenience of attorneys and judges, but to further the goal of good patient care, "everyone" expects that clinicians will keep records. "Everyone" means your patients, your professional society's ethics board, your professional discipline's licensing board, the newspapers, the general public, and perhaps most relevant for us . . . the courts. Courts know what everyone else knows, and courts expect clinicians to keep records documenting their work.[20]

To ensure appropriate content in documentation, practitioners should consider several issues. A primary function of documentation is to serve and protect all parties. The content, however, must tread a careful line, striking a balance between too much and too little information. In a crisis situation, practitioners need to observe some precautions when recording case information. Furthermore, they should follow specific guidelines for documenting services to families and couples and the extent to which individual members may be privy to that information.

*Serve and protect.* Practitioners' first rule of thumb when documenting cases should be to include sufficient detail to facilitate the delivery of services and protect themselves in the event of an ethics complaint or lawsuit. In clinical settings, such details involve social histories, assessments, and treatment plans; informed-consent procedures (including consent related to remote service delivery); information provided to clients concerning confidentiality and exceptions; information given to clients regarding practitioners' social media policies (including information about use of online social networking sites, text messages, e-mail, and online search engines to locate information about clients); contacts with clients (type, date, and time); contacts with third parties; consultation with other professionals; decisions made and services provided; critical incidents; instructions, recommendations, advice, and referrals to specialists; failed and canceled appointments; previous or current psychological, psychiatric, and medical evaluations; information concerning fees, charges, and payments; termination of services; final assessment; and other relevant documents.

Behavioral health supervisors should document the date, time, and content of supervision sessions, including specific recommendations, critical incidents, and consultations. As noted earlier, they should document supervision agreements they have with supervisees, including supervisees' responsibility to share ethics-related concerns. Behavioral health managers and administrators should document key discussions, consultations, and meetings that address ethical and legal issues. For example, they should note the steps taken to determine whether to disclose confidential information without a client's consent to protect a third party from harm, to manage complex boundary issues, to address an employee's impairment or unethical conduct, or to develop conflict-of-interest guidelines for agency personnel. David Gould, a veteran malpractice attorney who has defended several mental health practitioners, writes:

> These types of cases, like almost all medical negligence cases, are won or lost by what is contained, or not contained, in the medical record. It has been my experience that mental health notes, particularly in the outpatient setting,

are, more often than not, deficient. . . . Inadequate notes leave the clinician at the mercy of a plaintiff's attorney, especially when he is asked years later to recall an event that is poorly documented, if at all.[21]

*Strike a balance.* Documenting too much or too little can be perilous. For example, in clinical settings too little detail about a client's suicidal ideation may compromise the quality of services provided by an on-call colleague who reviews incomplete or vague entries in the client's chart. Furthermore, practitioners who do not include sufficient detail concerning the steps they took to address a client's crisis are likely to have difficulty defending their actions in the event of an ethics complaint or negligence lawsuit.

In contrast, too much detail—a client's fantasies or involvement in a crime committed many years earlier, for instance—could be used against the client if that client's spouse subpoenas the record as part of a child custody dispute. Admittedly, distinguishing between too much and too little detail can be difficult. It requires experience and reasoned decision-making. Practitioners should strive for a reasonable balance, considering what information is clinically essential to properly assess clients' needs; plan, coordinate, deliver, supervise, and evaluate services; and be accountable to clients, insurers, agencies, other providers, courts, and utilization review bodies.

*Avoid overdocumentation in a crisis.* Practitioners also need to strive for balance during crises, avoiding the temptation to overdocument. Including excessive detail in a case record in the context of a crisis can be a red flag when records are reviewed during an ethics hearing or litigation. A practitioner's claim that she handled the matter in a manner that is consistent with prevailing standards in the profession may be challenged in the face of inordinate detail in the case record. Such detail may in fact suggest that the case was handled in an extraordinary or unusual way. As Berner asserts, it is far more important in a clinical crisis to "write smarter, not longer. . . . Writing smarter means being succinct."[22]

*Use caution with personal notes.* Clinical practitioners, supervisors, managers, and administrators sometimes maintain separate personal (or "shadow") notes to keep track of details that do not belong in an official agency record. Practitioners sometimes assume—mistakenly—that such personal notes will always be treated as confidential and that adversarial parties cannot gain access to them; for example, in a malpractice lawsuit.

In fact in most court jurisdictions, lawyers can subpoena practitioners' personal notes during legal proceedings. Thus, practitioners who maintain personal notes assume some risk. Information in personal notes could be used against a client. For example, information contained in the notes may become central during divorce, termination of parental rights, or child custody proceedings. Personal notes can also be used against the supervisor, manager, or administrator who documents potentially embarrassing details concerning interstaff relationships. Practitioners who maintain personal notes should word entries without an expectation of privacy and with the assumption that someday the notes may be reviewed by third parties whose interests may be adversarial.

Illinois is one state whose law includes explicit protection for behavioral health professionals' personal notes. The Illinois Mental Health and Developmental Disabilities Confidentiality Act of 1981 (and subsequent amendments) addresses the issue of personal notes by stating that the client's record "does not include the therapist's notes, if such notes are kept in the therapist's sole possession for his own personal use and are not disclosed to any other person, except the therapist's supervisor, consulting therapist or attorney. If at any time such notes are disclosed, they shall be considered part of the . . . record." The act (40 ILCS 110/2) goes on to say that the therapist's personal notes may include "information disclosed to the therapist in confidence by other persons on condition that such information would never be disclosed to the recipient or other persons; information disclosed to the therapist by the recipient which would be injurious to the recipient's relationship to other persons; and the therapist's speculations, impressions, hunches, and reminders."[23] In fact in 1998, the Illinois Appellate Court held that a psychiatrist's personal notes were protected from discovery in a malpractice claim against him (see *In re* Estate of Bagus). State laws differ in their definition of personal notes.

Although the support for such personal notes may provide practitioners with some comfort, they must realize that outside Illinois a lawyer *could* subpoena such notes, along with formal agency or private practice records (*subpoena duces tecum*). Lawyers have in fact subpoenaed such items as appointment books, scraps of paper, calendars, any other documents on which the practitioner may have written notes related to the matter at hand, and electronically stored information (such as e-mail, text messages, and online posts). Also, most states do not distinguish between professional and personal notes. According to Madden:

> Many therapists wonder about the legality of keeping two sets of records, the
> official record, and a second file including personal notes, hypotheses, subjective comments, or other information not directly relevant to the reason
> for treatment. Although a few states do allow separate working notes (see,
> e.g., Illinois Mental Health and Developmental Disabilities Confidentiality
> Act, 1996), this practice is generally discouraged. Except where protected
> by statute, personal notes are subject to a subpoena and lawyers routinely
> include reference to personal notes when requesting client records. These
> subjective or speculative notes may contain information that can be used to
> undercut the conclusions in the formal file. If case notes are carefully written, there should be no reason to keep a separate set of notes.[24]

*Be cautious in documenting services provided to families and couples.*
Behavioral health practitioners who counsel families and couples are often
in an untenable position: if they maintain a single record for the family
and couple, they risk exposing confidential information in the event the
record is subpoenaed; careful redaction is essential. Maintaining separate
records for all parties, on the other hand, is cumbersome and inconsistent
with practitioners' belief that the family or couple as a whole is the client.
According to Barker and Branson:

> There are advantages and disadvantages to whichever choice this worker, or
> any worker, makes. The only virtue in having separate files—but it is a significant one—is in the event that members of the client-group have major
> disputes. When their disputes lead to legal action, one client or another may
> seek the worker's files. An individual may be able legally to have access to his
> or her own records, but what about when the information is intertwined
> with that of another person, especially another person who is now an opponent in a lawsuit? If the files are written separately, then every person can
> claim access only to their own files, and the worker's position is much less
> uncomfortable.[25]

Some practitioners compromise by maintaining separate records for
sensitive information that must be protected and joint files for more routine assessments and summaries of services provided. For example, a practitioner who provides an individual counseling session to one member of a

couple, as a supplement to counseling the couple, can create a separate file for that client in which private issues, such as a report of struggles with sexual orientation, family violence, infidelity, or substance abuse, are recorded. In the couple's joint file, the practitioner would record their having sought marital counseling to address "relationship issues." Maintaining separate records in these circumstances may help the practitioner protect each client in the event that a dispute arises—a child custody dispute or divorce, for example. The practitioner has a duty to explain at the outset her role during the case and to anticipate and minimize potential conflicts of interest.

*Do not air agency dirty laundry.* Details concerning understaffed programs, conflicts among staffers, or personal opinions about the competence of a colleague do not belong in a client's record. Documentation of personnel and staffing problems should appear in administrative files. Including such detail in clients' records may expose agencies to considerable risk in the event of a negligence lawsuit.

Furthermore, behavioral health clinicians, supervisors, managers, and administrators who become involved in disputes among staff members— a disagreement about an agency policy or administrative order, for example— should not include documentation about the dispute in clients' records. When there is reason to create a paper trail, relevant opinions, decisions, and actions can be documented in administrative memoranda or logs. Put simply, evidence of jousting among staff should not appear in clients' records.

### Language and Terminology

Wording in documentation is just as important as the substance of the content. Loose and casual language and terminology can be catastrophic to the practitioner, the supervisor, and the agency. Practitioners must choose their words carefully, taking care to be clear, to fully support conclusions drawn, to avoid defamatory language, and to write knowing there is always an audience.

*Writing with clarity.* Practitioners should use clear, specific, unambiguous, and precise wording. Lack of clarity, specificity, and precision provides considerable opportunity for adversarial parties to raise doubts about practitioners' claims, observations, and interpretations. In addition, these shortcomings in a report may confuse colleagues who are depending on the notes to provide follow-up services to clients. Conversely, clear, specific, unambiguous, and precise wording enhances the delivery of services and strengthens practitioners' ability to explain and defend previous decisions and actions.

In addition to using precise wording, practitioners should avoid the use of professional jargon, slang, or abbreviations that may be misunderstood. For example, the abbreviation BPD could mean bipolar disorder or borderline personality disorder. SA could mean substance abuse, suicide attempt, or sexual assault. Such ambiguity could prove disastrous if the abbreviations are misinterpreted by a colleague or debated in an ethics hearing, licensing-board inquiry, or litigation. Some organizations maintain an approved list of abbreviations to prevent ambiguity.

*Drawing conclusions.* Documenting conclusions with terms or phrases such as "the client was confused" or "the unit counselor behaved aggressively toward the client" without including supporting details is risky. Today's practitioner therefore needs to always include details that support a conclusion or assertion. Summary statements about the mental health status or behavior of a client, employee, or colleague should always be supported with sufficient specific information. Terms such as *hostile, under the influence*, or *incompetent* should always be followed by a phrase along the lines of "as evidenced by," with appropriate details included.

*Avoiding defamatory language.* Practitioners should also take steps to avoid using language that might constitute libel or slander, the two forms of defamation of character. As noted earlier, libel (the written form of defamation) and slander (the oral form of defamation) occur when practitioners write or say something about a client, colleague, or third party that is not true, the practitioner knew to be untrue or should have known was untrue, and harmed the individual who was the subject of the written or oral communication. Examples include untrue statements alleging mental illness, substance abuse, incompetence, criminal conduct, or inappropriate behavior. Use of quotation marks to reflect clients' verbatim statements can be effective and protect against defamation claims.

*Writing for an audience.* Practitioners should expect managed-care authorities, utilization review personnel, and third-party payers to review documents and records. Poorly worded and inadequate documentation may affect payment for services to clients. Also, practitioners should protect clients' privacy when they share records with such outside parties.

### Credibility

When disputes arise concerning the appropriateness of practitioners' actions—whether they conducted adequate assessments of clients, maintained proper boundaries, terminated services appropriately, obtained needed consultation, used technology appropriately, or provided proper supervision, for example—case records and administrative files provide essential evidence. Without thorough documentation, practitioners may have difficulty defending their actions. Thoroughness, however, is not sufficient. Even thorough documentation needs to be credible, and the credibility of practitioners' documentation can be enhanced or compromised in several ways. Time is of the essence when documenting cases, but practitioners must take care not to jump the gun and record events that are only anticipated. Likewise, the writing in documentation must always be professional. Finally, when a mistake is made, a credible practitioner will be forthright and honest. Consulting with colleagues is prudent if you are unsure about the best way to document an encounter.

*Documenting in a timely fashion.* Few behavioral health practitioners relish the task of documentation, whether for clinical, supervisory, management, or administrative purposes. Careful documentation takes time and often looms as an onerous task—a necessary evil associated with professional life. As a result, practitioners sometimes put off documenting their interventions, decisions, and actions.

Delayed documentation can compromise the credibility of practitioners' claims about what the notes reflect. Adversarial parties, especially opposing legal counsel, can use evidence of delayed documentation to challenge the credibility of practitioners' testimony. According to Barsky and Gould:

> The timing of note taking can have great legal significance. Ideally, notes should be made contemporaneously with the events being recorded (i.e., during a session with a client, immediately following, or within 24 hours). Evidentiary rules assume that information recorded contemporaneously with the events is more likely to be accurate. Behavioral science research supports the fact that notes contemporaneously taken are more accurate than those recorded at a later time, even if it is later the same day.[26]

*Avoiding prognostic documentation.* In an effort to save time and expedite documentation, practitioners occasionally record notes in advance of an intervention or event. Sometimes, however, the planned interventions or events do not occur (perhaps due to an emergency) or they unfold differently than expected. The prematurely recorded notes would therefore not accurately reflect what happened and thus would undermine the practitioner's credibility.

Further, in some instances practitioners may be tempted to forecast clients' outcomes. This is a mistake. An example is a practitioner who conducts an initial assessment of a mother who has lost custody of her child because of the mother's mental health and substance use challenges and writes in the record, "Based on this assessment, it is highly unlikely that this mother will be able to parent this child." The reality is that clinicians cannot always forecast client outcomes accurately. Some clients with poor prognoses do well. Some clients with favorable prognoses encounter major obstacles that interfere with their progress.

*Striving for professional prose.* Practitioners do not always pay close attention to the legibility of handwritten notes, the accuracy of electronic notes, or grammatical correctness of their documentation. Colleagues may have difficulty understanding or may misinterpret illegible or poorly worded entries and may miss important cues that are essential for proper intervention, supervision, management, or administration. Therefore, it is imperative that practitioners ensure the accuracy of their notes and use proper grammar when recording case information. Copies of practitioners' documentation typically become tangible evidence and exhibits during ethics hearings, licensing-board inquiries, pretrial depositions, and courtroom proceedings (often displayed prominently on LED screens for all parties to see). Illegible or poorly worded entries and a pattern of grammatical and spelling errors are a professional embarrassment to the practitioner and the agency represented. Such inattention to detail severely weakens credibility. Worse, it could also result in the provision of misleading information.

*Acknowledging errors.* To err is human, and every practitioner is capable of inadvertently inserting incorrect facts in, and omitting important facts from, case documentation. Ethics committee members, licensing boards, lawyers, and judges recognize that any professional can make occasional errors.

To avoid undermining their credibility, practitioners should never attempt to cover up or camouflage their errors. Such efforts can backfire. For example, sometimes opposing lawyers can access documents before practitioners attempt to conceal the errors. Practitioners who alter records in anticipation of legal proceedings or after legal proceedings have been initiated therefore assume great risk and public humiliation if the inconsistencies are brought to light. As Barsky and Gould observe, "If a clinician is aware of an impending legal process or has been subpoenaed, doctoring or destroying documents can result in such charges as contempt of court or obstruction of justice, malpractice suits, and professional disciplinary actions."[27] Instead, practitioners should always acknowledge their errors, making clear that the new entry occurred after the error was discovered. In clinical settings that use paper records, practitioners should enter a new note that acknowledges and corrects the error or draw a thin line through the error and insert the correction, along with the practitioner's initials, the date, and the word *error*. Practitioners should ensure that errors in electronic records are acknowledged forthrightly and corrected. Clyde Bergstresser, a seasoned malpractice attorney, emphasizes:

> Do not change or lose your records. Do not make "additions" or "corrections" to clarify what you meant. You would be amazed at how many people cannot resist the temptation to make sure that in hindsight the records say what was meant. When you get caught, your credibility will be destroyed, and it is very likely you will be caught. Copies of "lost" records have a habit of cropping up when you least expect it. Document experts are now very sophisticated in their ability to determine from writing patterns whether an entry was made all in one sitting, even from a copy.[28]

### Access to Records and Documents

Behavioral health practitioners generally assume that case records and documents will remain confidential. In reality, a truly confidential case record does not exist. An extraordinarily wide array of laws, regulations, contracts, and court rules require or permit disclosure of otherwise confidential documents.

Furthermore, practitioners need to be cognizant of security risks associated with the widespread use of electronic behavioral health records. Thus, practitioners should be familiar with the various circumstances under which records and documents may be disclosed. Practitioners need to know how to respond to subpoenas, need to be familiar with applicable state and federal laws and regulations, and need to know how to secure documentation for future access.

*Know how to respond to a subpoena.* Perhaps the most frequent trigger for the disclosure of documents is the subpoena. A *subpoena duces tecum* requires a party who is in control of relevant documents, including electronically stored information, to disclose them to the requesting party and bring them to a deposition or court hearing. Practitioners should not confuse subpoenas to appear with documents and a court order to disclose the documents' contents. Subpoenas and court orders are entirely different phenomena. Practitioners should always take steps to protect the confidentiality of relevant documents during legal proceedings to the extent permitted by law. When a court of law or other legally authorized body orders practitioners to disclose confidential or privileged information without a client's consent and such disclosure could cause harm to the client, practitioners should request that the court withdraw the order or limit the order as narrowly as possible or maintain the records under seal, unavailable for public inspection. Put briefly, practitioners should not release any confidential information contained in documents unless they are sure they are authorized to do so—based on client consent or in response to a court order, for example.

*Know relevant statutes and regulations.* Many federal and state statutes and regulations govern the handling of confidential documents. For example, the federal Health Insurance Portability and Accountability Act, or HIPAA, and its regulations address the protection of personal health-related information (known as PHI, or protected health information). Practitioners should be especially familiar with explicit HIPAA provisions that are unique to psychotherapy notes. As noted earlier, the regulations define these specifically as notes recorded in any medium by a health-care provider who is a mental health professional documenting or analyzing the contents of conversation during a private counseling session or a group, joint, or family counseling session, and which are separated from the rest of the individual's medical record. Further, the Health Information Technology for Economic and Clinical Health (HITECH) Act provides the U.S. Department of Health and Human Services with the authority to establish programs to improve health-care quality, safety, and efficiency through the promotion of health information technology, including electronic health records and private and secure electronic health information exchange.

Under the 21st Century Cures Act, various categories of clinical notes created in an electronic health record (EHR) may need to be made available to clients immediately through a secure online portal.

Other key federal regulations govern the handling of confidential documents related to privacy of personally identifiable information about individuals in records maintained by federal agencies (Privacy Act of 1974 as amended), substance use disorder treatment records, and school records. Records maintained by behavioral health professionals employed in military settings and by the U.S. Department of Veterans Affairs are governed by unique federal laws. States also have specific laws and regulations governing the release of confidential documents contained in health, mental health, school, and child welfare records.

*Secure records.* Practitioners should store records (clinical, personnel, supervisory, and administrative) in secure locations to prevent unauthorized access. When using electronic media, practitioners should exercise caution to ensure that this information cannot be accessed by unauthorized parties (e.g., with strict log-in protocols and firewalls). Practitioners should consult relevant federal and state statutes, regulations, codes of ethics, and contracts (e.g., insurance company and managed-care contracts) to determine the length of time that documents should be retained. If and when records are destroyed or disposed of, care must be taken so that the disposal still protects client confidentiality.

Behavioral health practitioners should keep a number of criteria in mind with respect to recording. In particular, the practitioner should record the following:

- Informed-consent procedures, enclosing in the file signed consent forms for release of information and treatment.
- Clients' consent for remote delivery of services, including potential benefits and limitations, confirmation of the client's geographical location during clinical sessions (to ensure that the practitioner is properly licensed in that jurisdiction), emergency protocols, advice about what to do in the event of technology failure, the importance of using a secure Wi-Fi or other connection, privacy risks, the practitioner's policy regarding recording of clinical sessions and the presence of third parties off-camera.
- All contacts made with third parties (such as family members, acquaintances, and other professionals), whether in person, by telephone, text

message, or e-mail. The record should include a brief description of the contacts and any significant events surrounding them.

- Collateral agreements signed by individuals who join counseling sessions but who are not considered clients and who should be advised about pertinent confidentiality policies and guidelines (e.g., clients' family members or acquaintances).
- Any consultation with other professionals, including the date that the client was referred to another professional for services.
- A copy of the document given to clients explaining the practitioner's social media policies related to online social networking communications, online searches for information about clients, and use of text messages or e-mails by clients in the event of an emergency.
- A complete social history, assessment, and treatment plan, stating the client's problems and challenges, the reason for requesting service, objectives and relevant timetable, intervention strategy, planned number and duration of contacts, assessment and evaluation of progress, termination plan, and reasons for termination. Practitioners should update their records as needed (e.g., when assessments and treatment plans change).
- Documents pertaining to compliance with the federal No Surprises Act. This law requires practitioners to give uninsured and self-pay clients a good faith estimate of costs for services that they offer.
- A brief description of the practitioner's reasoning for all decisions made during the course of intervention.
- Any instructions, recommendations, and advice provided to the client, including referral to and suggestions to seek consultation from a specialist.
- A description of all clinically relevant contacts with the client, including type of contact (e.g., in person versus telephone or video, e-mail or text message; individual, family, couples, group) and dates and times of contacts. The record also should include notation of failed or canceled appointments and any previous or current psychological, psychiatric, or medical evaluations relevant to the practitioner's intervention.

The record should not contain information regarding a client's political, religious, or other personal views unless this detail is directly relevant to the intervention or clinical work. Intimate, gossipy, and other personal details that are not directly germane to service delivery should be omitted, as should any information that could in any way be used against the client in a court of law.

State statutes, federal regulations, and insurance company contracts may specify a retention period for records. Case records pertaining to minors ordinarily should be kept longer because the statute of limitations may not begin to run until the child reaches the age of majority.

As I discussed in chapter 2, practitioners would also be wise to prepare a will that includes plans for the transfer or disposition of cases in the event of death or incapacitation. Some experts suggest providing for an executor or trustee to maintain records for a specified period (e.g., thirty days).

As noted earlier, practitioners assume considerable risk if they keep minimal notes. Some argue that the absence of records would be particularly helpful when practitioners are subpoenaed to court, where in principle they could claim that they do not fully remember what happened in the case. Professionals generally agree, however, that maintaining minimal records would create more problems, legal and otherwise, than it would solve. The absence of thorough, carefully written notes may compromise the practitioner's credibility and expose the practitioner to rigorous, possibly devastating, cross-examination by opposing legal counsel.

Although the vast majority of practitioners agree that keeping good case notes is important, some do not do so. In chapter 5, for example, I described a case involving a behavioral health practitioner who was a partner in a private practice and was sued under the doctrine of *respondeat superior* in connection with mistakes alleged to have been made by a former nurse whom the practitioner had hired. In that case, the plaintiff alleged that the former nurse, who was originally hired to conduct eating disorder assessments and evaluations of children, provided incompetent counseling services to her before the former nurse had completed her formal education in a counseling program and before she was licensed as a counselor. The plaintiff also claimed that the practitioner should be held liable both because the former nurse provided the counseling and in relation to the monitoring and intervention in the case by the practitioner, which the suit claimed was inadequate. The specific allegations included claims that the former nurse promoted the client's dependency on her; involved the client in her side business, which was completely unrelated to counseling; traveled out of state with the client; and otherwise was involved in inappropriate dual relationships with the client. The client and her husband sued, claiming that she had been manifesting serious symptoms, including depression and suicidal ideation.

One key issue involved in the case, which was settled before trial, concerned the claim that during the intervention neither the former nurse nor the practitioner maintained notes about the case. When the plaintiff's attorney deposed the former nurse, the following dialogue took place, beginning with the lawyer:

Q: What kinds of clients do you tend to see?

A: What do you mean?

Q: Do you specialize in certain kinds of problem areas?

A: No, not really. I see lots of different kinds of clients.

Q: Do you have case notes on all of your clients?

A: Some yes, some no.

Q: What about [the plaintiff in this case]? Why didn't you keep notes in this case?

A: You have to understand that this is a very complicated case. There were two other clinicians involved, plus lots of other service providers outside of our own agency. This wasn't my case primarily, so I didn't feel the need to keep detailed notes. There were so many others involved, it just didn't seem necessary. I was usually in touch with the other counselors. So I just didn't think there was a problem.

Q: Well, frankly, I am confused about this. I am trying to imagine what it must be like to keep track of so many clients. I can't imagine keeping it all in my head. What if I get a call from a client I haven't seen in some time? How am I supposed to remember all those details? It seems to me that any professional who provides services to clients—or patients—ought to keep careful notes to keep track of all the details of the case. Suppose you get sick or have to go away in an emergency? What happens if some colleague of yours needs to know what's happening in the case? Don't you think you have a responsibility here?

A: I guess we see these things differently. I've been operating this way for years. I think I have the ability to remember the important things that are going on in my clients' lives. I guess it's possible that I'd forget something, but I've never considered it a problem. In this particular case I was in pretty close touch with my colleagues involved with [the plaintiff]. Whenever I felt the need for some consultation I would contact one of my colleagues here. That happened a lot. Maybe it would have been a good idea to write all this stuff down, but I didn't. I just didn't think I needed to.

The next week, the practitioner (the partner in the private practice who had hired the former nurse), who was being sued under the doctrine of *respondeat superior*, was also deposed, and here too the plaintiff's lawyer pursued the subject of recording and note taking:

Q: Let me ask you this question, Ms. [mentions the practitioner's name].
   Do you ordinarily keep detailed case notes?

A: It depends, but usually not.

Q: What do you think about that?

A: What do you mean?

Q: I mean, do you think that's standard procedure in social work?

A: Look, I don't really know what standard procedure is in general. I know what I do and what I think is acceptable. I've never kept detailed case notes on every client.

Q: You've always practiced this way?

A: Yes, since day one. I've never felt the need to handle my practice any differently.

Q: Is this what you were taught to do when you went to school to become a social worker?

A: Not really. It's never been a problem before.

Q: Well, I'm not really concerned about problems before now. I want to know whether there was a problem in this case.

A: I guess we have a different view of this.

Q: Is it ever necessary for you to keep case notes?

A: Only if there's something highly unusual.

Q: Highly unusual?

A: Like a suicidal client—something like that.

Sometimes practitioners whose records are subpoenaed are tempted to alter the record in order to fill in any gaps or to correct errors. In some instances, practitioners have actually destroyed all or a portion of a record in order to cover up some error. This is a serious mistake. In addition to engaging in deception (see chapter 7), the practitioner may be held liable because of the altered or destroyed record.

Issues pertaining to altered records arose in the Florida case that I discussed earlier, which involved a health-care provider who was sued after a patient committed suicide; the suit alleged that the health-care provider had failed to refer the man to a psychiatrist and had failed to recommend hospitalization. In that case, the primary health-care provider had referred the client to a psychologist, who had treated him. The psychologist's chart indicated that he had recommended referral of the client to a psychiatrist and for hospitalization. The plaintiff challenged the authenticity of the psychologist's record, and a document analyst concluded that the disputed entries had been made at least several weeks *after* the man committed suicide.

Practitioners should also be familiar with the legal concept of spoliation. Spoliation is the destruction or alteration of evidence resulting from a party's failure to preserve evidence relevant to litigation or an investigation. Practitioners involved in litigation may face severe sanctions for intentionally destroying paper documents and electronically stored information (ESI) that may be relevant to a lawsuit or government investigation after the practitioner's duty to preserve is triggered. The court may sanction a spoliating party by fining the practitioner; issuing a contempt citation; permitting an adverse-inference jury instruction; striking the party's pleadings in whole or in part; prohibiting the party from introducing certain evidence; or dismissing the party's claims or defenses.

*Understand clients' right to access their own records.* As I discussed earlier, clients generally have a right to examine their own records, although there are some narrow exceptions. And, under the 21st Century Cures Act, many practitioners are obligated to provide clients with remote access to their electronic records, excluding psychotherapy notes and certain recognized exceptions. Practitioners who are concerned that clients' access to their records could cause serious misunderstanding or harm to the client should provide assistance in interpreting the records and consultation with the client regarding the records. Practitioners should limit clients' access to their records or portions of their records only in exceptional circumstances when compelling evidence exists that such access would cause serious harm to the client. In a Texas case, the state licensing board disciplined a social worker "related to failure to respond to, and provide information to a patient regarding a request for patient records."[29]

# CHAPTER 7

# Deception and Fraud

When I conducted a workshop in a large midwestern city on ethics and liability issues in the field of behavioral health, a participant approached during a break to ask me a question. She explained that she was a therapist in solo private practice in a nearby suburban community. She complained that insurance companies often will not approve psychotherapy for "adjustment disorders," which occur when people have difficulty coping with stress and trauma. She explained that because her livelihood depended on third-party payment, she felt compelled to camouflage her treatment of adjustment disorders by changing the coding for clients' diagnoses to codes for which insurance companies will authorize therapy (e.g., major depressive disorder, generalized anxiety disorder, acute stress disorder). The practitioner asked whether I thought she could, as a result, "get in trouble." "Yes," I replied.

Many circumstances in the field of behavioral health provide opportunities for some form of deception or fraud; that is, a deliberate attempt by a practitioner to give a false impression to a client, colleague, insurance provider, employer, or some other party. Fraud—which often, but not always, involves financial transactions—is typically considered in the law as an intentional tort.

Practitioners who engage in deception and fraud do so for various reasons and with various motives. Some practitioners—a small percentage—are simply dishonest and attempt to take advantage of others for reasons of greed, malice, or self-protection. Other practitioners engage in deceit and fraud for what appear to be more altruistic reasons; that is, to be as helpful as they can be to their clients and agencies.

## SELF-INTERESTED DECEPTION AND FRAUD

The vast majority of behavioral health practitioners enter the profession with remarkably pure motives. For a variety of reasons, they are moved to help vulnerable people. Some practitioners have been influenced by an admired mentor and some by family values. Some enter a behavioral health profession as a result of their own personal trauma or experience as a client. Whatever the reasons, most practitioners are attracted to the profession for noble purposes—to assist people who are experiencing serious problems in living that are related to poverty, mental illness, substance abuse, child or elder abuse, aging, family conflict or violence, physical disability or illness, and so on.

However, some practitioners enter the profession with ignoble motives or develop them along the way. Consider these prominent examples of behavioral health practitioners who were convicted in federal court and sentenced to prison for engaging in health-care fraud:

• In a Medicare fraud case, Alton Bates, an attorney in Baton Rouge, Louisiana, was sentenced in federal court to thirty-four months in prison, to pay restitution of $1,063,873 to Medicare, to forfeit the gross proceeds of his scheme to defraud Medicare, and to three years supervised release after imprisonment. The judge also sentenced Robert Ivory Levy, a licensed clinical social worker, to fifteen months imprisonment, to pay restitution of $120,946.89 to Medicare, and to three years supervised release after imprisonment. The defendants schemed to defraud the Medicare program by submitting false and fraudulent claims for psychotherapy services that were not provided. In total, the defendants' participation in this scheme involved more than 7,700 false claims seeking Medicare payments totaling $3,052,838. Because of the scheme, the Medicare program paid more than $1,000,000 to Above and Beyond, LLC, the Baton Rouge company operated by the defendants between 2003 and 2005.[1]

• Wyoming psychologist Gibson Buckley Condie was sentenced in federal court to serve three years in prison for felony health-care fraud involving mental health services falsely billed to Wyoming Medicaid. Condie was also ordered to pay approximately $2.28 million in restitution to the Wyoming Department of Health and the US Department of Health and Human Services and to forfeit certain assets traceable to the proceeds of his fraud.

Condie, who was a licensed psychologist, had been indicted by a federal grand jury for a scheme to defraud Wyoming Medicaid. Condie admitted to operating a scheme involving a number of misrepresentations and false statements intended to cause Medicaid to pay for mental health services for which he knew Medicaid would not pay if he truthfully reported the facts. Specifically, Condie claimed to be the treating provider even though almost all services were provided by unenrolled, and often unlicensed, persons who could not provide mental health services under Wyoming Medicaid.

Condie also routinely endorsed mental health assessments, which claimed that a Medicaid beneficiary had a qualifying mental health disorder, when in fact Condie had neither performed nor properly supervised the assessments. These assessments were often done by individuals who did not have the required training or license to diagnose mental health disorders. Condie then submitted false bills for these assessments and submitted bills for other treatment services on the basis of these improper assessments. Finally, Condie billed for life-skills training, psychosocial rehabilitation, and adult case management services even though the beneficiaries had not received a proper diagnosis of a mental health disorder, the activities billed for did not qualify as medically necessary therapy, and he did not operate a qualified community mental health center. As a result of Condie's false statements and misrepresentations, Wyoming Medicaid paid Condie $2,283,792.49 for mental health services that did not qualify for Medicaid reimbursement. Condie in turn distributed a portion of this money to the unenrolled, and often untrained and unlicensed, individuals who actually spent time with the beneficiaries.[2]

• Nina Jafari, a licensed clinical social worker in New York, was convicted of health-care fraud and sentenced to thirty months in prison. According to federal prosecutors, Jafari defrauded Blue Cross Blue Shield of Western New York by submitting reimbursement claim forms to the insurance provider for services that were not rendered. The government's evidence included tape-recorded conversations between the defendant and a client. In those conversations, Jafari instructed the client not to share any information with Blue Cross Blue Shield regarding dates of service. The amount that the defendant defrauded the insurance carrier totaled approximately $138,000.[3]

• Louisiana social worker Carla Clark was sentenced in federal court to twenty-one months imprisonment, two years of supervised release following imprisonment, and ordered to pay $413,109 in restitution for her role in a health-care fraud scheme involving two Louisiana companies. The sentencing stemmed from a health-care fraud scheme involving two companies known as Fusion Services, L.L.C. ("Fusion"), and Grace Social Services, L.L.C. ("Grace"), which operated in Alexandria, Louisiana, and the surrounding areas. Clark was a licensed clinical social worker who worked with Sonya Williams, the owner of the two companies.

Clark participated in creating false and misleading medical records for Fusion indicating that Medicare beneficiaries had received individual, face-to-face psychotherapy when, in fact, no such services had been provided. Williams then prepared false claims for the purported psychotherapy services to elderly patients and submitted them to Medicare for reimbursement. Medicare paid Fusion and Grace approximately $349,715 as a result of the billings, and much of the profit was deposited into Williams's personal accounts. In addition to the term of imprisonment, Judge Jackson ordered Clark to pay restitution in the amount of $413,109 to the Department of Health and Human Services/Centers for Medicare and Medicaid Services for her role in the fraudulent conduct involving Fusion, Grace, and other health-care entities.[4]

• Anthony D. Jackson, owner of Pantherview Sober House LLC, was sentenced in federal court to forty-two months in prison and three years of supervised release. The sentencing is in addition to court-ordered restitution of $5,122,886 following a previous guilty plea to conspiring with others to commit health-care fraud. Jackson—owner of the Boynton Beach, Florida, substance abuse recovery residence and a certified addiction counselor—accepted kickbacks and bribes from Kenneth Chatman, owner and chief operating officer of Reflections Treatment Center, for referring Pantherview patients to Reflections for treatment. Jackson, who also served as the program director at Reflections, led therapy sessions and completed clinical notes related to the sessions. He then copied and pasted the same notes into the records of other patients who did not attend and later billed the patients' insurance for therapy sessions that did not occur. Along with others, Jackson and Chatman provided kickbacks to the insured patients who did attend the sessions in the form of free or reduced rent, cigarettes, and other items.[5]

State licensing boards have also disciplined behavioral health practitioners who have engaged in fraud, especially financial fraud. For example, the state board in Ohio revoked the license of a social worker who pleaded guilty in federal court to embezzlement and theft of federal funds in connection with her position as director of a social service program.[6] In another case, New Jersey suspended the license of a social worker who was convicted of Medicaid fraud when, in his position as executive director of a behavioral health program, he billed for therapy services that were never provided.[7]

In most fraud cases, evidence shows that financial greed and self-interest led to the misconduct. In other cases, no direct financial motive is involved; for example, when practitioners fraudulently declare to licensing boards that they have completed mandated continuing education courses. The Iowa licensing board disciplined a social worker who, when she submitted her application for license renewal, stated that she had completed required continuing education, when she had not.[8] In another case, Alabama revoked the license of a social worker who submitted fraudulent forms to the board indicating she had received clinical social work supervision.[9] In Maryland, the state board suspended the license of a practitioner who, while working as a therapist at a mental health clinic, forged the signature of a client's guardian on a treatment plan.[10]

As I discussed in chapter 4, a number of impaired behavioral health practitioners, particularly those who sexually abuse clients, may use their power, status, and authority as professionals to seek opportunities to meet their own needs by exploiting clients. Practitioners who have addictions— whether to gambling or substances such as alcohol or other drugs—may use their professional positions to extort or steal money from impressionable or incompetent clients or use deceit and undue influence to persuade clients to enter into agreements primarily designed to benefit the practitioner.

> Paul S. was a behavioral health caseworker at Community Services of Boone County. He had been employed at the agency as a case coordinator for five years. Paul S. provided case management and crisis services for a caseload of twenty-five clients. Several clients had been declared incompetent. Most, however, were able to participate in the management of their affairs.
>
> One of his clients was a seventy-six-year-old man, John M., who struggled with clinical depression, among other challenges. John M. had been a client of the agency for three years, and Paul S. had gotten to know him quite well during that time. In fact, the two men had become so close that John M. often referred to Paul S. as the "son I always wanted."

John M. was living in a congregate housing development where he had a small private apartment and shared kitchen facilities with six other residents. Before his retirement at age seventy, he had been a highly successful furniture manufacturer. He had developed a large furniture factory, ultimately employing about three hundred people. When he sold the business, John M. became a relatively wealthy man.

Recently, John M. received a diagnosis of liver cancer. Paul S. spent quite a bit of time with him, reminiscing about John M.'s life and talking about his impending death. Clearly, John M. was dying and becoming more and more confused. The psychiatric consultant said that John M. would probably need to be placed on psychotropic medication to help him with his confusion.

At about this time, Paul S., the case manager, was having serious financial problems. A couple of years earlier, he had taken his brother-in-law's advice and, without his wife's knowledge, had invested most of their savings in the options market. Within a year, however, he had lost nearly everything. Paul S. had two children in private school and was feeling guilty and desperate about the money that he had lost.

During one conversation with John M., Paul S. said that he was worried about one of his daughters who, Paul S. lied, was gravely ill and disabled. Over three days, Paul S., who had become quite important to John M., convinced John M. to rewrite his will to include Paul S. as a beneficiary.

In a notorious case that received national publicity, psychiatrist Isaac Herschkopf allegedly abused his relationship with a patient to exploit the patient for personal gain. According to reports, Herschkopf used his influence to gain control of one patient's bank account and hijack his Hamptons home on Long Island, New York, and talked patients into writing his family into their wills.[11]

Not all cases of this sort, in which unscrupulous practitioners use undue influence and deceit to benefit themselves, involve incompetent or close-to-incompetent clients. In many cases, clients are competent but vulnerable and impressionable. A counselor providing psychotherapy to a client who originally sought counseling for a serious self-esteem problem may find a ripe opportunity to convince the client to include the practitioner as a partner in her thriving business. The practitioner may deceitfully convince the client that nothing about this relationship is inappropriate. Or, a counselor who has serious financial problems may use fraud to convince an impressionable client to invest in a legitimate-sounding limited partnership that in actuality is a Ponzi scheme (a swindle in which an initial investment provides a quick return paid out of funds from new investors).

Other forms of self-interested deceit and fraud are more straightforward. One more common form involves practitioners—albeit a relatively small percentage—who submit fraudulent information on claim forms to third-party payers and insurance companies. Insurance companies may be billed for counseling sessions that did not occur. Or, practitioners may collude with a psychiatrist who for a fee signs forms attesting to the client's diagnosis and treatment when the psychiatrist was virtually uninvolved in the case and had no contact with the client. In one widely publicized signing-off case, a social worker in private practice spent a weekend in jail after pleading guilty in an insurance fraud case. She was also ordered to perform 720 hours of community service.[12]

In the chapter 5 discussion of *respondeat superior* and problems related to staff supervision, I described a case involving a behavioral health professional who was a partner in a private practice and who was accused of improper supervision of an employee, a former nurse who was providing counseling services. Another aspect of that case involved allegations that a physician was signing insurance claim forms attesting to his involvement in the practitioner's cases when in fact his involvement was minimal. The formal lawsuit included the following allegations, among others:

> Plaintiffs further show that [the private practice] submitted numerous charges to plaintiffs' insurer which were signed by Dr. A. [identity deleted by author].
>
> Plaintiffs further show that said insurance claim forms suggest and imply that the therapy listed thereon was provided by Dr. A.
>
> Plaintiffs show that Dr. A. provided no such services to plaintiff.

As the following excerpt shows, the plaintiffs' attorney pursued this issue aggressively during the deposition conducted with the practitioner defendant:

> Q: I'm rather confused by what I see here on the forms. These numbers here, is that a diagnostic code for the insurance company? Is that what you have to put down to get reimbursed by the insurance company?

A: Yes, that's what the number's for. That was Dr. A.'s diagnosis.

Q: Dr. A. gave a diagnosis in this case?

A: Yes. He's my consulting psychiatrist, and he gives the diagnoses in the cases we discuss.

Q: So he's the one that came up with this diagnostic category? Dr. A.'s the one who said you should put this number down?

A: Sort of. We came up with the number during our discussion.

Q: Is it safe for me to assume that Dr. A. examined the client?

A: No.

Q: No what? What do you mean?

A: I mean Dr. A. never saw the client.

Q: Is that typical?

A: Typical of what?

Q: For Dr. A. to sign the form without examining the client?

A: Are you asking whether he does this all the time?

Q: I'm asking whether he usually does this with your clients.

A: Yes, it's routine practice with us. As far as I know this is pretty common. Are we really that different?

Q: I'm just trying to figure out how you handled these procedures. You're saying that this is what usually happened?

A: That's right.

Q: So when Dr. A. signed these forms he was saying, in effect, that in his professional judgment, based on his medical and psychiatric background, that this is the right diagnosis?

A: Yes.

Q: And was he saying that this person needed psychotherapy?

A: Yes.

Q: But how could he know this if he never met the client?

A: Well, Dr. A. would often attend our agency staff meetings, so he would learn what was going on in different cases. He knew a lot about what was happening with clients.

Q: Do you see a problem here, with this arrangement?

A: What do you mean?

Q: I mean I'm puzzled about this arrangement where you had a psychiatrist signing a form about what a particular client needs, his or her psychiatric and therapy needs, but this psychiatrist never actually saw the client.

A: This is pretty common.

Q: That doesn't mean it's right or acceptable, does it?
A: No.

Allegations of improper billing also arose in *Suslovich v. New York State Education Department*.[13] In this case, a psychologist's license was suspended after the clinician submitted insurance reimbursement forms for ten client sessions, although the client attended only five.

In some cases, behavioral health organizations—as opposed to individual practitioners—are charged with fraud. In one prominent federal court case in which I served as an expert witness, a large behavioral health organization allegedly submitted false claims for reimbursement by the Commonwealth of Massachusetts program that provides coverage for low-income clients. The Massachusetts Attorney General's Office alleged that the organization named in the complaint suffered significant gaps in licensing and supervision of therapists. The investigation by the attorney general's office revealed that the organization had a widespread pattern of employing unlicensed, unqualified, and unsupervised staff at its mental health facilities in violation of state regulations. The case resulted in a $25 million settlement.[14]

Another serious problem concerns behavioral health practitioners' designation of diagnostic codes on insurance or other third-party payer claim forms. Many third-party payers rely on the American Psychiatric Association's *Diagnostic and Statistical Manual of Mental Disorders* (*DSM*) classifications. Most claim forms require the practitioner to list one or more diagnostic codes to qualify for reimbursement. Some diagnostic classifications, however, are not reimbursable, and as a result some practitioners use bogus—but reimbursable—diagnostic codes on claims forms.[15]

An important study by Kirk and Kutchins documented the extent of this form of deception and fraud among practitioners. These authors set out to investigate the extent of deliberate misdiagnosis by clinicians: "Such acts are legal and ethical transgressions involving deceit, fraud, or abuse. Charges made for services not provided, money collected for services to fictitious patients, or patients encouraged to remain in treatment longer than necessary are examples of intentional inaccuracy."[16]

Kirk and Kutchins surveyed a random sample that included 10 percent of the individuals listed in the National Association of Social Workers'

*Register of Clinical Social Workers.* At the time of their survey, the *Register* included the names of more than 8,000 experienced clinical social workers. These practitioners held master's degrees, had at least two years of experience, and were members of the Academy of Certified Social Workers or were licensed by their respective states at an equivalent level. Respondents completed a lengthy questionnaire that focused on their attitudes and opinions about psychiatric diagnosis, actual diagnostic practices that they had observed in their professional work, the frequency of and reasons for their use of the *DSM*, and their professional background. Open-ended comments were also invited.

The respondents were clearly familiar with the *DSM*. One-fourth of the sample reported daily use of the *DSM*, and another fourth reported using the book at least once a week. Thirty percent of the sample reported using the *DSM* several times each month.

To explore the incidence of misdiagnosis, Kirk and Kutchins presented the clinicians with a list of various diagnostic practices. Respondents were then asked to report the extent to which they had observed these practices.

Respondents said that in many instances, clinicians use a more serious diagnosis than is warranted by the client's clinical profile. About three-fifths of the sample (59 percent) stated that they report significant clinical diagnoses (the major mental disorders) to insurance companies, although they are not warranted clinically. Nearly three-fourths of the sample (72 percent) reported being aware of cases in which more-serious-than-warranted diagnoses were used to qualify for reimbursement. About one-fourth of the sample reported that this practice occurs frequently. Eighty-six percent of the clinicians reported being aware of instances of listing diagnoses for individuals, although the focus of treatment was on the family (some third-party payers do not reimburse for family treatment). More than 80 percent indicated that third-party payer requirements often influence diagnosis. Kirk and Kutchins conclude that "these data suggest that deliberate misdiagnosis occurs frequently in the mental health professions."[17]

The temptation of course is to argue that deliberate overdiagnosis is done primarily to benefit clients. That is, clients may not receive needed services unless their psychotherapists can qualify for reimbursement. Hence, deliberate overdiagnosis is a form of beneficent lying. As Kirk and

Kutchins appropriately conclude, however, in many cases the practitioner's self-interest may be a driving force behind fraudulent billing:

> The manifest function of underdiagnosis is to protect clients; with overdiagnosis, the accurate diagnosis is replaced by a deliberately inaccurate one in order to deceive others. In particular, misdiagnosis is used so that the therapist's services will qualify for third-party reimbursement. Here the rationale is also nonclinical, but the argument that the therapist is acting only for the client's benefit is strained. The rationale that it is being done so that the client can obtain needed service is colored by the obvious self-interest of the therapist. Agencies, both public and private, also benefit when they obtain reimbursement as a result of such diagnostic practices.[18]

Behavioral health practitioners who market or advertise their credentials and services also need to be particularly careful to avoid deception and fraud. In one prominent case, the director of a Massachusetts hospital-based social service department resigned after evidence emerged that she falsified her professional credentials on her resume. As the *Boston Globe* reports:

> The state Department of Public Health has launched a sweeping review of how it verifies the licenses of employees at public hospitals following the resignation of the director of social services at the state-operated Lemuel Shattuck Hospital in Jamaica Plain over allegations that she falsified her academic credentials and licenses. . . .
>
> Sarah Pawa, who ran a department of seven people at a hospital geared toward the indigent and mentally ill, resigned last week after her superiors received an anonymous letter alleging that Pawa had lied on her resume.
>
> Pawa—hired on June 20, 2002—listed a doctorate in education and a master's degree in social work from Boston University on the resume she gave hospital officials when she applied for the job. BU officials confirmed for the *Globe* this week that she holds no degree from their school, though she did attend classes.
>
> Pawa, 44, also said on her resume that she was a practicing psychologist and clinical social worker. She said in a letter that accompanied her resume that she treated patients with "significant addiction issues and trauma history" in private practice. State licensing officials said this week that she has never held either license in Massachusetts.[19]

Although most behavioral health practitioners provide fair and accurate descriptions of their services and expertise, some practitioners who advertise intentionally or unintentionally misrepresent their programs, effectiveness, qualifications, education, or skills. Examples include advertising or other publicity material that essentially promises effective treatment; falsely portrays the practitioner's training, credentials, or expertise; or promises services the practitioner does not intend to provide.

In a widely publicized case, James Kirk, president of a Louisiana correspondence school, LaSalle University, which granted unaccredited degrees, admitted that he conspired to commit fraud by misleading prospective students and telling them that the school was accredited by a fictitious organization, the Council on Post-Secondary Christian Education.[20] Kirk was sentenced to five years in federal prison.

Allegations of fraud related to marketing arose in a Washington, D.C., case that I discussed in chapter 3. This case involved an attorney who sued an educational-psychological training program for injuries that he claimed he sustained while participating in a five-day program of lectures, guided fantasies, and experiential psychological exercises. In addition to claiming intentional infliction of emotional distress, his suit alleged that the program engaged in fraud through its representations of the nature of the program. The jury awarded him $297,387 after finding the program liable for negligence and fraud.[21]

Behavioral health practitioners must also avoid deception and fraud when applying for liability insurance, employment, a license, or some other form of certification. In *Gares v. New Mexico Board of Psychologist Examiners*, for example, the state Board of Psychologist Examiners revoked a practitioner's certificate because of fraud and deception in applying for certification, and the psychologist appealed the court order affirming revocation of his license. The state certification board had revoked his license after finding that his certification application had involved a statement indicating that he had not engaged "in any activities which misrepresented his professional qualifications, affiliation, or purposes or those of the institutions with which he was associated." The clinician had been sexually involved with three female clients during the course of treatment and had represented to the clients that such sex was a component of their therapy.[22]

Falsification of records and official documents takes other forms as well. One involves staff members who falsify records to cover their tracks, so to speak. In these cases, practitioners typically alter or falsify records to create the impression that they provided services or supervision that they never actually provided or that they obtained informed consent when they had not done so. In some cases, practitioners falsify records to camouflage a genuine mistake. In other instances, however, no mistake was made. Rather, the practitioner knowingly and intentionally failed to provide the service or supervision, for instance, and simply falsified or altered the record to cover up the negligence.

In a dramatic case, a behavioral health practitioner was sentenced to seventeen-and-a-half years in federal prison after a criminal court judge found that she had committed record-keeping fraud. According to court records, the practitioner directed the day-to-day operations of a Philadelphia-funded social service agency. A child with cerebral palsy who was served by the agency died. The agency had been hired to provide in-home services to families at risk of abuse or neglect. As the *Philadelphia Inquirer* reports:

> Authorities said that after [fourteen-year-old Danieal] Kelly died, [Michal] Kamuvaka, who is known as "Dr. K" and who has a doctorate from the University of Pennsylvania, orchestrated a fraud to backdate and falsify records in an attempt to fool city auditors into thinking that the agency [MultiEthnic Behavioral Health Inc.] had been making visits to children, including Kelly, that never occurred.
>
> When the feds began investigating, prosecutors said Kamuvaka convinced one former MultiEthnic co-worker to lie to federal agents and schemed to obstruct the federal grand jury's investigation by withholding and shredding agency records related to Kelly and dumping them into a trash bin.
>
> Before imposing sentence, Dalzell said Kamuvaka's stewardship of Multi-Ethnic was so "lackadaisical" that it was "just a matter of time" before one of the children under its care would die.
>
> The judge also said that Kamuvaka and Manamela had engaged in an "orgy of document fabrication" and that neither defendant appreciated the "full import" of the crimes.[23]

Several years ago, I conducted in-depth training for a group of experienced practitioners employed in a private child welfare agency. Most were involved in protective services cases that had been referred by the state child welfare agency. The training I conducted focused primarily on ethical and liability issues that arise in child welfare settings. During the discussion that addressed deception and fraud in child welfare, one practitioner, a supervisor, shared the following experience:

> I sure am glad you brought up this topic. I've been stewing about this for months and haven't really discussed it with anyone. I think I need to bring it up now. Perhaps my colleagues can help me figure out how to handle this problem I've had with one of my caseworkers.
>
> One of my caseworkers is supposed to spend most of his time conducting follow-up home visits to families whose children have been returned to them from temporary foster placement. The typical situation involves a child who has been placed in foster care because of alleged or substantiated abuse or neglect. Often, of course, when allegations are unfounded or a family has participated in treatment and received various services, the child is returned.
>
> As a condition of the child's return home, the family must agree to announced and unannounced visits from one of our caseworkers. During the child's return home a caseworker may visit as many as five times per week.
>
> One of my caseworkers was out of work because of a death in his family, and because we were short-staffed I took over his caseload. I went to visit a particular family, which included a five-month-old girl and her mother. The infant had been returned to her mother from foster care about three months earlier. The child was placed initially because of evidence of neglect (failure to thrive).
>
> I visited the family and had the impression that things were going reasonably well. During the visit I asked the mother whether she was finding my caseworker's recent visits at all helpful. The mother gave me a puzzled look and indicated that she hadn't seen the caseworker in about seven weeks. I tried to keep my composure and tried not to show my dismay.
>
> When I got back to my office I carefully reviewed the record and discovered that the caseworker had made entries indicating that he had been making regular home visits to the family during the recent seven-week period. When the caseworker returned to work, I confronted him with my discovery. He confessed that he had not in fact made the recent home visits, despite the entries in the record. With considerable trepidation he confessed that he had a serious alcohol problem and had not been functioning well at all.
>
> What do you folks think I should do?

One can only begin to imagine the liability risks involved here. If the child were neglected or abused during the period when the agency was supposed to have been making home visits, the agency quite likely would be vulnerable. The noncustodial father, for example, might sue the agency, alleging failure to supervise properly and to protect the child (see chapter 3). The casework supervisor might also have been vulnerable under the doctrine of *respondeat superior*.

Sometimes practitioners may believe that they are being pressured to alter records to protect their employing organization as well as themselves. Consider this case involving a practitioner who was employed at a public psychiatric hospital. According to the practitioner, who sued the hospital for wrongful termination of her employment, the director of her department asked her and several members of the staff to amend records if necessary before a site visit from a national accreditation organization. According to the suit, on which I consulted, the director had sent a memo to staff members instructing each person to review a random sample of a colleague's case records to ensure that they included all appropriate information, such as assessment information, treatment plans, progress notes, and discharge plans. The suit alleged that the memo reiterated instructions that the director had given at an earlier staff meeting. According to the plaintiff, the director instructed each staff member to review the case records and to add any missing information, although the staffers would be reviewing cases for which they had not been responsible. The memo included the following text:

As you know [the accreditation organization] will be here this Thur./Fri.—so we must be caught up and on target with our work.

I will be reviewing every active chart in the hospital, paying particular attention to MTP's [master treatment plans] (being individualized) and documentation of discharge planning notes.

Please re-check your charts and make any additions/deletions changes necessary. The purpose of this is not a witch hunt, but for us all to be ready for the survey!

In addition, for QA [quality assurance], each of you will need to do 10 charts before Thursday.

[mentions a staffer's name]—any 10 from 4W

[a second staffer's name]—any 10 from 2W

[a third staffer's name]—I will get with you—if you have time—5 charts from 3W.

I will cover 3W and 5th floor. For this month's QA, do not just note probs [problems], but where you can—actually make the changes on the chart.

This does not mean changing dates, etc. It means if the MTP does not have individualized strategies, then add them. If a signature is needed on the plan, go get it!!

If there are no DC [discharge] planning notes, review the chart and add a final social services DC note.

Any questions, see me. Realize that these are things we SHOULD ALREADY HAVE BEEN DOING. Thank you.

The practitioner plaintiff claimed that the memo constituted a directive to the staff to alter the records, if necessary, to cover up any omissions. She said that the director did not instruct the staff to indicate that the record had been amended and claimed that the director wanted staff to participate in his attempt to deceive the accreditation team. Her view was that making entries in records of cases on which they had not worked was unconscionable and that this was what the director was asking staff to do.

The practitioner plaintiff claimed that she was forced to resign her position because of her refusal to participate in the director's plan. She alleged that she was given an ultimatum to either quit her job or be fired. In the lawsuit, she alleged that she lost wages, her career was interrupted, and she experienced serious mental anguish as a result of the incident and her employment termination.

The department director defended his actions and the statements in his memo. The director claimed that aspects of the staffer's job performance were unacceptable and that on one occasion the worker had violated patients' privacy rights. What follows is an excerpt from the director's deposition, conducted by the practitioner's attorney (I have excerpted a significant portion of this deposition to illustrate the fine detail that is often examined during this aspect of legal proceedings, usually called pretrial discovery):

Q: Can you tell me what happened that led to her [the plaintiff's] termination then in September?
A: On September 20th we were having a group Social Service meeting. We had invited—there were two Social Work interns—I'm not sure if it was their first day, but possibly the first day they had ever seen or been in [the hospital]—and they were invited to also attend the meeting. And we had a survey approaching, I think with [the accreditation organization], I'm not sure if it was—yeah, it was [the accreditation organization].

Q: That's the national psychiatric hospital group you referred to at the beginning?

A: You know what that is.

Q: Okay.

A: And in that meeting, what I—I told each of the employees to make—part of QA [quality assurance]—back to QA—is an ongoing, where you check your active charts to make sure that treatment plans accurately reflect the services that are being provided. So, I encouraged all of the Social Workers to continue to do that.

Q: So, in other words, keep your charts up to snuff?

A: Well, what that would mean would be: if a patient was receiving medication. And where you see that would be in the Process Notes and the Progress Notes. If a nurse administered the meds it's documented. If a patient gets activities therapy, it's documented. If nursing encourages and gets a patient's feelings, she'll document it. And if the Master Treatment Plan does not document those procedures and services that are being performed, then we have an inaccurate record.

Q: And that was the Social Worker's responsibility?

A: Correct.

Q: To make sure that the Master Treatment Plan reflected what was actually happening?

A: Correct.

Q: Okay.

A: I instructed them on their active charts to make sure and do that. And I also told each of them to pull ten charts of discharged patients and to review the Progress Notes and compare it to the treatment plan to see if there were any procedures that had been done which were not documented on the treatment plan, which would be an inaccurate chart. And if they were documented, the Progress Notes, to add those procedures on to the treatment plan, to document what was actually being done.

Q: Was this like the usual treatment, a QA, if they didn't do their own or did they do other people's?

A: This was like when they were doing other people's; ten random charts.

Q: So, this was on patients they had never seen?

A: Correct.

Q: Now, [what] was usual procedure on QA?

A: I would usually get feedback from QA on exactly those same issues routinely, and they would routinely do that on the active charts.

Q: So, they would routinely do it on the active charts which are their own, or other people's?

A: Their own.

Q: Okay. And this was different in that these were not their own?

A: They would routinely give feedback on those exact issues whether it was an active record or closed charts which were not their own.

Q: But in this case, they're going to the medical records you've described, picking out random charts, and they are to see whether the Progress Notes and treatment notes matched, and if they don't, they're to add them—

A: Not if they match.

Q: Not if they match?

A: See, if there is—to see if there's documentation of services or procedures received in the Progress Notes that that is also documented on the Master Treatment Plan.

Q: Okay. But these were patients who had closed charts?

A: Correct. Actually, it wasn't a closed chart, really, until they did that, because it was inaccurate record.

Q: But, routinely, it was the job of the Social Worker who worked with that patient to do this, not people who had never seen them?

A: Routinely, on the active charts the Social Workers would do that and they would routinely give me feedback on those same issues on closed charts . . .

Q: Why was this time, on the 20th of September, any different than what had been done in the past? Why did you ask them to do this?

A: I probably should have done that all along. Because what was leaving was— they would give me the feedback—I was leaving inaccurate records. I was leaving a treatment plan which didn't accurately reflect what actually happened to the patients. So in retrospect, I probably should have had them do it all of the time.

Q: Go back in and fix up closed charts?

A: No, go back in and make sure the treatment plan reflects accurately the procedures that are actually performed as documented in the Progress Notes.

Q: On open charts?

A: No, on closed charts.

Q: Okay. So, your view is you should have been doctoring closed charts all of the time?

A: No, no, that's not what I said. My view is, if a closed chart—in the Progress Notes, the patient receives antidepressant medication every day and if the Master Treatment Plan, which is supposed to be a summary of all of the services that are being provided, and the patient's responses to it, doesn't document that they are receiving antidepressant medication, it's an inaccurate chart.

Q: Right. But these are supposed to be contemporaneous records, correct?

A: I'm not sure what you mean.

Q: These things are supposed to be documented at the time the patient's in the hospital, not after the chart's gone to the record room?

A: The chart—it's preferable if as—it is preferable if the chart, on an ongoing basis, accurately reflects what is being performed. That is preferable, if the plan reflects that.

Q: Was this your idea or did someone suggest you do this?

A: This was my idea.

Q: No one suggested it to you?

A: Initially, it was my idea . . .

Q: Now these are closed charts?

A: Correct . . .

Q: And you wanted them to go through the record and add summaries or individual strategies—which you've described as if they were receiving medication or activity—and they were to add them?

A: If there was documentation that they were receiving them.

Q: Okay. How, physically, were they supposed to do that in the record? This is all handwritten?

A: Correct.

Q: And they were just to stick it in where it belonged?

A: To put in under—if it was a medical intervention that was being done and it was documented in the Progress Notes, to add it in the appropriate place on the Master Treatment Plan.

Q: Would anyone looking at this have known that it was added later?

A: I'm not sure.

Q: So, it's possible that there was nothing to say it was or wasn't added later where it was done?

A: I am not sure.

Q: You did some of them didn't you?

A: Yes.

Q: Was there any way, on the ones you did, to tell—for anyone to tell that they were added at a later time then [*sic*] when the chart was closed?

A: Probably not . . .

The staffer who sued was not successful. The lower court dismissed the case, and the staffer lost her subsequent appeal to the state's supreme court, which ruled that there was insufficient evidence that the department director's instructions to his staff were inappropriate.

In general, if a practitioner finds that accurate details were inadvertently omitted, a possibility in every practitioner's professional life, the information can be added, but the record should clearly show that the entry was made subsequently. The practitioner should sign and date the change to show that it is an emendation (revision). It is hard to imagine any circumstance in which it would be appropriate for practitioners to fill in gaps or make other entries in records for cases on which they did not work.

A troubling form of deceit and fraud that I have encountered concerns behavioral health administrators who produce false accounts of expenditures and other allocations of agency resources. Administrators often need to juggle budget categories in order to enhance productivity, access to services, and effectiveness. It is one of the enduring challenges of administrative positions.

However, administrators occasionally have been too creative with their budgets, sometimes for self-serving reasons, and end up being deceitful or fraudulent to cover their tracks. The anecdote that follows describes a set of circumstances that I encountered in one program.

Joanne M. was the executive director of a mental health center that served a county of about 120,000 residents. Joanne M. had been director of the program for six years. She was well regarded in the community and by her board of directors. Several staff members, however, were critical of Joanne M.'s administrative style and leadership.

The mental health agency depended on federal funds and an annual grant from the state behavioral health agency to provide casework services to low-income people who struggle with chronic mental illness. The funds were used to pay the salaries of three caseworkers and overhead involved in the delivery of services.

During a recent four-month period, the program operated with only two caseworkers. One caseworker had been on unpaid leave to take care of an ailing relative. As a result, the agency saved about $39,000 in staff salaries.

Joanne M. decided to use the savings to purchase computer equipment that she could use in her own home for, she said, work-related purposes. The funding guidelines, however, prohibited use of the funds for capital expenditures. In her annual accounting and report to the state behavioral health agency, Joanne M. did not report the one caseworker's leave of absence. She also did not report that the federal and state funds were used to purchase computer equipment. The unauthorized appropriation of funds was uncovered in a random audit by the state auditor general's office. The deputy auditor general then informed Joanne M. that the auditor general was considering taking both civil and criminal action against her.

Although administrators can often justify reallocation of funds to meet agency needs, they must abide by funders' guidelines concerning changes made after the initial allocation. Some funders provide administrators with a margin of flexibility; for example, a 5 percent shift of funds among specified categories, such as personnel or equipment lines. Some funders, however, prohibit any allocation changes without formal authorization. Of course, no funders would permit administrators to siphon funds for their personal use. Any departure from established funding guidelines and administrative practices may expose a behavioral health administrator to civil suits and/or criminal charges.

In a widely publicized case of fraud and conflict of interest, the former president of a mental health clinic was sentenced to nearly seven years in federal prison for perpetrating a multiyear fraud scheme through which the former agency director stole more than $2 million dollars that was supposed to be spent to help some of the most at-risk individuals in her community.

A federal court jury found Renee Tartaglione of Philadelphia, Pennsylvania, guilty on fifty-three counts of conspiracy, fraud, theft, and tax crimes. In addition to the prison sentence, the judge ordered Tartaglione to forfeit $2.4 million in proceeds from her scheme and to pay $2,076,024 in restitution to the Pennsylvania Attorney General's Office.

According to the evidence presented at trial, between 2007 and 2015, Tartaglione, as president of the Board of Directors of the Juniata Community Mental Health Clinic ("JCMHC"), defrauded and stole money from JCMHC through a series of actions designed to benefit her personally at the expense of the clinic. For example, Tartaglione purchased the building on 3rd Street in Philadelphia that housed the clinic and then proceeded to raise the rent repeatedly, causing the clinic's rent for the 3rd Street building to increase from $4,500 per month to $25,000 per month.

Additionally, Tartaglione's company acquired an interest in another building in Philadelphia, and Tartaglione caused the clinic to spend money to fix up that building. In December 2012, Tartaglione leased that building to JCMHC under a lease that called for rent of $35,000 per month for the first two years and $75,000 per month for the next three years. The rent Tartaglione charged the nonprofit clinic at both buildings was wildly in excess of the market rent.

None of the JCMHC rent increases or the lease agreements were approved by JCMHC's board of directors. Tartaglione and her co-conspirators created false and fictitious documents in an attempt to make the transactions appear legitimate.[24]

### DECEPTION AND FRAUD MOTIVATED BY ALTRUISM

In some instances, behavioral health practitioners engage in deceit and fraud primarily to help clients. For example, they may eschew damaging diagnostic labels on insurance claim forms to avoid stigmatizing clients. In addition to documenting the extent of overdiagnosis, as described earlier, Kirk and Kutchins gathered evidence that practitioners sometimes underdiagnose, presumably to benefit clients. Some practices observed and reported by Kirk and Kutchins's sample suggest that professionals often misdiagnose to help clients; that is, to avoid labeling them. For example, most respondents in their sample (87 percent) indicated that a less serious diagnosis than clinically indicated was used frequently or occasionally to avoid labeling clients. Seventy-eight percent reported that they frequently or occasionally used only the least serious of several appropriate diagnoses on official records. Most (82 percent) acknowledged that they frequently or occasionally used the diagnosis of adjustment disorder when a more serious diagnosis might be more accurate.

Practitioners might intentionally deceive to benefit clients in other ways as well. Imagine, for example, a psychotherapist who has been providing counseling services to a client, a forty-one-year-old woman, who had been manifesting relatively modest anxiety symptoms. On occasion, the client experienced panic attacks, although the attacks tended to be rather mild.

The client originally sought counseling from the practitioner to help her cope with a conflict-ridden divorce.

After being in counseling with the practitioner for about four months, the client one day asked the practitioner to write a letter in support of her application for disability benefits. The client said that she was "sick and tired" of her job as a store manager and was finding it difficult to work during the divorce proceedings. The client told the practitioner that she—the therapist—would probably need to embellish her letter in order to make a convincing case for disability. The client conceded that a candid report from the practitioner would not be helpful, in light of the client's rather mild anxiety symptoms.

The practitioner wanted to be supportive of her client and decided to write a convincing, albeit largely embellished, letter to the client's disability insurer. Shortly thereafter, an insurance company representative contacted the practitioner and at first politely challenged the therapist's assessment of her client's disability. Toward the end of the conversation, the insurance company representative told the practitioner that she had substantial evidence that the client was not in fact disabled and that the insurance company was concerned that the therapist was helping the client to perpetrate a fraud. The insurance company representative ended the conversation by saying that according to company policy, she was obligated to refer the case to the local insurance fraud investigation unit.

Although the practitioner was merely trying to be helpful, the embellished letter exposed her to considerable risk. Practitioners must be careful to include in letters written on clients' behalf only those details that practitioners can document and substantiate. To do otherwise, even for altruistic reasons, is quite risky.

Practitioners should exercise similar caution and reserve when writing reference letters on behalf of agency staff members who may be pursuing positions elsewhere. On occasion, practitioners will inflate their evaluations of a colleague in the agency to help that individual secure employment. Here too, practitioners incur considerable risk if they knowingly attest to skills and qualifications that the subject of the letter does not have. The other agency could hire this individual in part because of the practitioner's recommendation. If that individual ends up engaging in some negligent action that might have been avoided if the individual had actually had the skills endorsed in the practitioner's recommendation letter, the author of the letter could be at risk. While it may seem unlikely that the practitioner who wrote the reference letter would be named as a defendant in a lawsuit, this is not a risk worth taking. To be on the safe side, practitioners should include in recommendation or reference letters only those details they know to be true or have good reason to believe are true. Critical or negative comments are defensible if, in fact, they are true and can be backed up if challenged. Many behavioral health organizations require that staffers limit the content of letters to dates of employment.

Practitioners must also avoid altering dates of service to help clients obtain insurance reimbursement. In one case, a psychotherapy client left her job and, thus, lost her insurance coverage. The client asked her therapist to list false session dates that preceded the loss of coverage so that she could be reimbursed for sessions that took place after the loss of coverage. The insurance company detected the falsified dates and referred the clinician for criminal prosecution (insurance fraud).

One final form of deception and fraud concerns behavioral health administrators who fabricate research or program evaluation results to enhance the likelihood of obtaining or retaining funding from some out-side source. Administrators whose agencies depend on outside funding are under substantial pressure. They have a considerable incentive to present as positive a picture as possible about the agency's efficiency and effectiveness. However, such pressure can prove the downfall of an otherwise competent administrator.

Roland M. was the executive director of the Strathmore Substance Abuse Treatment Center. Strathmore was a private nonprofit agency that was about to begin its seventeenth year of service. The agency received about 60 percent of its revenue from the local Community Fund. The remaining funds were obtained from the state mental health agency's substance use disorders division (25 percent) and client fees (15 percent).

Several years earlier, the Community Fund implemented new guidelines for member agencies. The Community Fund insisted on program evaluation data to demonstrate the effectiveness of services provided with its money. Member agencies were to collaborate with Community Fund staff to determine an acceptable program evaluation strategy. Most consisted of relatively simple outcome measures using primary and secondary data.

In Strathmore's case, the Community Fund wanted program staff members to collect data on lengths of stays in the residential component of the program, relapse rates, and costs per unit of service.

Roland M. was nervous about the program evaluation. Given that he depended on the Community Fund for such a large portion of his budget, he felt he could not afford unfavorable results. At the suggestion of the Community Fund's staff, Roland M. and his board of directors retained an outside evaluator, a consultant from the local university. The consultant conducted the study over a nine-month period. Some of the most significant results were disappointing and unflattering. Roland M. was especially concerned about the discouraging data on relapse rates and program dropouts.

Unbeknown to the consultant, Roland M. modified several facts and figures in the consultant's final report to shed a more favorable light on the agency. However, an astute Community Fund staff member noticed a couple of inconsistencies in the report and telephoned the consultant for an explanation. The consultant and the Community Fund staff shortly found that Roland M. had altered some results. As a consequence, Strathmore lost its Community Fund subsidy, and the Community Fund threatened to sue to recover a portion of the current year's allocation that was based in part on the report's results.

Relatively few behavioral health administrators actively engage in deceit and fraud. Among those who do, some are motivated primarily by self-interest and greed. Their sleight of hand is designed to exploit others to line their own pockets or advance their own careers.

Others, however, have more altruistic intentions. These practitioners may be moved by the plights of clients or genuine concern about the financial stability and future of the agencies that they administer. Their more noble motives do not excuse whatever deceit and fraud they engage in, of course. Nonetheless, these practitioners' actions contrast markedly with those of their self-centered colleagues whose deceit and fraud are driven essentially by self-interest.

And, human nature being what it is, in many instances practitioners' deceitful and fraudulent activities depend on mixed motives. That is, practitioners are inspired by simultaneous concern about themselves and others. An example of this phenomenon is practitioners who submit fraudulent diagnoses to insurance companies to help clients obtain needed services and to enhance their own income.

Whatever the motives—whether singularly self-interested, altruistic, or mixed—behavioral health practitioners need to be cognizant of deceit and fraud in the ranks. They must avoid whatever temptation exists in their own work to deceive and defraud—if for no other reason than to avoid the accompanying liability risks—and they must engage in preventative efforts to discourage deception and fraud elsewhere in the profession.

# CHAPTER 8

# Interruption and Termination of Service

Malpractice and liability risks also arise in relation to interruption and termination of service. In my experience, the most frequent problems concern allegations that behavioral health professionals failed to terminate services properly, failed to continue needed services, or were unavailable to clients who were in need of care. Improper termination of service might occur, for instance, when a practitioner transfers to a new position or moves out of town without adequately preparing a client for the termination or without referring a client to a new service provider. Or, a practitioner might terminate services abruptly to a client who is noncompliant or because a client is unable to pay for the care. As noted in chapter 3, the advent of online and other remote counseling services introduces novel termination risks when practitioners are not available to assist clients they never meet in person.[1] Practitioners also risk liability when they are unavailable and have failed to properly instruct clients about how to handle emergencies that may arise.

## THE CONCEPT OF ABANDONMENT

A substantial portion of claims regarding termination of services involves allegations of abandonment. Abandonment is a legal concept that refers to instances when a professional is not available to a client when needed. Once a behavioral health practitioner begins to provide service to a client, whether in person or remotely (e.g., using online or other distance counseling services), the practitioner incurs an ethical and legal responsibility to sustain that service or to refer a client to an alternative service provider.

Practitioners are not, of course, obligated to serve every individual who requests assistance. The practitioner might not have room for a new client or may lack the specialized expertise a particular client may need.

However, once a practitioner begins service, she cannot terminate it abruptly. Rather, practitioners are obligated to conform to the profession's standard of care regarding termination of service and referral to other providers in the event the client is still in need. As Schutz suggests with respect to termination of psychotherapy services, "Once a patient makes a contact with a therapist and the therapist agrees to see him, he is that therapist's patient. The therapist then assumes the fiduciary duty not to abandon the patient. At the very least, therefore, he must refer the patient to another therapist if he elects to terminate the relationship."[2]

Behavioral health practitioners have to be careful not to extend services to clients beyond the point where they are warranted, clinically or otherwise. But as the case that follows illustrates, practitioners sometimes fail to terminate services when termination is in the client's best interest.

Scott N. was a mental health counselor in solo private practice. He had begun his private practice approximately six months earlier after working for seven years at a local community mental health center. Scott N. decided to begin his private practice to enhance his autonomy and to get away from what was beginning to feel like onerous bureaucracy at the community mental health center.

Scott N. knew that building up his client base would take a number of months and that his income would be modest during this period. He was concerned, however, about the relatively small number of referrals and inquiries that he had been receiving. The stagnant local economy exacerbated the problem because fewer people could afford private counseling services, and the relatively high unemployment rate in the community meant that fewer people had third-party coverage for mental health services.

With two children in college, Scott N. was getting more and more nervous about being able to pay his bills. One consequence was that he avoided terminating three clients who clinically were ready for termination. Scott N. intentionally prolonged their treatment in order to sustain the revenue that these clients generated.

Two different insurance companies, both of which had contracts with managed-care firms, covered the services for these clients. At specified junctures in the treatment process, Scott N. had to contact the managed-care companies to seek approval for additional sessions with these clients. In his communications with the managed-care representatives, Scott N. had to exaggerate their symptoms to make the case for such approval.

A practitioner who fails to terminate properly and in the process attempts to deceive an insurance company obviously incurs risk. Clients may be upset about the prolonged treatment, and third-party payers may sue to recover fees that they paid the practitioner and refer the case for criminal prosecution. Thus, practitioners must be particularly careful to avoid extending services beyond what is warranted, clinically or otherwise.

### PREMATURE TERMINATION

More common, however, are instances in which the practitioner or client terminates services prematurely. Premature termination can occur for several different reasons. First, clients may initiate the termination of services, perhaps against the advice of practitioners and other professionals involved in their care. Second, the practitioner or other professional might initiate the termination, as when the practitioner finds that a particular client is not making adequate progress or is unable to pay for services. In addition practitioners who find a particular client too difficult to handle are at risk of terminating services inappropriately. Clients who object to a practitioner's decision to terminate services may file a lawsuit or licensing-board complaint.

#### Client-Initiated Termination

Clients in residential and nonresidential programs sometimes decide unilaterally that they do not want to continue receiving services. Clients may leave residential programs against professional advice or may decide not to return for outpatient services.

In a South Dakota case, for example, a psychiatric patient who had a history of violence was taken on an outing and escaped, thereby terminating service. No one notified police of the man's dangerousness for about twelve hours after the escape. The patient broke into a home and killed a woman and her daughter. The plaintiff alleged that allowing the patient to go on the outing and not notifying law enforcement officials that the man was dangerous constituted negligence on the part of the psychiatrists in charge of the patient. The case was settled for $950,000.[3]

In *Boles v. Milwaukee County*, a woman with a history of mental illness was brought to a hospital emergency room after her sister observed her striking herself repeatedly. Because of this self-destructive behavior, emergency room personnel placed the woman in restraints. Within less than thirty minutes, the patient told a nurse that she felt better and wanted to return home. Before a psychiatrist arrived for a consultation, the woman left the hospital, shouted at cars, struck them with her hands, and was struck and killed by a car when she ran into the street. The woman's children sued the hospital, claiming that staff failed to properly detain her in order to make an appropriate assessment. The appellate court affirmed the lower court's finding in favor of the family, concluding that the hospital's failure to detain the patient until completion of the psychiatric examination was "palpably negligent."[4]

However, a Texas jury did not hold a hospital liable for injuries sustained by a patient who essentially terminated his own services by fleeing from the hospital. The plaintiff, a voluntary psychiatric patient at the hospital, and two other patients fled the building and were pursued by hospital employees. The plaintiff climbed a fence and ran along the shoulder of a highway, attempted to cross the lanes, tripped, and was hit by a truck. The plaintiff's leg was shattered and required extensive and repeated surgery. He argued that the hospital staff breached the standard of care in pursuing a voluntary patient and attempting to restrain him against his will.[5]

### Practitioner-Initiated Termination

In contrast, a practitioner's decision to terminate a client might result in premature termination. In residential programs, for example, staff members may terminate a client prematurely because they find that the client is not making adequate progress, is not complying with program rules or expectations, they want to open up a bed for a client who will generate a higher reimbursement rate because of insurance coverage, or the client's insurance benefits have run out. Of course, premature termination sometimes occurs because of poor clinical judgment about the client's readiness for community-based living.

In 1981, a Kansas man sued a hospital and its doctors, claiming that his son was discharged prematurely. The son had been involuntarily admitted to a state hospital after an assault on his grandparents. During the son's stay at the state hospital, staff members decided that he should be transferred to a hospital in Salem, Oregon. However, the Kansas hospital's clinical director, who had never had contact with the patient, sent a note to the leader of the treatment team at his hospital stating that the patient is "physically healthy and suffers from a character disorder and . . . furthermore is not motivated for treatment. It rather looks to me that we should discharge this patient." The patient was discharged and killed his mother and brother.

The defendants in the lawsuit disagreed about the reason for the discharge. The clinical director testified that the patient was discharged because he demonstrated no motivation for treatment; the treatment team, however, stated that he was discharged because he was "doing so well." The federal district court in Kansas held that the hospital and doctors were negligent in discharging the patient prematurely and in not conducting an adequate assessment to determine his readiness for discharge. The court awarded the father damages.[6]

A New York case raised similar issues. The plaintiff, a young woman, sued the New York City Health and Hospitals Corporation, alleging that a city hospital prematurely released and terminated services to a woman with serious psychiatric illness who subsequently injured the plaintiff. The plaintiff had been waiting on a subway platform in New York City when the woman, released from the hospital the previous month, pushed the plaintiff in front of an oncoming train. The plaintiff sustained serious injuries, including blindness in one eye and various other head injuries; she experienced memory loss and permanent injury to her head, face, arms, legs, hip, and abdomen.

In her lawsuit, the plaintiff claimed that the hospital had discharged her attacker prematurely. The week before her release, the woman had been restrained in a straitjacket after various acts of violence against herself and others. Just before her release, the hospital kept the woman in the highest form of security, and her treating physician noted her lack of understanding and concern about her treatment program upon release. The physician stated that he doubted the woman could succeed in her treatment program. A jury awarded the plaintiff $1.5 million.[7]

A Texas jury also entered a judgment against a hospital in the case of a son who killed his father. The father had sought emergency psychiatric care and detention for his son. The son had been hospitalized four times and had received a diagnosis of chronic schizophrenia. The son was prescribed neuroleptic (antipsychotic) medication but was released before anyone administered the medication or monitored its effectiveness. The next morning, the son killed his father. The plaintiffs claimed that the hospital was negligent because it failed to detain the son and follow through with proper treatment.[8]

An Indiana man sued an agency after he was discharged and then injured himself. The plaintiff had been admitted to a state hospital after a suicide attempt and was discharged the following day. Later the same day, he attempted suicide again by pouring flammable substances over his body and igniting them. He suffered extensive burns. The case was settled, with the state of Indiana's Patient Compensation Fund paying him $300,000 and the doctor's insurance company paying $100,000.[9]

In a Pennsylvania case, the plaintiff was a woman who had a history of self-destructive behavior and had been hospitalized for treatment of severe mental illness. She was then released to another individual's custody. The plaintiff locked her custodian out of the custodian's own house and then ingested lye. In her lawsuit, the plaintiff alleged that she had been released inappropriately, particularly given that the hospital and other defendants were aware of her history of mental illness, destructive behavior, and suicidal tendencies. The jury awarded damages against the hospital.[10]

Courts do not always find behavioral health staff and agencies liable when discharged clients subsequently harm another individual or themselves.

For example, in North Carolina, a mental health center and one of its psychiatrists were sued after a recently discharged client killed a fifty-eight-year-old man in a knife fight. The client, who had been admitted to the center in an intoxicated state, had been discharged after being examined by a staff psychiatrist. The plaintiffs alleged that releasing the client and terminating services to him constituted negligence. The defendants argued that they had no legal justification to continue involuntary commitment of the client. The jury found in the defendants' favor.[11]

A California court also found a hospital and its staff were not liable in injuries sustained by a patient injured in a suicide attempt. The plaintiff, a nineteen-year-old survivor of incest who had a history of suicide attempts and severe depression, was admitted voluntarily to the psychiatric unit of a local medical center. Shortly after admission, however, staff learned that the woman's insurance coverage would not cover the admission. The woman was discharged despite her adamant request to remain; she had promised to borrow the money to enable her to stay hospitalized.

Several hours after discharge, the woman attempted suicide by driving her automobile off a cliff. She suffered severe injuries that required hospitalization for three and one-half months. The woman claimed that her psychiatric treatment was inadequate and was inappropriately terminated in light of her suicidal symptoms. Hospital staff, however, argued that the woman's financial status was unrelated to the reasons for discharge and that termination of service was consistent with the standard of care.[12]

The liability risks associated with premature discharge when a patient's insurance benefits have been exhausted are addressed in a North Carolina case. The parents of a sixteen-year-old boy sued the hospital, claiming that their son's suicide was the result of premature discharge when the insurance coverage ran out. The boy had been admitted to the psychiatric hospital and remained there until two days after his insurance coverage was exhausted. Two weeks after discharge, the boy committed suicide by taking a drug overdose. The parents argued that they received no warning that their son was suicidal, that family therapy was not provided, and that the agency to which the hospital had referred the boy for follow-up care did not receive adequate information about his condition.

The psychiatrist involved in the case settled out of court. A jury awarded the parents $7.09 million against the hospital ($1.09 million in compensatory damages and $6 million in punitive damages), although the trial judge reduced the compensatory damage award slightly (to $1.03 million).[13]

In another North Carolina case, a twenty-five-year-old man was admitted to a hospital for treatment of suicidal ideation. The hospital determined that the man's insurance would cover a twelve-day stay. The patient expressed concern about being discharged but was released when his insurance coverage ran out. The next day, the man shot and killed himself. The plaintiffs alleged that the man had been discharged only because his insurance coverage ran out and not because of his clinical status. The parties reached a $3 million settlement.[14]

Behavioral health practitioners in outpatient settings have been known to terminate clients prematurely when they find them resistant, hostile, uncooperative, or otherwise difficult to handle. I am familiar with a case in which a practitioner was sued by a former client who claimed that the practitioner terminated her relationship with the client abruptly and precipitously. The severely disabled woman had sought counseling from a practitioner who specialized in treatment of people with physical disabilities. After several months of intervention, the practitioner found it extremely difficult to relate to the client. She claimed that the client was excessively demanding and hostile and was consuming inordinate amounts of her professional time. The practitioner said that the client telephoned her frequently and left angry voicemail messages when the practitioner did not return the call promptly.

The practitioner became more and more resentful of the client and during one particularly heated conversation told the client that she would no longer be able to serve her. The client mailed the practitioner a certified letter asking for an explanation, but the practitioner refused to accept the letter. In addition, the practitioner made no attempt to provide the client with names of other practitioners whom she could contact for assistance.

Although the practitioner's frustration in this case may be understandable, her virtual abandonment of her client, including her refusal to accept the client's letter, is not. Practitioners should take reasonable steps to avoid abandoning clients who are still in need of services. Practitioners should withdraw services precipitously only under unusual circumstances, giving careful consideration to all factors in the situation and taking care to minimize possible adverse effects. Practitioners should assist in making appropriate arrangements for continuation of services when necessary. Practitioners who anticipate the termination or interruption of services to clients should notify clients promptly and seek the transfer, referral, or continuation of services in relation to the clients' needs and preferences. As R. Cohen states:

> No doctor in private practice is legally compelled to accept any patient for treatment. The mental health professional may feel that he does not have the expertise to deal with a particular problem; he may not have the number of hours needed to provide adequate services; he may not see himself as able

to establish a good enough rapport with the patient; the patient may not be able to pay the doctor's fee, etc. But while there are any number of perfectly acceptable reasons for refusing to treat a patient, there is *no* reason to justify abandonment of a patient once treatment begins. Before accepting a new patient, the mental health professional would be wise to schedule an initial consultation for the purpose of a mutual evaluation of suitability. If a doctor accepts a patient but some time later believes he can no longer be of value (because, for example, he has discovered factors operating that are beyond his competence to deal with), "following through" would mean advising this patient of the state of affairs and referring him to an appropriate mental health professional.[15]

The reasons for termination of care were the central issue in a Missouri case. A thirteen-year-old boy was being seen as an outpatient at a state hospital. According to the plaintiffs—the boy's parents—they met with the treating physician two and one-half weeks before their son committed suicide and informed the doctor of their son's suicide threats. A psychiatric resident who had seen the boy had referred the parents to the physician. The physician diagnosed the boy's condition as panic anxiety accompanied by a preoccupation with death. He saw the boy during the next two days, prescribed medication, and removed himself from the case five days after his consultation with the boy's parents.

The resident's notes, however, did not indicate that the other physician had removed himself from the case or that the other physician had transferred the boy back to the original treatment team at the state hospital. Two original team members were no longer available (one had left the job and another was on vacation).

After discharge the boy committed suicide, just as he had threatened, by driving a car into a concrete embankment. Four teenage passengers in the car also died. The boy's family alleged, among other claims, that the treating physician's termination of his involvement in the case was improper. The doctor argued that he removed himself from the case because he thought the care provided by the treatment team would be adequate. He also claimed that his withdrawal from the case was not the proximate cause of the boy's death, that the death resulted from an accident, not suicide, and that the parents were at fault in allowing the boy to have access to car keys and in their monitoring of his medication. The jury awarded the parents

$750,000 but under the doctrine of comparative negligence reduced the award by 25 percent because of fault by the parents.[16]

Practitioners in managed-care settings need to be particularly careful about the ways in which they terminate services. If clients' insurance companies refuse to authorize services or an extension of services, practitioners should be sure to advise clients of their right to appeal the decision and offer to assist the client with the appeal process. Otherwise, practitioners may expose themselves to allegations that they abandoned their clients. According to Madden:

> The provider's duty is to give all of the care that is necessary to the client, regardless of the decision of the managed care company to authorize payment for the services. Although this may seem unduly burdensome on clinicians, particularly those in a private practice setting, these are important legal guidelines that protect clients while not causing undue financial hardship to the clinician. The decision to terminate treatment must be based on clinical evidence, not managed care authorization (Corcoran & Vandiver 1996). The duty of the clinician is to seek approval, through any and all appeals processes, if continued treatment is indicated. Further, the clinician should try to make arrangements with the client for payment including such options as reduced fee/sliding scale options (unless prohibited by the managed care or insurance company). Alternatively, the clinician may refer the client to an agency that provides reduced fee or free services. As noted above, the referral process should be carefully attended to so as to ensure that the client actually receives the services. This issue comes down to a decision by the mental health care provider to decide whether to run the risk of a malpractice suit by not providing treatment that is judged to be necessary by the clinician but not by the managed care company.[17]

Also, behavioral health practitioners should be scrupulous about the ways in which they handle clients who have not paid overdue bills for services rendered. In general, practitioners assume considerable risk if they let clients accumulate large debt. As the case of *Geis v. Landau* illustrates (see chapter 3), courts have been critical of practitioners who have allowed clients to build up large unpaid bills. However, practitioners can, in principle, terminate services to clients who have not paid their debts, so long as the practitioners do so ethically. Practitioners in fee-for-service settings may terminate services to clients who are not paying an overdue balance if the financial contractual arrangements have been made clear to the client, if the client does not pose an imminent danger to self or others, and if the clinical and other consequences of the current nonpayment have been addressed and discussed with the client.

Practitioners can also be liable for abandonment if they fail to provide clients with sufficient instructions about what to do when the practitioner is unavailable because of vacation, illness, or emergencies. This also applies to practitioners who provide remote counseling services online or through other means; for example, video counseling or telephone counseling. Practitioners should always provide clients with clearly stated information, including who to call and how to handle emergencies. I always recommend that practitioners provide these instructions to clients in writing and include in the case record a copy of the instructions, signed by the clients to acknowledge that they received the instructions and that the instructions were explained to them.

Practitioners should be especially careful to arrange for competent coverage when they know that they will not be available for a period of time. The colleagues who are to provide coverage should be given information about clients' status sufficient to enable them to provide adequate care should the need arise (after obtaining clients' consent to the release of such information consistent with the law, of course).

In light of modern technology, practitioners should also be careful about regularly checking their text, e-mail, and voicemail messages. It is important to refer clients to a colleague if they need immediate help and the practitioner is unavailable. Failure to retrieve messages and provide proper referral could result in a liability claim alleging abandonment.

### PREVENTION STRATEGY

Behavioral health practitioners should consider a number of protocols to avoid charges of client abandonment:

- Provide clients with the names, addresses, and telephone numbers of at least three appropriate referrals (if there are at least three options in the local community) when it is necessary to terminate services. Practitioners should write letters to their clients documenting their referrals, offering transition sessions, and explaining the reasons for termination.

- Follow up with a client who has been terminated. If the client does not go to the referral, write a letter to him or her about the risks involved should the client not follow through with the referral.
- Clients who will be terminated should be given as much advance warning as possible.
- When clients announce their decision to terminate prematurely, explain to them the risks involved and suggestions for alternative care. Include this information in a follow-up letter.
- Carefully document in the case record all decisions and actions related to termination of services.
- In cases involving discharge of clients from a residential facility, be sure that a comprehensive discharge plan has been formulated and significant others have been notified of the client's discharge (clients should be informed of this). In cases involving clients held in a residential facility by court order, seek legal consultation and court approval before terminating care.
- Provide clients with clear instructions to follow and telephone numbers and other contact information to use in the event of an emergency. Include a copy of the instructions in the client's case record. Clients should be asked to sign this copy, affirming that they received the instructions and that the instructions were explained to them.
- When away from the office for an extended period of time, call in regularly for messages. Practitioners who are away from the office should leave emergency contact information with an appropriate staff person, an answering service, or on voicemail. The voicemail box should be purged regularly to ensure there is room for new messages. Practitioners who anticipate that certain clients may need assistance during their absence (for e.g., clients in crisis) should refer those clients to a colleague who has appropriate expertise.
- Practitioners who provide remote counseling services should ensure that clients understand what steps they should take if they need emergency assistance.
- Practitioners who are leaving an employment setting (e.g., to start a new job) should inform clients of appropriate options for continuation of services (such as transferring to another service provider or continuing with the practitioner in her new employment setting) and of the benefits and risks of the options.

- Consult with colleagues and supervisors about a decision to terminate services. In some cases, addressing relevant issues can prevent termination. For example, practitioners may be able to address a client's reason for not paying an overdue balance and develop a workable payment plan. Practitioners whose clients are not making reasonable progress may be able to modify their intervention to enhance the client's progress.

Some employers will ask new employees to sign "noncompete" agreements when they are first hired. Typically, these agreements are designed to prevent practitioners from competing with the employer if the practitioner chooses to leave the agency's employment; for example, by having agency clients follow the employee to her or his new agency or private practice. These agreements pose significant ethical issues that, in principle, could lead to client abandonment if practitioners are unable to honor clients' wishes to follow the practitioner to a new setting. Ethically, practitioners should explain to clients that clients have several options, including remaining with the current agency and seeing a new provider, transferring to another agency with another practitioner, or following the current practitioner to her or his new location. That is, practitioners should respect clients' right to self-determination. For this reason, practitioners should do their best to avoid signing noncompete agreements. If the practitioner signed a noncompete or nonsolicitation agreement, she should consider communicating with her employer to develop a mutually satisfactory approach. This may involve a jointly prepared letter to clients informing them of their options and how to transfer or access records.

# CHAPTER 9

# Responding to Lawsuits and Board Complaints

Legal liability and licensing-board complaints are unfortunate risks associated with professional practice. They are also relatively rare occurrences. The vast majority of behavioral health practitioners will never be named as defendants in lawsuits or respondents in licensing-board complaints. As I discussed in chapter 1, however, the number of claims against practitioners is significant, as is the monetary value of related out-of-court settlements and judgments. In light of this trend, practitioners need to anticipate the possibility, however remote, that they will be named in a lawsuit or licensing-board complaint. Although this book discusses various causes and sources of risk, practitioners should also be acquainted with conventional advice about how to respond if they are named as a litigation defendant or licensing-board respondent or retained as an expert witness.

## IN THE EVENT OF A LAWSUIT OR LICENSING-BOARD COMPLAINT

Assuming a behavioral health practitioner named in a lawsuit holds a liability insurance policy—which every practitioner should—the insurance company will appoint an attorney to handle the case. Most popular liability insurance companies also cover legal costs associated with licensing-board complaints. Practitioners who lack liability coverage should consult an attorney as well, particularly one who specializes in health-care law, malpractice, and risk management; although this can be expensive, practitioners who proceed without skilled legal counsel do so at their own peril.

In fact, practitioners responding without the benefit of an attorney may inadvertently make unnecessary admissions or increase their exposure by causing a licensing board to expand the scope of the alleged misconduct. Keep in mind that disciplinary action is a public record and gets reported to the National Practitioner Data Bank, which is available to boards in other states. Skilled attorneys familiar with health-care law, litigation, and licensing boards can be remarkably helpful. When selecting a lawyer, practitioners would do well to follow Besharov's sound advice directed at social workers:

> Basically, selecting a lawyer is like selecting a doctor or a therapist. Personal recommendations from friends and colleagues are the best way to identify a qualified professional. Ask around. Find social workers or others who have been sued, find out who represented them, and ask whether they were satisfied with the representation they received. Do not be shy. Ask what the result was, and ask how expensive the lawyer was. Even workers who were represented by counsel provided by insurance companies can provide helpful leads. Most lawyers who handle insurance cases also handle individual clients. . . .
>
> As potential lawyers are being identified, the social worker will have to decide whether to hire a general practitioner or a specialist. Many lawyers still maintain general practices, handling a variety of commercial, tax, financial, real estate, and torts cases. In smaller communities, there may be no choice but to hire a general practitioner. In larger communities, though, there will be a wide choice of specialists. (In fact, some lawyers specialize in plaintiff's tort work, while others specialize in defense work.)
>
> A specialist is more likely to do a satisfactory job handling the case than is a generalist unfamiliar or only marginally familiar with the relevant area of the law.[1]

In many instances, a practitioner's employer will retain an attorney to handle the lawsuit. The practitioner should be sure to talk with the attorney about whether the attorney is planning to represent the practitioner or only the agency.

Practitioners who have been sued may be wise to retain their own lawyer because the attorney retained by the employer may be obligated, first and foremost, to protect the employer's interests. This could create a conflict of interest, particularly if the employer believes that the practitioner, not the employer, was somehow negligent. Having one's own malpractice and liability policy—apart from the policy held by one's employer—provides access to an attorney whose sole mission is defending the individual practitioner.

For a practitioner sued or named in a licensing-board complaint, reacting as calmly and thoughtfully as possible is important. This can be difficult, of course, given the traumatizing nature of adversarial legal proceedings. Ultimately, a carefully planned response will be more effective than an impulsive one.

The first step is to notify the insurer of the lawsuit or complaint. The importance of this step cannot be overestimated. The best course is to make a telephone call and to follow this with a certified letter and a copy of the letter sent by the plaintiff's attorney or, in the case of a licensing-board complaint, the letter and complaint sent by the board. Although it is often tempting to talk with the client (or whoever the plaintiff or complainant is) about the lawsuit or complaint, the practitioner should refrain from doing so. In fact, discussing the case with anyone other than the attorney retained to defend the practitioner is generally a mistake.

The plaintiff's attorney usually asks for copies of case record material and other relevant documents, including electronically stored information (e.g., text messages, e-mail messages, electronic health records, online social networking posts). As I discussed in chapter 7, practitioners must not alter records to fill in gaps or create false impressions. Not only is this wrong, but also the plaintiff's attorney may have already seen unaltered copies of this material and will detect the alteration. This would of course be disastrous. Practitioners accused of spoliation—the destruction or alteration of evidence relevant to litigation or an investigation—risk suffering serious consequences.

A practitioner named in a lawsuit commonly is asked to give a deposition, sworn testimony obtained in question-and-answer form before the trial (known as the discovery phase of litigation). A key goal of depositions is to promote settlement and minimize trial time. Some depositions are conducted remotely using videoconferencing technology, particularly when witnesses live a considerable distance from the lawyer's location. The plaintiff's attorney poses a series of questions, and the entire proceeding is recorded in order to prepare a transcript.

The primary purpose of a deposition is to obtain the practitioner's version of what happened in the case and to provide leads that may be relevant. Of course, the practitioner's attorney also has the option to depose the plaintiff and other parties who may be involved in the case (e.g., family members of the client, colleagues of the practitioner, or expert witnesses whose specialized knowledge may be drawn on by the plaintiff or defendant). Here is a series of helpful guidelines for handling a deposition (some of this discussion also pertains to testimony in court or a licensing-board hearing):[2]

1. The first rule is to be honest. You are under oath and should be telling the truth at all times. If you do not tell the truth, you may be subject to criminal charges. Additionally, if it can be demonstrated that there are falsehoods in your sworn testimony on any point (however minor), then your credibility on other points will be called into question.

2. Do not answer any question unless you are absolutely certain that you understand it fully. Do not be embarrassed to ask for as much clarification as you need or to say "I don't know."

3. If you are uncertain of your facts, state them as forthrightly as possible. On the other hand, if you are asked a question to which you really are not 100 percent certain of the facts, it is acceptable to use qualifiers such as "My best recollection is . . ."; "As best as I can recall . . ."; and "I believe . . ."

4. If you are concerned about how to answer the examiner on some sensitive aspect of the case or you believe that your answer might prove to be embarrassing, discuss the issue fully with your attorney before the deposition. Together you can decide if the matter is relevant to the case and, if so, what position to take.

5. The examiner may ask you what client charts, documents, textbooks, or other sources you have consulted in preparing for your deposition. If you are a witness appearing on someone else's behalf, the lawyer taking the deposition will probably ask you about the financial arrangements that have been made concerning your appearance at the deposition and your participation in the case. Be prepared for such questions by discussing them in advance with your attorney.

6. At any time during the deposition, you may ask to have a private conference with your attorney. Similarly, you may at any time ask for a break if you are becoming fatigued or uncomfortable.

7. The well-known army rule "never volunteer" is most appropriate in a deposition. Do not volunteer any information that you are not specifically

asked about. Often, short answers—"yes" or "no" when possible—are best. However, there are times when it becomes necessary to provide lengthier responses to address key issues in a case. Advance preparation with your attorney will provide invaluable guidance. Do not volunteer to look anything up, obtain any records, or do anything at all unless your attorney has advised you to do so. Do not volunteer the name of someone who might know the answer to a question, and do not volunteer opinions if you are not asked for them.

8. Be cautious about deciding on which client charts, notes, documents, or other memoranda you wish to bring with you into the deposition room, as the examiner may ask to look at such materials. It is therefore a good idea to have your attorney approve whatever it is you wish to bring with you.

9. If the examiner has in her possession a client's chart or some other document and she asks you questions about it, read it over carefully before replying.

10. It is usually a good idea to wait a moment or two before answering any question during the deposition (as opposed to the trial). The brief pause will provide you with additional time to get your answer the way you want it, and it will provide your attorney with the time to raise any objections she might have to the question. Listen carefully to the objections; these may guide you to problems with the questions, such as ambiguity as to the meaning of terms or the time frame, misstating your prior responses, misstating the facts or assuming facts not in evidence, or repeating questions to which you already responded in an effort to get you to change your answer. If your attorney instructs you not to answer the question, do not answer it, even if you think it will help your case to do so.

11. Speak slowly when answering all questions, and stop talking if your attorney interrupts. You may ask for some time to think about an answer to a question if the question is particularly difficult or complicated. Remember, the written transcript of your deposition will not reflect how long it took you to answer any questions, so do not feel pressured into giving quick answers. However, a video-recorded deposition will reveal delays in responses.

12. If the opposing lawyers get into an argument, stay out of it. You should, however, listen carefully to what is being said and be particularly attentive to the point that your own lawyer is trying to make. Such disagreements may alert you to an aspect of the case to which you may not have given due consideration before the deposition.

13. Some examiners may try to provoke you to the point where your judgment and memory are uncertain. Methods of rattling you will vary, but a common technique is to accuse you of being inconsistent in your testimony. Alternatively, the examiner may refer to some document or record that your testimony supposedly contradicts. Be prepared for such contingencies, and do not let the examiner succeed in his goal. Be courteous and professional at all times.

14. Some examiners may appear to be exceptionally concerned, friendly, and understanding. In some instances, this is a ploy designed to obtain more from you than you are willing to give. The examiner is not your buddy. During the deposition, the examiner will probably be sizing you up in terms of where your weak spots are as a witness on the stand. Therefore, you should be cordial but not overly friendly or anxious to please. If you are there to impress the examiner with anything, it is your credibility and self-confidence as a witness.

15. At some point in the deposition, the examiner may attempt to summarize what you have said. Listen carefully to what the attorney says when she or he is supposedly paraphrasing your testimony. Do not let the attorney put words in your mouth. If what she or he is saying is not what you meant to say, do not hesitate to say so. Also, be aware of the fact that you can have any portion of your testimony read back to you at your request.

One of my attorney friends also offers the following suggestions:

- Remember, you can't win a case in a deposition—you can only lose. Be a goalie.
- Depositions are not normal conversations. Everything counts.
- Do not show your anxiety by answering quickly. Pause before answering, and do not offer any visual cues to your uncertainty.

After the court reporter has prepared the deposition transcript, the practitioner should read a copy and correct any errors before signing it. However, if the practitioner becomes aware of an error during the deposition, she should correct it on the record and not wait. It is wise to review the transcript again before going to court to testify, should the case get that far.

While many suggestions concerning depositions also apply to actual courtroom testimony, some do not. For example, many trial attorneys believe that pausing or hesitating too much during courtroom testimony can raise doubt in a jury's mind about a witness's credibility. Also, how the practitioner appears at a trial—with regard to dress (conservative professional dress is usually recommended) and manner—counts much more than it does at a deposition. Jurors often react to subtleties related to a witness's physical appearance, gestures, and mannerisms.

On the witness stand, the practitioner must be careful not to use too much professional jargon or to appear cocky, cavalier, arrogant, condescending, evasive, argumentative, insincere, crude, overly technical, or overbearing. When responding to a question that is difficult to answer, saying simply "I don't know" is fine and often desirable. Contriving an answer in order to sound knowledgeable can backfire.

Maintaining composure on the witness stand, despite an opposing attorney's best efforts to be provocative, is especially important. Practitioners need to be aware that litigation is an adversarial process, and the job of opposing attorneys is to do their best to challenge and discredit the witness's testimony.

As Saltzman and Proch observe:

> Attorneys use a variety of tactics to discredit witnesses and their testimony during cross examination. They use leading questions which require a yes or no answer when no such simple answer is possible or when it would be misleading. They may be condescending, attacking, or overly friendly. They may ask repetitious questions in an attempt to make you answer inconsistently or they may badger you. They may reverse your words. And they may question you about your personal beliefs and your personal life to show possible bias or prejudice or motive to lie. . . .
>
> The important point to remember when faced with such tactics is that this is part of the system and not something that is happening to just you. Your best defense is to remain alert and calm. Resist being lulled into a false sense of security when an attorney seems overly friendly and resist becoming defensive or hostile when an attorney seems to be attacking you.[3]

A special problem sometimes arises when a behavioral health practitioner who is on the witness stand attempts to characterize a former client as having a major mental illness. This might occur if a former client sues a practitioner and during the trial the practitioner attempts to convey the impression that the client is unstable. R. Cohen refers to this as the "What's-wrong-with-that?" phenomenon:

> Many mental health professionals, to their detriment, make what might be termed "What's-wrong-with-that? (WWT)" errors in their court testimony. When a supposedly revealing statement about a patient's pathology compels the majority of the jury to ask themselves, "What's wrong with that?" a WWT error has been made.
>
> For example, suppose "Mr. Citizen," the patient, is forcibly taken from his home by the police, handcuffed, and packed into a police car in full view of his friends and neighbors. And suppose "Dr. Smith," a psychiatrist, testifies that the patient was verbally abusive and hostile to the therapist on admission. Jury members are likely to ask themselves, "What's wrong with that? Who wouldn't be verbally abusive and hostile under such conditions?" This is especially true if Mr. Citizen appears to be composed and "normal" in the courtroom. Smith may compound his WWT error by going on to say something like, "Further, Mr. Citizen denied that he was mentally ill." Again, jury members—who are more likely to identify with a patient than a psychiatrist—are likely to ask themselves, "What's wrong with that? I would deny it under the same circumstances."
>
> To weaken his testimony still further, Smith might testify that the patient's denial of mental illness demonstrated lack of insight, which was evidence of mental illness. Although all of Smith's statements might make sense to experienced mental health professionals, they will probably not make much sense to the lay people of the jury. WWT errors can be avoided with some forethought, factual documentation, and practice in presenting professional opinion to lay audiences.[4]

Practitioners need to be completely candid with their attorney to enable the attorney to prepare the strongest defense possible. Attorneys hate nothing more than surprises in the courtroom or licensing-board hearing, particularly when the opposing attorney reveals damaging information that the attorney's client—the practitioner—failed to disclose ahead of time. It is important to be completely forthright with your own attorney.

### THE ROLE OF THE EXPERT WITNESS

Behavioral health practitioners sometimes serve as expert witnesses. In litigation, practitioners may be expert witnesses on behalf of plaintiffs or defendants. In licensing-board cases, practitioners may be expert witnesses on behalf of respondents (practitioners accused of violating licensing standards) or a licensing board.

An expert witness is a witness who, by virtue of education, training, skill, or experience, is believed to have expertise and specialized knowledge in a particular subject beyond that of the average person. This expertise and specialized knowledge should enable others to officially and legally rely on the witness's specialized (scientific, technical, or other) opinion about an evidence or fact issue within the scope of her expertise to assist the fact finder (judge, jury, or licensing board).

In U.S. courts, under Federal Rule of Evidence 702, an expert witness must be qualified on the topic of testimony. In determining the qualifications of the expert, the Federal Rules of Evidence require that the expert have specialized education, training, or practical experience in the subject matter relating to the case. More specifically, Rule 702 states:

> A witness who is qualified as an expert by knowledge, skill, experience, training, or education may testify in the form of an opinion or otherwise if:
>
> (a) the expert's scientific, technical, or other specialized knowledge will help the trier of fact to understand the evidence or to determine a fact in issue;
>
> (b) the testimony is based on sufficient facts or data;
>
> (c) the testimony is the product of reliable principles and methods; and
>
> (d) the expert has reliably applied the principles and methods to the facts of the case.

Most courts of law follow what is known as the *Daubert* standard regarding the admissibility of testimony from an expert witness.[5] The trial judge uses the *Daubert* standard to make a preliminary assessment of whether an expert's scientific testimony is based on reasoning or methodology that is scientifically valid and can properly be applied to the facts at issue. Under this standard, the factors that may be considered in determining whether the methodology is valid are (1) whether the theory or technique in question can be and has been tested; (2) whether it has been subjected to peer review and publication; (3) its known or potential error rate; (4) the existence and maintenance of standards controlling its operation; and (5) whether it has attracted widespread acceptance within a relevant scientific community. Although the *Daubert* case is binding only on federal courts, the majority of state courts have adopted the *Daubert* reasoning for trials in their jurisdictions. Some courts also draw on the *Frye* standard, which refers more narrowly to the admissibility of scientific evidence.

### PREVENTING LAWSUITS AND LICENSING-BOARD COMPLAINTS: GOOD PRACTICE

As I said in the preface, it is unfortunate that this book is necessary. Everyone in the behavioral health field would prefer that practitioners merely go about their noble business of helping people in need. No practitioner wishes to be distracted by the annoying, burdensome, and distressing problems of professional malpractice and liability.

As in all professions, however, these phenomena are a reality in behavioral health. And much of the malpractice and liability risk in behavioral health is preventable. Throughout this discussion, I have reviewed a variety of practical ways in which professionals can reduce the chances of being sued or having a complaint filed against them. Examples include being careful to protect clients' privacy, managing digital and online communications carefully, complying with standard informed-consent procedures, understanding key confidentiality and privileged communication statutes, avoiding inappropriate dual relationships, documenting services provided to clients and supervision provided to staff, terminating services carefully, using technology properly, and seeking consultation when issues arise that are outside one's range of expertise.

These and the many other practical suggestions that appear throughout this discussion can certainly go a long way toward preventing malpractice and liability. By themselves, however, they constitute a rather shortsighted approach to prevention. Rather, knowledge of these specific ways to prevent malpractice and liability are but supplements to a firm grasp of two essential components of competent performance in the field of behavioral health: good practice and good ethics.

In my experience with respect to malpractice and liability problems in the field of behavioral health, I have been struck by the frequency with which good practice would have avoided lawsuits and licensing-board complaints. Certainly in some cases, good practice by itself would not prevent a complaint. A practitioner who is sued by a former client for having divulged confidential information to protect a third party from imminent violence threatened by the former client has not necessarily engaged in bad practice. In fact, the practitioner may very well have demonstrated good practice skills and made the right decision in deciding to breach confidentiality. That the client chose to sue the practitioner for the breach may simply be unfortunate.

Similarly, a practitioner who is sued or named in a licensing-board complaint for improper referral of a client to a specialist may have practiced good behavioral health. She may have followed proper referral procedures, including giving the client the names of several well-trained colleagues. However, one colleague may have sexually abused the client. The referring practitioner may have had no way to know that her colleague would violate a client in such a way; the perpetrator's behavior may not have been well known in the professional community. In fact, the assault may have been the first such occurrence in his career. Although the outcome was tragic, the referring practitioner may have been in no way at fault. Clearly, practitioners can be competent professionals and still get sued or named in a licensing-board complaint.

Nonetheless, professionals who understand sound practice principles and carry them out every day substantially reduce their chances of being sued. Practitioners who have a firm understanding of confidentiality and privileged communication issues, the assessment process, intervention techniques, termination and boundary issues, proper use of technology to serve clients, and the nature of supervision, consultation, and referral, for example, minimize the likelihood that they will make the sort of mistake that could trigger a complaint. Skillful practice is the most powerful preventative. As Besharov appropriately asserts, in the event of a lawsuit "good practice is the best defense."[6]

In addition, however, solid grounding in professional ethics is essential in order to prevent malpractice and liability. This is often the missing link in behavioral health practitioners' armamentarium.

### PREVENTING LAWSUITS AND LICENSING-BOARD COMPLAINTS: GOOD ETHICS

Professional values and ethics have always been a central ingredient in the prominent behavioral health professions. Historical accounts of the professions' development routinely dwell on the compelling importance of core values and ethical tenets. Over time, beliefs about professional values and ethics have served as the principal organizing theme of the professions' mission and as the normative linchpin in the professions' foundation.

Although the theme of values and ethics has endured in the professions, practitioners' conceptions of what these terms mean, and of their bearing on practice, have changed considerably. However, only recently, relatively speaking, have behavioral health practitioners devoted serious attention to ethical issues as they pertain to professional malpractice and liability.

Many malpractice risks and licensing-board complaints stem from ethical decisions that practitioners make in these circumstances. For example, whether a practitioner should divulge confidential information against a client's wishes to prevent harm to a third party or how a practitioner who lives and works in a small community manages complex boundaries requires keen understanding of the nature of ethical dilemmas and various ways of addressing them. Although reasonable people may disagree with a behavioral health practitioner's particular decision in the case, a practitioner who can explain to a court or licensing board how she went about examining and addressing this ethical dilemma may prevent a judgment against her. Being able to demonstrate such familiarity with literature and concepts in ethical decision-making; relevant code of ethics standards, practice standards, and laws; consultation with experts on the subject; and documentation of efforts in this regard may convince a jury that the practitioner acted in a manner consistent with the profession's standard of care. Moreover, familiarity with the general subject of professional ethics, ethical dilemmas, and ethical decision-making can, by itself, enhance the likelihood that practitioners will make sound judgments—which may, after all, be the most powerful preventative of malpractice claims and licensing-board complaints.

### ETHICAL DILEMMAS AND DECISION-MAKING

In many instances, behavioral health practitioners' ethical responsibilities are clear and uncomplicated. Ordinarily, practitioners understand their duty, for example, to respect clients' right to confidentiality and to protect the general welfare of members of society. These ethical principles are set forth rather clearly in professional codes of ethics.

On occasion, however, such duties conflict in ways that might generate a lawsuit or licensing-board complaint. A practitioner whose client informs him during a counseling session that she plans to harm her estranged spouse must make a difficult choice between the client's right to confidentiality and protection of a third party. Assuming clinical intervention fails to resolve the issue and evidence exists that the client plans to carry out her threat, the practitioner must choose between two competing duties that practitioners are ordinarily expected to fulfill.

Hence, ethical dilemmas in the field of behavioral health include those instances in which practitioners face conflicting duties or obligations. Three major categories of ethical dilemmas are particularly relevant to behavioral health practitioners and to malpractice and licensing-board risks. The first major category includes ethical dilemmas related to intervention with individuals, couples, families, and groups. Prominent dilemmas in this area concern issues of confidentiality, boundaries and dual relationships, client self-determination, paternalism, and truth telling. As I have discussed, with regard to confidentiality, behavioral health practitioners need to understand the extent of clients' rights and the limits of confidentiality, particularly when clients threaten to harm themselves or a third party. Under what circumstances should practitioners breach clients' right to privacy in order to protect third parties from clients or the clients from themselves?

Similar dilemmas arise with regard to clients' right to self-determination. Ordinarily, practitioners respect clients' right to self-determination and help them pursue goals that are meaningful to them. Instances arise, however, in which practitioners must consider limiting clients' right to self-determination because such actions threaten to harm clients themselves or third parties. Consider, for example, a practitioner whose client is a domestic violence survivor. After a period of separation from her abusive partner, who has beaten the client on several previous occasions, the client informs the practitioner of her intention to once again live with her partner. The practitioner feels strongly that the client is quite likely to be abused again. Empirically based literature on the phenomenon also supports the practitioner's hunch. To what extent should the practitioner respect the client's right to self-determination and help her pursue her chosen goal, as opposed to actively attempting to dissuade her from her plans to move in again with her partner? Understanding these issues may help to prevent a lawsuit or licensing-board complaint alleging improper treatment or inappropriate use of coercion.

Further, how should practitioners respond to severely mentally or physically disabled clients who have decided to end their lives because of the chronic emotional or physical pain that they experience? Should practitioners summarily reject the possibility of "rational suicide" and discourage clients from further consideration of the possibility? Is it ever defensible for practitioners to respect the decision of a distressed but competent client who has decided to commit suicide? Practitioners' answers to these complex questions may have important bearing on the likelihood that they will be sued or named in a licensing-board complaint for causing or failing to prevent a client's suicide.

Debate concerning the limits of clients' right to self-determination in instances in which their actions seem self-destructive inevitably leads to discussion of the concept of professional paternalism. Whether practitioners acted assertively enough with clients who harmed themselves is a common issue in lawsuits and licensing-board complaints.

Paternalism is ordinarily defined as interference with an individual's intentions or mental state in order to protect the individual from herself. Common examples of paternalism include prohibiting swimming at beaches when lifeguards are not on duty, requiring members of certain religious groups to receive lifesaving blood transfusions, permitting involuntary civil commitment to a psychiatric facility, and legislating against suicide. The general presumption in behavioral health is that practitioners should respect clients' right to self-determination and that interference with this right requires truly exceptional circumstances where clients pose a serious threat of harm to themselves or others.

Behavioral health practitioners concerned about preventing lawsuits and licensing-board complaints, in addition to protecting clients, face several types of ethical dilemmas involving paternalism. First are those instances in which practitioners decide whether to physically interfere with clients for their own protection. Should a practitioner require a resourceful but troubled homeless individual to go to a shelter against his wishes when the temperature is below freezing? How a practitioner handles this predicament may affect the chances of being sued for false imprisonment.

Second are those instances in which practitioners decide whether to withhold information from a client because of a belief that the client's knowledge of that information will be harmful. Is it justifiable, for example, for a hospital-based practitioner to withhold from a critically ill patient the information that his child was just killed in an automobile accident?

Is paternalism, in the form of withholding personally relevant information, justified in order to protect the hospital patient from harm?

Third are those instances in which practitioners decide whether to deliberately give clients inaccurate information, or to lie to clients, in order to protect clients from harm. Is it justifiable on paternalistic grounds for a practitioner to lie to a child about the reason for her father's arrest by the police in order to preserve as much as possible the child's relationship with her father? Is it permissible to give inaccurate information to a suicidal client in an effort to prevent suicide? Would such actions breach the standard of care in the profession and expose a practitioner to a liability claim or licensing-board complaint?

Dilemmas involving paternalism frequently raise issues concerning truth telling. Although practitioners are typically inclined to be truthful with clients, truth telling may seem to be harmful at times. Whether deception can ever be justified is an important matter to debate.

The second major category of ethical dilemmas in behavioral health pertains to the ways in which practitioners design and administer policies and programs. Practitioners also encounter dilemmas concerning their duty to obey laws, agency rules, and public or private agency regulations. In all states, for example, behavioral health practitioners are required to report suspected cases of child abuse and neglect to protective service officials. Despite this mandate, however, practitioners sometimes do not report such cases on the ground that they are in a better position than public officials to intervene effectively or that they do not want to betray the client's trust. As I have discussed, practitioners who fail to report suspected abuse or neglect risk being sued for failure to consult a specialist.

Complicated ethical dilemmas also arise with respect to compliance with regulations and agency policy. Many behavioral health agencies, for instance, depend on reimbursement for their services from insurance carriers or other third-party payers. To receive reimbursement, agency staff members typically need to provide insurers with documentation of reimbursable services provided. Because some of the agency's services may not be reimbursable under the insurer's guidelines, practitioners may struggle with their obligation to provide truthful claims information. The viability of the agency and its services may be at stake. Of course, a practitioner who decides to submit bogus information to obtain reimbursement risks criminal charges, a lawsuit filed by the insurer, and licensing-board discipline.

The third major category of ethical dilemmas involves relationships among professional colleagues. The most common, perhaps, concerns instances in which behavioral health practitioners encounter impaired or incompetent colleagues. These circumstances—when a practitioner has evidence that a colleague is abusing alcohol, drugs, or clients, for example—involve troubling ethical issues in regard to whistle-blowing. Under what circumstances is whistle-blowing (e.g., notifying an employer or licensing board about an impaired colleague) justifiable? What conditions should first be met? How much professional and personal risk should the whistle-blower be willing to assume?[7] On the one hand are liability risks if a practitioner fails to confront an impaired employee who subsequently injures a client. On the other hand, confronting an impaired colleague in the presence of third parties and discussing the problem with other agency staff may lead to a defamation-of-character lawsuit or licensing-board complaint.

Ethical dilemmas can also arise in relationships among colleagues with respect to the use of deception. Behavioral health organizations may be competitors, and such competition may sometimes tempt administrators to engage in deceptive practices to win new grants or undermine competitors' advantages in order to ensure their own agency's fiscal health or survival. Deception may also be contemplated in order to surreptitiously gather information to document suspected wrongdoing by colleagues.

Behavioral health practitioners today have greater access to literature and instruction on ethical decision-making. Especially since the mid-1970s, the growth in literature and teaching on ethical decision-making has been substantial. Practitioners can consult a wide range of resources that provide useful introductions to and overviews of various ethical theories and frameworks for ethical decision-making and for analyzing ethical dilemmas in practice.

No precise formula for resolving ethical dilemmas exists. Reasonable, thoughtful practitioners can disagree about the ethical principles and criteria that ought to guide ethical decisions in any given case. But ethicists generally agree on the importance of approaching ethical decisions systematically, by following a series of steps to ensure that all aspects of an ethical dilemma are addressed. Following a series of clearly formulated steps allows behavioral health practitioners to enhance the quality of the ethical decisions they make. In my experience, practitioners attempting to resolve ethical dilemmas find the following steps helpful:

1. Identify the ethical issues, including the behavioral health values and duties, that conflict.
2. Identify the individuals, groups, and organizations likely to be affected by the ethical decision.
3. Tentatively identify all viable courses of action and the participants involved in each, along with the potential benefits and risks for each.
4. Thoroughly examine the reasons in favor of and against each course of action, considering relevant:
   (a) codes of ethics and legal principles;
   (b) ethical theories, principles, and guidelines;
   (c) behavioral health practice theory, principles, and widely embraced practice standards; and
   (d) personal values (including religious, cultural, and ethnic values and political ideology), particularly those that conflict with one's own.
5. Consult with colleagues and appropriate experts (such as agency staff, supervisors, agency administrators, attorneys, and ethics scholars).
6. Make the decision and document the decision-making process.
7. Monitor, evaluate, and document the decision.

### CONDUCTING AN ETHICS AUDIT

One of the most effective ways to prevent malpractice and licensing-board complaints is to conduct an ethics audit.[8] An ethics audit provides practitioners and agencies with a framework for examining and critiquing the ways in which they address a wide range of ethical issues. More specifically, an ethics audit provides behavioral health practitioners with an opportunity to achieve the following:

- Identify pertinent ethical issues in their practice settings that are unique to the client population, treatment and intervention approach, setting, program design, and staffing pattern.
- Review and assess the adequacy of their current ethics-related policies, practices, and procedures.
- Design a practical strategy to modify current practices, as needed, to prevent lawsuits and licensing-board or other complaints.
- Monitor the implementation of this quality assurance strategy.

Conducting an ethics audit involves several key steps:

1. In behavioral health organizations, a staff member should assume the role of chair of the ethics audit committee. Appointment to the committee should be based on demonstrated interest in the organization's ethics-related risk management policies and practices. Ideally, the chair would have formal education or training related to professional ethics and risk management. Practitioners in private or independent practice may want to consult with knowledgeable colleagues or a peer supervision group.

2. Using the list of major ethical risks as a guide (client rights, confidentiality and privacy, informed consent, service delivery, use of technology to serve clients, boundary issues and conflicts of interest, documentation, defamation of character, client records, supervision, staff development and training, consultation, client referral, fraud, termination of services, practitioner impairment), the committee should identify specific ethics-related risk management issues on which to focus. In some settings, the committee may decide to conduct a comprehensive ethics audit, one that addresses all the topics. In other organizations, the committee may focus on specific ethical issues that are especially important in those settings.

3. The ethics audit committee should decide what kind of data it will need to conduct the audit. Sources of data include documents and interviews conducted with agency staff that address specific issues contained in the audit. For example, staff may examine the forms the agency uses to explain clients' rights and informed consent when providing services to clients remotely. In addition, staff may interview or administer questionnaires to key personnel in the agency about such matters as the extent and content of ethics-related risk management training that they have received or provided, specific ethical issues that need attention, and ways to address compelling ethical issues. Committee members may want to consult a lawyer about legal issues (e.g., the implications of federal or state confidentiality regulations and laws or key court rulings) and agency documents (e.g., the appropriateness of agency informed-consent and release-of-information forms to provide services to clients remotely). Also, committee members should review all relevant regulations and laws (federal, state, and local) and ethics codes in relation to confidentiality, privileged communication, informed consent, client records, termination of services, supervision, use of technology to serve clients, licensing, personnel issues, and professional misconduct.

4. Once the committee has gathered and reviewed the data, it should assess the risk level associated with each topic. The assessment for each topic has two parts: policies and procedures. The ethics audit assesses the adequacy of various ethics-related policies and procedures. Policies may be codified in formal agency documents or memoranda (e.g., official policy concerning confidentiality, digital and online communications, informed consent, dual relationships, conflicts of interest, and termination of services). Procedures include practitioners' actual handling of ethical issues in their relationships with clients and colleagues (e.g., concrete steps that staff members take to address ethical issues involving confidentiality or boundaries, routine explanations provided to clients concerning agency policies about informed consent and confidentiality, ethics consultation obtained, informed-consent forms completed, documentation placed in case records in ethically complex cases, and supervision and training provided on ethics-related topics).

5. The committee should assign each topic addressed in the audit to one of four risk categories: no risk—current policies and practices are acceptable and do not require modification; minimal risk—current policies and practices are reasonably adequate, but minor modifications would be useful; moderate risk—current policies and practices are problematic, and modifications are necessary to minimize risk; and high risk—current policies and practices are seriously flawed, and significant modifications are necessary to minimize risk.

6. Once the ethics audit is complete, behavioral health practitioners need to take assertive steps to make constructive use of the findings. Practitioners should develop a plan for each risk area that warrants attention, beginning with high-risk areas that jeopardize clients and expose practitioners and their agencies to serious risk of lawsuits and ethics complaints. Areas that fall into the categories of moderate risk and minimum risk should receive attention as soon as possible.

7. Practitioners should establish priorities among the areas of concern on the basis of the degree of risk involved and available resources. Spell out specific measures that need to be taken to address the problem areas identified. Examples include reviewing all current informed-consent and release-of-information forms and creating updated versions; writing new comprehensive confidentiality and social media policies; creating a client rights statement; inaugurating training of staff responsible for supervision; strengthening staff training on documentation and on boundary issues;

developing state-of-the-art policies and protocols concerning staff use of digital and other technology to serve clients; and preparing detailed procedures for staff to follow when terminating services to clients.

8. Practitioners should identify all the resources needed to address the risk areas, such as agency personnel, publications, staff development time, appointment of a committee or task force, legal consultants, and ethics consultants.

9. Practitioners should identify which staff will be responsible for the various tasks and establish a timetable for completion of each. Have a lawyer review and approve policies and procedures to ensure compliance with federal and state laws, regulations, and court opinions. Identify a mechanism for following up on each task to ensure its completion and for monitoring its implementation.

10. Practitioners should document the complete process involved in conducting the ethics audit. This documentation may be helpful in the event of a lawsuit alleging ethics-related negligence (in that it provides evidence of the agency's or practitioner's conscientious effort to address specific ethical issues).

Agency administrators can also conduct a "management audit" to ensure the agency's compliance with widely embraced standards.[9] The typical management audit verifies the following:

- The agency's government licenses (such as those from government agencies) are in good standing.
- The agency's papers of incorporation and bylaws fully authorize the current scope of practice and service.
- The state licenses and current registrations of all professional staff are active.
- Protocols for handling emergencies (e.g., fire drills, involuntary client hospitalization, staff safety, unusual incident reporting) are well known and updated.
- Premiums for all forms of casualty and professional insurance are paid and current, and the coverage for programs, staff, and settings is adequate.
- Procedures for maintaining and safeguarding client records are sound (including state-of-the-art cybersecurity).
- Staff evaluations are conducted and reviewed regularly.
- Records for fiscal disbursements are properly authorized and maintained.
- Insurance reimbursement forms are completed in a timely fashion and are authenticated in accordance with contractual requirements.

Although behavioral health practitioners might prefer to avoid the topic of professional malpractice and risk management, practitioners need to understand the risks involved and ways to mitigate them. Given the complexity of the legal, ethical, and practice issues involved, the tendency may be for practitioners to become preoccupied with the technical aspects of professional malpractice and liability. These high-anxiety issues often lead practitioners to dwell on the trees—the mechanics of lawsuits and licensing-board complaints, and the mistakes, oversights, and improprieties that may give rise to them—rather than on the forest, the need to engage in good and ethical practice. In the final analysis, however, skillful and ethical practice is the most effective way to prevent and manage risk. This is also the hallmark of a professional.

# Sample Forms

*Note*: These are sample forms. Behavioral health practitioners and agencies should use these only as a general guide. Revisions may be necessary on the basis of practitioners' and agencies' specific settings, client populations, services, and state law and regulations where practitioners are licensed. Agencies that serve clients for whom English is not the primary language should translate these forms into languages that their clients can understand. Accommodations may be necessary for clients with disabilities or other special needs. The text of several forms contains instructions in square brackets that are addressed to the agency or independent practitioner; that is, the agency or practitioner should insert the information before asking the client to read and sign the form.

### OVERVIEW OF PSYCHOTHERAPY POLICIES AND PROCEDURES

Welcome to my practice. This document contains important information about my professional services and business policies. The federal Notice of Privacy Practices, widely available online, provides you with information about your privacy protections and client rights under the Health Insurance Portability and Accountability Act (HIPAA).[1] The law requires that I obtain your signature acknowledging that I have provided you with this information. I ask that you review both documents before our next session, at which time I will be happy to discuss any questions that you might have about these documents. When you sign this document, it will represent an agreement between us.

#### Counseling Services

Psychotherapy is not easily described in general statements. It varies depending on the personalities of the therapist and the client, and the particular challenges you are experiencing. There are many different methods I may use to deal with the challenges that you hope to address. Psychotherapy is not like a medical doctor visit. Instead, it calls for a very active effort on your part. In order for the therapy to be successful, you will have to work on things we talk about both during and outside of our sessions.

Psychotherapy can have benefits and risks. Because therapy often involves experiencing unpleasant or problematic aspects of your life, you may experience uncomfortable feelings like sadness, guilt, anger, frustration, loneliness, and helplessness. On the other hand, psychotherapy also has been shown to have many benefits. Therapy often leads to better relationships, solutions to specific problems, and significant reductions in feelings of distress; however, there are no guarantees of what you will experience and what you will accomplish.

Our first few sessions will involve my asking a lot of questions to learn more about you and your needs. As time goes on, I will be able to offer my impressions of what might be helpful in your situation and what our work might include if you decide to continue with therapy. You should evaluate this information along with your own opinions of whether you feel comfortable working with me. Therapy involves a commitment of time and energy, as well as a financial commitment, so you should be very careful about the therapist you select. If you have questions about my approach, we should discuss them whenever they arise. If your doubts persist, I will be happy to help you identify another mental health professional who can offer a second opinion or with whom you may feel more comfortable continuing with psychotherapy.

## Sessions

I generally expect that it will take from two to four sessions for both of us to decide whether I am the best person to provide the services you need in order to meet your goals. We generally will schedule fifty-minute sessions at times that we agree on, and at a frequency that we agree on, although some sessions may be longer. Once an appointment time is scheduled, you will be expected to pay for it unless you provide twenty-four hours advance notice of cancellation, unless we both agree that you were unable to attend because of circumstances beyond your control. You will be asked to pay a fee of $_____ for a missed session with no phone call or $_____ for a session cancelled with less than twenty-four-hour notice from the starting time of that session. Please be aware that insurance companies do not provide reimbursement for missed sessions. I am committed to our work together and know that treatment is most effective when sessions are held at regular intervals. For this reason, multiple no-shows or frequent last-minute cancellations may result in a suspension of treatment.

## Contacting Me

Because of my work schedule, I am often not immediately available by telephone. While I am usually in my office on _____, I will not answer the telephone when I am with a client. When I am unavailable during work hours, my telephone is answered either by my secretary or by voicemail that I monitor frequently. I will make every effort to return your call on the same day you make it, with the exception of weekends and holidays. If you are difficult to reach, please inform me of some times when you will be available. In the event that you experience a psychiatric emergency, in which you need immediate professional consultation, you may call 911 or report to your local hospital emergency room. Alternatively, I have arranged to share on-call services with several trusted and experienced colleagues.

### Limits of Confidentiality

The law protects the privacy of most communications between a client and a therapist. In most situations, I can only release information about your treatment to others if you sign a written authorization form that meets certain legal requirements imposed by HIPAA or with your advance consent. I may occasionally find it helpful to consult other health or mental health professionals about a case. During a consultation, I make every effort to avoid revealing the identity of my client. The other professionals are also legally bound to keep the information confidential. If you do not object, I will not tell you about these consultations unless I feel that it is important to our work together. I generally note consultations in your clinical record. Disclosures required by health insurers are discussed elsewhere in this overview.

There are some situations where I am permitted or required by law or the code of ethics to disclose information without either your consent or authorization. Following are examples of some of these situations:

- If you are involved in a court proceeding and a request is made for information concerning your diagnosis and treatment, such information is generally protected by the therapist-client privilege law. I cannot provide my information without your (or your legal representative's) written authorization or a court order. For example, in some proceedings involving child custody and those in which your emotional condition is an important issue, a judge may order my testimony if he or she determines that the issues demand it. If you are involved in or contemplating litigation, you should consult with your attorney to determine whether a court would be likely to order me to disclose information.
- If a government agency is requesting the information for health oversight activities, I may be required to provide it to the agency.
- If a client files a complaint or lawsuit against me, I may disclose relevant information regarding that client in order to defend myself.
- If a client files a workers' compensation claim, I must, upon appropriate request, provide appropriate information, including a copy of the client's record, to the client's employer, the insurer, or the Department of Workers' Compensation.

There are some situations in which I am legally obligated to take actions that I believe are necessary to attempt to protect you and others from harm, and I may have to reveal some information about a client's treatment. These situations are unusual in my practice. Following are examples of some of these situations:

- If I have reasonable cause to believe that a child under age eighteen is suffering physical or emotional injury resulting from abuse inflicted upon him or her which causes harm or substantial risk of harm to the child's health or welfare (including sexual abuse) or from neglect (including malnutrition), the law requires that I file a report with the Department of Children, Youth and Families. Once such a report is filed, I may be required to provide additional information.
- If I have reason to believe an elderly or disabled individual is suffering from abuse, the law requires that I report to the Division of Elderly Affairs. Once such a report is filed, I may be required to provide additional information.
- If a client communicates an immediate threat of serious physical harm to an identifiable victim or if a client has a history of violence and the apparent intent and ability to carry out the threat, I may be required to take protective actions. These actions may include notifying the potential victim, contacting the police, and/or seeking hospitalization for the client.
- If a client threatens to harm himself or herself, I may be obligated to seek hospitalization for him or her or to contact family members or others who can help provide protection.

The Notice of Privacy Practices also describes exceptions to confidentiality. There are also exceptions described in the [cite relevant state law(s)].

If such a situation arises, I will make every effort to fully discuss it with you before taking any action, and I will limit my disclosure to what is necessary.

While this written summary of exceptions to confidentiality should prove helpful in informing you about potential problems, it is important that we discuss any questions or concerns that you may have now or in the future. The laws governing confidentiality can be quite complex, and I am not an attorney. In situations where specific advice is required, formal legal advice may be needed.

### Professional Records

The laws and standards of my profession require that I keep treatment records. You should be aware that, pursuant to HIPAA, I keep protected health information (PHI) in your clinical record. This record includes your diagnosis, treatment and progress, any past records that I receive from other providers, reports of professional consultations, your billing records, and any reports that have been sent to anyone, including reports to your insurance carrier. This record also includes psychotherapy notes I have made regarding our conversations. Because these are professional records, they can be misinterpreted and/or upsetting to untrained readers. HIPAA does not provide clients with the right of access to separately maintained psychotherapy notes. If you wish to see your records, I recommend that you let me know, and I can determine the extent to which we can discuss the contents. You may examine and/or receive a copy of your clinical record if you request it in writing unless I believe that the access requested is reasonably likely to endanger the life or physical safety of you or another person or if the information is contained in separately maintained psychotherapy notes. In those situations, you may have a right to a summary and to have your record sent to another mental health provider or your attorney. If I refuse your request for access to your records, you have a right of review, which I will discuss with you upon your request. This is described fully in the attached Notice of Privacy Practices.

### Client Rights

HIPAA provides you with several new or expanded rights with regard to your clinical record and disclosures of protected information. These rights include requesting that I amend your record; requesting restrictions on what information from your clinical record is disclosed to others; requesting an accounting of most disclosure or protected health information that you have neither consented to nor authorized; determining the location to which protected information disclosures are sent; having any complaints you make about my policies and procedures recorded in your records; and the right to a paper copy of this overview and the attached Notice of Privacy Practices. I am happy to discuss any of these rights with you.

### Electronic Communications

In order to maintain clarity regarding our use of electronic modes of communication during your treatment, I have developed the following policy.

The use of various types of electronic communications is common in our society, and many individuals believe this is the preferred method of communication with others, whether their relationships are social or professional. Many of these common modes of communication, however, put your privacy at risk and can be inconsistent with the law and with the standards of my profession. Consequently, this policy has been prepared to ensure the security and confidentiality of your treatment and to ensure that it is consistent with ethics and the law. If you have any questions about this policy, please feel free to discuss this with me.

### E-MAIL AND TEXT MESSAGING COMMUNICATIONS

I use e-mail communication and text messaging only with your permission and only for administrative purposes unless we have made another agreement. That means e-mail exchanges and text messages with my office should be limited to things like setting and changing appointments, billing matters, and other related issues. Please do not e-mail or text me about clinical matters because e-mails and texts are not completely secure or confidential ways to contact me. If you need to discuss a clinical matter with me, please feel free to call me so we can discuss it on the telephone or wait so we can discuss it during your therapy session. The telephone or face-to-face context simply is much more secure and clinically effective as a mode of communication.

If you choose to communicate with me by e-mail or text, be aware that all e-mails are retained in the logs of your and my Internet service or cellular telephone providers. While it is unlikely that someone will be looking at these logs, they are, in theory, available to be read by the system administrator(s) of the Internet service or cellular telephone provider. You should also know that any e-mails or texts I receive from you and any responses that I send to you may become a part of your legal record.

### SOCIAL MEDIA[2]

I do not accept friend or contact requests or otherwise communicate with or contact current or former clients on any social media platforms like Twitter, Facebook, or LinkedIn. In addition, if I discover that I have accidentally established an online relationship with you, I will cancel that relationship. I believe that adding clients as friends or contacts on these sites can compromise your confidentiality and our respective privacy and can create significant security risks for you. These sites are not secure, and I may not read these messages in a timely fashion. Do not use "wall" postings, @replies, or other means of engaging with me in public online if we have an already established client-therapist relationship. Engaging with me this way could compromise your confidentiality. It may also create the possibility that these exchanges become a part of your legal medical record and will need to be documented and archived in your chart. It may also blur the boundaries of our therapeutic relationship. If you have questions about this, please bring them up when we meet, and we can talk more about it.

I participate on various social networks, but not in my professional capacity. If you have an online presence, there is a possibility that you may encounter me by accident. If that occurs, please discuss it with me during our time together. I believe that any communications with clients online have a high potential to compromise the professional relationship. In addition, please do not try to contact me in this way. I will not respond and will terminate any online contact no matter how accidental.

### WEBSITES

I have a website that you are free to access. I use it for professional reasons to provide information to others about me and my practice. You are welcome to access and review the information that I have on my website and, if you have questions about it, we should discuss this during your therapy sessions.

### WEB SEARCHES

I will not use web searches to gather information about you without your permission because I believe that this violates your privacy rights. Extremely rare exceptions may be made during times of crisis. If I have a reason to suspect that you are in danger and you have not been in touch with me via our usual means (coming to appointments, phone, or e-mail), there might be an instance in which using a search engine (to find you, find someone close to you, or to check on your recent status updates) becomes necessary as part of ensuring your welfare. These are unusual situations, and if I ever resort to such means, I will fully document it and discuss it with you when we next meet. However, I understand that you might choose to gather information about me in this way. In this day and age, there is an incredible amount of information available about individuals on the Internet, much of which may actually be known to that person and some of which may be inaccurate or unknown. If you encounter any information about me through web searches or in any other fashion for that matter, please discuss this with me during our time together so that we can deal with it and its potential impact on your treatment.

Recently, it has become fashionable for clients to review their health-care provider on various websites. Unfortunately, mental health professionals cannot respond to such comments and related errors because of confidentiality restrictions, whether it is positive or negative.

Many of these sites comb search engines for business listings and automatically add listings regardless of whether the business has added itself to the site. If you should find my listing on any of these sites, please know that my listing is NOT a request for a testimonial, rating, or endorsement from you as my client. If you encounter such reviews of me or any professional with whom you are working, please share it with me so we can discuss it and its potential impact on your therapy. Please do not rate my work with you while we are in treatment together on any of these websites. This is because it has a significant potential to damage our ability to work together. I urge you to take your own privacy as seriously as I take my commitment of confidentiality to you. You should also be aware that if you are using these sites to communicate indirectly with me about your feelings about our work, there is a good possibility that I may never see it.

If we are working together, I hope that you will bring your feelings and reactions to our work directly into the therapy process. This can be an important part of therapy, even if you decide we are not a good fit. None of this is meant to keep you from sharing that you are in therapy with me wherever and with whomever you like. Confidentiality means that I cannot tell people that you are my client, and my code of ethics prohibits me from requesting testimonials. But you are more than welcome to tell anyone you wish that I am your therapist or how you feel about the treatment I provided to you, in any forum of your choosing.

### LOCATION-BASED SERVICES

If you use location-based services on your mobile phone, you may wish to be aware of the privacy issues related to using these services. I do not place my practice as a check-in location on various sites. However, if you have GPS tracking enabled on your device, it is possible that others may surmise that you are a therapy client due to regular check-ins at my office on a weekly basis. Please be aware of this risk if you are intentionally "checking in," from my office or if you have a passive location-based service (LBS) app enabled on your phone.

### SECURITY

My practice involves face-to-face therapy. I believe that this is the most clinically effective and most secure and confidential manner in which to conduct therapy. There may be limited occasions when we agree to communicate by a videoconferencing platform, such as VSee, Zoom, Skype, or Facetime. While I will take reasonable precautions to maintain confidentiality, as with all forms of electronic communication, there are risks that such communications can be intercepted, and your participation in such communications indicates that you assume the risks related to using such communications.

### Minors and Parents

Clients under eighteen years of age who are not emancipated and their parents should be aware that the law allows parents to examine their child's treatment records, unless I believe this review would be harmful to the client and his or her treatment. However, HIPAA does not provide parents with the right of access to separately maintained psychotherapy notes. Because privacy in psychotherapy is often crucial to successful progress, particularly with teenagers, it is sometimes my policy to request an agreement from parents that they consent to give up their access to their child's records. If they disagree, I will provide them only with general information about the progress of the child's treatment and his or her attendance at scheduled sessions. Any other communication will require the child's authorization, unless I feel that the child is in danger or is a danger to someone else, in which case I will notify the parents of my concern. Before giving parents any information, I will discuss the matter with the child, if possible, and do my best to handle any objections he or she may have.

### Marital/Couples Therapy

#### COURT PROCEEDINGS

It is understood that the purpose of marital/couples therapy is for the amelioration of distress within a relationship. Therefore, if both partners request my services as a therapist, they are expected not to use information given to me during the therapy process against the other party in a judicial setting of any kind, including civil or criminal. Likewise, neither party shall for any reason attempt to subpoena my testimony or my records to be presented in a deposition or court hearing of any kind for any reason, such as a divorce case.

### RELEASE OF RECORDS

There are times when the best treatment approach is for a client to be seen with his or her partner, with the relationship itself being the focus of treatment. When that occurs, both partners must provide their consent to release marital/couples counseling records. If one partner does not provide consent, I will not voluntarily release the records, subject to exceptions to confidentiality addressed elsewhere in this overview.

### NO SECRETS POLICY

When it is determined that therapy will be most helpful if a client is seen for treatment with his or her partner, the couple is considered to be one unit. This means that my allegiance is to the couple "unit" and not to either partner as individuals. I find this is particularly important in creating a space where both partners can feel safe. Therefore, I adhere to a strict "No Secrets" policy. This means I will not hold secrets for either partner. This policy is intended to allow me to continue to treat the couple or family by preventing, to the extent possible, a conflict of interest from arising where an individual's interests may not be consistent with the interests of the unit being treated.

On occasion during the counseling process, individual partners may be seen for an individual counseling session. In this case, the individual session is still considered as part of the couple's counseling relationship. Information disclosed during individual sessions may be relevant or even essential to the proper treatment of the couple or the family. If an individual chooses to share such information with me, I will offer the individual every opportunity to disclose the relevant information and will provide guidance in this process. If the individual refuses to disclose this information within the couple's session, I may determine that it is necessary to discontinue the counseling relationship with the couple. If there is information an individual desires to address within a context of individual confidentiality, I will be happy to

provide referrals to therapists who can provide concurrent individual therapy. This policy is intended to maintain the integrity of the couples/marital
counseling relationship.

### Professional Fees

If you choose to use your health insurance to pay for psychotherapy,
I will have my billing company pursue payment through your insurance. You will be responsible for paying me the co-pay fee at the time of
our session. You also will be responsible for paying me the full amount
allowed by your insurance company if you have not met your deductible.
You will also be responsible for the balance incurred if your insurance
lapses, you have not informed me, and we have not made an alternative
payment agreement. You should read the section in your insurance coverage booklet that describes mental health services and make sure that
any questions you have are answered either by me or by your insurance
company. It is often the case that an insurance company will authorize
only a limited number of sessions initially. If therapy continues beyond
this point, it is usually possible for me to seek approval from the insurance company for additional sessions. However, it is important for us
to discuss your options in the event that reimbursement is no longer
available. These options include keeping our goals within a short-term
therapy framework, considering the possibility of self-payment for sessions once benefits are exhausted, and placing therapy on hold until a
new benefit year begins.

You should also be aware that your contract with your health insurance
company requires that I provide it with information relevant to the services that I provide to you. I am required to provide a clinical diagnosis.
Sometimes I am required to provide additional clinical information, such
as treatment plans or summaries. In such a situation, I will make every
effort to release only the minimum information about you that is necessary
for the purpose requested. This information will become part of the insurance company files and will probably be stored in a computer. Though all
insurance companies claim they keep such information confidential, I have
no control over what they do with it once it is in their hands. I will provide
you with a copy of any report I submit, if you request it. Your signature on
the Consent to Bill Insurance Provider form, which you received in the

first session, gives permission for me to provide requested information to your carrier.

I appreciate your taking the time to read this Overview, and I look forward to discussing any questions or concerns you may have. If you decide to continue in psychotherapy with me, I hope that we will have a satisfying and productive working relationship.

Your signature below indicates that you have read the information in this document, have had the opportunity to ask questions about it, and agree to abide by its terms during our professional relationship.

_____

Name

_____

Date

## CLIENT RIGHTS

We want you to know that as a client of this agency you have certain rights. ABC Counseling Agency treats all people with dignity and respect. ABC Counseling Agency does not discriminate on the basis of race, ethnicity, national origin, color, sex, sexual orientation, gender identity or expression, age, marital status, political belief, religion, immigration status, and mental or physical disability. In addition, you have the following specific rights:

1. You have the right to privacy and confidentiality. All information that you disclose to agency staff members will be kept confidential in accordance with federal and state laws and relevant court orders. [*Note:* Agencies and practitioners may wish to add specific details concerning the confidentiality of information related to, for example, substance use disorders treatment, HIV/AIDS, abuse and neglect, threats to third parties, electronic records, minors, court orders, and disclosure of information to insurers or other parties.]

2. You have the right to know that information about you may be shared among staff members for the purposes of service planning, service coordination, supervision, consultation, and referral.

3. You have the right to receive information and to be informed in a language that you understand. If ABC Counseling Agency is unable to provide services in a language that you understand, we will do our best to refer you, with your permission, to an agency that can provide services in your language.

4. You have the right to know the title and professional qualifications of the staff members who provide services to you.

5. You have the right to be informed about decisions that staff members make concerning services provided to you. You have the right to participate in those decisions whenever feasible.

6. You have the right to ask for a second opinion concerning your services and decisions made about you.

7. You have a right to a copy of your clinical record, with limited exceptions, such as psychotherapy notes. Also, you have the right to request that protected health information contained in such records be amended, the right to an accounting of disclosures made of that protected health information, and the right to request a restriction or limitation on the use or disclosure

of your protected health information for treatment, payment, or health-care operations.

8. You have the right to appeal decisions about you made by agency staff.

9. You have the right to refuse services in accordance with federal and state laws and relevant court orders.

10. You have the right to ask for a referral to another agency or practitioner.

11. You have the right to receive a copy of the client handbook. This handbook includes descriptions of this agency's services, staff, confidentiality guidelines, emergency services, social media policies, and other important information.

12. You have the right to be informed of the cost of services. ABC Counseling Agency charges fees that are fair and reasonable. ABC Counseling Agency will take into consideration your ability to pay.

13. You have the right to ask to review the information in your agency record consistent with agency policy and relevant laws.

14. You have the right to refuse permission for agency staff to use technology such as one-way mirrors, video recorders, voice recorders, and still cameras.

15. You have the right to refuse to participate in any research or evaluation project that ABC Counseling Agency conducts or sponsors.

Client signature _____

Parent/Guardian signature _____

Date _____

## CONSENT FOR RELEASE OF CONFIDENTIAL INFORMATION

Client name_____

Date of birth_____

_____ I hereby authorize ABC Counseling Agency to release the record of my care to: [specify agency, practitioner, facility and address]

This information may be released via:

_____ U.S. Mail

_____ Telephone

_____ Fax

_____ E-mail

_____ Other (specify): _____

_____ I hereby authorize ABC Counseling Agency to obtain the record of my care from: _____ [specify agency, practitioner, facility and address]

_____ I hereby authorize ABC Counseling Agency to speak verbally regarding my care to: _____ [specify agency, practitioner, facility and address]

The information to be released shall include:

___ Assessments

___ Treatment plans

___ Treatment provided

___ Consultation reports

___ Medication records

___ Verification of attendance

___ Discharge plan

___ HIV/AIDS information (specify): _____

___ Substance use disorders information and treatment (specify): _____

___ Other information (specify): _____

Pertaining to services on or about _____ [specify date(s)].

This information is needed for the following purpose(s):

___ Treatment/continued care

___ Consultation

___ Legal purposes

___ Application for insurance
___ Payment of insurance claim
___ Disability determination
___ Other (specify): _____

I understand that my records are protected under [specify relevant state and local laws] and cannot be disclosed without my written consent except as otherwise specifically provided by law. I also understand that if my records involve substance use disorders treatment issues, treatment, or services, they are processed according to Federal Regulation 42 CFR Part 2, Confidentiality of Substance Use Disorder Patient Records. A general authorization for disclosure of medical or other information is not sufficient for this purpose. I understand that there will be separate authorization forms to obtain or release psychotherapy notes and substance use disorder records.

I understand that released information will not be relayed to any other party not specified in this consent, except as provided by law, which may include the admission or introduction of such information as evidence at any hearing held in connection with the above proceeding. I understand that this authorization is voluntary, that the information disclosed, except substance use disorder records, may be subject to re-disclosure and may no longer be protected by federal privacy regulations.

I understand that I may revoke this authorization at any time by notifying the ABC Counseling Agency in writing. Such revocation will not affect any actions taken before this revocation is received. This authorization expires [specify date or time period].

I understand I may refuse to sign this authorization.

I may inspect or copy any information disclosed under this authorization.

I have read this statement carefully, it has been explained to me in a language that I can understand, and I have had an opportunity to ask questions about it.

Client signature _____

Parent/Guardian signature _____

Signature of witness _____

Date _____

## COLLATERAL AGREEMENT

This document is to inform you about the risks, rights, and responsibilities of your participation as a collateral contact participating in the therapy and/ or evaluation of the client named _____.

Who and what is a collateral contact? A collateral contact is a partner, family member, friend, or other individual who participates in the therapy or evaluation of the identified client of a therapist or clinic. As a collateral contact, you are not considered to be a client of mine, and you are not the subject of the treatment or evaluation. Clinicians have certain legal and ethical responsibilities to their clients, including confidentiality and the overall privacy of the relationship; collateral contacts have less protection, as the clinician's first ethical and legal responsibilities are toward the client.

The role of collaterals in therapy. The role of collateral contacts can vary greatly. You might attend only one meeting to provide information or you might attend many therapy sessions, and your relationship with the client might even be a focus of the treatment. The meetings you attend may be alone or with the client. You may discuss your own problems in therapy, especially problems that are related to the issues of the identified client, but even then the therapeutic relationship still resides with the identified client, as you are not the client. If you desire your own personal therapy, you may ask for an appropriate referral. I will discuss your specific role in the treatment at our first meeting and other appropriate times.

Benefits and risks. Counseling services can evoke intense emotional experiences, and your participation may be distressing to you. It may also expose or create tension in your relationship with the client. While your participation can result in having a better understanding of the client or an improved relationship or may even help in your own growth and development, there is no guarantee that this will be the case.

Health records and release of information. No separate record or chart will be maintained on you personally in your role as a collateral contact. Because you are not a client, you will not carry a diagnosis, and there is no individualized treatment plan for you. It is sometimes possible to maintain the privacy of our communications. If that is your wish, we should discuss it before any information is communicated. Information that you share about yourself or about the client may be recorded in the client's chart. The client has the right to access the chart and the material contained therein, and it is possible that the client will know what you say during a collateral contact even if he or she was not present. In addition, the client may grant the therapist permission to exchange information with other health providers or other professionals (such as an attorney), and the therapist may then share information about your participation as a collateral contact. You have no right to access the client's chart without consent of the client. (An exception exists if you are a parent or legal guardian of the client and have inherent rights to medical information of your child in that role.)

Fees. As a collateral contact, you are not responsible for paying for my professional services unless you are financially responsible for the client.

Confidentiality. The confidentiality of information in the client's chart, including the information that you provide, is protected by both federal and state laws. It can only be released if the client specifically authorizes me to do so. There are some exceptions to this general rule. For example:

- I must report any knowledge or suspicion of abuse or neglect of a child or dependent adult.
- I am required by law to take action to protect you if you become an imminent danger to yourself. Action in this situation may include psychiatric hospitalization and/or notifying a loved one of your circumstances.
- By law, if you are a serious and imminent threat to another person or threaten violence at a specific location, I have a duty to protect that person and may warn that person and/or notify the police or other appropriate authorities.
- If I am directed by a judge in a court of law to reveal information, I may comply.
- If insurance is used to pay for the treatment, the client's insurance company may require me to submit information about the treatment for claims-processing purposes or for utilization review.
- To protect public health, you or I may at some point become legally required to disclose that we have been in contact (e.g., if either of us were to test positive for, or show signs of, COVID-19 infection). If I am legally compelled to disclose information, I will inform you and will only provide the minimum necessary information required by law (e.g., your name and the dates of our contact). I will not go into any details about the reason(s) for our contact.

- You are expected to maintain the confidentiality of the client in your role as a collateral contact. Thank you for accepting the invitation to assist in the identified client's treatment. By signing below, you are indicating that you have read and understand this document. Please feel free to ask me questions for clarification.

Signature of collateral contact: _____

Printed name: _____

Date: _____

**CONFIDENTIALITY AGREEMENT FOR MINOR CLIENTS**

What to expect:

The purpose of meeting with a counselor or therapist is to get help with problems in your life that are bothering you or that are keeping you from being successful in important areas of your life. You may be here because you wanted to talk to a counselor or therapist about these problems. Or, you may be here because your parent, guardian, doctor, teacher, or another adult had concerns about you. When we meet, we will discuss these problems. I will ask questions, listen to you, and suggest a plan for improving these problems.

It is important that you feel comfortable talking to me about the issues that are bothering you. Sometimes these issues will include things you don't want your parents or guardians to know about. For most people, knowing that what they say will be kept private helps them feel more comfortable and have more trust in their counselor or therapist. Privacy, also called confidentiality, is an important and necessary part of good counseling.

As a general rule, I will keep the information you share with me in our sessions confidential, unless I have your written consent to disclose certain information. There are, however, important exceptions to this rule that are important for you to understand before you share personal information with me in a therapy session. In some situations, I am required by law or by the guidelines of my profession to disclose information, whether or not I have your permission. I have listed some of these situations below.

Confidentiality cannot be maintained when:

- You tell me you plan to cause serious harm or death to yourself, and I believe you have the intent and ability to carry out this threat in the very near future. I must take steps to inform a parent or guardian of what you have told me and how serious I believe this threat to be. I must make sure that you are protected from harming yourself.
- You tell me you plan to cause serious harm or death to someone else who can be identified, and I believe you have the intent and ability to carry out this threat in the very near future. In this situation, I must inform your parent or guardian, and I may need to inform the person whom you intend to harm or other people in a position to prevent harm.

- You are doing things that could cause serious harm to you or someone else, even if you do not intend to harm yourself or another person. In these situations, I will need to use my professional judgment to decide whether a parent, guardian, or another adult should be informed.
- You tell me you are being neglected or abused—physically, sexually, or emotionally—or that you have been abused in the past. In this situation, I am required by law to report the abuse to child welfare officials.
- You are involved in a court case, and a request is made for information about your counseling or therapy. If this happens, I will not disclose information without your written agreement unless the court requires me to. I will do all I can within the law to protect your confidentiality, and if I am required to disclose information to the court, I will inform you that this is happening.

Communicating with your parent(s) or guardian(s):

Except for situations such as those mentioned above, I will not tell your parent or guardian specific things you share with me in our private therapy sessions. This includes activities and behavior that your parent or guardian would not approve of—or would be upset by—but that do not put you at risk of serious and immediate harm. However, if your risk-taking behavior becomes more serious, then I will need to use my professional judgment to decide whether you are in serious and immediate danger of being harmed. If I feel that you are in such danger, I will communicate this information to your parent or guardian.

Example: If you tell me that you have tried alcohol at a few parties, I would keep this information confidential. If you tell me that you are drinking and driving or that you are a passenger in a car with a driver who is drunk, I would not keep this information confidential from your parent or guardian. If you tell me or if I believe based on things you've told me that you are addicted to alcohol, I would not keep this information confidential.

Example: If you tell me that you are having protected sex with a boyfriend or girlfriend, I would keep this information confidential. If you tell me that, on several occasions, you have engaged in unprotected sex with people you do not know or in unsafe situations, I will not keep this information confidential. You can always ask me questions about the types of information I would disclose. You can ask in the form of "hypothetical situations," in other words: "If someone told you that they were doing _____, would you tell their parents?"

Even if I have agreed to keep information confidential—to not tell your parent or guardian—I may believe it is important for that person to know what is going on in your life. In these situations, I will encourage you to tell your parent or guardian and will help you find the best way to tell him or her. Also, when meeting with your parent or guardian, I may sometimes describe problems in general terms, without using specifics, in order to help that person know how to be more helpful to you.

You should also know that your parent or guardian may have the right to see any written records I keep about our sessions, with some limited exceptions. It is extremely rare that a parent or guardian would ever request to look at these records.

Communicating with other adults:

School: I will not share any information with your school unless I have your permission and permission from your parent or guardian. Sometimes I may request to speak to someone at your school to find out how things are going for you. Also, it may be helpful in some situations for me to give suggestions to your teacher or counselor at school. If I want to contact your school or if someone at your school wants to contact me, I will discuss it with you and ask for your written permission. A very unlikely situation might come up in which I do not have your permission but both I and your parent or guardian believe that it is very important for me to be able to share certain information with someone at your school. In this situation, I will use my professional judgment to decide whether to share any information.

Doctors: Sometimes your doctor and I may need to work together; for example, if you need to take medication in addition to seeing a counselor or therapist. I will get your written permission and permission from your parent or guardian in advance to share information with your doctor. The only time I will share information with your doctor even if I don't have your permission is if you are doing something that puts you at risk for serious and immediate physical/medical harm.[3]

Minor's assent: _____

Minor's name: _____

Date: _____

## CONFIDENTIALITY AGREEMENT FOR PARENTS OR
## GUARDIANS OF MINOR CLIENTS

Prior to beginning treatment, it is important for you to understand my approach to counseling with children and agree to some rules about your child's confidentiality during the course of his or her treatment. Counseling is most effective when a trusting relationship exists between the therapist and the client. Privacy is especially important in securing and maintaining that trust. One goal of treatment is to promote a stronger and better relationship between children and their parents. However, it is often necessary for children to develop a "zone of privacy" whereby they feel free to discuss personal matters with greater freedom. This is particularly true for adolescents who are naturally developing a greater sense of independence and autonomy, but also for younger children.

Although the laws of [this state] may give parents the right to see any written records I keep about your child's treatment, by signing this agreement, you are agreeing that your child or teen should have a "zone of privacy" in his or her meetings with me, and you agree not to request access to your child's written treatment records.

In order to authorize mental health treatment for your child, you must have either sole or joint legal custody of your child. If you are separated or divorced from the other parent of your child, please notify me immediately. I will ask you to provide me with a copy of the most recent custody decree that establishes custody rights of you and the other parent or otherwise demonstrates that you have the right to authorize treatment for your child.

If you are separated or divorced from the child's other parent, please be aware that it is my policy to notify the other parent that I am meeting with your child. I believe it is important that all parents have the right to know, unless there are truly exceptional circumstances, that their child is receiving mental health evaluation or treatment.

One risk of child therapy involves disagreement between parents and/ or disagreement between parents and the therapist regarding the child's treatment. If such disagreements occur, I will strive to listen carefully so that I can understand your perspectives and fully explain my perspective. We can resolve such disagreements or we can agree to disagree, so long as this enables your child's therapeutic progress. Ultimately, parents decide whether therapy will continue. If either parent decides that therapy should end, I will honor that decision, unless there are extraordinary circumstances. However, in most cases, I will ask that you allow me the option of having a few closing sessions with your child to appropriately end the treatment relationship.

In the course of my treatment of your child, I may meet with the child's parents or guardians either separately or together. Please be aware, however, that, at all times, my client is your child—not the parents or guardians nor any siblings or other family members of the child. If I meet with you or other family members in the course of your child's treatment, I will make notes of that meeting in your child's treatment records. Please be aware that those notes will be available to any person or entity that has legal access to your child's treatment record.

By signing this agreement, you will be waiving any right of access to your child's treatment records. It is my policy to provide you with general information about treatment status. I will not share with you what your child has disclosed to me without your child's consent, unless disclosure to you is warranted due to a health or safety risk. At the end of your child's treatment, I will provide you with feedback that will describe what issues were discussed, what progress was made, and what areas are likely to require intervention in the future.

It is possible that your child will reveal sensitive information regarding problematic behaviors. If I believe that your child is at serious risk of harming himself or herself or another, I will inform you.

You agree to treat anything that is said in a session in which you participate as confidential. You agree that you will not attempt to gain advantage in any legal proceeding from my involvement with your child. In particular, I need your agreement that in any such proceedings, you will not ask me to testify in court, whether in person or by affidavit. You also agree to instruct your attorneys not to subpoena me or to refer in any court filing to anything we have said or done.

Please note that your agreement may not prevent a judge from requiring my testimony, even though I will not do so unless legally compelled. If I am required to testify, I am ethically bound not to give my opinion about either parent's custody, visitation suitability, or fitness. If the court appoints a custody evaluator, *guardian ad litem*, or parenting coordinator, I will provide information as needed, if appropriate releases are signed or a court order is provided, but I will not make any recommendation about the final decision(s). Furthermore, if I am required to appear as a witness or to otherwise perform work related to any legal matter, the party responsible for my participation agrees to reimburse me at the rate of [$XXX] per hour for time spent traveling, speaking with attorneys, reviewing and preparing documents, testifying, being in attendance, and any other case-related costs.

I have read and understand all the information provided in this document. I have been offered an opportunity to ask questions.

Signature of parent: _____

Name of parent (print): _____

Date: _____

### GUIDELINES FOR GROUP CONFIDENTIALITY

As a member of this therapy group, I understand that I have an obligation to respect the privacy and confidentiality of other group members. I agree to keep confidential all information shared by other group members. I will not talk with others outside the group about what is shared during group discussions. I agree not to record any sessions.

Further, I understand that there is a risk of disclosure to people outside the group by people in the group. I agree to release ABC Counseling Agency from any claims or liability resulting from any disclosure of confidential information, by me or other group members, to parties outside the group and to hold ABC Counseling Agency harmless from any claims or liability resulting from any disclosure of confidential information, by me or other group members, to parties outside the group.

Client signature _____ _____

Parent/Guardian signature _____

Date _____

### CONSENT FOR REMOTE COUNSELING

The following information is provided to clients who are seeking remote counseling services (also known as tele-mental health counseling). This document covers your rights, risks, and benefits associated with receiving services, my policies, and your authorization. Please read this document carefully and ask questions for clarification.

Tele-mental health services means the remote delivery of counseling services via technology. This includes a wide array of clinical services and various forms of technology. The technology includes but is not limited to video, Internet, a smartphone, tablet, PC desktop system, or other electronic means. You are solely responsible for any cost to you to obtain any necessary equipment, accessories, or software to take part in tele-mental health. The delivery method must be secured by two-way encryption to be considered secure. Synchronous (at the same time) secure video chatting is my preferred method of service delivery. By signing this form, you acknowledge that you understand and agree to the following:

1. You have a right to confidentiality with regard to your treatment and related communications via telehealth under the same laws that protect the confidentiality of your treatment information during in-person psychotherapy. The same mandatory and permissive exceptions to confidentiality we have discussed regarding our counseling relationship also apply to telehealth services.

2. While telehealth services offer several advantages, such as convenience and flexibility, it is an alternative form of therapy or adjunct to therapy and thus may involve some disadvantages and limitations. For example, there may be a disruption to the service (e.g., loss of Internet connection or poor smartphone reception). This can be frustrating and interrupt the normal flow of personal interaction.

There is a risk of misunderstanding one another when communication lacks visual or auditory cues. For example, if video quality is lacking for some reason, I might not see various details such as facial expressions. Or if audio quality is lacking, I might not hear differences in your tone of voice that I could easily pick up if you were in my office. Additionally, in-person counseling decreases the likelihood of interruptions.

There are ways to minimize interruptions and maximize privacy and effectiveness. I will do everything I can to ensure secure and private counseling sessions and prevent miscommunication. You understand that there is a risk of being overheard by persons near you and that you are responsible for using a location that is private and free from distractions or intrusions.

The nature of electronic communications technologies is such that I cannot guarantee that our communications will be kept confidential or that other people may not gain access to our communications. You also understand that other people might be able to get access to our private conversation or stored data could be accessed by unauthorized people or companies. I will try to use updated encryption methods, firewalls, and backup systems to help keep your information private, but there is a risk that our electronic communications may be compromised, unsecured, or accessed by others. You should also take reasonable steps to ensure the security of our communications (e.g., only using secure networks for telepsychology sessions and having passwords to protect the device you use for tele-mental health).

3. You understand that at the beginning of each telehealth session, I am required to verify your full name and current location.

4. You understand that in some instances, telehealth may not be as effective or provide the same results as in-person therapy. You understand that if I believe you would be better served by in-person therapy, I will discuss this with you and refer you to in-person services as needed. If such services are not possible because of distance, health challenges, or other hardship, I will refer you to other therapists who can provide such services, to the extent possible.

5. You understand that while telehealth has been found to be effective in treating a wide range of emotional issues, there is no guarantee that telehealth is effective for all individuals. Therefore, you understand that while you may benefit from telehealth, results cannot be guaranteed.

6. You understand that some telehealth platforms allow for video or audio recordings and that neither you nor I may record the sessions without the other party's explicit permission.

7. You and I have discussed the fees charged for telehealth and you agree to them [or you and I have agreed that I will bill your insurance plan for telehealth and that you will be billed for any portion that is your responsibility (e.g., co-payments)].

8. We will develop a plan for dealing with crisis/emergency situations and technology failures when providing tele-mental health services. This plan should include things such as: how crisis/emergency situations will be addressed (local resources, hotlines, trusted people identified by you, etc.); how to confirm your location; how to deal with technology failures during sessions and in crisis situations; how to deal with billing in the event of technology failures; and similar considerations. You understand that I will make reasonable efforts to identify and provide you with information about emergency resources in your geographical area. You further understand that I may not be able to assist you in an emergency situation. If you require emergency care, you understand that you may call 911 or proceed to the nearest hospital emergency department for immediate assistance.

You acknowledge that you have read and understand the information provided above, have discussed it with me, and understand that you have the right to have all your questions regarding this information answered to your satisfaction. [For conjoint or family therapy, clients may sign individual consent forms or sign the same form.]

Client's Signature _____

Client's Printed Name _____

Date _____

## 1. PROFESSIONAL RISK MANAGEMENT: AN OVERVIEW

1  R. Carroll, ed., *Risk Management Handbook for Healthcare Organizations* (Hoboken, NJ: Wiley, 2011).

2  K. Austin, M. Moline, and G. Williams, *Confronting Malpractice: Legal and Ethical Dilemmas in Psychotherapy* (Newbury Park, CA: Sage, 1990); B. Cooke, E. Worsham, and G. Reisfield, "The Elusive Standard of Care," *Journal of the American Academy of Psychiatry and the Law* 45 (2017): 358–64; T. Hartsell and B. Bernstein, *The Portable Lawyer for Mental Health Professionals: An A-Z Guide to Protecting Your Clients, Your Practice, and Yourself*, 3rd ed. (Hoboken, NJ: Wiley, 2013); T. Maschi and G. Leibowitz, eds., *Forensic Social Work: Psychosocial and Legal Issues Across Diverse Populations and Settings*, 2nd ed. (New York: Springer, 2018); P. Moffett and G. Moore, "The Standard of Care: Legal History and Definitions: The Bad and Good News," *Western Journal of Emergency Medicine* 12 (2011): 109–12; B. Schutz, *Legal Liability in Psychotherapy* (San Francisco: Jossey-Bass, 1982); D. Vanderpool, "The Standard of Care," *Innovations in Clinical Neuroscience* 18 (2021): 50–51.

3  D. Hogan, *The Regulation of Psychotherapists: Volume I—A Study in the Philosophy and Practice of Professional Regulation* (Cambridge, MA: Ballinger, 1979).

4  Hogan, *The Regulation of Psychotherapists: Volume I*, 8.

5  Hogan, *The Regulation of Psychotherapists: Volume I*, 8–10.

6  S. Gifis, *Law Dictionary*, 6th ed. (Hauppauge, NY: Barron's, 2010), 460.

7  H. Michaud, *Tort Law: Concepts and Applications*, 2nd ed. (Boston: Pearson, 2014).

8  Michaud, *Tort Law*.

9  Hogan, *The Regulation of Psychotherapists: Volume I*, 9–10.

10  Hogan, *The Regulation of Psychotherapists: Volume I*, 318.

11  Michaud, *Tort Law*. F. Reamer, *Ethical Standards in Social Work: A Review of the NASW Code of* Ethics, 3rd ed. (Washington, DC: NASW, 2018); F. Reamer, *Social Work Values and Ethics*, 5th ed. (New York: Columbia University Press, 2018).

12  F. Reamer, *The Social Work Ethics Casebook: Cases and Commentary*, 2nd ed. (Washington, DC: NASW, 2018).

13  Michaud, *Tort Law: Concepts and Applications*.

14  "Inadequate Psychiatric Treatment Blamed for Woman Killing Son," *Mental Health Law News* 9, no. 10 (1994): 2.

15  "Psychiatric Nurse Seduced Woman into Lesbian Relationship; $460,000 Verdict, *Mental Health Law News* 10, no. 9 (1995): 3.

16  Michaud, *Tort Law*.

17  "Plaintiffs Claim Failure to Continue Hospitalization Led to Murder, Then Suicide: $363,000 Verdict," *Mental Health Law News* 9, no. 4 (1994): 2.

18  "Man Claims Inadequate Observation in Psychiatric Ward; Falls from Window," *Mental Health Law News* 9, no. 11 (1994): 3.

19  "Sexual Relationship Between Patient and Unlicensed Mental Health Worker Results in Lawsuit," *Mental Health Law News* 10, no. 5 (1995): 3.

20  "Alleged Sexual Misconduct by Psychotherapist Causes Stress Disorder," *Mental Health Law News* 9, no. 8 (1994): 6.

21  Michaud, *Tort Law*.

22  Michaud, *Tort Law*.

23  Michaud, *Tort Law*.

24  Michaud, *Tort Law*.

## 2. CONFIDENTIALITY AND PRIVILEGED COMMUNICATION

1  R. Meyer, E. Landis, and J. Hays, *Law for the Psychotherapist* (New York: Norton, 1988).

2  M. Fisher, *The Ethics of Conditional Confidentiality: A Practice Model for Mental Health Professionals* (New York: Oxford University Press, 2013); Meyer, Landis, and Hays, *Law for the Psychotherapist*.

3  Fisher, *The Ethics of Conditional Confidentiality*.

4  M. Lewis, "Duty to Warn Versus Duty to Maintain Confidentiality: Conflicting Demands on Mental Health Professionals," *Suffolk Law Review* 20 (1986): 579–615.

5  Lewis, "Duty to Warn Versus Duty to Maintain Confidentiality."

6   Hammonds v. Aetna Casualty & Surety Co., 243 F. Supp. 793, 801–2 (N.D. Ohio 1965).

7   Lewis, "Duty to Warn Versus Duty to Maintain Confidentiality," 597.

8   Fisher, *The Ethics of Conditional Confidentiality*; Lewis, "Duty to Warn Versus Duty to Maintain Confidentiality."

9   Fisher, *The Ethics of Conditional Confidentiality*; Lewis, "Duty to Warn Versus Duty to Maintain Confidentiality."

10  Fisher, *The Ethics of Conditional Confidentiality*; Lewis, "Duty to Warn Versus Duty to Maintain Confidentiality."

11  Tarasoff v. Board of Regents of the University of California, 551 P.2d 334, 336–37 (Cal. 1976 [*Tarasoff II*]).

12  The original *Tarasoff* case was decided by the California Supreme Court in 1974. The court then withdrew its first published opinion and in 1976 issued its second opinion, commonly known as *Tarasoff II*, which recognized a duty to protect third parties under certain circumstances.

13  See also "Patient's Threats Disclosed: Right to Privacy Not Violated," *Mental Health Law News* 8, no. 2 (1993): 6; "Psychiatrist and Psychologist Revealed Patient's Threat: No Invasion of Privacy," *Mental Health Law News* 10, no. 6 (1995): 1; "Psychologists Owed Duty to Protect Child from Sexual Abuse," *Mental Health Law News* 11, no. 4 (1996): 3; "Counselor Had No Duty to Warn Ex-wife of Patient Who Later Shot Her," *Mental Health Law News* 12, no. 11 (1997): 1; "Counseling Center Did Not Violate Patient's Confidentiality When It Disclosed Her Death Threats," *Mental Health Law News* 12, no. 5 (1997): 1; "Lack of Physician-Patient Relationship Did Not Provide Psychiatrist with Defense," *Mental Health Law News* 3, no. 4 (1998): 1; "Defendant's Admission to Therapist Not Protected: Expressed Threat of Future Criminal Conduct," *Mental Health Law News* 14, no. 9 (1999): 4; "Psychiatrist's Testimony About Patient's Threats Not Protected by Psychotherapist-Patient Privilege," *Mental Health Law News* 14, no. 12 (1999): 3; "Psychologist Immune from Liability for Warning About Threats," *Mental Health Law News* 16, no. 8 (2001): 1; "Hospital Had Duty to Protect Mother of Patient with Psychiatric Impairments," *Mental Health Law News* 16, no. 9 (2001): 1.

14  See also Perreira v. State, 768 P.2d 1198 (Colo. 1989); Schuster v. Altenberg, 424 N.W.2d 159 (Wis. 1988); and Naidu v. Laird, 539 A.2d 1064 (Del. 1988).

15  "Psychiatrist Did Not Owe Duty to Protect Prospective Victims of Former Patient," *Mental Health Law News* 10, no. 10 (1995): 4. See also "Hospital Has No Duty to Protect Unforeseeable Third Party Whom Patient Assaulted,"

*Mental Health Law News* 8, no. 5 (1993): 1; "Chemical Dependency Counselor Who Disclosed Client's Threats Immune from Liability," *Mental Health Law News* 8, no. 10 (1993): 2; "Claim for Injuries from Escaped Patient Dismissed: Claimant Not Readily Identifiable Victim," *Mental Health Law News* 9, no. 1 (1994): 3; "Therapists Have No Duty to Control Outpatients from Harming Unidentified Third Parties," *Mental Health Law News* 11, no. 9 (1996): 1; "No Duty to Warn Without Direct Threat of Specific Act Against Identifiable Victim," *Mental Health Law News* 14, no. 3 (1999): 6.

16  T. Lambert, "Tom on Torts." *Law Reporter* 39 (1996): 228–31.

17  Lambert, "Tom on Torts," 230. ATLA refers to the Association of Trial Lawyers of America. The citation is to the association's law reporter.

18  B. Schutz, *Legal Liability in Psychotherapy* (San Francisco: Jossey-Bass, 1982), 57.

19  "Psychotherapist Has No Duty to Warn Third Party of Patient's Threat of Violence," *Mental Health Law News* 7, no. 2 (1992): 3.

20  See also "Psychiatrist Did Not Owe Duty to Protect Prospective Victims of Former Patient," *Mental Health Law News* 10, no. 10 (1995): 4.

21  "Psychiatry Resident Has Improper Sexual Contact with Child," *Mental Health Law News* 14, no. 10 (1999): 3.

22  "Doctor Who Conducted Training Had Duty to Warn or Prevent Resident from Abusing Patient," *Mental Health Law News* 14, no. 4 (1999): 4.

23  V. Quinsey, G. Harris, M. Rice, and C. Cormier, *Violent Offenders: Appraising and Managing Risk* (Washington, DC: American Psychological Association, 2005).

24  M. Grossman, "Confidentiality: The Right to Privacy Versus the Right to Know," in *Law and the Mental Health Professions*, ed. W. Barton and C. Sanborn (New York: International Universities Press, 1978), 159–60.

25  Grossman, "Confidentiality," 163.

26  *Tarasoff v. Board of Regents*, 551 P.2d at 340.

27  Lewis, "Duty to Warn Versus Duty to Maintain Confidentiality," 588–89.

28  J. Piel and R. Opara, "Does Volk v. Demeerleer Conflict with the AMA Code of Medical Ethics on Breaching Patient Confidentiality to Protect Third Parties," *AMA Journal of Ethics*, (January 2018), https://journalofethics. ama-assn.org/article/does-volk-v-demeerleer-conflict-ama-code-medical-ethics-breaching-patient-confidentiality-protect/2018-01.

29  T. Chenneville, "HIV, Confidentiality, and Duty to Protect: A Decision-Making Model," *Professional Psychology: Research and Practice* 31 (2000): 661–70.

30 C. Kain, "To Breach or Not to Breach: Is That the Question?," *Journal of Counseling and Development* 66 (1988): 224–25.

31 D. Francis and J. Chin, "The Prevention of Acquired Immunodeficiency Syndrome in the United States," *Journal of the American Medical Association* 257 (1987): 1364.

32 Chenneville, "HIV, Confidentiality, and Duty to Protect"; D. Lamb et al., "Applying *Tarasoff* to AIDS-Related Psychotherapy Issues," *Professional Psychology: Research and Practice* 20 (1989): 37–43.

33 L. Gray and A. Harding, "Confidentiality Limits with Clients Who Have the AIDS Virus," *Journal of Counseling and Development* 66 (1988): 219–23.

34 "Malpractice: How to Sidestep the Pitfalls," *NASW News*, February 1997, 5.

35 Schutz, *Legal Liability in Psychotherapy*, 64.

36 Lewis, "Duty to Warn Versus Duty to Maintain Confidentiality," 614–15.

37 Lewis, "Duty to Warn Versus Duty to Maintain Confidentiality," 606.

38 R. Madden, *Legal Issues in Social Work, Counseling, and Mental Health* (Thousand Oaks, CA: Sage, 1998).

39 "Psychiatric Nurse's Disclosure of Confidential Treatment Records Justified License Suspension," *Mental Health Law News* 15, no. 8 (2000): 3.

40 F. Reamer, *Ethics and Risk Management Issues in Online and Distance Behavioral Health* (San Diego, CA: Cognella, 2021).

41 F. Reamer, "Ethical Issues in Integrated Health Care: Implications for Social Workers," *Health & Social Work*, 43 (2018): 118–24.

42 American Health Information Management Association, "Privacy and Security Audits of Electronic Health Information," accessed September 28, 2022, https://library.ahima.org/doc?oid=300276#.YnfmmejMK3A.

43 J. Alden, "Health Care Group Hit with California Privacy Law Breach Suit," Bloomberg Law, March 11, 2020, https://news.bloomberglaw.com/tech-and-telecom-law/health-care-group-hit-with-california-privacy-law-breach-suit?context=search&index=7.

44 A. Gross, "Misconfigured Webpage Exposed Patient Data," HIPAA Secure Now, April 30, 2019, https://www.hipaasecurenow.com/misconfigured-webpage-exposed-patient-data/

45 C. Chaffin, "More than 645,000 Oregonians Impacted by DHS Data Breach," *The Oregonian*, June 25, 2019, https://www.oregonlive.com/data/2019/06/more-than-645000-oregonians-impacted-by-dhs-data-breach.html.

46 Federal Trade Commission, "Electronic Health Records Company Settles FTC Charges It Deceived Consumers about Privacy of Doctor Reviews" [press release],

June 8, 2016, https://www.ftc.gov/news-events/press-releases/2016/06/electronic -health-records-company-settles-ftc-charges-it-deceived.

47  See https://www.hhs.gov/hipaa/for-professionals/privacy/guidance/extreme -risk-protection-orders/index.html.

48  L. Bradley, B. Hendricks, and D. Kabell, "The Professional Will: An Ethical Responsibility," *Family Journal* 20 (2012): 309–14.

49  Fisher, *The Ethics of Conditional Confidentiality*; R. Madden, *Essential Law for Social Workers* (New York: Columbia University Press, 2003); S. Wilson, *Confidentiality in Social Work* (New York: Free Press, 1978).

50  Meyer, Landis, and Hays, *Law for the Psychotherapist*, 51–52.

51  J. Wigmore, *A Treatise on the System of Evidence in Trials at Common Law* (Boston: Little, Brown, 1905).

52  R. Alexander, Jr., "Social Workers and Privileged Communication in the Federal Legal System," *Social Work* 42 (1997): 387–91.

53  Jaffe v. Redmond, 116 S. Ct. 1923, 1932 (1996).

54  Fisher, *The Ethics of Conditional Confidentiality*.

55  Madden, *Legal Issues in Social Work, Counseling, and Mental Health*, 80.

56  "Psychiatrist's Crime Tip Did Not Violate Physician-Patient Privilege," *Mental Health Law News* 5, no. 3 (1990): 1.

57  "No Violation of Confidentiality in Communicating Patient's Arson Confession," *Mental Health Law News* 5, no. 4 (1990): 4.

58  "Privilege Did Not Protect Defendant's Letter to Therapist Admitting Sexual Abuse of Daughter," *Mental Health Law News* 8, no. 8 (1993): 1.

59  Fisher, *The Ethics of Conditional Confidentiality*; Madden, *Legal Issues in Social Work, Counseling, and Mental Health*.

60  Meyer, Landis, and Hays, *Law for the Psychotherapist*.

61  "Man in Joint Counseling Session Did Not Waive Patient-Psychotherapist Privilege," *Mental Health Law News* 10, no. 4 (1995): 3.

62  F. Reamer, *Risk Management in Social Work: Preventing Professional Malpractice, Liability and Disciplinary Action* (New York: Columbia University Press, 2015), 67.

63  "Psychologist-Patient Privilege Did Not Protect Statements by Spouse During Counseling," *Mental Health Law News* 10, no. 7 (1994): 2.

64  "Psychiatrist Who Discloses Confidential Information Liable for Damages," *Mental Health Law News* 9, no. 4 (1994): 1.

65  "Psychologist Breaches Psychologist-Patient Privilege by Providing Testimony," *Mental Health Law News* 15, no. 2 (2000): 4.

66  Madden, *Legal Issues in Social Work, Counseling, and Mental Health*.

67  "Statements Made to Alcoholics Anonymous Volunteers Not Protected by Privilege," *Mental Health Law News* 12, no. 3 (1997): 1.

68  K. Austin, M. Moline, and G. Williams, *Confronting Malpractice: Legal and Ethical Dilemmas in Psychotherapy* (Newbury Park, CA: Sage, 1990), 70.

69  "Testimony from Social Worker and Psychologist Not Privileged," *Mental Health Law News* 11, no. 10 (1996): 6.

70  "Defendant's Admission to Child Molestation Not Protected by Therapist-Client Privilege," *Mental Health Law News* 14, no. 2 (1999): 2.

71  "Juvenile's Communications to Psychologist and Social Worker Not Privileged," *Mental Health Law News* 16, no. 8 (2001): 5.

72  In an effort to prevent this potential conflict of interest, many clinicians who serve couples have the parties sign an agreement that includes language such as: "All parties acknowledge that the goal of psychotherapy is the amelioration of psychological distress and interpersonal conflict, and that the process of psychotherapy depends on trust and openness during the therapy sessions. Therefore, it is understood by all parties that if they request my services as a psychotherapist, they are expected not to use information given to me during the therapy process for their own legal purposes or against any of the other parties in a court or judicial setting of any kind. If you are involved in a divorce or child custody dispute, I will not provide testimony in court on any subject other than your therapy. You must hire a different mental health professional for any evaluations you require."

73  Grossman, "Confidentiality," 245.

74  Grossman, "Confidentiality," 145.

75  Wilson, *Confidentiality in Social Work*, 138.

76  Austin, Moline, and Williams, *Confronting Malpractice*; C. Polowy and C. Gorenberg, *Client Confidentiality and Privileged Communications: Office of General Counsel Law Notes* (Washington, DC: National Association of Social Workers, 1997).

77  Austin, Moline, and Williams, *Confronting Malpractice*; Polowy and Gorenberg, *Client Confidentiality and Privileged Communications*.

78  Wilson, *Confidentiality in Social Work*, 100.

79  R. Cohen, *Malpractice: A Guide for Mental Health Professionals* (New York: Free Press, 1979), 146.

80  Grossman, "Confidentiality."

81  Austin, Moline, and Williams, *Confronting Malpractice*, 47.

82   Austin, Moline, and Williams, *Confronting Malpractice*, 52–53.
83   Austin, Moline, and Williams, *Confronting Malpractice*, 55.


3. THE DELIVERY OF SERVICES

1   President's Commission for the Study of Ethical Problems in Medicine and
    Biomedical and Behavioral Research, *Making Health Care Decisions: The Ethi-
    cal and Legal Implications of Informed Consent in the Patient-Practitioner Rela-
    tionship*, vol. 3. (Washington, DC: US Government Printing Office, 1982), 5.
2   President's Commission, *Making Health Care Decisions*, 4–5.
3   M. Pernick, "The Patient's Role in Medical Decision Making: A Social His-
    tory of Informed Consent in Medical Therapy," in President's Commission,
    *Making Health Care Decisions*, 28–29.
4   J. Berg, P. Appelbaum, C. Lidz, and L. Parker, *Informed Consent: Legal Theory
    and Clinical Practice*. 2nd ed. (New York: Oxford University Press, 2001).
5   K. Austin, M. Moline, and G. Williams, *Confronting Malpractice: Legal and
    Ethical Dilemmas in Psychotherapy* (Newbury Park, CA: Sage, 1990), 187.
6   Berg et al., *Informed Consent*.
7   F. Rozovsky, *Consent to Treatment: A Practical Guide* (Boston: Little, Brown,
    1984), 240.
8   D. Hester and T. Schonfeld, eds. *Guidance for Healthcare Ethics Committees*
    (New York: Cambridge University Press, 2012).
9   Berg et al., *Informed Consent*; Rozovsky, *Consent to Treatment*.
10  Berg et al., *Informed Consent*; Rozovsky, *Consent to Treatment*; President's
    Commission, *Making Health Care Decisions*.
11  Berg et al., *Informed Consent*; Rozovsky, *Consent to Treatment*; President's
    Commission, *Making Health Care Decisions*.
12  Rozovsky, *Consent to Treatment*, 18.
13  Rozovsky, *Consent to Treatment*, 26.
14  Berg et al., *Informed Consent*.
15  Rozovsky, *Consent to Treatment*, 89.
16  "Mental Health Center's Failure to Conduct Tests for Brain Tumor Make It
    Liable for Patient's Death," *Mental Health Law News* 7, no. 5 (1992): 2.
17  B. Schutz, *Legal Liability in Psychotherapy* (San Francisco: Jossey-Bass, 1982),
    25–26.
18  "Man Kills Woman, Then Commits Suicide: $1 Million Settlement on Claim
    of Failure to Diagnose," *Mental Health Law News* 9, no. 5 (1994): 3.

19 R. Cohen, *Malpractice: A Guide for Mental Health Professionals* (New York: Free Press, 1979).

20 Cohen, *Malpractice*, 164.

21 "Patient Admitted to Hospital for Detoxification; Attempted Suicide Results in Brain Damage," *Mental Health Law News* 5, no. 7 (1990): 2.

22 "Hospital Liable for Failure to Admit Suicidal Patient Who Killed Himself," *Mental Health Law News* 6, no. 8 (1991): 4.

23 Austin, Moline, and Williams, 167.

24 "Psychiatrist Not Negligent in Misdiagnosing and Releasing Patient Who Killed Third Party," *Mental Health Law News* 7, no. 10 (1992): 1.

25 "Wife Kills Self; Had Been Hospitalized for Earlier Suicide Attempt," *Mental Health Law News* 10, no. 2 (1995): 3.

26 M. Janofsky, "Therapists Are Sentenced in Girls' 'Rebirthing' Death," *New York Times*, June 19, 2001, https://www.nytimes.com/2001/06/19/us/therapists-are-sentenced-in-girl-s-rebirthing-death.html.

27 D. Barr, "Clinical Social Worker Disciplined by State, Sued Over Patient Relations," *Daily News-Record* (Harrisonburg, VA), November 14, 1997, 19.

28 "Psychologist's Unorthodox Treatment for Personality Disorder Results in $325,000 Settlement," *Mental Health Law News* 10, no. 3 (1995): 1.

29 E. McArdle, "New Cause of Action May Stem from California Verdict: Father Wins $500,000 for Daughter's 'False Memory' of Abuse," *Lawyers Weekly USA*, June 6, 1994, B3.

30 "Psychiatrist Sued: Recovered Repressed Memories of Patient's Childhood," *Mental Health Law News* 10, no. 4 (1995): 6.

31 "Woman Claims Psychological Counselor Implanted Memories of Satanic Rituals and Parental Incest," *Mental Health Law News* 10, no. 7 (1995): 3.

32 Austin, Moline, and Williams, *Confronting Malpractice*, 156–57.

33 "Patient Improperly Treated for Panic Disorder and Agoraphobia," *Mental Health Law News* 7, no. 7 (1992): 6.

34 Austin, Moline, and Williams, *Confronting Malpractice*, 155–56.

35 Florida Board of Clinical Social Work, Marriage and Family Therapy and Mental Health Counseling, "Department of Health vs. Deborah A. Hulbert," 2001, http:// ww2.doh.state.fl.us/FinalOrderNet/folistbrowse.aspx?LicId =4410&P roCde=5201&discpln=DISCPLN.

36 Wisconsin Department of Safety and Professional Services, "In the Matter of Disciplinary Proceedings Against Cheryl K. Rotherham," 2013, https:// online.drl.wi.gov/decisions/2013/ORDER0002561–00008687.pdf.

37  "Member Blows Whistle on Rx Refills." *NASW News*, June 1990, 11.

38  "Attorney Suffers Psychotic Breakdown from Lifespring Training," *Mental Health Law News* 6, no. 7 (1991): 1.

39  "Woman Claims Psychological Problems Following 'Seminar Training,'" *Mental Health Law News* 7, no. 2 (1992): 6.

40  Cohen, *Malpractice*, 164.

41  M. Maheu et al., "An Interprofessional Framework for Telebehavioral Health Competencies," *Journal of Technology in Behavioral Science* 3 (2018): 108–40.

42  National Association of Social Workers, Association of Social Work Boards, Council on Social Work Education, and Clinical Social Work Association, *Standards for Technology in Social Work Practice* (Washington, DC: National Association of Social Workers, 2017). I chaired the task force that developed these standards.

43  F. Reamer, *Boundary Issues and Dual Relationships in the Human Services*, 3rd ed. (New York: Columbia University Press, 2021).

44  A. Celenza, *Sexual Boundary Violations: Therapeutic, Supervisory, and Academic Contexts* (Lanham, MD: Aronson, 2007); Reamer, *Boundary Issues and Dual Relationships*; G. Syme, *Dual Relationships in Counselling and Psychotherapy* (London: Sage, 2003); O. Zur, *Boundaries in Psychotherapy: Ethical and Clinical Explorations* (Washington, DC: American Psychological Association, 2007); O. Zur, ed., *Multiple Relationships in Psychotherapy and Counseling* (New York: Routledge, 2017).

45  American Psychological Association, *Code of Ethics* (Washington, DC: American Psychological Association, 2017).

46  American Counseling Association, *Code of Ethics* (Alexandria, VA: American Counseling Association, 2014).

47  National Association of Social Workers, *Code of Ethics* (Washington, DC: National Association of Social Workers, 2021).

48  State of Ohio Counselor and Social Worker Board, "Consent Agreement Between Robert J. Carson and the State of Ohio Counselor, Social Worker, and Marriage and Family Therapist Board, 2009, http://cswmft.ohio.gov /DiscLic/I0009744.pdf.

49  R. Epstein, *Keeping Boundaries: Maintaining Safety and Integrity in the Psychotherapeutic Process* (Washington, DC: American Psychiatric Press, 1994); M. Gottlieb, "Avoiding Exploitive Dual Relationships: A Decision-Making Model," in *Ethical Conflicts in Psychology*, ed. D. N. Bersoff (Washington,

DC: American Psychological Association, 1995), 242–43; Reamer, *Boundary Issues and Dual Relationships*.

50  S. Gifis, *Law Dictionary*, 6th ed. (Hauppauge, NY: Barron's, 2010), 508.

51  Alabama State Board of Social Work Examiners, "In the Matter of Shirley Carter," 2003, http://www.socialwork.alabama.gov/pdfs/Carter%20Decision .pdf.

52  Austin, Moline, and Williams, *Confronting Malpractice*, 224–25.

53  D. Besharov, *The Vulnerable Social Worker: Liability for Serving Children and Families* (Silver Spring, MD: National Association of Social Workers, 1985), 180.

54  Austin, Moline, and Williams, *Confronting Malpractice*, 223.

55  J. Sadek, *A Clinician's Guide to Suicide Risk Assessment and Management* (New York: Springer International, 2019).

56  "$570,841 Judgment Returned; Man Committed Suicide After Leaving Psychiatric Facility," *Mental Health Law News* 6, no. 2 (1991): 3.

57  "Psychiatrists Liable for Patient's Attempted Suicide," *Mental Health Law News* 6, no. 3 (1991): 1.

58  R. Meyer, E. Landis, and J. Hays, *Law for the Psychotherapist* (New York: Norton, 1988), 38.

59  Meyer, Landis, and Hays, *Law for the Psychotherapist*, 38.

60  R. Cohen and W. Mariano, *Legal Guidebook in Mental Health* (New York: Free Press, 1982), 156.

61  "Nursing Home Liable in Attempted Suicide," *Mental Health Law News* 5, no. 1 (1990): 1.

62  "Psychiatrists Not Liable for Discharging Patient Who Later Committed Suicide," *Mental Health Law News* 4, no. 10 (1989): 2.

63  "Hospital Liable for Failure to Prevent Suicide of Psychiatric Patient," *Mental Health Law News* 5, no. 2 (1990): 2.

64  "Hospital Liable for Suicide of Psychiatric Patient," *Mental Health Law News* 5, no. 5 (1990): 2.

65  "Schizophrenic Patient Hangs Self," *Mental Health Law News* 6, no. 3 (1991): 6.

66  R. Madden, *Legal Issues in Social Work, Counseling, and Mental Health* (Thousand Oaks, CA: Sage, 1998), 76.

67  Austin, Moline, and Williams, *Confronting Malpractice*; Meyer, Landis, and Hays, *Law for the Psychotherapist*; Sadek, *A Clinician's Guide*; D. Worchel and

R. Gearing, *Suicide Assessment and Treatment: Empirical and Evidence-Based Practices* (New York: Springer 2010).

68  Sadek, *A Clinician's Guide.*

69  Sadek, *A Clinician's Guide*; Schutz, *Legal Liability in Psychotherapy.*

70  D. Pinals and D. Mossman, *Evaluation for Civil Commitment* (New York: Oxford University Press, 2012).

71  Cohen and Mariano, *Legal Guidebook in Mental Health*, 380.

72  Austin, Moline, and Williams, *Confronting Malpractice*, 201.

73  Austin, Moline, and Williams, *Confronting Malpractice*, 206.

74  Meyer, Landis, and Hays, *Law for the Psychotherapist*; E. R. Saks, *Refusing Care: Forced Treatment and the Rights of the Mentally Ill* (New York: Oxford University Press, 2002).

75  Cohen, *Malpractice*, 139.

76  Austin, Moline, and Williams, *Confronting Malpractice*, 207–8.

77  Meyer, Landis, and Hays, *Law for the Psychotherapist*, 120.

78  Besharov, *The Vulnerable Social Worker*; D. DePanfilis and M. Salus, *Child Protective Services: A Guide for Caseworkers* (Washington, DC: U.S. Department of Health and Human Services, 2003).

79  Besharov, *The Vulnerable Social Worker*, 28–29.

80  "Therapists Fail to Notify or Take Action Against Abuse of Group Home Residents," *Mental Health Law News* 16, no. 8 (2001): 2.

81  Besharov, *The Vulnerable Social Worker*, 32–33.

82  "Treating Therapist Falsely Reports Father's Molestation of Young Daughter," *Mental Health Law News* 12, no. 9 (1997): 4.

83  Besharov, *The Vulnerable Social Worker*, 41.

84  "Counselor Who Suspected Child Abuse Not Liable for Interfering with Family Rights," *Mental Health Law News* 5, no. 5 (1990): 4.

85  "Psychotherapist May Not Be Sued for Erroneous Child Abuse Diagnosis," *Mental Health Law News* 7, no. 11 (1992): 4.

86  Besharov, *The Vulnerable Social Worker*, 43–44.

87  P. Pecora et al., *The Child Welfare Challenge: Policy, Practice, and Research*, 4th ed. (New York: Routledge, 2019).

88  Besharov, *The Vulnerable Social Worker*, 58–59.

89  DeShaney v. Winnebago County Department of Social Services, 812 F.2d 298, 301 (7th Cir. 1987); 109 S. Ct. 998 (1989).

90  Besharov, *The Vulnerable Social Worker*, 70.

91  Besharov, *The Vulnerable Social Worker*, 79.

92 Besharov, *The Vulnerable Social Worker*, 94.

93 Pecora et al., *The Child Welfare Challenge*.

94 Besharov, *The Vulnerable Social Worker*, 111–115.

95 Besharov, *The Vulnerable Social Worker*, 120.

96 Gifis, *Law Dictionary*, 124.

97 K. Abraham, *The Forms and Functions of Tort Law*, 5th ed. (St. Paul, MN: Foundation Press, 2017).

98 Schutz, *Legal Liability in Psychotherapy*, 10.

99 Austin, Moline, and Williams, *Confronting Malpractice*, 91.

100 Besharov, *The Vulnerable Social Worker*, 41.

101 Besharov, *The Vulnerable Social Worker*, 79.

102 F. Reamer, *Ethics and Risk Management Issues in Online and Distance Behavioral Health* (San Diego: Cognella, 2021).

103 Zur, *Boundaries in Psychotherapy*, 133, 136.

104 K. Kolmes, "Social Media in the Future of Professional Psychology," *Professional Psychology: Research and Practice* 43 (2012): 606–12.

105 Reamer, *Ethics and Risk Management Issues in Online and Distance Behavioral Health*.

106 National Association of Social Workers et al., *Standards for Technology in Social Work Practice*.

107 L. Stevenson, "HCPC Sanctions Social Worker Over Facebook Posts," Community Care, September 10, 2014, https://www.communitycare.co.uk/2014/09/10/social-worker-given-conditions-practice-order-disrespectful-facebook-posts/.

108 Zur, *Boundaries in Psychotherapy*, 141.

109 Zur, *Boundaries in Psychotherapy*, 144–45.

## 4. IMPAIRED PRACTITIONERS

1 F. Reamer, "The Impaired Social Worker," *Social Work* 37 (1992): 165–70.

2 R. Coombs, *Drug-Impaired Professionals* (Cambridge, MA: Harvard University Press, 2000); R. Kilburg, F. Kaslow, and G. VandenBos, "Professionals in Distress," *Hospital and Community Psychiatry* 39 (1988): 723–25; E. Knutsen, "On the Emotional Well-Being of Psychiatrists: Overview and Rationale," *American Journal of Psychoanalysis* 37 (1977): 123–29; D. Laliotis and J. Grayson, "Psychologist Heal Thyself: What Is Available for the Impaired Psychologist?" *American Psychologist* 40 (1985): 84–96; B. McCrady, "The Distressed

or Impaired Professional: From Retribution to Rehabilitation," *Journal of Drug Issues* 19 (1989): 337–49.

3  H. Stadler, K. Willing, M. Eberhage, and W. Ward, "Impairment: Implications for the Counseling Profession," *Journal of Counseling and Development* 66 (1988): 258–60.

4  National Association of Social Workers (NASW), Commission on Employment and Economic Support, *Impaired Social Worker Program Resource Book* (Silver Spring, MD: National Association of Social Workers, 1987).

5  NASW, Commission on Employment and Economic Support, *Impaired Social Worker Program Resource Book*, 7.

6  NASW, Commission on Employment and Economic Support, *Impaired Social Worker Program Resource Book*, 6.

7  D. Lamb et al., "Confronting Professional Impairment During the Internship: Identification, Due Process, and Remediation," *Professional Psychology: Research and Practice* 18 (1987): 598.

8  NASW, Commission on Employment and Economic Support, *Impaired Social Worker Program Resource Book*, 4.

9  NASW, Commission on Employment and Economic Support, *Impaired Social Worker Program Resource Book*, 6.

10  L. Stoesen, "Recovering Social Workers Offer Support," *NASW News*, July 2002, 3.

11  J. Guy, P. Poelstra, and M. Stark, "Personal Distress and Therapeutic Effectiveness: National Survey of Psychologists Practicing Psychotherapy," *Professional Psychology: Research and Practice* 20 (1989): 48–50.

12  K. Pope, B. Tabachnick, and P. Keith-Spiegel, "Ethics of Practice: The Beliefs and Behaviors of Psychologists as Therapists," *American Psychologist* 42 (1987): 993.

13  B. Wood et al., "Impaired Practitioners: Psychologists' Opinions About Prevalence, and Proposals for Intervention," *Professional Psychology: Research and Practice* 16 (1985): 843–50.

14  B. A. Farber, ed., *Stress and Burnout in the Human Service Professions* (New York: Pergamon, 1983).

15  C. Deutsch, "A Survey of Therapists' Personal Problems and Treatment," *Professional Psychology: Research and Practice* 16 (1985): 305–15.

16  L. Bissell and P. Haberman, *Alcoholism in the Professions* (New York: Oxford University Press, 1984).

17 K. Pope, "How Clients Are Harmed by Sexual Contact with Mental Health Professionals: The Syndrome and Its Prevalence," *Journal of Counseling and Development* 67 (1988): 222–26.

18 D. Crombie, "Social Worker Sentenced in Assaults," *Providence Journal-Bulletin* (Providence, RI), April 20, 1989, B3.

19 Guy, Poelstra, and Stark, "Personal Distress and Therapeutic Effectiveness."

20 R. Thoreson, M. Miller, and C. Krauskopf, "The Distressed Psychologist: Prevalence and Treatment Considerations," *Professional Psychology: Research and Practice* 20 (1989): 153–58.

21 Lamb et al., "Confronting Professional Impairment During the Internship."

22 Wood et al., "Impaired Practitioners."

23 Kilburg, Kaslow, and VandenBos, "Professionals in Distress," 723.

24 F. Reamer, *Boundary Issues and Dual Relationships in the Human Services*, 3rd ed. (New York: Columbia University Press, 2021).

25 A. Brodsky, "The Distressed Psychologist: Sexual Intimacies and Exploitation," in *Professionals in Distress: Issues, Syndromes, and Solutions in Psychology*, ed. R. Kilburg, P. Nathan, and R. Thoreson (Washington, DC: American Psychological Association, 1986), 155.

26 S. Martelle, "Broken Trust," *Hour Detroit*, August 2009, http://www.hourdetroit. com/Hour-Detroit/August-2009/Broken-Trust/.

27 M. Romero, "Ex-Social Worker Sentenced to Prison for Sex with Teen Client," *Deseret News*, April 25, 2016, https://www.deseret.com/2016/4/25/20587263/ex-social-worker-sentenced-to-prison-for-sex-with-teen-client.

28 "Ex-Prison Psychologist Gets 3 Years Behind Bars," *Arkansas Democrat Gazette*, September 1, 2007, https://www.arkansasonline.com/news/2007/sep/01/ex-prison-psychologist-gets-3-years-behind-bars/.

29 "Former Social Worker Sentenced for Sex Crimes with Minors in Mississippi," Yahoo News, January 6, 2022, https://www.yahoo.com/news/former-social-worker-sentenced-sex-132843339.html.

30 J. Papp, "Child Psychologist Sentenced to Prison in Decade-Long Sexual Exploitation Case, *Augusta Chronicle*, March 2, 2022, https://www.augustachronicle.com/story/news/crime/2022/03/02/psychologist-sentenced-prison-decade-long-child-molestation-case/6978729001/.

31 C. Ward, "Former Social Worker at Elgin Mental Health Center Pleads Guilty to Sexual Misconduct with Patient, Sentenced to 180 Days in Jail," *Chicago Tribune*, September 9, 2019, https://www.chicagotribune.com/news

/breaking/ct-elgin-mental-health-center-worker-guilty-sex-crime-20190909
-g65tj33yjnht5lm2ofjnqcukcy-story.html.

32  M. Wenzke, "Ex-Marriage and Family Therapist in Pasadena Sentenced to
    Prison for Sexually Abusing 7 Patients," KTLA.com, January 21, 2021, https://
    ktla.com/news/local-news/ex-family-and-marriage-therapist-in-pasadena
    -sentenced-to-prison-for-sexually-abusing-7-patients/.

33  P. Stein, "Prison for Psychologist Who Had Sex with Patients," KRQE.com,
    January 12, 2018, https://www.krqe.com/news/crime/new-mexico-therapist
    -who-raped-clients-sentenced-to-12-years/.

34  A. Aisner, "Ex-Therapist Faces Prison for Assaulting Patients," *Ann Arbor News*,
    January 29, 2008, https://www.mlive.com/annarbornews/2008/01/extherapist
    _faces_prison_for_a.html.

35  "New Mexico Therapist Who Raped Clients Sentenced to 12 Years," KRQE.
    com, July 29, 2020, https://www.krqe.com/news/crime/new-mexico-therapist
    -who-raped-clients-sentenced-to-12-years/.

36  "Medicaid Fraud, Sexual Assault Results in Prison Term for Ex-Cheyenne
    Counselor," *Star Tribune*, November 28, 2021, https://trib.com/news/state
    -and-regional/crime-and-courts/medicaid-fraud-sexual-assault-results-in
    -prison-term-for-ex-cheyenne-counselor/article_6d24819c-1678-5eba-89fc
    -f243dcaf3c21.html.

37  A. Celenza, *Sexual Boundary Violations: Therapeutic, Supervisory, and Aca-
    demic Contexts* (Lanham, MD: Aronson, 2007); Reamer, *Boundary Issues
    and Dual Relationships*; A. Steinberg, J. Alpert, and C. Courtois, eds., *Sexual
    Boundary Violations in Psychotherapy: Facing Therapist Indiscretions, Trans-
    gressions, and Misconduct* (Washington, DC: American Psychological Asso-
    ciation, 2021); G. Syme, *Dual Relationships in Counselling and Psychotherapy*
    (London: Sage, 2003); O. Zur, *Boundaries in Psychotherapy: Ethical and Clin-
    ical Explorations* (Washington, DC: American Psychological Association,
    2007); O. Zur, *Multiple Relationships in Psychotherapy and Counseling* (New
    York: Routledge, 2017).

38  N. Gartrell et al., "Psychiatrist-Patient Sexual Contact: Results of a National
    Survey," *American Journal of Psychiatry* 143 (1986): 1126–31.

39  Brodsky, "The Distressed Psychologist," 157–58.

40  R. Reaves, "Legal Liability and Psychologists," in *Professionals in Distress:
    Issues, Syndromes, and Solutions in Psychology*, ed. R. Kilburg, P. Nathan, and
    R. Thoreson (Washington, DC: American Psychological Association, 1986),
    173–84.

41 "Woman Has Sexual Relationship with Therapist; $123,500 Award," *Mental Health Law News* 14, no. 12 (1999): 5.

42 Wisconsin Department of Safety and Professional Services, "In the Matter of Disciplinary Proceedings Against Jackie M. Morter," 2012, https://online.drl .wi.gov/ decisions/2012/ORDER0001302–00006751.pdf.

43 Alabama State Board of Social Work Examiners, "In the Matter of Michael Beddingfield," 2006, http://www.socialwork.alabama.gov/pdfs/Beddingfield .pdf.

44 New Jersey State Board of Social Work Examiners, "In the Matter of Daniel Cruz," 2000, http://www.state.nj.us/lps/ca/action/20000216_44SW01452900 .pdf.

45 Louisiana State Board of Social Work Examiners, "In the Matter of Kristin Richards," 2013, http://www.labswe.org/lms/ Files/606.pdf.

46 Maryland Board of Social Work Examiners, "In the Matter of Ava Barron-Shasho," 2012, http://dhmh.maryland.gov/bswe/Docs/Orders/Shasho-1735.pdf.

47 B. Schutz, *Legal Liability in Psychotherapy* (San Francisco: Jossey-Bass, 1982), 34–35.

48 Schutz, *Legal Liability in Psychotherapy*, 34–35.

49 Schutz, *Legal Liability in Psychotherapy*, 35.

50 "Psychologist Encourages Sexual Misconduct Between Patient and Psychiatrist," *Mental Health Law News* 4, no. 3 (1989): 2.

51 "Psychiatric Patient Has Sexual Relationship with Psychiatrist," *Mental Health Law News* 6, no. 11 (1989): 4.

52 "Psychiatrist Has Sex with Patient," *Mental Health Law News* 4, no. 11 (1989): 6.

53 "Marriage Therapist Has Affair with Patient," *Mental Health Law News* 5, no. 4 (1990): 3.

54 "Patient Sexually Abused by Psychologist," *Mental Health Law News* 5, no. 12 (1990): 3.

55 "Counselor Begins Sexual Relationship with Client," *Mental Health Law News* 6, no. 4 (1991): 1.

56 "Drug Treatment Counselor Has Affair with Patient's Mother," *Mental Health Law News* 7, no. 1 (1992): 3.

57 "Female Therapist Engages in Same-Sex Relationship with Patient," *Mental Health Law News* 15, no. 6 (2000): 3.

58 "Psychiatrist's License Suspended Six Months for Having Sexual Relations with Patient," *Mental Health Law News* 8, no. 3 (1993): 4; *Pundy v. Illinois Department of Professional Regulation*, 570 N.E.2d 458 (Ill. App. Ct. 1991).

59   "Court Affirms Suspension of Psychologist's License for Sexual Misconduct,"
     *Mental Health Law News* 12, no. 12 (1997): 3.
60   S. Twemlow and G. Gabbard, "The Love-Sick Therapist," in *Sexual Exploi-
     tation in Professional Relationships*, ed. G. O. Gabbard (Washington, DC:
     American Psychiatric Press, 1989), 71–87.
61   G. Schoener, "Assessments of Professionals Who Have Engaged in Boundary
     Violations," *Psychiatric Annals* 25 (1995): 95–99.
62   S. Olarte, "Sexual Boundary Violations," in *The Hatherleigh Guide to Ethics in
     Therapy* (New York: Hatherleigh, 1997), 205.
63   Olarte, "Sexual Boundary Violations," 204.
64   R. Simon, "Therapist-Patient Sex: From Boundary Violations to Sexual Mis-
     conduct," *Forensic Psychiatry* 22 (1999): 31–47.
65   R. Simon, "The Natural History of Therapist Sexual Misconduct: Identifica-
     tion and Prevention," *Psychiatric Annals* 25 (1995): 90–94.
66   Celenza, *Sexual Boundary Violations*.
67   G. VandenBos and R. Duthie, "Confronting and Supporting Colleagues
     in Distress," in *Professionals in Distress: Issues, Syndromes, and Solutions in
     Psychology*, ed. R. Kilburg, P. Nathan, and R. Thoreson (Washington, DC:
     American Psychological Association, 1986), 224–26.
68   R. Thoreson and J. Skorina, "Alcohol Abuse Among Psychologists," in *Profes-
     sionals in Distress: Issues, Syndromes, and Solutions in Psychology*, ed. R. Kil-
     burg, P. Nathan, and R. Thoreson (Washington, DC: American Psychological
     Association, 1986), 77–117.
69   H. Freudenberger, "Chemical Abuse Among Psychologists: Symptoms,
     Causes, and Treatment Issues," in *Professionals in Distress: Issues, Syndromes,
     and Solutions in Psychology*, ed. R. Kilburg, P. Nathan, and R. Thoreson
     (Washington, DC: American Psychological Association, 1986), 137–38.
70   Iowa Board of Social Work, "In the Matter of Brian C. Nedoba," 2013, http://
     www.idph.state.ia.us/IDPHChannelsService/file.ashx?file=B5221FE3-D8F1
     -4A02-B595-8C8878F8173A.
71   Texas Department of State Health Service, "Texas State Board of Social Worker
     Examiners Enforcement Actions—Disciplinary Actions," 2013, http://www
     .dshs.state.tx.us/socialwork/sw_cmp.shtm.
72   Arkansas Social Work Licensing Board, "Disciplinary Action," 2013, http://
     www.arkansas.gov/swlb/pdfs/Disciplinary_Action_Descending_Order.pdf.
73   Alabama State Board of Social Work Examiners, "In re Sally Baker," 1999,
     http://www.socialwork.alabama.gov/pdfs/Baker%20disciplinary%20action.pdf.

74  Guy, Poelstra, and Stark, "Personal Distress and Therapeutic Effectiveness."

75  Wood et al., "Impaired Practitioners."

76  VandenBos and Duthie, "Confronting and Supporting Colleagues in Distress," 212.

77  R. Thoreson, P. Nathan, J. Skorina, and R. Kilburg, "The Alcoholic Psychologist: Issues, Problems, and Implications for the Profession," *Professional Psychology: Research and Practice* 14 (1983): 670–84.

78  Deutsch, "A Survey of Therapists' Personal Problems and Treatment."

79  Brodsky, "The Distressed Psychologist," 164.

80  G. R. Schoener and J. Gonsiorek, "Assessment and Development of Rehabilitation Plans for Counselors Who Have Sexually Exploited Their Clients," *Journal of Counseling and Development* 67 (1988): 227–32; W. Sonnenstuhl, "Reaching the Impaired Professional: Applying Findings from Organizational and Occupational Research," *Journal of Drug Issues* 19 (1989): 533–39; VandenBos and Duthie, "Confronting and Supporting Colleagues in Distress."

81  Lamb et al., "Confronting Professional Impairment During the Internship."

82  Sonnenstuhl, "Reaching the Impaired Professional."

83  VandenBos and Duthie, "Confronting and Supporting Colleagues in Distress," 227–229.

84  P. Candilis D. Kim, and L. Sulmasy, "Physician Impairment and Rehabilitation: Reintegration into Medical Practice While Ensuring Patient Safety: A Position Paper from the American College of Physicians," *Annals of Internal Medicine* 170 (219): 871–79; R. DuPont et al., "How Are Addicted Physicians Treated? A National Survey of Physician Health Programs," *Journal of Substance Abuse Treatment* 37 (2009): 1–7; A. Winkler, "Treating Physicians for Addiction," *American Journal of Psychiatry* 12 (2017): 6–7.

85  M. Goby, N. Bradley, and D. Bespalec, "Physicians Treated for Alcoholism: A Follow-up Study," *Alcoholism: Clinical and Experimental Research* 3 (1979): 121–24.

86  D. Kliner, J. Spicer, and P. Barnett, "Treatment Outcome of Alcoholic Physicians," *Journal of Studies on Alcohol* 41 (1980): 1217–20.

87  R. Morse, M. Martin, W. Swenson, and R. Niven, "Prognosis of Physicians Treated for Alcoholism and Drug Dependence," *Journal of the American Medical Association* 251 (1984): 743–46.

88  R. Herrington, D. Benzer, G. Jacobson, and M. Hawkins, "Treating Substance-Use Disorders Among Physicians," *Journal of the American Medical Association* 247 (1982): 2253–57.

89  M. Pearson, "Psychiatric Treatment of 250 Physicians," *Psychiatric Annals* 12 (1982): 194–206.

90  J. Shore, "The Impaired Physician: Four Years After Probation," *Journal of the American Medical Association* 248 (1982): 3127–30.

91  Simon, "Therapist-Patient Sex," 32.

92  Celenza, *Sexual Boundary Violations*; Syme, *Dual Relationships in Counselling and Psychotherapy*; Zur, *Boundaries in Psychotherapy*; Zur, *Multiple Relationships in Psychotherapy and Counseling*.

93  T. Gutheil and G. Gabbard, "The Concept of Boundaries in Clinical Practice: Theoretical and Risk-Management Dimensions," *American Journal of Psychiatry* 150 (1993): 191.

94  Simon, "The Natural History of Therapist Sexual Misconduct."

95  Gutheil and Gabbard, "The Concept of Boundaries in Clinical Practice," 192.

96  Gutheil and Gabbard, "The Concept of Boundaries in Clinical Practice," 192.

97  Gutheil and Gabbard, "The Concept of Boundaries in Clinical Practice," 192.

98  Simon, "The Natural History of Therapist Sexual Misconduct."

## 5. SUPERVISION: CLIENTS AND STAFF

1  C. Beckett, *Supervision: A Guide for the Helping Professions* (Thousand Oaks, CA: Sage, 2021); M. Carroll, *Effective Supervision for the Helping Professions*, 2nd ed. (Thousand Oaks, CA: Sage, 2014); G. Corey, R. Haynes, P. Moulton, and M. Muratori, *Clinical Supervision in the Helping Professions: A Practical Guide*, 3rd ed. (Alexandria, VA: American Counseling Association, 2021); A. Kadushin and D. Harkness, *Supervision in Social Work*, 5th ed. (New York: Columbia University Press, 2014).

2  "Resident at Hospital for Mentally Retarded Receives Award for Negligent Treatment," *Mental Health Law News* 4, no. 3 (1989): 4.

3  "Psychiatric Patient Raped by Fellow Patient," *Mental Health Law News* 4, no. 3 (1989): 4.

4  "Patient Raped by Fellow Patient," *Mental Health Law News* 4, no. 11 (1989): 6.

5  "Hospital Not Negligent in Supervising Patient Who Attacked Another Patient," *Mental Health Law News* 7, no. 1 (1992): 3.

6  "School and Staff Not Liable for Injuries Sustained When Retarded Resident Was Attacked," *Mental Health Law News* 9, no. 5 (1994): 3.

7  "Patient Jumps from Hospital Window," *Mental Health Law News* 4, no. 12 (1989): 2.

8   "Suicidal Patient Not Restrained by Defendant Hospital," *Mental Health Law News* 5, no. 2 (1990): 3.

9   "Mental Patient Escapes and Is Struck by Car," *Mental Health Law News* 5, no. 11 (1990): 3.

10  "Psychiatric Patient Not Properly Monitored While Eating Chokes to Death," *Mental Health Law News* 5, no. 11 (1990): 4.

11  Kadushin and Harkness, *Supervision in Social Work*.

12  Beckett, *Supervision*; Carroll, *Effective Supervision*; Corey et al., *Clinical Supervision*; Kadushin and Harkness, *Supervision in Social Work*.

13  S. Gifis, *Law Dictionary*, 6th ed. (Hauppauge, NY: Barron's, 2010), 416–17.

14  Louisiana State Board of Social Work Examiners. "In the Matter of Donald Henry," 2013, http://www.labswe.org/lms/Files/625.pdf.

15  K. Austin, M. Moline, and G. Williams, *Confronting Malpractice: Legal and Ethical Dilemmas in Psychotherapy* (Newbury Park, CA: Sage, 1990), 232.

16  "Social Worker Engages in Sexual Relationship with Patient," *Mental Health Law News* 4, no. 5 (1999): 2.

17  "Hospital Liable for Employee's Sexual Assault on Psychiatric Patient," *Mental Health Law News* 7, no. 10 (1992): 6.

18  "Official of Alcohol Center Entered into Sexual Relationship with Woman One Month After She Left Program," *Mental Health Law News* 5, no. 7 (1990): 5.

19  "Employer May Be Held Liable for Psychotherapist's Sexual Misconduct," *Mental Health Law News* 5, no. 11 (1990): 1.

20  "Employer Not Vicariously Liable for Therapist's Sexual Misconduct," *Mental Health Law News* 4, no. 10 (1989): 1.

21  B. Schutz, *Legal Liability in Psychotherapy* (San Francisco: Jossey-Bass, 1982), 50.

22  G. Robinson, "Discussion," *American Journal of Psychiatry* 118 (1962): 780.

23  R. Woody, *Legally Safe Mental Health Practice* (Madison, CT: Psychosocial Press, 1997).

24  Woody, *Legally Safe Mental Health Practice*.

25  Schutz, *Legal Liability in Psychotherapy*, 50.

26  "Negligent Care of Mental Patient Alleged in Suicide Death; $317,500 Verdict," *Mental Health Law News* 16, no. 2 (2001): 2.

27  R. Cohen and B. DeBetz, "Responsive Supervision of the Psychiatric Resident and Clinical Psychology Intern," *American Journal of Psychoanalysis* 37 (1977): 55.

28  C. Falender and E. Shafranske, *Clinical Supervision: A Competency-Based Approach*, 2nd ed. (Washington, DC: American Psychological Association, 2021).

## 6. CONSULTATION, REFERRAL, DOCUMENTATION, AND RECORDS

1  National Association of Social Workers and Association of Social Work Boards, *Best Practice Standards in Social Work Supervision* (Washington, DC: National Association of Social Workers, 2013).
2  G. Fredman, A. Papadopoulou, and E. Worwood, eds., *Collaborative Consultation in Mental Health: Guidelines for the New Consultant* (London: Routledge, 2018).
3  A. Kadushin, *Consultation in Social Work* (New York: Columbia University Press, 1977), 25–26.
4  "Physician Fails to Properly Treat Depression or Make Timely Referral," *Mental Health Law News* 7, no. 10 (1992): 2.
5  R. Marchant, "Police: Greenwich Child Psychologist Charged with Failing to Report Alleged Abuse or Neglect to Authorities," *Greenwich Time*, December 28, 2021, https://www.greenwichtime.com/news/article/Police-Greenwich-child-psychologist-charged-with-16733352.php.
6  B. Schutz, *Legal Liability in Psychotherapy* (San Francisco: Jossey-Bass, 1982), 47.
7  R. Meyer, E. Landis, and J. Hays, *Law for the Psychotherapist* (New York: Norton, 1988), 50–51.
8  Meyer, Landis, and Hays, *Law for the Psychotherapist*, 50.
9  "State Disciplines Psychiatrist for Making Improper Referral," *Providence Journal-Bulletin* (Providence, RI), December 1, 1992, B3.
10  "Psychological Counselor Refers Patients to Unqualified 'Colleague,'" *Mental Health Law News* 6, no. 8 (1991): 6.
11  "Therapist Begins Personal Relationship with Wife While Still Seeing Husband," *Mental Health Law News* 9, no. 6 (1994): 4.
12  R. Cohen, *Malpractice: A Guide for Mental Health Professionals* (New York: Free Press, 1979), 239.
13  "Failure to Refer to Psychiatrist and to Hospital Alleged in Suicide," *Mental Health Law News* 10, no. 5 (1995): 6.
14  K. Austin, M. Moline, and G. Williams, *Confronting Malpractice: Legal and Ethical Dilemmas in Psychotherapy* (Newbury Park, CA: Sage, 1990), 30.

15  Texas Department of State Health Service, "Texas State Board of Social Worker Examiners Enforcement Actions—Disciplinary Actions," 2013, http://www.dshs.state.tx.us/socialwork/sw_cmp.shtm.

16  Arkansas Social Work Licensing Board, "Disciplinary Action," 2013, http://www.arkansas.gov/swlb/pdfs/Disciplinary_Action_Descending_Order.pdf.

17  Louisiana State Board of Social Work Examiners, "In the Matter of Jennifer Gordon," 2013, http://www.labswe.org/lms/ Files/580.pdf.

18  J. D. Kagle and S. Kopels, *Social Work Records*, 3rd ed. (Long Grove, IL: Waveland Press, 2008); E. Luepker, *Record Keeping in Psychotherapy and Counseling*, 2nd ed. (New York: Routledge, 2022); N. Sidell, *Social Work Documentation: A Guide to Strengthening Your Case Recording*, 2nd ed. (Washington, DC: NASW Press, 2015).

19  J. Kagle, "Recording in Direct Practice," in *Encyclopedia of Social Work*, 18th ed. (Silver Spring, MD: National Association of Social Workers, 1987), 463.

20  M. Berner, "Write Smarter, Not Longer," in *The Mental Health Practitioner and the Law: A Comprehensive Handbook*, ed. L. Lifson and R. Simon (Cambridge, MA: Harvard University Press, 1998), 60–61.

21  D. Gould, "Listen to Your Lawyer," in *The Mental Health Practitioner and the Law: A Comprehensive Handbook*, ed. L. Lifson and R. Simon (Cambridge, MA: Harvard University Press, 1998), 345.

22  Berner, "Write Smarter, Not Longer," 54.

23  Mental Health and Developmental Disabilities Confidentiality Act, https://www.ilga.gov/legislation/ilcs/ilcs3.asp?ActID=2043&ChapterID=57.

24  R. Madden, *Legal Issues in Social Work, Counseling, and Mental Health* (Thousand Oaks, CA: Sage, 1998), 31–32.

25  R. Barker and D. Branson, *Forensic Social Work: Legal Aspects of Professional Practice* (New York: Taylor & Francis, 2000), 154–55.

26  A. Barsky and J. Gould, *Clinicians in Court: A Guide to Subpoenas, Depositions, Testifying and Everything Else You Need to Know* (New York: Guilford, 2002), 135.

27  Barsky and Gould, *Clinicians in Court*, 145.

28  C. Bergstresser, "The Perspective of the Plaintiff's Attorney," in *The Mental Health Practitioner and the Law: A Comprehensive Handbook*, ed. L. Lifson and R. Simon (Cambridge, MA: Harvard University Press, 1998), 342.

29  Texas Department of State Health Service, "Texas State Board of Social Worker Examiners Enforcement Actions—Disciplinary Actions," 2013, http://www.dshs.state.tx.us/socialwork/sw_cmp.shtm.

## 7. DECEPTION AND FRAUD

1  US Department of Justice, "Three Sentenced to Prison for Scheme to Defraud Medicare" [press release], 2011, http://www.justice.gov/usao/lam/press/press1101.html.

2  US Department of Justice, "Powell, Wyoming Psychologist Sentenced to Three Years in Prison for Health Care Fraud" [press release], 2018, https://www.justice.gov/usao-wy/pr/powell-wyoming-psychologist-sentenced-three-years-prison-health-care-fraud-0.

3  US Department of Justice, "Social Worker Sentenced for Defrauding Blue Cross Blue Shield" [press release], 2015, https://www.justice.gov/usao-wdny/pr/social-worker-sentenced-defrauding-blue-cross-blue-shield.

4  US Department of Justice, "Licensed Clinical Social Worker Sentenced to Prison for Health Care Fraud" [press release], 2015, https://www.justice.gov/usao-mdla/pr/licensed-clinical-social-worker-sentenced-prison-health-care-fraud-0.

5  US Department of Labor, "Florida Substance Abuse Recovery Center Owner Receives Prison Sentence, Ordered to Make $5,122,886 in Restitution for Healthcare Fraud" [news release], June 28, 2018, https://www.dol.gov/newsroom/releases/ebsa/ebsa20180628.

6  State of Ohio Counselor and Social Worker Board, "In the Matter of Charlea M. Harbert," 1996, http://cswmft.ohio.gov/DiscLic/S0001133.pdf.

7  New Jersey State Board of Social Work Examiners, "In the Matter of Paul Steffens," 2004, http://www.state.nj.us/lps/ca/action/20040123_44SW00652000.pdf.

8  Board of Social Work of the State of Iowa, "In the Matter of Natalie Montross," 2012, http://www.idph.state.ia.us/IDPHChannelsService/file.ashx?file=FC7595BF-3B2B-4DA0-A9C4-C09006AF88E7.

9  Alabama State Board of Social Work Examiners, "In the Matter of Sharon J. Jones," 2009, http://www.socialwork.alabama.gov/pdfs/S.%20Jones%20Discip.%20doc.pdf.

10  Maryland Board of Social Work Examiners, "In the Matter of Lachandra Colbert," 2013, http://dhmh.maryland.gov/bswe/Docs/Orders/colbert-1775.pdf.

11  D. Lewak, "How a Celebrity Shrink Allegedly Conned Himself into Patients' Wills," *New York Post*, June 8, 2019, https://nypost.com/2019/06/08/how-a-celebrity-shrink-allegedly-conned-himself-into-patients-wills/.

12  National Association of Social Workers, " 'Signing Off' Fraud Charge Warns Kentucky Clinicians," *NASW News*, June 1987, 1.

13  Suslovich v. New York State Education Department, 571 N.Y.S.2d 123 (N.Y. App. Div. 1991).

14  Massachusetts Office of Attorney General, "Private Equity Firm and Former Mental Health Center Executives Pay $25 Million Over Alleged False Claims Submitted for Unlicensed and Unsupervised Patient Care" [press release], 2021, https://www.mass.gov/news/private-equity-firm-and-former-mental -health-center-executives-pay-25-million-over-alleged-false-claims-submitted -for-unlicensed-and-unsupervised-patient-care.

15  S. Kirk, ed., *Mental Disorders in the Social Environment: Critical Perspectives* (New York: Columbia University Press, 2005).

16  S. Kirk and H. Kutchins, "Deliberate Misdiagnosis in Mental Health Practice," *Social Service Review* 62 (1988): 226.

17  Kirk and Kutchins, "Deliberate Misdiagnosis in Mental Health Practice," 231.

18  Kirk and Kutchins, "Deliberate Misdiagnosis in Mental Health Practice," 232.

19  B. Ballou, "Licensing of Hospital Officials Under Review: Resume at Issue, Official Resigns," *Boston Globe*, June 8, 2007, http://www.boston.com/news /local/massachusetts/articles/2007/06/08/licensing_of_hospital_officials _under review/?page=full.

20  "Issuer of Degrees Pleads to Fraud," *NASW News*, February 1997, 9.

21  "Attorney Suffers Psychotic Breakdown from Lifespring Training," *Mental Health Law News* 6, no. 7 (1991): 1.

22  "Psychologist's License Properly Revoked for Deception in Application," *Mental Health Law News* 6, no. 5 (1991): 6.

23  M. Hinkelman, "Two Social-Service Administrators Get Long Jail Terms in Danieal's Death," *Philadelphia Inquirer*, June 11, 2010, http://articles.philly .com/2010–06–11/news/24966642_1_danieal-kelly-social-services-long-jail -terms.

24  US Department of Justice, "Renee Tartaglione Sentenced to 82 Months in Federal Prison for Fraud Scheme That Looted Millions of Dollars from Nonprofit Clinic" [press release], 2018, https://www.justice.gov/usao-edpa/pr/renee -tartaglione-sentenced-82-months-federal-prison-fraud-scheme-looted-millions.

## 8. INTERRUPTION AND TERMINATION OF SERVICE

1  F. Reamer, *Ethics and Risk Management Issues in Online and Distance Behavioral Health* (San Diego: Cognella, 2021).

2  B. Schutz, *Legal Liability in Psychotherapy* (San Francisco: Jossey-Bass, 1982), 50.

3  "Patient Escapes and Commits Murder," *Mental Health Law News* 5, no. 10 (1980): 6.

4  "Hospital Liable for Failing to Detain Mentally Ill Emergency Room Patient," *Mental Health Law News* 5, no. 1 (1990): 4.

5  "Psychiatric Patient Injured Trying to Flee Hospital," *Mental Health Law News* 5, no. 4 (1990): 5.

6  K. Austin, M. Moline, and G. Williams, *Confronting Malpractice: Legal and Ethical Dilemmas in Psychotherapy* (Newbury Park, CA: Sage, 1990), 215–17.

7  "Government Liable for Premature Release of Psychiatric Patient," *Mental Health Law News* 7, no. 3 (1992): 4.

8  "Man Murdered by Son Following Son's Dismissal from Hospital After Evaluation," *Mental Health Law News* 7, no. 3 (1992): 6.

9  "Man Claims Improper Discharge Following Suicide Attempt," *Mental Health Law News* 5, no. 11 (1990): 6.

10 "Patient Released from Mental Hospital Ingests Lye," *Mental Health Law News* 4, no. 11 (1989): 3.

11 "Mental Health Facility Not Liable for Release of Patient," *Mental Health Law News* 5, no. 4 (1990): 2.

12 "Woman Claims She Was Improperly Discharged from Psychiatric Ward Due to Inadequate Insurance," *Mental Health Law News* 4, no. 11 (1989): 2.

13 "Teenager Commits Suicide by Taking Drug Overdose After Hospital Discharge," *Mental Health Law News* 7, no. 4 (1992): 1.

14 "Man Discharged from Psychiatric Facility Commits Suicide: $3 Million Settlement," *Mental Health Law News* 9, no. 8 (1994): 4.

15 R. Cohen, *Malpractice: A Guide for Mental Health Professionals* (New York: Free Press, 1979), 273.

16 "Parents Allege Failure to Document Treatment Withdrawal from Case Contributed to Son's Suicide," *Mental Health Law News* 5, no. 11 (1990): 4.

17 R. Madden, *Legal Issues in Social Work, Counseling, and Mental Health* (Thousand Oaks, CA: Sage, 1998), 141–42.

9. RESPONDING TO LAWSUITS AND BOARD COMPLAINTS

1  D. Besharov, *The Vulnerable Social Worker: Liability for Serving Children and Families* (Silver Spring, MD: National Association of Social Workers, 1985), 199–200.

2  This list of tips draws on R. Cohen, *Malpractice: A Guide for Mental Health Professionals* (New York: Free Press, 1979), 277–78.

3  A. Saltzman and K. Proch, *Law in Social Work Practice* (Chicago: Nelson-Hall, 1990), 61.

4  Cohen, *Malpractice*, 280–281.

5  The *Daubert* standard was established in Daubert v. Merrell Dow Pharmaceuticals (509 U.S. 579 [1993]), in which two minor children and their parents alleged that the children's serious birth defects had been caused by the mothers' prenatal ingestion of Bendectin, a prescription drug marketed by a pharmaceutical company. The district court granted the company summary judgment on the basis of a well-credentialed expert's affidavit concluding, upon reviewing the extensive published scientific literature on the subject, that maternal use of Bendectin has not been shown to be a risk factor for human birth defects. Although the plaintiffs had responded with the testimony of eight other well-credentialed experts, who based their conclusion that Bendectin can cause birth defects on animal studies, chemical structure analyses, and the unpublished reanalysis of previously published human statistical studies, the court determined that these experts were basing their testimony on evidence that did not meet the applicable "general acceptance" standard and so could not be considered by the court. The district court's decision later was upheld by the U.S. Supreme Court.

6  Besharov, *The Vulnerable Social Worker*, 168.

7  F. Reamer, "The Ethics of Whistle Blowing," *Journal of Mental Health Ethics* 10 (2019): 1–19.

8  F. Reamer, *The Social Work Ethics Audit: A Risk Management Tool* (Washington, DC: NASW Press, 2001).

9  P. Kurzman, "Professional Liability and Malpractice," in *Encyclopedia of Social Work*, 19th ed. (Washington, DC: NASW Press, 1995), 1921–27.

## APPENDIX

1  The federal privacy practices notice can be found here, among other places: https://www.hhs.gov/hipaa/for-professionals/privacy/guidance/privacy-practices-for-protected-health-information/index.html

2  Social media policy guidelines have been adapted from K. Kolmes, "My Private Practice Social Media Policy," 2010, https://www.drkkolmes.com/docs/socmed.pdf.

3  This form has been adapted from Center for Ethical Practice, "Adolescent Informed Consent Form," https://centerforethicalpractice.org/ethical-legal-resources/practice-resources/sample-handouts/adolescent-consent-form/ (accessed April 25, 2022).

## REFERENCES

Abraham, K. *The Forms and Functions of Tort Law*. 5th ed. St. Paul, MN: Foundation Press, 2017.

Aisner, A. "Ex-Therapist Faces Prison for Assaulting Patients." *Ann Arbor News*, January 29, 2008. https://www.mlive.com/annarbornews/2008/01/extherapist_faces_prison_for_a.html.

Alabama State Board of Social Work Examiners. "In re Sally Baker." 1999. http://www.socialwork.alabama.gov/pdfs/Baker%20disciplinary%20action.pdf.

Alabama State Board of Social Work Examiners. "In the Matter of Michael Beddingfield." 2006. http://www.socialwork.alabama.gov/pdfs/Beddingfield.pdf.

Alabama State Board of Social Work Examiners. "In the Matter of Sharon J. Jones." 2009. http://www.socialwork.alabama.gov/pdfs/S.%20Jones%20Discip.%20doc.pdf.

Alabama State Board of Social Work Examiners. "In the Matter of Shirley Carter." 2003. http://www.socialwork.alabama.gov/pdfs/Carter%20Decision.pdf.

Alden, J. "Health Care Group Hit with California Privacy Law Breach Suit." Bloomberg Law, March 11, 2020. https://news.bloomberglaw.com/tech-and-telecom-law/health-care-group-hit-with-california-privacy-law-breach-suit?context=search&index=7.

Alexander, R., Jr. "Social Workers and Privileged Communication in the Federal Legal System." *Social Work* 42 (1997): 387–91.

"Alleged Sexual Misconduct by Psychotherapist Causes Stress Disorder," *Mental Health Law News* 9, no. 8 (1994): 6.

American Counseling Association, *Code of Ethics*. Alexandria, VA: American Counseling Association, 2014.

American Psychological Association, *Code of Ethics*. Washington, DC: American Psychological Association, 2017.

Arkansas Social Work Licensing Board. "Disciplinary Action." 2013. http://www.arkansas.gov/swlb/pdfs/Disciplinary_Action_Descending_Order.pdf.

"Attorney Suffers Psychotic Breakdown from Lifespring Training." *Mental Health Law News* 6, no. 7 (1991): 1.

Austin, K., M. Moline, and G. Williams. *Confronting Malpractice: Legal and Ethical Dilemmas in Psychotherapy*. Newbury Park, CA: Sage, 1990.

Ballou, B. "Licensing of Hospital Officials Under Review: Resume at Issue, Official Resigns." *Boston Globe*, June 8, 2007. http://www.boston.com/news/local /massachusetts/articles/2007/06/08/licensing_of_hospital_officials_under _review/?page=full.

Barker, R., and D. Branson. *Forensic Social Work: Legal Aspects of Professional Practice*. New York: Taylor & Francis, 2000.

Barr, D. "Clinical Social Worker Disciplined by State, Sued Over Patient Relations." *Daily News-Record* (Harrisonburg, VA), November 14, 1997, 19.

Barsky, A., and J. Gould. *Clinicians in Court: A Guide to Subpoenas, Depositions, Testifying and Everything Else You Need to Know*. New York: Guilford, 2002.

Beckett, C. *Supervision: A Guide for the Helping Professions*. Thousand Oaks, CA: Sage, 2021.

Berg, J., P. Appelbaum, C. Lidz, and L. Parker. *Informed Consent: Legal Theory and Clinical Practice*. 2nd ed. New York: Oxford University Press, 2001.

Bergstresser, C. "The Perspective of the Plaintiff's Attorney." In *The Mental Health Practitioner and the Law: A Comprehensive Handbook*, ed. L. Lifson and R. Simon, 329–43. Cambridge, MA: Harvard University Press, 1998.

Berner, M. "Write Smarter, Not Longer." In *The Mental Health Practitioner and the Law: A Comprehensive Handbook*, ed. L. Lifson and R. Simon, 54–71. Cambridge, MA: Harvard University Press, 1998.

Besharov, D. *The Vulnerable Social Worker: Liability for Serving Children and Families*. Silver Spring, MD: National Association of Social Workers, 1985.

Bissell, L., and P. Haberman. *Alcoholism in the Professions*. New York: Oxford University Press, 1984.

Board of Social Work of the State of Iowa. "In the Matter of Natalie Montross." 2012. http://www.idph.state.ia.us/IDPHChannelsService/file.ashx?file=FC7595BF -3B2B-4DA0-A9C4-C09006AF88E7.

Bradley, L., B. Hendricks, and D. Kabell. "The Professional Will: An Ethical Responsibility." *Family Journal* 20 (2012): 309–14.

Brodsky, A. "The Distressed Psychologist: Sexual Intimacies and Exploitation." In *Professionals in Distress: Issues, Syndromes, and Solutions in Psychology*, ed. R. Kilburg, P. Nathan, and R. Thoreson, 153–71. Washington, DC: American Psychological Association, 1986.

Candilis P., D. Kim, and L. Sulmasy, "Physician Impairment and Rehabilitation: Reintegration into Medical Practice While Ensuring Patient Safety: A Position Paper from the American College of Physicians." *Annals of Internal Medicine* 170 (2019): 871–79.

Carroll, M. *Effective Supervision for the Helping Professions*. 2nd ed. Thousand Oaks, CA: Sage, 2014.

Carroll, R., ed. *Risk Management Handbook for Healthcare Organizations*. Hoboken, NJ: Wiley, 2011.

Celenza, A. *Sexual Boundary Violations: Therapeutic, Supervisory, and Academic Contexts*. Lanham, MD: Aronson, 2007.

Center for Ethical Practice. "Adolescent Informed Consent Form." Accessed April 25, 2022. https://centerforethicalpractice.org/ethical-legal-resources /practice-resources/sample-handouts/adolescent-consent-form/.

Chaffin, C. "More than 645,000 Oregonians Impacted by DHS Data Breach." *The Oregonian*, June 25, 2019. https://www.oregonlive.com/data/2019/06/more -than-645000-oregonians-impacted-by-dhs-data-breach.html.

"Chemical Dependency Counselor Who Disclosed Client's Threats Immune from Liability." *Mental Health Law News* 8, no. 10 (1993): 2.

Chenneville, T. "HIV, Confidentiality, and Duty to Protect: A Decision-Making Model." *Professional Psychology: Research and Practice* 31 (2000): 661–70.

"Claim for Injuries from Escaped Patient Dismissed: Claimant Not Readily Identifiable Victim." *Mental Health Law News* 9, no. 1 (1994): 3.

Cohen, R. *Malpractice: A Guide for Mental Health Professionals*. New York: Free Press, 1979.

Cohen, R., and B. DeBetz. "Responsive Supervision of the Psychiatric Resident and Clinical Psychology Intern." *American Journal of Psychoanalysis* 37 (1977): 51–64.

Cohen, R., and W. Mariano. *Legal Guidebook in Mental Health*. New York: Free Press, 1982.

Cooke, B., E. Worsham, and G. Reisfield. "The Elusive Standard of Care." *Journal of the American Academy of Psychiatry and the Law* 45 (2017): 358–64.

Coombs, R. *Drug-Impaired Professionals*. Cambridge, MA: Harvard University Press, 2000.

Corcoran, K., and V. Vandiver. *Maneuvering the Maze of Managed Care*. New York: Free Press, 1996.

Corey, G., R. Haynes, P. Moulton, and M. Muratori. *Clinical Supervision in the Helping Professions: A Practical Guide*. 3rd ed. Alexandria, VA: American Counseling Association, 2021.

"Counseling Center Did Not Violate Patient's Confidentiality When It Disclosed Her Death Threats." *Mental Health Law News* 12, no. 5 (1997): 1.

"Counselor Begins Sexual Relationship with Client." *Mental Health Law News* 6, no. 44 (1991): 1.

"Counselor Had No Duty to Warn Ex-wife of Patient Who Later Shot Her." *Mental Health Law News* 12, no. 11 (1997): 1.

"Counselor Who Suspected Child Abuse Not Liable for Interfering with Family Rights." *Mental Health Law News* 5, no. 5 (1990): 4.

"Court Affirms Suspension of Psychologist's License for Sexual Misconduct." *Mental Health Law News* 12, no. 12 (1997): 3.

Crombie, D. "Social Worker Sentenced in Assaults." *Providence Journal-Bulletin* (Providence, RI), April 20, 1989, B3.

"Defendant's Admission to Child Molestation Not Protected by Therapist-Client Privilege." *Mental Health Law News* 14, no. 2 (1999): 2.

"Defendant's Admission to Therapist Not Protected: Expressed Threat of Future Criminal Conduct." *Mental Health Law News* 14, no. 9 (1999): 4.

DePanfilis, D., and M. Salus. *Child Protective Services: A Guide for Caseworkers.* Washington, DC: US Department of Health and Human Services, 2003.

Deutsch, C. "A Survey of Therapists' Personal Problems and Treatment." *Professional Psychology: Research and Practice* 16 (1985): 305–15.

"Doctor Who Conducted Training Had Duty to Warn or Prevent Resident from Abusing Patient." *Mental Health Law News* 14, no. 4 (1999): 4.

"Drug Treatment Counselor Has Affair with Patient's Mother." *Mental Health Law News* 7, no. 1 (1992): 3.

DuPont, R., A. McLellan, G. Carr, M. Gendel, and G. Skipper. "How Are Addicted Physicians Treated? A National Survey of Physician Health Programs." *Journal of Substance Abuse Treatment* 37 (2009): 1–7.

"Employer May Be Held Liable for Psychotherapist's Sexual Misconduct." *Mental Health Law News* 5, no. 11 (1990): 1.

"Employer Not Vicariously Liable for Therapist's Sexual Misconduct." *Mental Health Law News* 4, no. 10 (1989): 1.

Epstein, R. *Keeping Boundaries: Maintaining Safety and Integrity in the Psychotherapeutic Process.* Washington, DC: American Psychiatric Press, 1994.

"Ex-Prison Psychologist Gets 3 Years Behind Bars." *Arkansas Democrat Gazette,* September 1, 2007. https://www.arkansasonline.com/news/2007/sep/01/ex -prison-psychologist-gets-3-years-behind-bars/.

"Failure to Refer to Psychiatrist and to Hospital Alleged in Suicide." *Mental Health Law News* 10, no. 5 (1995): 6.

Falender, C., and E. Shafranske. *Clinical Supervision: A Competency-Based Approach.* 2nd ed. Washington, DC: American Psychological Association, 2021.

Farber, B. A., ed. *Stress and Burnout in the Human Service Professions.* New York: Pergamon, 1983.

Federal Trade Commission. "Electronic Health Records Company Settles FTC Charges It Deceived Consumers about Privacy of Doctor Reviews" [press release]. June 8, 2016. https://www.ftc.gov/news-events/press-releases/2016/06/electronic-health-records-company-settles-ftc-charges-it-deceived.

"Female Therapist Engages in Same-Sex Relationship with Patient." *Mental Health Law News* 15, no. 6 (2000): 3.

Fisher, M. *The Ethics of Conditional Confidentiality: A Practice Model for Mental Health Professionals.* New York: Oxford University Press, 2013.

"$570,841 Judgment Returned; Man Committed Suicide After Leaving Psychiatric Facility." *Mental Health Law News* 6, no. 2 (1991): 3.

Florida Board of Clinical Social Work, Marriage and Family Therapy and Mental Health Counseling. "Department of Health vs. Deborah A. Hulbert." 2001. http:// ww2.doh.state.fl.us/FinalOrderNet/folistbrowse.aspx?LicId=4410&ProCde=5201&discpln=DISCPLN.

"Former Social Worker Sentenced for Sex Crimes with Minors in Mississippi." Yahoo News, January 6, 2022. https://www.yahoo.com/news/former-social-worker-sentenced-sex-132843339.html.

Francis, D., and J. Chin. "The Prevention of Acquired Immunodeficiency Syndrome in the United States." *Journal of the American Medical Association* 257 (1987): 1357–66.

Fredman, G., A. Papadopoulou, and E. Worwood, eds. *Collaborative Consultation in Mental Health: Guidelines for the New Consultant.* London: Routledge, 2018.

Freudenberger, H. "Chemical Abuse Among Psychologists: Symptoms, Causes, and Treatment Issues." In *Professionals in Distress: Issues, Syndromes, and Solutions in Psychology,* ed. R. Kilburg, P. Nathan, and R. Thoreson, 135–52. Washington, DC: American Psychological Association, 1986.

Gartrell, N., J. Herman, S. Olarte, M. Feldstein, and R. Localio. "Psychiatrist-Patient Sexual Contact: Results of a National Survey." *American Journal of Psychiatry* 143 (1986): 1126–31.

Gifis, S. *Law Dictionary.* 6th ed. Hauppauge, NY: Barron's, 2010.

Goby, M., N. Bradley, and D. Bespalec. "Physicians Treated for Alcoholism: A Follow-up Study." *Alcoholism: Clinical and Experimental Research* 3 (1979): 121–24.

Gottlieb, M. "Avoiding Exploitive Dual Relationships: A Decision-Making Model." In *Ethical Conflicts in Psychology*, ed. D. Bersoff, 242–43. Washington, DC: American Psychological Association, 1995.

Gould, D. "Listen to Your Lawyer." In *The Mental Health Practitioner and the Law: A Comprehensive Handbook*, ed. L. Lifson and R. Simon, 344–56. Cambridge, MA: Harvard University Press, 1998.

"Government Liable for Premature Release of Psychiatric Patient." *Mental Health Law News* 7, no. 3 (1992): 4.

Gray, L., and A. Harding. "Confidentiality Limits with Clients Who Have the AIDS Virus." *Journal of Counseling and Development* 66 (1988): 219–23.

Gross, A. "Misconfigured Webpage Exposed Patient Data." HIPAA Secure Now, April 30, 2019. https://www.hipaasecurenow.com/misconfigured-webpage-exposed -patient-data/.

Grossman, M. "Confidentiality: The Right to Privacy Versus the Right to Know." In *Law and the Mental Health Professions*, ed. W. Barton and C. Sanborn, 137–84. New York: International Universities Press, 1978.

Gutheil, T., and G. Gabbard. "The Concept of Boundaries in Clinical Practice: Theoretical and Risk-Management Dimensions." *American Journal of Psychiatry* 150 (1993): 188–96.

Guy, J., P. Poelstra, and M. Stark. "Personal Distress and Therapeutic Effectiveness: National Survey of Psychologists Practicing Psychotherapy." *Professional Psychology: Research and Practice* 20 (1989): 48–50.

Hartsell, T., and B. Bernstein, *The Portable Lawyer for Mental Health Professionals: An A-Z Guide to Protecting Your Clients, Your Practice, and Yourself.* 3rd ed. Hoboken, NJ: Wiley, 2013.

Herrington, R., D. Benzer, G. Jacobson, and M. Hawkins. "Treating Substance-Use Disorders Among Physicians." *Journal of the American Medical Association* 247 (1982): 2253–57.

Hester, D., and T. Schonfeld, eds. *Guidance for Healthcare Ethics Committees.* New York: Cambridge University Press, 2012.

Hinkelman, M. "Two Social-Service Administrators Get Long Jail Terms in Danieal's Death." *Philadelphia Inquirer*, June 11, 2010. http://articles.philly .com/2010-06-11/news/24966642_1_danieal-kelly-social-services-long-jail -terms.

Hogan, D. *The Regulation of Psychotherapists: Volume I—A Study in the Philosophy and Practice of Professional Regulation*. Cambridge, MA: Ballinger, 1979.

"Hospital Had Duty to Protect Mother of Patient with Psychiatric Impairments." *Mental Health Law News* 16, no. 9 (2001): 1.

"Hospital Has No Duty to Protect Unforeseeable Third Party Whom Patient Assaulted." *Mental Health Law News* 8, no. 5 (1993): 1.

"Hospital Liable for Employee's Sexual Assault on Psychiatric Patient." *Mental Health Law News* 7, no. 10 (1992): 6.

"Hospital Liable for Failing to Detain Mentally Ill Emergency Room Patient." *Mental Health Law News* 5, no. 1 (1990): 4.

"Hospital Liable for Failure to Admit Suicidal Patient Who Killed Himself." *Mental Health Law News* 6, no. 8 (1991): 4.

"Hospital Liable for Failure to Prevent Suicide of Psychiatric Patient." *Mental Health Law News* 5, no. 2 (1990): 2.

"Hospital Liable for Suicide of Psychiatric Patient." *Mental Health Law News* 5, no. 5 (1990): 2.

"Hospital Not Negligent in Supervising Patient Who Attacked Another Patient." *Mental Health Law News* 7, no. 1 (1992): 3.

"Inadequate Psychiatric Treatment Blamed for Woman Killing Son." *Mental Health Law News* 9, no. 10 (1994): 2.

Iowa Board of Social Work. "In the Matter of Brian C. Nedoba." 2013. http://www.idph.state.ia.us/IDPHChannelsService/file.ashx?file=B5221FE3-D8F1-4A02-B595-8C8878F8173A.

"Issuer of Degrees Pleads to Fraud." *NASW News*, February 1997, 9.

Janofsky, M. "Therapists Are Sentenced in Girls' 'Rebirthing' Death," *New York Times*, June 19, 2001, https://www.nytimes.com/2001/06/19/us/therapists-are-sentenced-in-girl-s-rebirthing-death.html.

"Juvenile's Communications to Psychologist and Social Worker Not Privileged." *Mental Health Law News* 16, no. 8 (2001): 5.

Kadushin, A. *Consultation in Social Work*. New York: Columbia University Press, 1977.

Kadushin, A., and D. Harkness. *Supervision in Social Work*. 5th ed. New York: Columbia University Press, 2014.

Kagle, J. "Recording in Direct Practice." In *Encyclopedia of Social Work*. 18th ed. 463–67. Silver Spring, MD: National Association of Social Workers, 1987.

Kagle, J., and S. Kopels. *Social Work Records*. 2nd ed. Long Grove, IL: Waveland Press, 2008.

Kain, C. "To Breach or Not to Breach: Is That the Question?" *Journal of Counseling and Development* 66 (1988): 224–25.

Kilburg, R., F. Kaslow, and G. VandenBos. "Professionals in Distress." *Hospital and Community Psychiatry* 39 (1988): 723–25.

Kirk, S., ed. *Mental Disorders in the Social Environment: Critical Perspectives.* New York: Columbia University Press, 2005.

Kirk, S., and H. Kutchins. "Deliberate Misdiagnosis in Mental Health Practice." *Social Service Review* 62 (1988): 225–37.

Kliner, D., J. Spicer, and P. Barnett. "Treatment Outcome of Alcoholic Physicians." *Journal of Studies on Alcohol* 41 (1980): 1217–20.

Knutsen, E., "On the Emotional Well-Being of Psychiatrists: Overview and Rationale." *American Journal of Psychoanalysis* 37 (1977): 123–29.

Kolmes, K. "My Private Practice Social Media Policy." 2010. http://www.drkkolmes.com/docs/socmed.pdf.

Kolmes, K. "Social Media in the Future of Professional Psychology." *Professional Psychology: Research & Practice* 43 (2012): 606–12.

Kurzman, P. "Professional Liability and Malpractice." In *Encyclopedia of Social Work.* 19th ed., 1921–27. Washington, DC: NASW Press, 1995.

"Lack of Physician-Patient Relationship Did Not Provide Psychiatrist with Defense." *Mental Health Law News* 3, no. 4 (1998): 1.

Laliotis, D., and J. Grayson. "Psychologist Heal Thyself: What Is Available for the Impaired Psychologist?" *American Psychologist* 40 (1985): 84–96.

Lamb, D., N. Presser, K. Pfost, M. Baum, V. Jackson, and P. Jarvis. "Confronting Professional Impairment During the Internship: Identification, Due Process, and Remediation." *Professional Psychology: Research and Practice* 18 (1987): 597–603.

Lambert, T., "Tom on Torts." *Law Reporter* 39 (1996): 228–31.

Lewak, D. "How a Celebrity Shrink Allegedly Conned Himself into Patients' Wills." *New York Post*, June 8, 2019. https://nypost.com/2019/06/08/how-a-celebrity-shrink-allegedly-conned-himself-into-patients-wills/.

Lewis, M. "Duty to Warn Versus Duty to Maintain Confidentiality: Conflicting Demands on Mental Health Professionals." *Suffolk Law Review* 20 (1986): 579–615.

Louisiana State Board of Social Work Examiners. "In the Matter of Donald Henry." 2013. http://www.labswe.org/lms/Files/625.pdf.

Louisiana State Board of Social Work Examiners. "In the Matter of Jennifer Gordon." 2013. http://www.labswe.org/lms/ Files/580.pdf.

Louisiana State Board of Social Work Examiners. "In the Matter of Kristin Richards." 2013. http://www.labswe.org/lms/ Files/606.pdf.

Luepker, E. *Record Keeping in Psychotherapy and Counseling*. 2nd ed. New York: Routledge, 2022.

Madden, R. *Essential Law for Social Workers*. New York: Columbia University Press, 2003.

Madden, R. *Legal Issues in Social Work, Counseling, and Mental Health*. Thousand Oaks, CA: Sage, 1998.

Maheu, M., K. Drude, K. Hertlei, R. Lipschutz, K. Wall, and D. Hilty. "An Interprofessional Framework for Telebehavioral Health Competencies." *Journal of Technology in Behavioral Science* 3 (2018): 108–40.

"Malpractice: How to Sidestep the Pitfalls." *NASW News*, February 1997, 5.

"Man Claims Improper Discharge Following Suicide Attempt." *Mental Health Law News* 5, no. 11 (1990): 6.

"Man Claims Inadequate Observation in Psychiatric Ward; Falls from Window." *Mental Health Law News* 9, no. 11 (1994): 3.

"Man Discharged from Psychiatric Facility Commits Suicide: $3 Million Settlement." *Mental Health Law News* 9, no. 8 (1994): 4.

"Man in Joint Counseling Session Did Not Waive Patient-Psychotherapist Privilege." *Mental Health Law News* 10, no. 4 (1995): 3.

"Man Kills Woman, Then Commits Suicide: $1 Million Settlement on Claim of Failure to Diagnose." *Mental Health Law News* 9, no. 5 (1994): 3.

"Man Murdered by Son Following Son's Dismissal from Hospital After Evaluation." *Mental Health Law News* 7, no. 3 (1992): 6.

Marchant, R. "Police: Greenwich Child Psychologist Charged with Failing to Report Alleged Abuse or Neglect to Authorities." *Greenwich Time*, December 28, 2021. https://www.greenwichtime.com/news/article/Police-Greenwich-child -psychologist-charged-with-16733352.php.

"Marriage Therapist Has Affair with Patient." *Mental Health Law News* 5, no. 4 (1990): 3.

Martelle, S. "Broken Trust." *Hour Detroit*, August 2009. http://www.hourdetroit . com/Hour-Detroit/August-2009/Broken-Trust/.

Maryland Board of Social Work Examiners. "In the Matter of Ava Barron-Shasho." 2012. http://dhmh.maryland.gov/bswe/Docs/Orders/Shasho-1735.pdf.

Maryland Board of Social Work Examiners. "In the Matter of Lachandra Colbert." 2013. http://dhmh.maryland.gov/bswe/Docs/Orders/colbert-1775 .pdf.

Maschi, T., and G. Leibowitz, eds. *Forensic Social Work: Psychosocial and Legal Issues Across Diverse Populations and Settings*. 2nd ed. New York: Springer, 2018.

Massachusetts Office of Attorney General. "Private Equity Firm and Former Mental Health Center Executives Pay $25 Million Over Alleged False Claims Submitted for Unlicensed and Unsupervised Patient Care" [press release]. 2021. https://www.mass.gov/news/private-equity-firm-and-former-mental-health-center-executives-pay-25-million-over-alleged-false-claims-submitted-for-unlicensed-and-unsupervised-patient-care.

McArdle, E. "New Cause of Action May Stem from California Verdict: Father Wins $500,000 for Daughter's 'False Memory' of Abuse." *Lawyers Weekly USA*, June 6, 1994, B3.

McCrady, B. "The Distressed or Impaired Professional: From Retribution to Rehabilitation." *Journal of Drug Issues* 19 (1989): 337–49.

"Medicaid Fraud, Sexual Assault Results in Prison Term for Ex-Cheyenne Counselor." *Star Tribune*, November 28, 2021. https://trib.com/news/state-and-regional/crime-and-courts/medicaid-fraud-sexual-assault-results-in-prison-term-for-ex-cheyenne-counselor/article_6d24819c-1678-5eba-89fc-f243dcaf3c21.html.

"Member Blows Whistle on Rx Refills." *NASW News*, June 1990, 11.

Mental Health and Developmental Disabilities Confidentiality Act. https://www.ilga.gov/legislation/ilcs/ilcs3.asp?ActID=2043&ChapterID=57.

"Mental Health Center's Failure to Conduct Tests for Brain Tumor Make It Liable for Patient's Death." *Mental Health Law News* 7, no. 5 (1992): 2.

"Mental Health Facility Not Liable for Release of Patient." *Mental Health Law News* 5, no. 4 (1990): 2.

"Mental Patient Escapes and Is Struck by Car." *Mental Health Law News* 5, no. 11 (1990): 3.

Meyer, R., E. Landis, and J. Hays. *Law for the Psychotherapist*. New York: Norton, 1988.

Michaud, H. *Tort Law: Concepts and Applications*. 2nd ed. Boston: Pearson, 2014.

Moffett, P., and G. Moore. "The Standard of Care: Legal History and Definitions: The Bad and Good News." *Western Journal of Emergency Medicine* 12 (2011): 109–12.

Morse, R., M. Martin, W. Swenson, and R. Niven. "Prognosis of Physicians Treated for Alcoholism and Drug Dependence." *Journal of the American Medical Association* 251 (1984): 743–46.

National Association of Social Workers. *Code of Ethics*. Rev. ed. Washington, DC: National Association of Social Workers, 2021.

National Association of Social Workers. Commission on Employment and Economic Support. *Impaired Social Worker Program Resource Book*. Silver Spring, MD: National Association of Social Workers, 1987.

National Association of Social Workers. "'Signing Off' Fraud Charge Warns Kentucky Clinicians." *NASW News*, June 1987, 1.

National Association of Social Workers and Association of Social Work Boards. *Best Practice Standards in Social Work Supervision*. Washington, DC: National Association of Social Workers, 2013.

National Association of Social Workers, Association of Social Work Boards, Council on Social Work Education, and Clinical Social Work Association. *Standards for Technology in Social Work Practice*. Washington, DC: National Association of Social Workers, 2017.

"Negligent Care of Mental Patient Alleged in Suicide Death; $317,500 Verdict." *Mental Health Law News* 16, no. 2 (2001): 2.

New Jersey State Board of Social Work Examiners. "In the Matter of Daniel Cruz." 2000. http://www.state.nj.us/lps/ca/action/20000216_44SW01452900.pdf.

New Jersey State Board of Social Work Examiners. "In the Matter of Paul Steffens." 2004. http://www.state.nj.us/lps/ca/ action/20040123_44SW00652000.pdf.

"New Mexico Therapist Who Raped Clients Sentenced to 12 Years." KRQE.com, July 29, 2020. https://www.krqe.com/news/crime/new-mexico-therapist-who-raped-clients-sentenced-to-12-years/.

"No Duty to Warn Without Direct Threat of Specific Act Against Identifiable Victim." *Mental Health Law News* 14, no. 3 (1999): 6.

"No Violation of Confidentiality in Communicating Patient's Arson Confession." *Mental Health Law News* 5, no. 4 (1990): 4.

"Nursing Home Liable in Attempted Suicide." *Mental Health Law News* 5, no. 1 (1990): 1.

"Official of Alcohol Center Entered into Sexual Relationship with Woman One Month After She Left Program." *Mental Health Law News* 5, no. 7 (1990): 5.

Olarte, S. "Sexual Boundary Violations." In *The Hatherleigh Guide to Ethics in Therapy*, 195–209. New York: Hatherleigh, 1997.

Papp, J. "Child Psychologist Sentenced to Prison in Decade-Long Sexual Exploitation Case." *Augusta Chronicle*, March 2, 2022. https://www.augustachronicle.com/story/news/crime/2022/03/02/psychologist-sentenced-prison-decade-long-child-molestation-case/6978729001/.

"Parents Allege Failure to Document Treatment Withdrawal from Case Contributed to Son's Suicide." *Mental Health Law News* 5, no. 12 (1990): 4.

"Patient Admitted to Hospital for Detoxification; Attempted Suicide Results in Brain Damage." *Mental Health Law News* 5, no. 7 (1990): 2.

"Patient Escapes and Commits Murder." *Mental Health Law News* 5, no. 10 (1990): 6.

"Patient Improperly Treated for Panic Disorder and Agoraphobia." *Mental Health Law News* 7, no. 7 (1992): 6.

"Patient Jumps from Hospital Window." *Mental Health Law News* 4, no. 12 (1989): 2.

"Patient Raped by Fellow Patient." *Mental Health Law News* 4, no. 11 (1989): 6.

"Patient Released from Mental Hospital Ingests Lye." *Mental Health Law News* 4, no. 11 (1989): 3.

"Patient Sexually Abused by Psychologist." *Mental Health Law News* 5, no. 12 (1990): 3.

"Patient's Threats Disclosed: Right to Privacy Not Violated." *Mental Health Law News* 8, no. 2 (1993): 6.

Pearson, M. "Psychiatric Treatment of 250 Physicians." *Psychiatric Annals* 12 (1982): 194–206.

Pecora, P., J. Whittaker, R. Barth, S. Borja, and W. Vesneski. *The Child Welfare Challenge: Policy, Practice, and Research*. 4th ed. New York: Routledge, 2019.

Pernick, M. "The Patient's Role in Medical Decision Making: A Social History of Informed Consent in Medical Therapy." In President's Commission, *Making Health Care Decisions*, 1–35.

"Physician Fails to Properly Treat Depression or Make Timely Referral." *Mental Health Law News* 7, no. 10 (1992): 2.

Piel, J., and R. Opara. "Does Volk v. Demeerleer Conflict with the AMA Code of Medical Ethics on Breaching Patient Confidentiality to Protect Third Parties." *AMA Journal of Ethics* (January 2018). https://journalofethics.ama-assn.org /article/does-volk-v-demeerleer-conflict-ama-code-medical-ethics-breaching -patient-confidentiality-protect/2018-01.

Pinals, D., and D. Mossman. *Evaluation for Civil Commitment*. New York: Oxford University Press, 2012.

"Plaintiffs Claim Failure to Continue Hospitalization Led to Murder, Then Suicide: $363,000 Verdict." *Mental Health Law News* 9, no. 4 (1994): 2.

Polowy, C., and C. Gorenberg. *Client Confidentiality and Privileged Communications: Office of General Counsel Law Notes*. Washington, DC: National Association of Social Workers, 1997.

Pope, K. "How Clients Are Harmed by Sexual Contact with Mental Health Professionals: The Syndrome and Its Prevalence." *Journal of Counseling and Development* 67 (1988): 222–26.

Pope, K., B. Tabachnick, and P. Keith-Spiegel. "Ethics of Practice: The Beliefs and Behaviors of Psychologists as Therapists." *American Psychologist* 42 (1987): 993–1006.

President's Commission for the Study of Ethical Problems in Medicine and Biomedical and Behavioral Research. *Making Health Care Decisions: The Ethical and Legal Implications of Informed Consent in the Patient-Practitioner Relationship.* Vol. 3. Washington, DC: US Government Printing Office, 1982.

"Privilege Did Not Protect Defendant's Letter to Therapist Admitting Sexual Abuse of Daughter." *Mental Health Law News* 8, no. 8 (1983): 1.

"Psychiatric Nurse's Disclosure of Confidential Treatment Records Justified License Suspension." *Mental Health Law News* 15, no. 8 (2000): 3.

"Psychiatric Nurse Seduced Woman into Lesbian Relationship; $460,000 Verdict." *Mental Health Law News* 10, no. 9 (1995): 3.

"Psychiatric Patient Has Sexual Relationship with Psychiatrist." *Mental Health Law News* 6, no. 11 (1989): 4.

"Psychiatric Patient Injured Trying to Flee Hospital." *Mental Health Law News* 5, no. 4 (1990): 5.

"Psychiatric Patient Not Properly Monitored While Eating Chokes to Death." *Mental Health Law News* 5, no. 11 (1990): 4.

"Psychiatric Patient Raped by Fellow Patient." *Mental Health Law News* 4, no. 3 (1989): 4.

"Psychiatrist and Psychologist Revealed Patient's Threat: No Invasion of Privacy." *Mental Health Law News* 10, no. 6 (1995): 1.

"Psychiatrist Did Not Owe Duty to Protect Prospective Victims of Former Patient." *Mental Health Law News* 10, no. 10 (1995): 4.

"Psychiatrist Has Sex with Patient." *Mental Health Law News* 4, no. 11 (1989): 6.

"Psychiatrist Not Negligent in Misdiagnosing and Releasing Patient Who Killed Third Party." *Mental Health Law News* 7, no. 10 (1992): 1.

"Psychiatrist's Crime Tip Did Not Violate Physician-Patient Privilege." *Mental Health Law News* 5, no. 3 (1990): 1.

"Psychiatrists Liable for Patient's Attempted Suicide." *Mental Health Law News* 6, no. 3 (1991): 1.

"Psychiatrist's License Suspended Six Months for Having Sexual Relations with Patient." *Mental Health Law News* 8, no. 3 (1993): 4.

"Psychiatrists Not Liable for Discharging Patient Who Later Committed Suicide." *Mental Health Law News* 4, no. 10 (1989): 2.

"Psychiatrist's Testimony About Patient's Threats Not Protected by Psychotherapist-Patient Privilege." *Mental Health Law News* 14, no. 12 (1999): 3.

"Psychiatrist Sued; Recovered Repressed Memories of Patient's Childhood." *Mental Health Law News* 10, no. 4 (1995): 6.

"Psychiatrist Who Discloses Confidential Information About Patient Liable for Damages." *Mental Health Law News* 9, no. 4 (1994): 1.

"Psychiatry Resident Has Improper Sexual Contact with Child." *Mental Health Law News* 14, no. 10 (1999): 3.

"Psychological Counselor Refers Patients to Unqualified 'Colleague.'" *Mental Health Law News* 6, no. 8 (1991): 6.

"Psychologist Breaches Psychologist-Patient Privilege by Providing Testimony." *Mental Health Law News* 15, no. 2 (2000): 4.

"Psychologist Encourages Sexual Misconduct Between Patient and Psychiatrist." *Mental Health Law News* 4, no. 3 (1989): 2.

"Psychologist Immune from Liability for Warning About Threats." *Mental Health Law News* 16, no. 8 (2001): 1.

"Psychologist-Patient Privilege Did Not Protect Statements by Spouse During Counseling." *Mental Health Law News* 10, no. 7 (1994): 2.

"Psychologist's License Properly Revoked for Deception in Application." *Mental Health Law News* 6, no. 5 (1991): 6.

"Psychologists Owed Duty to Protect Child from Sexual Abuse." *Mental Health Law News* 11, no. 4 (1996): 3.

"Psychologist's Unorthodox Treatment for Personality Disorder Results in $325,000 Settlement." *Mental Health Law News* 10, no. 3 (1995): 1.

"Psychotherapist Has No Duty to Warn Third Party of Patient's Threat of Violence." *Mental Health Law News* 7, no. 2 (1992): 3.

"Psychotherapist May Not Be Sued for Erroneous Child Abuse Diagnosis." *Mental Health Law News* 7, no. 11 (1992): 4.

Quinsey, V., G. Harris, M. Rice, and C. Cormier. *Violent Offenders: Appraising and Managing Risk*. Washington, DC: American Psychological Association, 2005.

Reamer, F. *Boundary Issues and Dual Relationships in the Human Services*. 3rd ed. New York: Columbia University Press, 2021.

Reamer, F. *Ethical Standards in Social Work: A Review of the NASW Code of Ethics*. 3rd ed. Washington, DC: NASW Press, 2018.

Reamer, F. *Ethics and Risk Management Issues in Online and Distance Behavioral Health*. San Diego: Cognella, 2021.

Reamer, F. "The Ethics of Whistle Blowing." *Journal of Mental Health Ethics* 10 (2019): 1–19.

Reamer, F. "The Impaired Social Worker." *Social Work* 37 (1992): 165–70.

Reamer, F. *Risk Management in Social Work: Preventing Professional Malpractice, Liability and Disciplinary Action*. New York: Columbia University Press, 2015.

Reamer, F. *The Social Work Ethics Audit: A Risk Management Tool*. Washington, DC: NASW Press, 2001.

Reamer, F. *The Social Work Ethics Casebook: Cases and Commentary*. 2nd ed. Washington, DC: NASW, 2018.

Reamer, F. *Social Work Values and Ethics*. 5th ed. New York: Columbia University Press, 2018.

Reaves, R. "Legal Liability and Psychologists." In *Professionals in Distress: Issues, Syndromes, and Solutions in Psychology*, ed. R. Kilburg, P. Nathan, and R. Thoreson, 173–84. Washington, DC: American Psychological Association, 1986.

"Resident at Hospital for Mentally Retarded Receives Award for Negligent Treatment." *Mental Health Law News* 4, no. 3 (1989): 4.

Robinson, G. "Discussion." *American Journal of Psychiatry* 118 (1962): 780.

Romero, M. "Ex-Social Worker Sentenced to Prison for Sex with Teen Client." *Deseret News*, April 25, 2016. https://www.deseret.com/2016/4/25/20587263/ex-social-worker-sentenced-to-prison-for-sex-with-teen-client.

Rozovsky, F. *Consent to Treatment: A Practical Guide*. Boston: Little, Brown, 1984.

Sadek, J. *A Clinician's Guide to Suicide Risk Assessment and Management*. New York: Springer International, 2019.

Saks, E. *Refusing Care: Forced Treatment and the Rights of the Mentally Ill*. New York: Oxford University Press, 2002.

Saltzman, A., and K. Proch. *Law in Social Work Practice*. Chicago: Nelson-Hall, 1990.

"Schizophrenic Patient Hangs Self." *Mental Health Law News* 6, no. 3 (1991): 6.

Schoener, G. "Assessments of Professionals Who Have Engaged in Boundary Violations." *Psychiatric Annals* 25 (1995): 95–99.

"School and Staff Not Liable for Injuries Sustained When Retarded Resident Was Attacked." *Mental Health Law News* 9, no. 5 (1994): 3.

Schutz, B. *Legal Liability in Psychotherapy*. San Francisco: Jossey-Bass, 1982.

"Sexual Relationship Between Patient and Unlicensed Mental Health Worker Results in Lawsuit." *Mental Health Law News* 10, no. 5 (1995): 3.

Shore, J. "The Impaired Physician: Four Years After Probation." *Journal of the American Medical Association* 248 (1982): 3127–30.

Sidell, N. *Social Work Documentation: A Guide to Strengthening Your Case Recording.* 2nd ed. Washington, DC: NASW Press, 2015.

Simon, R. "Therapist-Patient Sex: From Boundary Violations to Sexual Misconduct." *Forensic Psychiatry* 22 (1999): 31–47.

"Social Worker Engages in Sexual Relationship with Patient." *Mental Health Law News* 4, no. 5 (1999): 2.

Sonnenstuhl, W. "Reaching the Impaired Professional: Applying Findings from Organizational and Occupational Research." *Journal of Drug Issues* 19 (1989): 533–39.

Stadler, H., K. Willing, M. Eberhage, and W. Ward. "Impairment: Implications for the Counseling Profession." *Journal of Counseling and Development* 66 (1988): 258–60.

"State Disciplines Psychiatrist for Making Improper Referral." *Providence Journal-Bulletin* (Providence, RI), December 1, 1992, B3.

State of Ohio Counselor and Social Worker Board. "Consent Agreement Between Robert J. Carson and the State of Ohio Counselor, Social Worker, and Marriage and Family Therapist Board." 2009. http:// cswmft.ohio.gov/DiscLic /I0009744.pdf.

State of Ohio Counselor and Social Worker Board. "In the Matter of Charlea M. Harbert." 1996. http://cswmft.ohio.gov/DiscLic/S0001133.pdf.

"Statements Made to Alcoholics Anonymous Volunteers Not Protected by Privilege." *Mental Health Law News* 12, no. 3 (1997): 1.

Stein, P. "Prison for Psychologist Who Had Sex with Patients." KRQE.com, January 12, 2018. https://www.krqe.com/news/crime/new-mexico-therapist-who-raped -clients-sentenced-to-12-years/.

Steinberg, A., J. Alpert, and C. Courtois, eds. *Sexual Boundary Violations in Psychotherapy: Facing Therapist Indiscretions, Transgressions, and Misconduct.* Washington, DC: American Psychological Association, 2021.

Stevenson, L. "HCPC Sanctions Social Worker Over Facebook Posts." Community Care, September 10, 2014. https://www.communitycare.co.uk/2014/09/10 /social-worker-given-conditions-practice-order-disrespectful-facebook-posts/.

Stoesen, L. "Recovering Social Workers Offer Support." *NASW News*, July 2002, 3.

"Suicidal Patient Not Restrained by Defendant Hospital." *Mental Health Law News* 5, no. 2 (1990): 3.

Syme, G. *Dual Relationships in Counselling and Psychotherapy.* London: Sage, 2003.

"Teenager Commits Suicide by Taking Drug Overdose After Hospital Discharge." *Mental Health Law News* 7, no. 4 (1992): 1.

"Testimony from Social Worker and Psychologist Not Privileged." *Mental Health Law News* 11, no. 10 (1996): 6.

Texas Department of State Health Service. "Texas State Board of Social Worker Examiners Enforcement Actions—Disciplinary Actions." 2013. http://www .dshs.state.tx.us/socialwork/sw_cmp.shtm.

"Therapist Begins Personal Relationship with Wife While Still Seeing Husband." *Mental Health Law News* 9, no. 6 (1994): 4.

"Therapists Fail to Notify or Take Action Against Abuse of Group Home Residents." *Mental Health Law News* 16, no. 8 (2001): 2.

"Therapists Have No Duty to Control Outpatients from Harming Unidentified Third Parties." *Mental Health Law News* 11, no. 9 (1996): 1.

Thoreson, R., and J. Skorina. "Alcohol Abuse Among Psychologists." In *Professionals in Distress: Issues, Syndromes, and Solutions in Psychology*, ed. R. Kilburg, P. Nathan, and R. Thoreson, 77–117. Washington, DC: American Psychological Association, 1986.

Thoreson, R., M. Miller, and C. Krauskopf. "The Distressed Psychologist: Prevalence and Treatment Considerations." *Professional Psychology: Research and Practice* 20 (1989): 153–58.

Thoreson, R., P. Nathan, J. Skorina, and R. Kilburg. "The Alcoholic Psychologist: Issues, Problems, and Implications for the Profession." *Professional Psychology: Research and Practice* 14 (1983): 670–84.

"Treating Therapist Falsely Reports Father's Molestation of Young Daughter." *Mental Health Law News* 12, no. 9 (1997): 4.

Twemlow, S., and G. Gabbard. "The Love-Sick Therapist." In *Sexual Exploitation in Professional Relationships*, ed. G. O. Gabbard, 71–87. Washington, DC: American Psychiatric Press, 1989.

US Department of Justice. "Licensed Clinical Social Worker Sentenced to Prison for Health Care Fraud" [press release]. 2015. https://www.justice.gov/usao-mdla /pr/licensed-clinical-social-worker-sentenced-prison-health-care-fraud-0.

US Department of Justice. "Powell, Wyoming Psychologist Sentenced to Three Years in Prison for Health Care Fraud" [press release]. 2018. https://www .justice.gov/usao-wy/pr/powell-wyoming-psychologist-sentenced-three-years -prison-health-care-fraud-0.

US Department of Justice. "Renee Tartaglione Sentenced to 82 Months in Federal Prison for Fraud Scheme That Looted Millions of Dollars from Nonprofit

Clinic" [press release]. 2018. https://www.justice.gov/usao-edpa/pr/renee
-tartaglione-sentenced-82-months-federal-prison-fraud-scheme-looted-millions.

US Department of Justice. "Social Worker Sentenced for Defrauding Blue Cross
Blue Shield" [press release]. 2015. https://www.justice.gov/usao-wdny/pr/social
-worker-sentenced-defrauding-blue-cross-blue-shield.

US Department of Justice. "Three Sentenced to Prison for Scheme to Defraud Medicare" [press release]. 2011. http://www.justice.gov/usao/lam/press/press1101
.html.

US Department of Labor. "Florida Substance Abuse Recovery Center Owner
Receives Prison Sentence, Ordered to Make $5,122,886 in Restitution for Health-
care Fraud" [news release]. June 28, 2018. https://www.dol.gov/newsroom
/releases/ebsa/ebsa20180628.

VandenBos, G., and R. Duthie. "Confronting and Supporting Colleagues in Distress." In *Professionals in Distress: Issues, Syndromes, and Solutions in Psychology*,
ed. R. Kilburg, P. Nathan, and R. Thoreson, 211–31. Washington, DC: American Psychological Association, 1986.

Vanderpool, D. "The Standard of Care." *Innovations in Clinical Neuroscience* 18
(2021): 50–51.

Ward, C. "Former Social Worker at Elgin Mental Health Center Pleads Guilty to
Sexual Misconduct with Patient, Sentenced to 180 Days in Jail." *Chicago Tribune*,
September 9, 2019. https://www.chicagotribune.com/news/breaking/ct-elgin
-mental-health-center-worker-guilty-sex-crime-20190909-g65tj33yjnht5l-
m2ofjnqcukcy-story.html.

Wenzke, M. "Ex-Marriage and Family Therapist in Pasadena Sentenced to Prison
for Sexually Abusing 7 Patients." KTLA.com, January 21, 2021. https://ktla
.com/news/local-news/ex-family-and-marriage-therapist-in-pasadena-sentenced
-to-prison-for-sexually-abusing-7-patients/.

"Wife Kills Self; Had Been Hospitalized for Earlier Suicide Attempt." *Mental
Health Law News* 10, no. 2 (1995): 3.

Wigmore, J. *A Treatise on the System of Evidence in Trials at Common Law*. Boston: Little, Brown, 1905.

Wilson, S. *Confidentiality in Social Work*. New York: Free Press, 1978.

Wisconsin Department of Safety and Professional Services. "In the Matter of
Disciplinary Proceedings Against Jackie M. Morter." 2012. https://online.drl
.wi.gov/ decisions/2012/ORDER0001302-00006751.pdf.

Wisconsin Department of Safety and Professional Services. "In the Matter of Disciplinary Proceedings Against Cheryl K. Rotherham." 2013. https://online.drl
.wi.gov/decisions/2013/ORDER0002561-00008687.pdf.

"Woman Claims Psychological Counselor Implanted Memories of Satanic Rituals and Parental Incest." *Mental Health Law News* 10, no. 7 (1995): 3.

"Woman Claims Psychological Problems Following 'Seminar Training.'" *Mental Health Law News* 7, no. 2 (1992): 6.

"Woman Claims She Was Improperly Discharged from Psychiatric Ward Due to Inadequate Insurance." *Mental Health Law News* 4, no. 11 (1989): 2.

"Woman Has Sexual Relationship with Therapist; $123,500 Award." *Mental Health Law News* 14, no. 12 (1999): 5.

Wood, B., S. Klein, H. Cross, C. Lammers, and J. Elliott. "Impaired Practitioners: Psychologists' Opinions About Prevalence, and Proposals for Intervention." *Professional Psychology: Research and Practice* 16 (1985): 843–50.

Woody, R. *Legally Safe Mental Health Practice.* Madison, CT: Psychosocial Press, 1997.

Worchel, D., and R. Gearing. *Suicide Assessment and Treatment: Empirical and Evidence-Based Practices.* New York: Springer, 2010.

Zur, O. *Boundaries in Psychotherapy: Ethical and Clinical Explorations.* Washington, DC: American Psychological Association, 2007.

Zur, O., ed. *Multiple Relationships in Psychotherapy and Counseling.* New York: Routledge, 2017.

*Abille v. United States*, 482 F. Supp. 703 (N.D. Cal. 1980).

*Alberts v. Devine*, 479 N.E.2d 113 (Mass. 1985).

*Alexander v. Knight*, 177 A.2d 142 (Pa. 1962).

*Almonte v. New York Medical College*, 851 F. Supp. 34 (D. Conn. 1994).

*Baker v. United States*, 226 F. Supp. 129 (D. Iowa 1964).

*Bellah v. Greenson*, 146 Cal. Rptr. 535 (Cal. Ct. App. 1978).

*Belmont v. California State Personnel Board*, 111 Cal. Rptr. 607 (Cal. Ct. App. 1974).

*Berry v. Moench*, 331 P.2d 814 (Utah 1958).

*Birkner v. Salt Lake County*, 771 P.2d 1053 (Utah 1989).

*Boles v. Milwaukee County*, 443 N.W.2d 679 (Wis. Ct. App. 1989).

*Boyer v. Tilzer*, 831 S.W. 2d 695 (Mo. Ct. App. E.D. 1992).

*Boynton v. Burglass*, 590 So. 2d 446 (Fla. Dist. Ct. App. 1991).

*Brady v. Hopper*, 570 F. Supp. 1333 (D. Colo. 1983).

*Bramlette v. Charter-Medical-Columbia*, 393 S.E.2d 914 (S.C. 1990).

*Cabrera v. Cabrera*, 23 Conn. App. 330 (Conn. App. Ct. 1990).

*Caesar v. Mountanos*, 542 F.2d 1064 (9th Cir. 1976).

*Cairl v. State*, 323 N.W.2d 20 (Minn. 1982).

*California v. Cabral*, 15 Cal. Rpt. 2d 866 (Cal. Ct. App. 1993).

*California v. Gomez*, 185 Cal. Rpt. 155 (Cal. Ct. App. 1982).

*California v. Kevin F.*, 261 Cal. Rptr. 413 (Cal. Ct. App. 1989).

*Cameron v. Montgomery County Welfare Services*, 471 F. Supp. 761 (E.D. Pa. 1979).

*Carr v. Howard, Massachusetts*, Norfolk County Super. Ct., No. 94–97, March 5, 1996.

*Chatman v. Millis*, 517 S.W.2d 504 (Ark. 1975).

*Chrite v. United States*, 564 F. Supp. 341 (D. Mass. 1983), Civ. No. 81–73844.

*Cohen v. State*, 382 N.Y.S.2d 128 (N.Y. App. Div. 1976).

*Currie v. United States*, 644 F. Supp. 1074 (M.D.N.C. 1986).

*Cutter II v. Brownbridge*, 228 Cal. Rptr. 545 (Cal. Ct. App. 1986).

*Darrah v. Kite*, 301 N.Y.S.2d 286 (N.Y. App. Div. 1969).

*Daubert v. Merrell Dow Pharmaceuticals, Inc.*, 509 U.S. 579 (1993).

*Davis v. Lhim*, 124 Mich. App. 291 (Mich. Ct. App. 1983).

*DeShaney v. Winnebago County Department of Social Services*, 812 F.2d 298 (7th
    Cir. 1987), 109 S. Ct. 998 (1989).

*Dill v. Miles*, 310 P.2d 896 (Kan. 1957).

*Doe v. Roe*, 400 N.Y.S.2d 668 (N.Y. Sup. Ct. 1977).

*Doe v. Samaritan Counseling Center*, 791 P.2d 344 (Alaska 1990).

*Dymek v. Nyquist*, 128 Ill. App. 3d 859 (Ill. App. Ct. 1984).

*Elliott v. North Carolina Psychology Board*, 485 S.E.2d 882 (N.C. Ct. App. 1997).

*Estate of Davies v. Reese*, 248 N.W.2d 344 (Neb. 1977).

*Fedell v. Wierzbieniec*, 485 N.Y.S.2d 460 (N.Y. Sup. Ct. 1985).

*Ferrara v. Galluchio*, 152 N.E.2d 249 (N.Y. 1958).

*Frye v. United States*, 293 F. 1013 (D.C. Cir. 1923).

*Garamella v. New York Medical College*, 23 F. Supp. 2d 153 (D. Conn. 1998).

*Gares v. New Mexico Board of Psychologist Examiners*, 798 P.2d 190 (N.M. 1990).

*Geis v. Landau*, 458 N.Y.S.2d 1000 (N.Y. Civ. Ct. 1983).

*Green v. State*, 309 So. 2d 706 (La. Ct. App. 1975).

*Hague v. Williams*, 181 A.2d 345 (N.J. 1962).

*Hammer v. Rosen*, 165 N.E.2d 756 (N.Y. 1960).

*Hammonds v. Aetna Casualty & Surety Co.*, 243 F. Supp. 793 (N.D. Ohio 1965).

*Heinmiller v. Department of Health*, 903 P.2d 433 (Wash. 1995).

*Hess v. Frank*, 367 N.Y.S.2d 30 (N.Y. App. Div. 1975).

*Holt v. Nelson*, 523 P.2d 211 (Wash. Ct. App. 1974).

*Horne v. Patton*, 287 So. 2d 824 (Ala. 1974).

*Hothem v. Fallsview Psychiatric Hospital*, 573 N.E.2d 803 (Ohio Ct. Cl. 1989).

*Hulsey v. Stotts, Barclay, Pettus, Moore, Whipple and Dugan, Inc.*, 155 F.R.D. 676
    (N.D. Okla. 1994).

*Humphrey v. Norden*, 359 N.Y.S.2d 733 (1974).

*In re* Estate of Bagus, 691 N.E.2d 401 (Ill. App. Ct. 1998).

*In re* Lifschutz, 467 P.2d 557 (Cal. 1970).

*In re* Quinlan, 355 A.2d 647 (N.J. 1976).

*In the Matter of Kathleen Quigley Berg and Eugene E. Berg*, 152 N.H. 658, 886 A.2d
    980 (N.H. 2005).

*Jablonski v. United States*, 712 F.2d 391 (9th Cir. 1983).

*Jaffe v. Redmond*, 116 S. Ct. 1923 (1996).

*Kavanaugh v. Indiana*, 695 N.E.2d 629 (Ind. Ct. App. 1998).

*Kleber v. Stevens*, 249 N.Y.S.2d 668 (N.Y. 1964).

*Kogensparger v. Athens Mental Health Center*, 578 N.E.2d 916 (Ohio Ct. Cl. 1989).

*Lee v. Alexander*, 607 So.2d 30 (Miss. Supt. Ct. 1992).

*Leedy v. Hartnett*, 510 F. Supp. 1125 (M.D. Pa. 1981), Civ. No. 80-0201.

*Lipari v. Sears, Roebuck*, 497 F. Supp. 185, Civ. No. 77-0-458 (D. Neb. 1980).

*Little v. Utah State Division of Family Services*, 667 P.2d 49 (Utah 1983).

*Lovett v. Superior Court*, 203 Cal. App. 3d 521 (Cal. Ct. App. 1988).

*Lux v. Hansen*, 886 F.2d 1064 (8th Cir. 1989).

*MacDonald v. Clinger*, 446 N.Y.S.2d 801 (N.Y. App. Div. 1982).

*Maas v. UPMC Presbyterian Shadyside*, 234 A.3d 427 (Pa. 2020).

*Mammo v. Arizona*, 675 P.2d 1347 (Ariz. Ct. App. 1983).

*Marvulli v. Elshire*, 27 Cal. App. 3d 180 (Cal. Ct. App. 1972).

*Mavroudis v. Superior Court*, 162 Cal. Rptr. 724 (Cal. Ct. App. 1980).

*McIntosh v. Milano*, 168 N.J. Super. 466, 403 A.2d 500 (N.J. 1979).

*McNamara v. Honeyman*, 546 N.E.2d 139 (Mass. 1989).

*Meier v. Ross General Hospital*, 445 P.2d 519 (Cal. 1968).

*Merchants National Bank v. United States*, 272 F. Supp. 409 (D. N.D. 1967).

*Minnesota v. Andring*, 342 N.W.2d 128 (Minn. 1984).

*Minogue v. Rutland Hospital*, 125 A.2d 796 (Vt. 1956).

*Missouri v. Beatty*, 770 S.W.2d 387 (Mo. Ct. App. 1989).

*Missouri v. Edwards*, 918 S.W.2d 841 (Mo. Ct. App. 1996).

*Naidu v. Laird*, 539 A.2d 1064 (Del. 1988).

*Narcarato v. Grob*, 180 N.W.2d 788 (Mich. 1970).

*Norton v. Argonaut Insurance Co.*, 144 So. 2d 249 (La. 1962).

*O'Connor v. Donaldson*, 422 U.S. 563 (1975).

*Patterson v. Jensen*, 17 N.W.2d 423 (Wis. 1945).

*Perreira v. State*, 768 P.2d 1198 (Colo. 1989).

*Pisel v. Stamford Hospital*, 430 A.2d 1 (Conn. 1980).

*Porter v. Maunnangi*, 764 S.W.2d 699 (Mo. App. 1988).

*Pundy v. Illinois Department of Professional Regulation*, 570 N.E.2d 458 (Ill. App. Ct. 1991).

*Redding v. Virginia Mason Medical Center*, 878 P.2d 483 (Wash. Ct. App. 1994).

*Reif v. Weinberger*, 372 F. Supp. 1196 (D. D.C. 1974).

*Rennie v. Klein*, 462 F. Supp. 1131 (D. N.J. 1978).

*Renzi v. Morrison*, 618 N.E.2d 794 (Ill. App. Ct. 1993).

*Rogers v. South Carolina Department of Mental Health*, 377 S.E.2d 125 (S.C. Ct. App. 1989).

*Rule v. Chessman*, 317 P.2d 472 (Kan. 1957).

*Runyon v. Smith*, 730 A.2d 881 (N.J. Super. Ct. App. Div. 1999).

*Salgo v. Stanford University Board of Trustees*, 317 P.2d 170 (Cal. Ct. App. 1957).

*Samuels v. Southern Baptist Hospital*, 594 So. 2d 571 (La. Ct. App. 1992).

*Sayes v. Pilgrim Manor Nursing Home*, 536 So. 2d 705 (La. Ct. App. 1988).

*Schloendorff v. Society of New York Hospital*, 211 N.Y. 125 (1914).

*Schuster v. Altenberg*, 424 N.W.2d 159 (Wis. 1988).

*Sears v. U.S.*, 497 F. Supp. 185 (N.E.D. Neb. 1980).

*Seavy v. State*, 250 N.Y.S.2d 877 (N.Y. App. Div. 1964), 216 N.E.2d 613 (N.Y. 1966).

*Shaw v. Glickman*, 415 A.2d 625 (Md. Ct. Spec. App. 1980).

*Simonsen v. Swenson*, 177 N.W. 831 (Neb. 1920).

*Smith v. Yohe*, 194 A.2d 167 (Pa. 1963).

*Snyder v. Mouser*, 272 N.E.2d 627 (Ind. Ct. App. 1971).

*Superintendent of Belchertown v. Saikewicz*, 370 N.E.2d 417 (Mass. 1977).

*Suslovich v. New York State Education Department*, 571 N.Y.S.2d 123 (N.Y. App. Div. 1991).

*Tarasoff v. Board of Regents of the University of California*, 529 P.2d 553 (Cal. 1974, also known as *Tarasoff I*); 551 P.2d 334 (Cal. 1976, also known as *Tarasoff II*).

*Thompson v. County of Alameda*, 614 P.2d 728 (Cal. 1980).

*Underwood v. United States*, 356 F.2d 92 (5th Cir. 1966).

*Vassiliades v. Garfinckel's*, 492 A.2d 580 (D.C. 1985).

*Vaughn v. North Carolina Department of Human Resources*, 252 S.E.2d 792 (N.C. 1979).

*Vineyard v. Craft*, 828 S.W.2d 248 (Tex. Ct. App. 1992).

*Volk v. DeMeerleer*, 386 P.3d 254, 187 Wn.2d 241 (2016).

*Walker v. Parzen*, 24 Ass'n. of Trial Lawyers of America L. Rep. 232 (June 1983).

*Whitree v. State*, 290 N.Y.S.2d 486 (N.Y. Ct. Cl. 1968).

*Winfrey v. Citizens & Southern National Bank*, 254 S.E.2d 725 (Ga. Ct. App. 1979).

*Wood v. Samaritan Institution*, 26 Cal. 2d 847, 853, 161 P.2d 556 (1945).

*Yorsten v. Pennell*, 153 A.2d 255 (Pa. 1959).